FINANCIAL
WORLD
Publishing

INVESTMENT MANAGEMENT

Jane Cowdell, Mark Billings
& Paul Cowdell

Financial World Publishing
IFS House
4-9 Burgate Lane
Canterbury
Kent
CT1 2XJ
United Kingdom

T   01227 818687
F   01227 479641
E   editorial@ifslearning.com
W   www.ifslearning.com

Financial World Publishing publications are published by The Chartered Institute of Bankers, a non-profit making registered educational charity.

Typeset by Kevin O'Connor

Printed by Selwood Printing, Burgess Hill, Sussex

© Jane Cowdell 2001

ISBN 0-85297-613-5

FINANCIAL
WORLD
Publishing
THE CHARTERED INSTITUTE OF BANKERS

CONTENTS

Contents

Contents

Contents

Contents

Contents

INTRODUCTION

The concept of the course

This study text has been written for students of The Chartered Institute of Bankers' ACIB/BSc subject Investment Management, and also for practitioners in financial services who are looking for a practical refresher.

Each chapter is divided into sections and contains learning objectives and clear, concise topic-by-topic coverage.

Syllabus

The key sections of the Investment Management syllabus are:

- Types of security and security markets
  - Insurance
  - Investments
  - Pensions
- Investment and portfolio theory and analysis
  - The trading of securities in world markets including procedures and settlement of the London Stock Exchange
  - Investment theory, security and market analysis and efficiency
  - Practical investment considerations
  - Investment by trustees
- Portfolio management
  - Managing client portfolios

Note: the syllabus is reviewed every year. Please make sure you have the most up-to-date version.

Your contribution

Although this study text is designed to stand alone, as with most topics, certain aspects of this subject are constantly changing. Therefore it is very important that you keep up-to-date with these key areas. For example, you should read the quality press and financial journals and look out for relevant websites.

We anticipate that you will study this course for one session (six months), reading through and studying approximately one chapter every week. However, note that as topics vary in size and as knowledge tends not to fall into uniform chunks, some chapters are unavoidably longer than others.

Study plan

If you are a distance learning student and have not received your study plan by the beginning of the session, please contact the *ifs* Student Learning Support team:

T   01227 818637

F   01227 453547

E   sls@ifslearning.com

1

OVERVIEW OF INVESTMENT

Objectives

After studying this chapter, the reader should be able to:

● analyse the motives for saving and investing;

● assess the factors that influence investment strategy;

● consider the various attitudes to risk and the implications of risk, time and return;

● differentiate between saving, speculation, investment and gambling;

● differentiate between 'direct investment' and 'indirect investment';

● define real and financial assets;

● list and briefly describe the types of financial asset held by investors.

1.1　Introduction

Investors and potential investors need to understand the importance of effective investment management. From the small investor just starting to plan for the future, to the largest investment companies in the world, an effective strategy of investment management must be implemented.

Many private individuals have become 'accidental' investors in the stock market from the demutualization of building societies and insurance companies. Although the amount of money involved for each investor may be modest, it is vital that investors understand their options and match these to their own needs.

Other people have investment needs because of, for example, redundancy payments, early retirement, an inheritance, or winning a large sum of money from the National Lottery or Premium Savings Bonds. Many smaller investors purchased shares issued by former public corporations as part of the government's privatization programme or from an employee share option scheme.

Planning for the future is a key motivator in developing an investment strategy. People may wish to set aside regular or occasional sums of money to build up funds for the future, which may be long term, e.g. saving for a house, or short term, e.g. saving for a holiday. They may also wish to provide for a comfortable retirement and for protection for their family.

There is a wide choice of financial institutions offering savings and investment products and services. The economist Andrew Bain divides these into three categories:

● Banks, building societies and National Savings, which generally provide capital-guaranteed savings and investment accounts offering ready access to funds and a rate of interest.

● Life assurance and pension funds, the former providing savings and financial protection in the event of early death, the latter doing the same in the event of lengthy survival. These institutions are differentiated from the first group in that early surrender or lapse of investments may result in a capital loss or having funds 'locked in'.

● Unit trusts, investment trusts, OEICs (open-ended investment companies) and stocks and shares. The capital value of these assets can change on daily basis. Their value can rise or fall. Investors may receive dividends, but the amounts and frequency of such payments are not guaranteed in any way.

Traditionally, each set of financial institutions had a highly defined role in the provision of personal savings and investment products and services. This was partly due to their respective specializations and expertise, but also due to government controls. These demarcations have largely broken down since 1980, with institutions making inroads into the markets of their competitors. Most of the retail and mortgage banks and all of the large building societies now provide a full range of services for savers and investors, often through specialist subsidiary and associated companies.

For these reasons, many customers are now able to approach a single financial institution to meet a wide range of financial needs instead of having to go to different organizations for each individual need.

1.2   Motives for saving and investing

The economist John Maynard Keynes, writing in his famous 1936 *General Theory*, identified three reasons for holding financial assets:

● Precautionary - saving for a rainy day.

● Transactionary - to accommodate day-to-day needs.

● Speculative - moving between money and non-monetary assets in anticipation of a financial return.

More recently, the monetarist Milton Friedman proposed his portfolio theory as to why people hold different financial assets. This suggests that people will satisfy their cash demands before considering any other assets. They will then fulfil their needs for highly liquid accounts (those that can be quickly converted to cash, such as current and deposit accounts), then less liquid but potentially higher return assets.

The motive for saving or investing has an effect on responses to changes in market conditions. For example, in a period of high inflation:

● Those saving for a specific future purchase will probably spend now and withdraw savings, if necessary borrowing the difference between price and savings balance, in the fear that the price of the purchase will increase in the future.

● Those saving for a rainy day will save more as they perceive that the value of their savings is no longer adequate in real terms for the purpose intended.

Another perspective on saving is the so-called 'life cycle' hypothesis. Like all 'economic models' it is a representation of reality and will not apply to everybody. Nevertheless, it does help us to understand savings and investment behaviour.

This view suggests that individuals move through different periods of life which affect their savings or investment behaviour. Young adults will generally have no savings (or negative savings i.e. net debt), because they will have relatively low incomes, spend a large proportion of those incomes, be starting families etc. Incomes are then likely to rise quite rapidly and individuals will feel the need to establish some financial security by taking out life insurance, starting pensions etc. As they move into middle age, life will become more comfortable as basic personal needs will have been met and children are perhaps leaving home. In this phase of the life cycle savings will reach a peak. In retirement the lack of earnings will be compensated for by running down savings accumulated during a working lifetime or drawing on the income generated by these savings.

This view of the 'life cycle' or 'the ages of man' is one that underlies much of the discussion later in this book about the role of investment in planning for the needs of the individual investor.

1.3   Factors affecting investment strategy

When saving and investing, people are driven by various stimuli. These vary according to personal need and preference, as well as factors such as attitude to risk.

The following factors usually drive demand for products offered by financial institutions:

● Rate of interest;

● Potential for capital growth;

● Risk of capital loss.

Additional factors which can vary from individual to individual are:

● Liquidity requirements (the perceived need to be able to convert the asset back into cash);

● Simplicity — the ease with which the product or service can be understood by the customer;

● Tax efficiency — some products are tax free such as PEPs (which have now been withdrawn but are still held by investors), NSCs and ISAs; others deduct income tax at source (bank and building society accounts) while others pay gross interest (offshore funds).

1.4   Attitudes towards risk

Different people have different attitudes towards risk. The attitudes generally identified are:

- Risk averse: people who dislike risk, prefer certainty to risk or uncertainty and may be prepared to pay to eliminate risk (e.g. through insurance);

- Risk neutral: people who are indifferent to risk or uncertainty, providing their average returns are not affected;

- Risk preferring: people who like taking risks e.g. gamblers.

Although this is a conventional classification there are problems with such categorization. Attitudes to risk may depend on circumstances. We cannot assume that an individual will always fall into the same one of these categories – it does not follow that an individual who is risk-averse in one situation will always be risk-averse in another. Also, where do we draw the boundaries between these categories? Perhaps it would be better to say that there is a spectrum of attitudes to risk. Nevertheless, it will be useful to bear this classification in mind as we think a little more about the motives for saving and investment. Risk, and its link with the potential return from an investment, is a key factor in investment management, and illustrations of this concept will appear throughout the book.

1.5   Risk, time and return

Requirements of different investors

Different investors have different risk and time preferences. A person with only £500 to invest will not wish to take much risk, and will probably require the money to be readily available to meet any sudden bills. This investor will have entirely different requirements to an investor with an existing portfolio of about £200,000 who has just won £5,000 on the National Lottery. This latter investor is more likely to have a greater willingness to accept a high-risk, long-term investment in the hope of a higher return.

The link between risk, time and return

Generally speaking, the greater the risk and time involved, the greater the potential return if all goes well. (Risk and return are covered fully in Chapter 9.)

1.6 Differences between saving, speculation, investment and gambling

Saving – short term: safety/low risk

Saving is putting money aside so that it is readily available for any sudden financial emergency. The saver has a low risk and short time preference. Examples of savings vehicles are bank and building society accounts. These funds are often called 'cash investments'. The best 'home' for savings is the account that gives the best after-tax return for the particular investor, coupled with low risk and ready accessibility. The return is usually purely in the form of interest, with the capital remaining at its face value.

Speculation – short term: higher risk

Speculation involves a short timescale with a potentially high reward by way of capital gain. An example of speculation was seen with the dot.com shares floated on the stock market. Many investors bought these shares with a view to reselling them quickly at a profit. In some cases the share price collapsed, and these shares ceased to be listed shares a very short time after flotation. However, a number of the remaining dot.coms did show phenomenal price rises in a short period. If it appears likely that demand for the shares will exceed the number of shares available with a new issue, then the shares will start trading at a higher price than when they were issued.

Another form of speculation is purchasing very low-priced equities which are called 'penny shares'. The Personal Investment Authority (now superseded by the Financial Services Authority) defined penny shares as: 'shares with a bid-offer spread of 10% or more of the offer price' (the bid price is the price at which the market maker will buy the shares from the shareholder. The offer price in the price the market maker will sell the shares at to a purchaser. Thus the bid price is the lower of the two prices quoted for a share). These shares are in companies that could quite possibly fail but where there is just a chance of a dramatic change of fortune. If a share is priced at 20p and the investor puts £500 into these shares he or she will receive 2,500 shares (£500 ÷ 20p). If one month later the shares rise to 22p each and he sells them he will receive 2,500 x 22p = £550 (ignoring dealing costs). Thus he has made a profit of £50. If the shares rise by 2p in the period of one month then the profit is equal to an annual interest rate of 120%. If he had however invested £500 in shares costing 200p each he would have received 250 shares. If the price had risen over the period of one month to 202p (i.e. the same rise of 2p a share) he would have received only £505 (ignoring dealing costs). This profit would have been equal to an annual interest rate of just 12%. Other forms of speculative investments are warrants, options and traded options (all of which fall into the category of derivatives, which we examine in Chapter 9).

Investment – longer term: low to high risk/reward

Investment has a higher risk and longer timescale than saving, and the return can come in the form of income or capital gain, or a mixture of the two. When you come to consider portfolio planning in Chapters 18 and 19, you will see that nobody should invest until he has adequate savings to meet any unforeseen financial emergency. One form of investment is equities (ordinary shares) because in the long term, say five years or more, the capital value of equities and their dividends should grow as the economy grows and should normally outperform competing investments over such a timespan.

Gambling – very short term, extremely high risk: little chance of reward

Gambling involves a very high risk with a very short timescale. It is usually an 'all or nothing' situation when you either lose all of your stake or may make a large gain. Gambling winnings are free of income and capital gains tax.

1.7   Direct and indirect investment, real and financial assets

Financial assets are those represented by a piece of paper, whereas real assets can be seen, touched and enjoyed personally. The following tables give examples that help you to understand the differences.

Financial assets	Real assets
Pension plans	Property (owner-occupied)
Life insurance policies	Property (not owner-occupied)
Unit trusts/Investment trusts/OEICs (open-ended investment companies)	Chattels (e.g. paintings, antiques, jewellery, fine wines)
Equities/ordinary shares	
Loan stocks (including gilts, local authority loan stocks and company loan stock)	
National Savings investments	
Cash investments (e.g. bank and building society accounts)	
Property bonds	
Individual savings accounts (ISAs)	

Direct investment	Indirect investment
Equities/ordinary shares	Unit trusts / Investment trusts / OEICs
Loan stocks (as described above)	Insurance policies (qualifying and non-qualifying)
National Savings investments	Pension plans
Property	Friendly society bonds
Chattels	Property bonds

Note: ISAs (individual savings accounts) could be classed as direct or indirect investments, depending on the rules of the particular plan under consideration.

1.8 Summary of differences between the above types of investment

Direct investments are ones that the individual investor personally selects, and ones that are registered in his name. Indirect investments are those made in pools of investments managed on behalf of a number of investors by professional managers. An example of a direct investment would be a property bought by an investor in the hope of acquiring rental income and a capital gain on subsequent sale. All decisions are taken by the investor. One indirect investment alternative is a property bond which is an investment in a diversified portfolio of commercial property, professionally managed by an institution on behalf of a number of investors.

Another example of an indirect investment is a unit trust. The managers select and manage stock exchange investments. Investors buy units in the trust and the units have a value based on the value of the underlying stocks and shares. The unit trust managers do not select investments that meet a specific investor's needs, but select them to meet the objectives specified in the trust deed (which governs the operations of the unit trust). A trust might be aimed at generating income or capital growth, or investing in a certain overseas market, or geographical area, or industry sector.

Note: full details of all the indirect and direct investments mentioned above are covered later in the book.

1.9 Difference between equities, loans, property and chattels

The terms stocks and shares tend to be used interchangeably. In UK terminology, strictly speaking, a 'stock' is a financial instrument carrying a fixed rate of interest whereas a 'share' is an equity (see below). To confuse matters, US usage is different – a stock can either be an equity or a fixed-interest security and equities are often referred to as 'common stock'.

Equities (commonly known as ordinary shares)

A shareholder is a part owner of a limited company but he has no personal liability for the company's debts provided the shares are fully paid. The cash return on equities, known as a dividend, depends on the profits of the company and on the policy of the directors. Full details of equities and other forms of company securities are given in Chapter 8.

Loan stocks

The holder of a loan stock has lent money to the government, local authority, public body or limited company that has issued the stock. He has no right to say how the money he has lent is used. In return he receives a fixed rate of interest or interest linked to a benchmark such as base rate. Government stocks, commonly called gilts, have a separate sub-group which pay interest linked to the Retail Price Index (RPI). Most loan stocks carry a date when they will be redeemed; i.e. the investor will receive back the nominal value (the face value – usually the amount originally lent). Some stocks carry two dates that means that they will be redeemed at the borrower's option at some time between the two dates. There are also some 'undated' gilts and local authority stocks that need never be redeemed. Full details of British government securities are given in Chapter 7 and full details of all other loan stocks are given in Chapter 8.

Property

Apart from an owner-occupied house, property is purchased with the intention of gaining a rental income and a capital gain on any subsequent sale. The basic difference between owning property, as opposed to owning equities or loans, is that property is a tangible asset which the owner can manage on a day-to-day basis. As we shall see in Chapter 8, ordinary shareholders in practice have very little control over the day-to-day operations of companies in which they hold shares.

Chattels

Examples of chattels are stamp collections, jewellery, antiques, fine wine or objets d'art. No income is generated, but the owner usually hopes to make a capital gain on ultimate disposal. (A more detailed examination of both property and chattels can be found in Chapter 11.) Chattels are also purchased to give pleasure as well as capital appreciation.

1.10   The principal types of asset held by UK residents

The principal types of financial investments held by UK residents and their suitability for short-term or long-term savings are as follows:

Cash investments

These are bank and building society accounts, National Savings Products, ISAs, money market and finance house deposits. All of these are short-term investments, because the capital invested always remains the same and the sum invested, or any part of it, can be withdrawn either immediately or at short notice.

National Savings products (NSPs)

These include items such as National Savings Certificates and Pensioners Guaranteed Income Bonds. These can always be encashed (sold) without loss of capital, but they really should be held for their full term, to obtain the optimal return. One example of such an investment is National Savings Certificates, on which the maximum return is gained by holding them to the end of their 5-year term.

Life insurance policies

These take various forms ranging from policies that pay out only if the investor dies before a certain date to those that pay out, at a set date or death, if earlier, a minimum sum plus 'profits' (i.e. a share of the total gains – income and capital gains – that the insurance company has made and allocated to the individual policies). Those policies that share in the profits are long-term investments, the minimum period for this type of policy being 10 years.

Pension plans

These are a form of long-term saving whereby the investor saves a certain amount each month or year starting at any time from the time his employment begins until he retires. Some pensions are non-contributory, i.e. the employer makes all the payments into the pension scheme, with none from the employee. But the pension belongs to the individual, even in non-contributory schemes.

Unit trusts, investment trusts and OEICs (open-ended investment companies)

With these an investor can either save on a regular basis or invest a lump sum. The money invested is added to money invested by others in these trusts and is used by the managers to purchase stocks and shares. This is an indirect form of investment, with professional managers employed to look after the money invested. Because the underlying investments are stocks and shares whose value fluctuates over time, this type of investment should be undertaken only as a long-term investment.

Equities and loan stocks

These are direct investments, where the investor himself decides which equities or loan stocks to purchase. These are long-term investments, because their prices fluctuate in the short-term and you can never be sure that you will get back as much as you invested. In the long-term, though, prices have shown an upward trend.

Individual savings accounts (ISAs)

ISAs are really a convenient way of packaging other investments in a tax-free savings vehicle. The investments that can be held in an ISA are cash, stocks and shares, life insurance and certain national savings products. ISAs are a tax-efficient way of investing, because the investor has is not liable to income tax or capital gains tax for investments held within an ISA. The maximum amount that an individual can invest in an ISA is £7,000 each year (Finance Act 2000). See Chapter 17 for further details about ISAs.

2

THE LONDON STOCK EXCHANGE

Objectives

After studying this chapter, the reader should be able to:

- appreciate the role of financial markets in analysing the performance of companies in the markets for goods and services;

- evaluate the role of the London Stock Exchange as a primary market; and as a secondary market;

- differentiate between the different types of capital raised on the London Stock Exchange;

- appreciate the other functions of the London Stock Exchange;

- differentiate between 'personal investors' and 'institutional investors';

- appreciate the role of institutional investors in the context of corporate governance;

- assess the significance of recent trends in share ownership;

- differentiate between the functions of the members of the London Stock Exchange.

2.1 The role of financial markets in analysing the performance of companies in the markets for goods and services

Obviously, since the advent of delivery channels such as the Internet, the days when all markets had a physical form are no longer with us. However, the purpose of any market, whether a financial market or a market for goods and services, is to bring buyers and sellers together. Markets not only facilitate exchange, they also generate information. The most valuable market information is price. Prices established by transactions in a free and competitive market are considered by many to be a fundamental measure of economic value. Such prices transmit signals to businesses which influence decisions such as whether to produce more or less of a particular good or service, and such prices can also influence the saving and spending plans of consumers.

The managers of companies are expected to make carefully considered decisions regarding the investment of the company's funds in the markets for goods and services. These investments by the company in goods and services markets will produce a payoff (hopefully positive) for the company. It can be difficult for outsiders to access information in the markets for goods and services, so it may be possible for company managers to exploit some competitive advantage to make abnormal profits for the company in these markets.

In financial markets, investors buy and sell stocks and shares in companies in order to increase their wealth. When the market participants believe that a particular company can exploit a competitive advantage in the markets for goods and services, they will buy the shares, thus raising the company's share price. Thus prices in financial markets can sometimes be taken as an indication of the view of market participants on the expertise of the managers in the markets for goods and services.

Markets are said to exhibit two forms of efficiency. Allocative efficiency implies that there is no alternative allocation of resources that will increase consumer satisfaction. Information efficiency reflects the speed with which prices adjust to new information. As a general rule, prices in financial markets react to new information much more quickly than prices in the markets for goods and services.

If financial markets exhibit information efficiency, then this should result in allocative efficiency in the markets for goods and services, since resources will tend to flow to companies whose share price is rising, and the cause of the share price upswing is the skill of the company managers in dealing in the markets for goods and services.

Financial markets consist of primary markets for raising new funds, and secondary markets where financial claims on companies can be traded. These functions are discussed below in connection with the London Stock Exchange.

2.2   Background to the London Stock Exchange (LSE) and its development

The LSE was originally established in 1773 as a market in which stocks and shares could be bought and sold, in much the same way that markets exist for commodities such as wheat, tea, wool and metals. By the 19th century more than 20 stock exchanges were operating around the country. Initially these exchanges operated independently of the LSE, but the developing market resulted in the need for amalgamation into one single exchange, which occurred in 1973. The LSE has continued to adapt to the changing needs of both the markets and investors and IT-based systems have ensured that the LSE remains at the forefront of the world's stock exchanges.

2.3   Functions of the LSE - Overview

The LSE has the following broad functions, all of which will be described in detail in this chapter.

- It enables capital to be raised by the government and by companies. This is achieved by the government issuing loan stock more commonly known as gilts and by companies issuing various classes of securities. The latter can be shares, representing equity (part ownership) investments in companies, or loan capital such as company loan stocks, representing the stake of long-term creditors in those businesses.

- It provides a secondary market through which existing securities can be bought and sold by shareholders and loan stock holders.

- It advertises security prices, enabling investors to follow the progress of quoted stocks and shares.

- It protects investors against fraud. The Main Market (formally called the 'Official List') is a guarantee that securities meet stringent entry requirements, and that the company is reputable at the time of listing. Permission to deal is not given unless the regulatory requirements of the LSE are met. Once shares in a company are admitted to the Main Market, if there is any doubt about the company's probity the LSE will suspend dealing.

- It serves as a barometer of the health of the economy. Movements in the market can provide important indicators of the prospects of quoted, industry group companies, e.g. retailers, and of the country as a whole.

2.4 The LSE as a primary market and a secondary market

A primary market is one which raises new capital for companies or for the government. A secondary market is one that deals in stocks and shares that have already been issued.

If you consider the example of British Telecom (now known as BT), the original subscribers for the shares were participants in the primary market, whereas subsequent sales by these subscribers took place on the secondary market.

There is a close connection between the two markets. Without an effective secondary market the primary market would fail, because investors subscribe to new issues only if they are hopeful of being able to sell at a profit at some time in the future. Equally, a healthy secondary market requires a flow of new companies obtaining listings to replace companies which leave the secondary market because they fail, are taken over, or withdraw from the LSE by 'going private'.

The LSE as a primary market

The mechanics of this market, where new money is raised, are covered in Chapter 3. There are several distinct facets of this market:

- New issue market in British government securities and in ordinary shares (sometimes known as Initial Public Offerings);

- Privatizations;

- Demutualizations;

- Rights issues (sometimes known as Secondary Offerings);

- New fixed-interest capital.

New issue market in British government securities

The largest market by far is the new issue market in British government securities, more commonly called 'gilts' (or gilt-edged securities). In the past government expenditure has often exceeded government income, and the government has had to borrow to meet the difference, which is known as the Public Sector Net Cash Requirement (PSNCR). In raising new funds the government also has to take account of redemptions (i.e. the repayment of debt already in issue). Other considerations also affect the decisions to issue new gilts, but detailed examination of money supply and interest-rate policy is beyond this syllabus.

Some idea of the figures involved can be gained from the final three columns of Table 1. Finance can be raised very quickly by this method – new gilts can always be sold by the government because British government debt is considered a very safe investment, but the interest rate paid on new debt will reflect current market rates of interest.

Privatizations

Privatization is another example of the use of the primary market to raise new funds for the government. In the 1980s the Conservative government started the policy of selling state-owned assets. The method normally used was to transform these organizations into public limited companies, shares in which were then issued, and a quotation on the LSE gained, usually by an offer for sale. See Chapter 3 for a more detailed explanation of this process.

The first BT issue in 1984 was a watershed for privatization, because failure would have embarrassed the government and jeopardized future privatizations. Since that issue, vast sums have been raised by privatization.

While the majority of shares offered in privatization issues were taken up by institutional investors, the Conservative government was keen to see wider share ownership, i.e. more individuals owning shares directly. In order to encourage wider share ownership various incentives were given on privatization issues. The main incentives have been:

- Priority application for private investors, particularly for customers of the concern, e.g. in the privatizations of the water companies and electricity companies;

- Bill vouchers for use against future bills from the company, e.g. British Telecom, British Gas and electricity companies;

- Free shares if the investor holds the shares for a preset number of years, e.g. BAA, British Telecom;

- Instalment payments whereby the investor pays only a small amount initially and the balance is paid at one or two dates several months later, e.g. the electricity companies, British Telecom;

- Cheap dealing services, or share shops, which have agreed to provide low rates of commission on sales of the privatized shares.

Incentives have also been used by a few, non-privatized, companies when they have their shares listed. For example, when Thomson Travel Group floated its shares in a new issue (it has since been taken over), it created a 'Founders Club' for investors, which provides discounts on Thomson holidays.

Demutualizations

Building societies and many life insurance companies were set up on a mutual basis. The owners of a mutual organization are its members – usually account holders (savers and borrowers) or policyholders. The financial services industry has seen major changes because a considerable number of 'mutuals' have gained a listing on the Stock Exchange. Organizations such as the Halifax and Norwich Union (now CGNU) are two examples of large-value demutualizations. Other mutuals have lost that status because they have been taken over by quoted companies.

The members of the demutualized companies receive monetary compensation or shares as an incentive to vote for demutualization. These forms of compensation are known as 'windfalls'.

Rights issue

The most successful activity on the primary market has been the rights issue. Rights issues involve already-quoted companies selling new shares to existing shareholders. Undoubtedly, the fact that the companies have a track record and are selling to existing shareholders has helped these issues to succeed. There are, however, occasions when rights issues do fail, usually because the shareholders are uncertain of the likely success of the venture for which the money was being raised, or because stock market conditions in general have deteriorated between the time of announcing the rights issue and the time for investors to make their decision as to whether to invest.

New fixed-interest capital

In 2000 £4.2bn was raised by UK listed companies through issues of convertibles, debentures, other loan stocks and preference shares. Although these are large sums of money, even more money was raised via issues of ordinary shares.

Even when interest rates were relatively low in 2000, companies tended to raise new equity capital, rather than new loan capital which carries more obligations to the issuing company than equities. In 2000 £21.2bn was raised by new issues of equity (ordinary shares) by UK listed companies, of which £11bn was raised by new companies listing and £10.2bn by companies already listed. (See Chapter 8 for more details of these classes of stocks and shares).

How successful is the primary market?

We have already said that the primary market is successful as regards new issues of gilts, equities for well-established companies and rights issues. There was another area in which the LSE was conspicuous by its absence, and that was in the raising of new equity capital for new companies. In the 1970s much of North Sea oil exploration was financed by bank loans, rather than by new issues of shares, because few of the companies involved had a track record.

In 1980 the LSE created a new market, the Unlisted Securities Market (USM), in an attempt to help new companies to raise new equity finance. However, the USM faced problems and the majority of the companies found that the USM failed to match up to its early promise. In 1995 there was an announcement that the USM would close in the following year and it has been replaced by the Alternative Investment Market (AIM), which will be considered in Chapter 3.

Money raised by new issues

Money raised by new issues of shares, rights issues and British government securities (gilts) 1993 - 2000 are given in Table 1, which shows the importance of the primary market function to industry and the Government.

Table 1: Money raised by new issues

	Money raised from new issues of equity, loan stock and other issues (excluding eurobonds) by listed UK companies	Money raided from rights issues (included in column (1) totals)	Money raised by the issue of British government securitites	Redemptions of British government securities	Net funds raised by the issue of British government securities
	(1)	(2)	(3)	(4)	(5)=(3)–(4)
1993	24389.1	11377.6	57230.2	6265.0	50965.2
1994	25462.3	7103.7	32640.0	9290.0	23350.0
1995	12807.3	5059.1	29720.0	7619.8	22100.2
1996	19531.4	4746.6	43813.8	12763.7	31050.1
1997	13568.8	2195.8	31911.4	16074.5	15836.9
1998	10975.9	1211.1	12768.6	12635.0	133.6
1999	15270.2	2570.3	15888.2	8201.6	7686.6
2000	25378.0	3926.4	8206.8	17281.6	(9074.8)

All figures in £m

Source: Fact File 2000, London Stock Exchange web site

2.5   The secondary market

The need for a secondary market

It is on the secondary market that investors who hold existing shares, gilts or loan stocks can sell them to other investors. Without an efficient secondary market the primary market would fail. People who invest in new issues or new gilts need to know that they could in turn sell them to someone else if the need were ever to arise. This market is successful in that gilts or quoted shares can always be sold at the current price and that the market makers are honest.

The progress of the secondary market can be assessed from the two main indices, the FTSE Actuaries Share Indices, and the FTSE 100 Indices, and other indices covered in Chapter 19.

Sales on the secondary market

A shareholder or the owner of a quoted stock or share can normally sell his holding very quickly on the LSE. The problem is that he will have to sell at the prevailing market price.

Current prices can always be ascertained from a stockbroker or on-line broker. In addition prices can be obtained from Ceefax and Teletext, but there is approximately a 20-minute delay in these prices being updated. If an investor is forced to sell at an unfavourable time, he may well end up by making a loss.

2.6   Other functions of the secondary market

Share price movements

The Stock Exchange acts as a 'barometer' of the health of the economy. If the market as a whole expects economic prospects to improve, share prices will rise and vice versa. In 1987 the FT indices rose to record levels until Monday 19 October when the world stock markets crashed, triggered by worries over the US economy. This was known as 'Black Monday' and heralded the first major fall in UK equity prices since 1972-74.

However, the UK stock market is still very volatile and large upward and downward movements in share prices are regularly seen. Factors such as announcements of interest-rate rises or falls in the USA by the Federal Reserve, or an expectation of slowing economic growth in the USA can have an adverse (or positive), if short-term, effect on UK share prices. Such large movements are caused because investors feel that there could be an impact on the strength of the UK economy.

An individual company's share price movements should, in theory, reflect the prospects of that company. This is not always the case in practice because a company's share price is often influenced by general market sentiment. At other times an individual company's share price may fall when record profits have been announced. This paradox is explained by the fact that the market had anticipated even higher profits and was disappointed by the outcome.

How share prices are determined

Share prices are set by the market forces of supply and demand.

Supply is affected by the amount of new issues being made at a particular time. It is further affected by the amount of shares or gilts that are being sold by investors. At times of panic, such as 1974-75, many investors decide to sell their shares. As a result the Financial Times Ordinary Index reached its lowest level for many years, falling from over 500 in the early 1970s to 146 at its lowest point in January 1975. Even after the October 1987 crash, the FT Ordinary Index still stood at 1,527.3 on 21 October 1987, and on 1 February 2001 it had further risen to 3,568.8.

Demand is influenced by how investors view economic prospects. It could be said that share prices are set 'at the margin' – in other words a very limited number of people – those wishing to buy or sell at a particular moment – effectively determine share prices. Thus share prices, and their movements, may not always seem rational, but we shall consider this further in Chapter 13.

Factors that tend to influence supply and demand for shares in general are:
- Political prospects;

- Government actions such as tax changes, controls over companies, dividend controls, credit restrictions, wage freezes;

- Balance of payment statistics;

- Economic statistics such as money supply figures. (If money supply figures are 'good' it could mean that there is scope for a fall in interest rates.) Other statistics include the inflation rate, exchange rate, and level of industrial production;

- The amount of money invested by institutional investors;

- Changes in consumer spending levels or patterns.

Factors that tend to affect supply and demand for a particular share are:
- Changes in dividends, profits or net assets values;

- Announcement by the company of expected good or poor trading figures or variation of announced figures from market expectations;

- Adverse or favourable press comment;

- A takeover bid;

- The development or introduction of new products or services or discovery of a new area of business, e.g. oil or gas fields for energy companies;

- New management;

- Large purchases or sales of shares by institutional investors.

Remember that all the factors affecting share prices in general can have effects on specific companies and therefore their share price.

Programme trading

Programme trading arises from the use of computer-based systems which are programmed to generate buy or sell orders if individual stock or share prices, or the market as a whole, or particular indices reach a certain price or fluctuate by a certain percentage. The October 1987 crash was partly blamed on US fund managers who use this technique very heavily on Wall Street. As share prices fell so rapidly the computers were triggering sales, thus worsening the situation. The USA 'pulled the plug' on the computers – but not before the effects were felt throughout the world.

Some stock markets in the USA and elsewhere have now employed 'uptick and downtick' rules which restrict trading if prices move up or down by a certain percentage in a given period. These are called 'circuit breakers' in the UK. Opinion on whether these serve any useful purpose is divided. Some argue that circuit breakers can remove the volatility caused by rapid and sudden changes in market sentiment, whereas others regard them as a means of delaying the inevitable, because the forces of supply and demand will eventually bring about changes whatever artificial constraints are used.

Derivatives

A derivative is an instrument whose price is affected by (or 'derived' from) an underlying market. When these derivatives seem to be 'cheap' compared with the stock market, shares are sold and the derivatives are bought. Derivatives that relate to shares and equity indices are analysed in Chapter 9.

2.7   The various types of investor: the private investor and the institutional investor

The bulk of stocks and shares by value (50.9% of UK equities in 1999) are owned by institutional investors, which consist of pension funds, insurance companies, unit trusts, investment trusts, and other financial institutions. Overseas investors (classified as 'rest of the world') accounted for 29.3% of total equity in 1999, with individual investors accounting for 15.3%, and the remaining 4.5% being held by charities, private non-financial corporations, the public sector and banks.

However, the pattern of share ownership has changed dramatically since 1963 as shown in the following table, which is derived from the latest available figures from 'The Share Ownership Report – Dec. 1999', National Statistics, Crown Copyright 2001.

Table 2: Changing patterns of share ownership per cent of equity owned – 31 December 1999

		1963	1975	1991	1999	% change 1963 - 1999
Institutional Investors	Insurance companies	10	15.9	20.8	21.6	+116%
	Pension funds	6.4	16.8	31.3	19.6	+205%
	Unit trusts	1.3	4.1	5.7	2.7	+109%
	Investment trusts and other financial institutions	11.3	10.5	2.3	7	-38%
	Rest of the world	7	5.6	12.8	29.3	+320%
	Charities	2.1	2.3	2.4	1.3	-38%
	Individuals	54	37.5	19.9	15.3	-71.7
	Private non-financial corporations, public sector and banks	7.9	8.6	4.8	3.3	-58%
		100	100	100	100.1 (sic)	

The 15.3% of total equity owned by private investors was worth £275.8bn in money terms at 31 December 1999. Table 3 shows the beneficial ownership of shares by value in 1989 and 1999 (earlier figures are not available).

Table 3: Beneficial ownership of shares by value £ billion December 1989 and 1999

Extracted from *The Share Ownership Report – Dec. 1999*, National Statistics) Crown Copyright 2001.

		1989	1999	% change 1989 - 1999
Institutional Investors	Insurance companies	93.9	389.6	+314.9%
	Pension funds	154.8	353.8	+128.5%
	Unit trusts	29.7	47.9	+61.3%
	Investment trusts and other financial institutions	13.7	126.2	+821%
	Rest of the world	64.5	530.3	+722.1%
	Charities	11.7	24.0	+105%
	Individuals	104.3	275.8	+164.4%
	Private non-financial corporations, public sector and banks	32.8	59.5	+81.4%
	Total	505.4	1807.2	+257.6%

The 15.3% of shares owned by individuals includes shares in the demutualized companies. Individuals own a significantly higher percentage of the share capital of these companies. *The Share Ownership Report* states that in 1999, 45.2% of shares in the recently demutualized companies were owned by individuals, the value of which totalled £17.2bn. The percentage of shares in these companies owned by individual investors fell from 60.6% in 1997 to 48.5% in 1998 and 42.5% in 1999. This fall was not unexpected because many individuals sold their 'windfall' shares to spend the money on consumer goods, holidays, and to invest in other types of investment.

Although the percentage of shares owned by individuals is low when compared to the institutional holdings, this equates to 12 million people owning shares – more than 25% of the adult population.

2.8 Reasons for the shift in share ownership from private individuals to institutional investors

Redistribution of wealth

Before World War II a relatively small number of wealthy individuals owned a large proportion of the country's wealth, while the ordinary working person had just about enough pay to survive on. After World War II a Labour government was elected which had as one of its major policies the redistribution of wealth. It achieved this objective by putting a heavy tax burden on the wealthy through high levels of income tax, capital gains tax and death duties (now called inheritance tax). This resulted in large tax bills that the wealthy could pay only by selling some of their assets – the most easily saleable being stocks and shares.

At the same time the real income of the ordinary working man increased and he began to have more money than he actually needed just to survive and he wanted to find a home for his savings. He looked first towards the areas he knew and understood, life insurance and pension funds. Then, as he became more financially aware, he began to look at other institutional investments as a way of making his money work. He began to invest in unit and investment trusts.

2.9 Growth of the institutional investors

Insurance companies

Even prewar the ordinary working man was familiar with life insurance through the weekly payment of small sums that would provide, on death, enough to pay the funeral expenses. As living standards began to improve after the war, other insurance policies became more popular. These policies were investment vehicles rather than providers of 'death cover'. People were able to invest in life policies that paid out a guaranteed amount if the individual lived until a certain age, or died prior to that date. The government made this form of saving even more attractive by allowing tax relief on the premiums paid on life policies. This tax relief was abolished for new policies taken out after March 1984, and this has had the effect of making certain types of life insurance less attractive to investors. As a result, the premium income of life insurance companies fell, which caused them to rethink their marketing strategies. Many of the major life insurance companies launched unit trusts and developed other savings-based products in order to try to attract funds back.

Pension funds

Many private and public-sector employers provide pensions for their employees. Over the last 40 years or so pension funds have grown into one of the most important of the institutional investors. Many smaller companies use commercial pension fund managers rather than 'in-house' managers, simply because they do not have the resources to manage a pension fund effectively.

The UK pension funds have freedom to invest in UK stocks and shares, overseas stocks and shares, index-linked investment, cash and property. However, their largest area of investment is UK equities.

Pensions are a tax-efficient way of saving for retirement. Contributions are tax deductible, and the pension fund itself pays no direct tax, but tax credits on dividends cannot be reclaimed.

On receipt of a pension, the pensioner is liable to tax on his regular pension payments at his marginal rate of income tax .

Unit trusts, investment trusts and OEICs (Open Ended Investment Companies)

These organizations provide professional management, simplified paperwork and diversified portfolios of stocks and shares. The majority of private investors lack the time and expertise to manage direct holdings of stocks and shares, but many wish to have stock-market investments in their portfolios. These organizations provide a simple way to achieve this aim.

As a result of the growth of the institutional investor, virtually all people in employment (and many who are not) have an interest in the stock market, although they may not realize this. If they hold pension plans or life insurance, the amount they receive will depend on the success of the institutions' investment policies. Thus at one remove 'the man in the street' is affected by stock-market conditions.

Nationalization

The postwar Labour government nationalized, i.e. brought into public ownership, many companies. The major companies nationalized were the Bank of England and the gas, electricity, coal, railway, steel and air/aviation companies. To pay for this nationalization the government issued £3,500 million of British government securities (gilts). Most of these companies were owned by private investors, who received the money, but did not reinvest directly into the stock market in large numbers. However, subsequent privatizations have returned these companies to private ownership and provided the government of the day with cash which was used to reduce the Public Sector Borrowing Requirement (now called the Public Sector Net Cash Requirement) at the time.

2.10   Corporate governance

In 1992 The Cadbury Report on Corporate Governance was published. Sir Adrian Cadbury was responsible for chairing the committee on 'The Financial Aspects of Corporate Governance'. Paragraph 2.5 of the Cadbury Report defines corporate governance as: 'the system by which companies are directed and controlled'. The report covered a wide range of issues and produced a 'Code of Best Practice' which, it recommended, should be adopted by all listed companies in the UK. This code has now been superseded by the 'Combined Code on Corporate Governance' (the Combined Code), in June 1998. The Combined Code now reflects the Turnbull report on Internal Control issued in September 1999.

The issue of corporate governance has grown in prominence for a number of reasons:

- The effects of the recession in the late 1980s and early 1990s on listed companies, and the discovery that financial reporting and controls were not always adequate (as was seen in relation to Queens Moat House Hotels);

- The standards of internal control and accountability seen in cases such as the failures of Barings Bank and BCCI, and the Maxwell case;

- Controversies over directors' ('fat cat') pay;

- Greater activism by shareholders and shareholder groups.

Although the Combined Code covers the areas that companies should be addressing, such as regularity of board meetings, the appointment of non-executive directors, full disclosure of executive directors' total emoluments, and reporting and control procedures, especially in relation to establishing an audit committee, it is not legally binding at present. This is where the role of the shareholder comes into play. The institutions are the major shareholders in virtually all UK quoted companies, thus it falls to these shareholders to 'encourage' companies to adopt, and indeed go beyond, the Combined Code. Shareholders should find improved standards where the Combined Code is followed, thus it is in their interests to encourage its adoption. The LSE requires all listed companies to adopt the Combined Code.

Institutional investors can collectively apply pressure on companies to improve corporate governance and there are two main organizations that do this – the Association of British Insurers (ABI) and the National Association of Pension Funds (NAPF). It is not the main role of either of these organizations to take on the job of improving corporate governance, but is a role they exercise effectively. Pressure by institutional investors is usually applied very discreetly but companies may be subjected to more public pressure from other organizations such as environmental or human or animal rights activists.

2.11 The effects of the change to institutional ownership of shares

Many private individuals now have an indirect interest in the stock market. The value of life policies, pension plans or unit or investment trusts or OEICs will depend in the long run on the performance of the stock market. There are now far more people affected by stock-market conditions than ever before because of their indirect investments in the stock-market.

Ownership is divorced from control. A shareholder in theory is part owner of a company, but in the past institutions tended to favour a 'hands-off' approach, except when takeovers were involved. However, institutions now intervene to prevent abuses, e.g. the institutions tend to scrutinize very carefully any 'golden handshakes' paid to directors who have been fired for incompetence.

The 'weight of money' theory says that much of the vast cash flow of the institutions will be invested in the stock market, thus keeping prices from falling. However, the institutions are not bound to invest in UK equities merely because they are cash rich, and they will invest in this way only if they are confident that prospects are good.

However, against this is the well known 'herd instinct' whereby all the institutions tend to act in the same way (i.e. all buy or all sell a particular company's shares). This herd instinct could account for the volatility of share prices.

The conclusion seems to be that there is a 'floor price' below which shares will not fall, but there will be violent fluctuations above this minimum level. When market prospects seem good, the cash from institutions will tend to be invested in UK shares, thus raising share prices.

2.12   The fall and rise of the private investor

In 1975 the FT Ordinary Share Index had fallen to 146 from 500 in 1972 (we discuss indices and their use in Chapter 19). The private investor sold his shares and left the market but has now been tempted back to a certain extent. Although Table 2 shows that individual investors now own only 15.3% of equities listed on the LSE, the number of individual shareholders in demutualized companies is still very high with 42.5% of the shares owned by individuals.

Much has been done over a long period to encourage wider share ownership by individuals. For many investors share ownership means owning shares in only one or two companies. One of the aims has been to encourage deeper share ownership, i.e. people having a number of different shares instead of one or two.

Many of the actions since 1979 to encourage wider share ownership can be directly attributed to government initiatives. These actions include:

● Privatization of businesses previously state-owned;

● Favourable tax treatment for employee share option schemes (ESOPs);

● More favourable tax treatment for private investors, e.g. abolition of the 'investment income surcharge', the introduction of indexation allowances for capital gains, the reduction of income tax levels;

● Introduction of personal equity plans (PEPs) and latterly individual savings accounts (ISAs);

● Reduction in stamp duty charge on share purchases from 2% to 0.5% (although this remains at a higher level than similar taxes in many overseas equity markets);

● Abolition of exchange control, leading to greater freedom to invest overseas;

● The property market has made people wealthy on paper, and as elderly parents die, or people trade down for retirement, large sums of money have been released for individual investment in equities;

● There has been a gradual increase in the income of individuals who have started to invest, albeit modestly, in shares. This was encouraged particularly by the privatization issues which offered payment in instalments and other perks such as bill vouchers for BT;

- There has been an increase in the amount of financial information available in the popular press, on television, and on the world-wide web, so people are finding it easier to understand the stock market;

- Banks and other financial institutions have become more involved in buying and selling shares. Some banks have computer-based dealing screens in branches, making dealing quicker and cheaper;

- The demutualization of building societies and insurance companies has resulted in more private share ownership. This has been facilitated in part by legislative change.

There are several factors that could reverse the trend in share ownership and reduce the amount of shares directly held by individuals:

- A rise in commission rates due to the increased costs of broking firms, although this has been offset by the cheap dealing services available by telephone and on-line brokers such as TD Waterhouse;

- A fall in the number of broking firms that are willing to deal with the small, private investor, because the firms do not consider the business to be profitable;

- The growth of personal pension plans due to the attractive tax treatment of premiums may make investors turn to a longer-term, indirect investment rather than shares.

- 'Dematerialization' of share certificates, meaning share ownership is evidenced electronically rather than by certificates. This is thought to favour investors other than individuals.

- The shortening of settlement periods (this is discussed in more detail in Chapter 5).

2.13 The functions of members of the Stock Exchange

Introduction
LSE member firms conduct their business from screen-based systems at various locations, and the Stock Exchange floor is no longer used for the trading of stocks and shares. A variety of types of member firms exist and these are described below.

Broker/dealers
Technically, all LSE firms are broker/dealers, i.e. a combination of the old functions of broker and jobber, but not all firms will wish to act in this dual capacity.

Market makers
Market makers fulfil the traditional wholesaler role previously taken by 'jobbers'.

Market makers will fill securities orders from their 'book' which is a common term used to describe stocks or shares owned by the market makers themselves. These organizations will take positions in stocks by increasing their 'book' in shares that are expected to rise in price, and reducing their book in shares that are expected to fall. The profitability, or otherwise, of a market maker will depend on correct anticipation of market movements.

A market maker is committed to making a buying or selling price on demand, but technically he need only quote prices on SEAQ (Stock Exchange Automated Quotation system) for small quantities of shares, and deal in up to the minimum quote size (see Chapter 5). Some firms will choose to be market makers in a small number of equities, rather than being obliged to quote prices in every quoted share on the market.

Usually a market maker will deal 'net'. This means that an investor who deals directly with the market maker will simply pay the market maker's selling price (offer price), or receive the market maker's buying price (bid price) without any commission being charged.

The function of a market maker is to provide liquidity, so that investors can always deal either way (i.e. buy or sell) at the current market price. Inter-dealer brokers (IDBs) act as intermediaries between market makers, thus aiding liquidity.

Agency broker

The agency broker is more commonly called a stockbroker. He will act as an intermediary between the investor and the market maker, will give advice and will charge a fee for this service. Some stockbrokers, however, have moved away from giving advice and have instead chosen to act as 'execution-only' brokers, i.e. purely taking orders and carrying out deals but not providing advice.

Because there are no fixed rates of commission, these 'execution-only' brokers have chosen to charge very low fees – well below those charged by ordinary agency brokers. These execution-only brokers provide a cheap dealing service for the private investor who knows exactly what he wants.

You may wonder why any investor would wish to use an intermediary (even an execution-only broker) who charges commission, when he could deal directly with the market maker on a 'net' basis. There are four reasons:

● The fund managers managing institutions' funds want the best City brokers to survive because they need the brokers' research, ideas, and market knowledge, especially about smaller companies;

● There are no conflicts of interest when an agency broker is used because the function of this member of the LSE is to act in his client's (i.e. the investor's) best interests. Hence the broker will shop around for the best deal, whereas a market maker is in business for himself and maintains his own market position which will influence the prices he quotes;

● The private investor loses access to the research facilities of the broker if he deals directly with the market maker;

● Market makers will deal only with very large orders given directly by a client. Effectively, the client will have to be an institutional investor because they are the major buyers and sellers of stocks and shares.

2.14 The gilts market

Market makers in the gilts market

The gilts market functions through direct dealings between the Bank of England and a gilt-edged market maker (GEMM). The function of a GEMM is to make, on demand and in any trading conditions, continuous and effective two-way prices at which they stand committed to deal. Only organizations that have given an undertaking to the Bank of England to act in this way will be designated as GEMMs. Their profits will in the main be derived from gains between their selling and buying prices. The market maker who makes most money will be the one who best anticipates the market movements.

Operation of the gilts market

GEMMs also operate in the primary or new issues market for gilts.

Gilt-edged auctions for new issues of gilts were introduced in May 1987. The Bank of England asks GEMMs to make competitive tenders for new issues of the gilts, and the Bank will respond to each bid entirely at its discretion. The Bank will prevent any single purchaser from acquiring more than 25% of a particular new issue of a gilt. There is no minimum price at an auction and successful bidders will be issued with the stock at the actual price they offer. Most bids come via GEMMs, but applications for new issues of gilts can be made by anyone, not just GEMMs, subject to a minimum application of £1,000.

As a concession to private investors they can apply at the 'non-competitive bid price' (the average price paid by all successful competitive bidders). Institutions can also trade on a 'when-issued' basis after an auction has been announced – announcements are made 17 calendar days before an auction). 'When-issued' means that institutions instruct the GEMMs that they will purchase at x price 'when issued', i.e. when the gilt begins trading.

Many new issues of gilts are made in partly paid form. For example, 63% Treasury 2010 was sold through an auction, with £50 per £100 nominal stock payable on application (closing date being 10 a.m. on 26 January 1994), and the balance of £50 per £100 nominal payable on 14 March 1994. If the non-competitive sale price is less than £100 per £100 nominal the excess is refunded by cheque. If the non-competitive sale price is above £100 per £100 nominal applicants have to pay the excess on receipt of a letter from the Bank of England (thus, effectively it is added to the first instalment). Allotment letters are issued after the closing date when the first instalment is received and any excess or refund is paid.

GEMMs make secondary markets in gilts and the Bank will deal with the GEMMs in the secondary market if it wishes. GEMMs will inevitably go 'over bought' or 'over sold' in a particular stock at some time or other (i.e. they will hold more or less than they would ideally like). Such positions can be unwound by selling an 'over bought' stock to another GEMM, or buying an 'oversold' stock from another GEMM. There would be problems in direct deals between GEMMs, because they are in fierce competition with each other. The Bank of England's solution to this dilemma was to bring into being an organization called an inter-dealer broker (IDB). Any GEMM who wishes to deal with another GEMM will do so through an IDB. (It is estimated that 90% of gilts business goes through IDBs.)

Individual investors can trade gilts through the Bank of England Brokerage Service (see Chapter 7) thus avoiding the use of a broker, but this method can be more time-consuming and market opportunities may be missed.

3

THE NEW ISSUE MARKET (INITIAL PUBLIC OFFERINGS)

Objectives

After studying this chapter, the reader should be able to:

- evaluate the benefits and drawbacks of a listing of the shares on the London Stock Exchange;

- understand the broad regulatory requirements for companies that wish to have their shares listed on the Stock exchange;

- differentiate between an initial public offering (new issue) and a secondary offering (rights issue);

- differentiate between the requirements for obtaining a listing on the Stock Exchange, AIM (the Alternative Investment Market) and techMARK;

- describe the procedure prior to issue;

- assess the significance of the role and functions of an sponsor/nominated advisor;

- appreciate the significance of underwriting and stabilization;

- assess the importance of the role and functions of a company broker;

- explain how a listing can be withdrawn;

- list and describe each of the methods of obtaining a listing;

- evaluate the information available in an initial public offering so as to assess the prospects of the issue;

- evaluate the various strategies which could be employed by an investor in connection with a new issue;

- define bulls, bears and stags and understand the effects of the activities of each of these types of investors on the market.

3.1 Benefits for companies from a stock market listing

These apply equally to a full listing and an AIM listing. The benefits are that:

- The existing shareholders may wish to sell some of their shares in order to receive a cash sum. While still retaining control, they can enjoy the results of their work in building the business up to its current size.

- The company gains prestige from being quoted. The rigorous inspections carried out before a listing is granted engender confidence in the company from both prospective investors and prospective customers.

- The company may wish to raise new finance by way of an equity issue either to fund new developments or to repay existing loans.

- The company may want its shares to become freely marketable so that at some time in the future it can use its shares as consideration for a takeover.

- The company may find it easier to raise debt finance due to greater confidence being generated by its quotation.

- The company should find it relatively easy to raise further share capital by secondary offerings (see below).

- Improved marketability of the company's shares can aid the establishment of an employee share option scheme as an additional incentive to employees to perform well.

- The introduction of outside shareholders, coupled with the potential threat of a hostile takeover, will provide the directors with an incentive to perform.

- A ready market can be gained for disposal of shares for inheritance tax purposes.

3.2 Disadvantages of a stock market listing

The Financial Services Authority (FSA) and the Stock Exchange require a high level of disclosure of information. Any adverse factors are quickly brought to the attention of investors and are quickly reflected in the share price.

Because the financial press will be reporting on any facts appertaining to the company that may be relevant to the public, the company must ensure that all it says or does is without reproach. A casual aside may well be repeated and misunderstood out of context, thus damaging the company's image, and probably its share price as well. Some readers may remember the devastating effect that some 'off the cuff' remarks from Gerald Ratner had on the Ratner share price.

Shareholders will wish to see their dividends increasing, especially as the company expands. This can result in a dividend policy that may not necessarily be in the best interests of the company, but may be the only way the directors can maintain their seats on the board.

With an unquoted company the shares and hence control are in the hands of just a few directors, but once the company is listed there will be many outside shareholders totally unconnected with the company. This dilution of control means that directors do not have a completely free hand to run the company as they wish, because they are responsible to the shareholders. One entrepreneur who found the dilution of control too onerous was Richard Branson who had his Virgin shares delisted because he did not wish to have his activities circumscribed by the requirement to satisfy external shareholders.

Because the directors are elec' ed by the shareholders they need to balance the interests of the
the shareholders. This can, of course, result in a less than
unities must be forgone in the interests of one or other party.

xpensive process to obtain a listing.

d regulatory requirements for
he UK Listing Authority)

ibility for the competent authority for listing transferred from
ancial Services Authority (FSA) and the responsible body is
\uthority (UKLA). One reason for this was the possible
Exchange, whereby it would become a public limited company
embers. The London Stock Exchange saw the demutualization
ts customers' needs and by handing over the listing regulatory
flicts of interest when its own shares were to be listed.

ies that want their shares listed is that the shares need to be
the UKLA and also have to be admitted to trading by the
rocesses are complete, the securities are officially listed on the

The objectives of the Stock Exchange as regards its formal requirements for listing are set out in its Admissions and Disclosure Standards booklet (May 2001) and are:

- To provide companies with access to markets for their listed securities
- To promote investor confidence in the market as a whole
- To maintain the quality and attractiveness of the markets for investors
- To operate orderly markets
- To minimize any overlap with the UKLA's listing rules.

3.4 Initial public offering (new issues) and secondary offerings (rights issues)

Now that we have looked at the benefits and drawbacks of a listing, let us see how listing procedures are regulated and how they operate.

The FSA Fact Sheet (December 2001) calls what was formerly termed a 'new issue' an initial public offering (IPO). The fact sheet explains 'To fund expansion and development, private companies can raise money by offering securities to the public. This is called an IPO (initial public offering). If a public company then needs to raise further funds, it may offer further securities for sale. This is called a secondary offering'.

An unquoted company may raise funds by an offer for sale, offer for subscription, placing or introduction, on the main market, the Alternative Investment Market (AIM) or techMARK.

3.5 The three markets

A company can obtain a listing on one of the three markets operated by the Stock Exchange. The market it chooses will depend on various factors such as company size and track record. The largest companies will gain a full listing on the Main Market; smaller companies will obtain a listing on the AIM. In addition companies involved in 'innovative technology' can join techMARK, a new market WITHIN the main market. To join techMARK, unquoted or AIM companies must obtain a listing on the Main Market. The size of the companies listed on techMARK will vary from very large to relatively small companies.

The Main Market (previously called the Official List)

For a company to gain a listing on the Stock Exchange, it will have to comply with the United Kingdom Listing Authority's (UKLA) Listing Rules. The UKLA is part of the Financial Securities Authority which has a legal responsibility to oversee the listing process. In addition to satisfying the UKLA's rules companies must also satisfy the requirements of the Stock Exchange's own set of admission and disclosure standards. These two sets of requirements are designed to work together in order to make the process of gaining a listing as straightforward as possible.

The requirements for a full listing are laid down in the 'Listing Rules', commonly called the 'Purple Book'. Examples of the requirements for a listing on the main market are:

● A minimum of 25 % of the company's shares must be in public hands.

● Normally a 3-year track record is required, but the exception to this rule is for innovative high-growth companies without a 3-year track record when the minimum market capitalization required is £50m.

● The company's rules must require prior shareholder approval for substantial acquisitions and disposals.

- The UKLA will have to give prior approval to the admission documents.

- Sponsors, reputable organizations approved by the UKLA under its Sponsors Eligibility Criteria of May 2000, can assist the company in complying with the UKLA requirements. For some types of IPO sponsors are compulsory.

- There will be minimum market capitalization requirements.

Once a company has had its shares admitted to listing on the main market, it must adhere to the continuing obligations in order to retain its listing. The main obligations are:

- Prompt notification to the Quotation Department of information necessary for investors to appraise the company's position. This is particularly important where the information could be 'price sensitive', i.e. cause a movement in the share price. Information about profits, dividends, rights issues or issues of any new types of securities must be given to the Quotation Department immediately after the meeting sanctioning such items.

- Issue of proxy forms with provision for two-way voting (i.e. for or against the resolution).

- Submission of circulars and announcements to shareholders.

- Issue of interim reports, which are required half-yearly. The interim report is unaudited.

- Prompt registration of transfers of stocks and shares and issue of certificates.

- Prior approval of members to any issues of equity capital (or similar) for cash other than to existing equity shareholders.

The Alternative Investment Market (AIM)

The Alternative Investment Market (AIM) commenced trading on 19 June 1995 and is designed to provide companies with an opportunity to raise capital, a trading facility for their shares and a way of placing a market value on their shares.

The type of company likely to be traded in AIM includes young and fast-growing businesses such as management buy-outs and buy-ins and family-owned companies.

The rules for joining AIM are fewer and simpler than for a full listing:

- Member companies must appoint and retain a nominated adviser to guide them on rules and procedures. They must also appoint and retain a broker to make a market in the company's shares.

- To join the AIM the company must produce a prospectus containing detailed financial information on the company. This must be sufficient and suitable for an informed assessment of the company's financial health to be made.

- There is no requirement for a minimum percentage of shares to be in public hands.

- The company's rules do not need to insist on prior shareholder approval for substantial acquisitions and disposals.

- There is no minimum market capitalization.

As a member of AIM, the company must keep investors fully informed. It must publish audited accounts each year along with information on dividends, changes in shareholders and directors. Any 'price-sensitive' information must also be published.

Companies that are members of AIM can represent a higher risk to investors than those quoted on the Main Market. The AIM is therefore more suited to the experienced professional investor.

Shares quoted on AIM are traded on SEATS PLUS – the Stock Exchange Automated Trading Services PLUS, which provides facilities for both market makers and order-driven trading. This helps to provide liquidity (i.e. the ability to buy and sell shares easily).

techMARK – the 'market within a market'

techMARK was created to provide a market for innovative technology companies listed on the Main Market from among the FTSE 100 companies right down to the smallest companies listed on the Main Market. Companies in computer hardware, computer services, Internet, semiconductors, software and telecommunications equipment are automatically admitted to techMARK. Other companies quoted on the Main Market or joining the Main Market can apply to join techMARK provided they can satisfy the Stock Exchange that they are involved in significant technological innovation.

Although a company wishing to join the Main Market would normally have a minimum of 3 years track record, for innovative high-growth companies seeking a listing onto the Main Market and joining techMARK, the rules have been relaxed. However these companies must have a minimum market capitalization of £50m and be selling a minimum of £20m of shares on flotation.

3.6   Procedure prior to issue

This is the same for both full and AIM listings.

- The company approaches a sponsor/nominated advisor in order to gain their support and expertise.

- The sponsor/nominated advisor and the directors agree the terms of reference of the accountant's report. The accountants chosen by the sponsor/nominated advisor will normally be one of the top firms, and the purpose of their report is to give a professional view on the affairs of the company, to protect both the public and the sponsor/nominated advisor.

- The sponsor/nominated advisor will have to be satisfied from the report that the company is suitable for flotation on the Stock Exchange, and the report will help decide the offer price of the new shares.

- If the sponsor/nominated advisor decides it is necessary, a new chairman will be appointed who has the necessary reputation and expertise to gain investor confidence.

- The issue price is provisionally agreed. This will be within one week of the issue date and the final price is agreed a day or two before issue date.

- The whole process from start to gaining a listing can take up to 2 years.

3.7   The role of the sponsor/nominated advisor

A sponsor/nominated advisor can be a merchant bank, a stockbroker or other financial institution. Sponsors/nominated advisors are organizations that specialize in the arrangement of IPOs (new issues). These sponsors/nominated advisors are staffed by financial experts who guide the company through the necessary procedures to obtain a listing. Because the sponsor/nominated advisor has a reputation to maintain, it will look very closely at the company it has been asked to assist. It may require certain changes to be made so that the company will be attractive to the investors.

The timing of the new issue is vital, as is the pricing, and method of issue. The sponsor/nominated advisor will advise on these, using its knowledge of the prevailing conditions to time the issue correctly at an attractive price, and to use the most appropriate method of issue.

The sponsor/nominated advisor acts in one of two roles regarding the issue, as agent or as principal.

- As agent it will distribute the listing particulars and allot shares on application. In return it earns a commission.

- As principal it will purchase the whole of the issue from the company and then offer it for sale to the public or to its own clients (placing).

- When the sponsor/nominated advisor acts as principal it does not charge a commission for its services; it makes its profit by selling the shares at a higher price than it paid. From the company's point of view this means that it knows exactly how much cash it will receive because the whole issue has been taken up. The danger to the sponsor/nominated advisor in this operation is that if the shares do not find buyers it will be left holding shares that it has already paid for and cannot sell.

3.8   Underwriting

The danger that the company (or sponsor/nominated advisor if acting as a principal) runs is that the whole of the share issue may not be taken up. This means that less money is received than is expected, and can seriously affect the future plans of the company. To prevent this occurrence the issue can be underwritten.

Underwriters are organizations that agree to subscribe for any shares not taken up at the time of issue. It is usually the sponsor/nominated advisor that underwrites the whole issue, and it will then arrange with sub-underwriters for a proportion of the issue to be taken. Sub-underwriters are usually banks, broker/dealers, unit trusts, investment trusts, insurance companies and pension funds. In return for underwriting an issue the underwriter receives a commission related to the value of the issue.

The majority of issues are fully subscribed, in which case the underwriters and sub-underwriters will just take their commission. However, in the event of the issue being under subscribed, the underwriters and sub-underwriters will have to buy the shares themselves. In order to recoup their losses, they may sell the shares on the market over a period of time, or they may hold them for a lengthy period until the market has picked up. The choice of action will depend on many factors, but the main one will be the reason for the failure of the issue. If the failure was caused by short-term market sentiment affecting the market in general rather than the company in particular, then the share price should improve quickly and a sale should soon be possible at a reasonable price. If the failure was caused by adverse news about the company or its market sector then the course of action would be rather more difficult to decide.

3.9 Stabilization of IPOs

Under FSA rules, the sponsor of an IPO can be allowed to buy shares in the market for a limited period, known as the stabilization period, after they have been issued. For shares the stabilization period lasts for

- 30 days after the closing date or
- 60 days after the allotment of securities to the investors.

This process of stabilization tries to reverse or halt any fall in the share price below its original issue price once the shares have been issued. Stabilization can be used to support the price, it can never be used to drive the price down.

Normally, manipulation of markets is considered contrary to acceptable standards of market conduct. However, stabilization has been sanctioned by the FSA in the case of IPOs to facilitate an orderly operation of the market. By improving the confidence of companies that the market price of IPOs can be supported, companies should be more willing to seek finance from the Stock Exchange.

3.10 The functions of a company broker

Every quoted company must have a formal link-up with a broker. If the formal link is severed, the company must find another broker very quickly or it will lose its Stock Exchange listing.

When a company first comes to the market the company broker will advise on the methods of obtaining a listing, and it will ensure that all legal formalities are complied with.

Once a company is officially listed, the obligations of a company broker are to ensure that formal announcements of results, acquisitions and disposals are made in accordance with the rules of the Stock Exchange and the UK Listing Authority.

3.11 Withdrawal of listing

The Stock Exchange can withdraw a listing either for a temporary period (called 'suspended') or permanently (called 'cancelled'). The company can itself also request that its listing be suspended or cancelled.

A listing may be cancelled if only a small number of securities remain in public hands, for example, following a takeover. It will also be cancelled if the company goes into liquidation.

A listing can be suspended for anything from a few hours to a few months. This occurs in order to protect investors who are not in full possession of all the relevant information about the company. This may be due to financial difficulties, fraud, takeover or merger with the company concerned. A suspension is often seen if there is takeover activity in the share and the Stock Exchange feels that a false market is being created in the share due to the takeover activity. In such a case a suspension will be for a short period of time to take the heat out of the situation. If the suspension has continued for a very long period (over a year), the listing may be cancelled.

3.12 Methods of obtaining a listing

There are four methods of obtaining a listing: an offer for subscription, offer for sale, placing and introduction.

Offer for subscription

An offer for subscription can be either fixed price or by tender and occurs where the issuing authority offers the shares directly to the public without using an intermediary.

This method can be used by the government for issuing gilts, or by a company. Most companies use the intermediary method, but some investment trusts have issued their shares directly to the public using this method.

Offer for sale

With the offer for sale the sponsor/nominated advisor purchases the securities from the original shareholders, and resells them at a slightly higher price to the general public. This is the most frequently used method of obtaining a listing for shares. The resale can be either fixed price or by tender.

Full details of the contract between the sponsor/nominated advisor and the company are published in the listing particulars.

It is not uncommon for this type of issue to occur when a reorganization of the share capital is undertaken. Often the issue does not raise any new capital for the company, but is used to allow the existing shareholders (usually the directors) to reduce their financial commitment to the company and realize some of the wealth they have tied up in the company.

Placing

A City organization, known as a 'sponsor', buys the whole issue and then agrees terms for sale of 50-95% (depending on the value of the issue) to its own clients. Technically these shares are 'placed' with the clients of the sponsor. The percentage of the issue that can be placed depends on the value of the issue.

The remaining unplaced shares must be sold to a second broker, known as an intermediary. The terms of this sale will have been agreed before the issue comes to market and the price will have been prearranged.

For all practical purposes the private investor has little chance of obtaining shares offered by a placing unless he is a client of the sponsor or intermediary.

All placings must be advertised by means of at least one advertisement in one national newspaper. For a medium and large offer the advertisement must include the full listing particulars or AIM particulars, a mini-prospectus, an offer notice and an application form. For a small offer the advertisement merely needs to advertise the availability of listing or AIM particulars.

Introduction

This method is available only to companies that already have a good spread of shareholders. It is not uncommon for AIM companies to graduate to a full listing by this means, because they often have a reasonable number of shareholders (100 or more). The other type of company commonly to gain a listing via an introduction is one that is already quoted on an overseas stock exchange.

With an introduction no new capital is raised. The existing shares are merely granted a listing. The advantage is with the shareholders who benefit from the increased marketability of their shares that comes with a listing.

The Stock Exchange does encourage the company to make some of its shares available on the market for any interested parties, but this is not compulsory.

Tender issues (applies to both offer for sale and offer for subscription)

Offers for sale or subscription are usually on a fixed-price basis but some issues are offered for tender. With a tender the public is invited to make an offer at or above a minimum stipulated price for the shares. It is usual for a minimum tender price to be fixed, below which offers will not be accepted.

Some gilts have been sold by means of a tender issue, and some company issues also use this method.

If a tender issue is expected to be successful, investors will tender at higher than the minimum tender price. If the offer is oversubscribed then the issuing authority will take the highest bids first and work downwards until all the shares are allotted. The lowest accepted price is called the striking price. Investors who offer above the striking price will receive their shares in full, plus a refund of the difference between their offered price and the striking price. Investors who tendered at lower than the striking price will receive a refund because their bids will not have been accepted.

Example of calculation of the striking price

A company offers 3,000,000 shares for sale by tender at a minimum price of 175p. The issue is oversubscribed and offers are received as detailed below:

400,000	184p
600,000	183p
700,000	182p
800,000	181p
500,000	180p 3,000,000 shares applied for
700,000	179p
600,000	177p
800,000	175p

In this case the striking price would be 180p.

In reality there will never be tenders for exactly the number of shares offered. When the offer is oversubscribed, those who tendered at above the striking price receive their shares in full, and the remaining tenders at striking price are balloted. A variation on this is to ballot all the tenders at or above striking price to allot the shares. The details of the method to be used will be laid down in the listing particulars. In some cases the listing particulars have specified that if the price tendered is above the 'striking price' then the shares are sold to the individual or institution at the price they have tendered. This factor needs to be borne in mind by investors who are subscribing via a tender issue. The best advice in all cases is not to tender a price higher than you are prepared to pay for the shares as a long-term investment.

3.13 Summary of common points between the four methods

These are:

●   If the new issue is undersubscribed the shares will commence trading at a lower price than that paid by the initial shareholder. If undersubscription occurs the 'successful' shareholder will make an immediate capital loss when trading starts.

- If the new issue is oversubscribed the shares are usually allotted by ballot. The successful shareholder receives his shares, the unsuccessful ones receive a refund of the money they submitted.

- If the new issue is oversubscribed the shares will open at a premium to the price paid. This is due to the effects of supply and demand. Institutional investors who do not receive all the shares they require will have to buy them on the Stock Market, thus driving up prices because demand exceeds supply.

- Provided the company (or sponsor/nominated advisor, depending on method of issue used) has had the issue underwritten, it will receive the full amount of cash expected regardless of the success or failure of the issue.

3.14 Information that investors would wish to study before investing in an IPO

The Stock Exchange lays down its listing requirements in the 'Purple Book' (the Listing Rules). All companies must comply with these conditions before their securities can be quoted on the Stock Exchange. In addition, the Financial Services Authority in its role as the UK Listing Authority has a legal obligation to oversee the listing process.

Listing particulars contain the published information made available to prospective investors prior to a new issue. Although the format of the listing particulars will vary depending on the business of the company, there are certain requirements that must be included. The listing particulars are extremely detailed and easily run to 40 or more pages. Summaries of the main points, together with comments on their significance, are shown below.

- The name of the sponsor/nominated advisor/broker. This is of great interest to a prospective investor, because certain sponsors/ nominated advisors/brokers have built up their reputations over the years in dealing with new issues of certain types of company. Thus the good name of these organizations is at risk if the issue should fail.

- Details of the capital structure of the company and the price of the shares being issued.

- Names and addresses of directors, secretary, bankers, solicitors, auditors. As with the sponsors, these firms and people are putting their reputation on the line and the prospective investors will be looking for names with a good reputation.

- The history of, description of, and analysis of the company. The growth should be shown as steady and new developments must be shown to be well researched.

- Prospects, profits and dividends, including earnings and dividends per share over the last three years.

- Accountant's report. This analyses the balance sheets and trends in the company over the past three years. Again the name of the accountants will carry great weight for the prospective investor, and it should be one of the top five firms in order to generate investor confidence.

For a listing on the Main Market or AIM the details are contained in a the listing particulars. An abbreviated form of the listing particulars is often published in the press and this is also known as a 'prospectus'. The price of the shares can be set just before launch date in the light of prevailing market conditions.

3.15   Investor strategy with new issues

The strategy adopted by the prospective investor depends entirely on the method of issue used.

Offer for subscription

A deadline is set, after which no applications will be accepted. The investor should wait for as long as possible before deciding whether or not to invest and how many shares to purchase. He must read the financial press for their comments on the issue, and obtain a broker's opinion on the prospects of both the company and the degree of success that the issue is likely to achieve.

If the investor then decides that the issue is likely to be oversubscribed, he needs to decide which course of action to adopt. He could:

● Apply for more shares than he wanted on the basis that the applications will be scaled down; or

● Apply for an odd number of shares, e.g. 5,200 instead of 5,000. If the issue is oversubscribed and a ballot is used to allocate the shares, the odd number may place him in a higher balloting bracket and increase his chances of obtaining shares. (The reason for this is that there are fewer applications for a large number of shares, thus the chances of successful inclusion in the ballot are higher.)

The danger with both these methods occurs if the issue is not fully subscribed. If this happens the investor will be allotted all the shares he applied for, and this may mean a cost that is in excess of the investor's financial capability to pay. It will also mean that the shares will commence trading at a lower price than he paid. Thus the shareholder will incur an immediate capital loss if he sells the shares at this time.

Offer for sale

Even though the sponsor/nominated advisor is acting as principal for the issue, rather than as an agent, the strategy to adopt is the same as for an offer for subscription.

Placing

The private investor has little opportunity unless he is a client of the sponsor or of the intermediary. The best hope for a private investor is to try to acquire the shares in the 'after market'.

Introduction

With this method of issue a document containing information similar to that in the listing particulars is circulated in the Extel Statistical Service. If the investor wishes to purchase these shares he must contact his broker immediately, because only a few shares may be made available.

The Stock Exchange does not lay down rules regarding the percentage of shares to be made available to the general public, but it does exert pressure on the sponsor/nominated advisor to satisfy demand from market makers. This 'satisfaction of demand' will last only a short while, so time is of the essence.

Tender issues (both offer for sale and offer for subscription)

The same detailed look at the company is needed for this method of issue as for all others, but with the additional feature that the investor must decide on the price he will tender for the shares.

If the investor tenders a price higher than he actually wishes to pay it is quite probable that he will obtain the shares. However, if the striking price is set at a higher level than he would have wished, because the offer is heavily oversubscribed and other investors have used the same strategy, then he must pay the full amount regardless.

If the issue is undersubscribed then the investor will pay the minimum tender price (which will become the striking price). However, the shares will commence trading at a lower price than he paid and he will incur an immediate capital loss if he sells the shares at that time.

The safest strategy is to tender the price he is willing to pay for the shares as a medium-term (5 to 10 years) investment. If the offer is heavily oversubscribed and the striking price is set above the level he has tendered, he will receive no shares. If the striking price is below the price tendered, he will be allotted the shares plus a refund of the difference between the price tendered and the striking price. The timing of the tender is the same as for an offer for sale or subscription, i.e. he should wait until the last possible moment before putting in his tender.

Note: the investor must initially check to see whether the price tendered will be the price paid, or whether one striking price will apply to all successful applicants.

3.16   Factors affecting the decision to invest in new issues

The investor must bear in mind that it is illegal to make multiple applications for a new issue of shares. In all cases detailed study of the financial press is necessary to judge the mood of the market regarding the issue.

A broker's opinion should be sought on the issue, especially if the financial press seems uncertain as to the outcome. The broker can also provide advice based on the listing particulars which are rather long and are too involved for most investors to study with any degree of comprehension. In addition, the investor must watch the timing of his application, looking at the points covered in Chapter 13.

3.17 Stags

Along with bulls and bears, stags are one of the 'animals' of the Stock Exchange. Stags are investors who apply for new issues of shares with the intention of selling them as soon as, or shortly after, dealings commence. Effectively, they are speculators whose intention is to make a quick profit on the shares. If they are successful (which means they have been allotted shares that commence trading at a price higher than they paid) they do not have to pay out any money. The reason for this is that new issues are dealt with on the Stock Exchange for 'cash', i.e. the investor receives the sale proceeds the day after the sale is made. The investor's cheque, which accompanies his application for the shares, usually takes several days to clear, and it is thus usual for the cheque to be cleared after the sale proceeds have been received.

Staging of new issues is a mixed blessing. It does ensure that an issue is fully subscribed because stags go only for issues that look successful. The other advantage is that it does make shares available on the market for unsuccessful applicants (or those who 'missed the boat' with their timings).

The problem, however, is with fixed-price issues that are heavily stagged. The oversubscription causes a tremendous amount of paperwork in allotting the shares, and it does prevent the genuine investor from obtaining shares at the outset.

4

CAPITALIZATION ISSUES, RIGHTS ISSUES AND ALLOTMENT LETTERS

Objectives

After studying this Chapter, the reader should be able to:

- describe a capitalization issue and the effect it has on a company's balance sheet and share price;

- evaluate the motives that might influence a company to make a capitalization issue;

- differentiate between a share split, a share consolidation and a scrip issue;

- describe the features of a renounceable certificate;

- explain what is meant by a rights issue (also called a secondary offering) and the reasons for a company to make a rights issue;

- understand the timetable for a rights issue;

- list and explain the courses of action a shareholder can take in relation to a rights issue;

- describe a deep-discounted rights issue;

- in relation to a rights issue, be able to calculate:

    - the ex rights price

    - nil paid price

    - value of the rights and explain what each of these means;

- describe a vendor placing;

- describe an open offer;

- describe the functions of an allotment letter;

- describe the choices an investor has in relation to an allotment letter.

4.1   Introduction

In Chapter 3 we discussed new issues of shares for companies that did not already have a Stock Exchange quotation. In this chapter we examine capitalization and rights issues which are new issues of shares for companies already quoted on the Stock Exchange. In both capitalization and rights issues the new shares are first offered to the existing shareholders on a pro rata basis. At the end of the chapter you will study renounceable certificates and allotment letters which form part of the administrative procedures for these issues.

4.2   Capitalization issues

There are some alternative names for this capitalization issues – 'bonus issues' or 'scrip issues'. All three names mean exactly the same, although the technically correct term is 'capitalization issue'.

What is a capitalization issue?

A capitalization issue is made by a company, not to raise new capital but to increase the number of shares in issue. This operation is usually carried out where the price of a single share is extremely high and the company feels that its shares are less attractive to investors due to the high unit price. A capitalization issue will cause the price per share to fall (see example below).

A capitalization issue is simply a book-keeping exercise where a proportion of a company's reserves in the balance sheet are transferred to share capital. Reserves can consist of share premium account, reserves from the revaluation of fixed assets or from retained profits (sometimes shown as the profit and loss balance in the balance sheet). If a company has a share premium account this will be used first, ahead of other reserves.

Example

A company's balance sheet prior to a capitalization issue could be:

	£000		£000
600,000 ordinary shares of £1 each	600	Net assets	1,200
Share premium account	60		
Reserves	540		
	1,200		1,200

The company may decide to make a one-for-one capitalization issue, which means that every shareholder will receive one new fully-paid share for every one he owns, and no money will be paid to the company for the 'privilege'.

After completion of the capitalization issue, the company's balance sheet will appear as follows (assuming no other factors apply):

	£000		£000
1,200,000 ordinary shares of £1 each	1,200	Net assets	1,200
	1,200		1,200

The balance sheet above is deliberately simplified to highlight the effect or, to be more accurate, the non-effect of a bonus issue. As can be seen, the balance sheet is neither stronger nor weaker than before, because the net assets remain unchanged. All that has happened is that there has been a change in the way shareholders' funds are shown, and such changes are merely cosmetic. Share capital, reserves and retained profits are regarded as a single item by lending bankers and other creditors.

4.3   Effect on the share price

Other things being equal, the price of the shares after the capitalization (known as the 'ex cap' price) will fall in direct proportion to the increase in share capital. In our example, if the quoted share price immediately before the capitalization issue had been 300p, the ex cap price would have been expected to fall to 150p, because there are twice the number of shares, but only the same asset backing and earning capacity.

This explanation began with the words 'other things being equal', but of course they rarely are equal. The lower price per share makes the shares more marketable. There is no logical reason for it, but private investors particularly find a lower-priced share more attractive than one with a higher price. If the new shares are more attractive, then under the basic law of supply and demand their price must rise.

Nobody can explain why the lower price makes the shares more marketable, but one explanation could be that an investment of £12,000 (ignoring costs) in the pre-capitalization shares would purchase 4,000 shares, while the same amount invested in the shares ex cap would result in acquisition of 8,000 shares, which makes the investor feel he has more for his money. If the company operates an employee share option scheme, whereby relatively small amounts are saved over a five-year period, then a highly-priced share may be less attractive to the employee.

Generally speaking, capitalization issues can be made only when a company has been successful in the past. Shares could only have been issued at a premium if buyers were confident of success. Revenue reserves can be acquired only from undistributed profits, and revaluations of fixed assets at least mean that the company's property has risen in value. In addition to all this, a capitalization issue is often accompanied by a good profits forecast.

Thus an aura of success generally surrounds a capitalization issue, and this, together with increased marketability, usually ensures that the ensuing ex cap price is above the one that would be expected from a simple mathematical calculation.

4.4 Why does a company make a capitalization issue?

There are no obvious tangible benefits to a company from a capitalization issue, but possible intangible benefits are:

- A capitalization issue can be a useful public relations exercise, bringing the past successes and future forecasts to the attention of shareholders and others.

- The issued share capital shown in the balance sheet can come more into line with net asset value.

- The rate of dividend per share can remain unchanged, but actual dividends can be increased. In our example the original 600,000 shares were doubled to 1,200,000 shares. Before the bonus issue a dividend of 5p net per share would have resulted in a total payment to shareholders of £30,000, whereas after the issue a dividend of 5p per share would have resulted in a total payment of £60,000.

- When negotiating with consumers or other interested parties there can be problems if the other party is aware that the dividend rate has doubled. However, these problems are likely to be less if the dividend rate remains constant but the number of shares has increased.

4.5 Difference between a capitalization issue, share split and a share consolidation

Share Split

A share split occurs when the company's total nominal capital remains unchanged, but when the nominal value per share is reduced. Let us recall our simplified pre-capitalization balance sheet which was:

	£000		£000
600,000 ordinary shares of £1 each	600	Net assets	1,200
Share premium	60		
Reserves	540		
	1,200		1,200

Quoted price per share 300p.

Using the appropriate resolution, the directors could authorize a one-for-one share split. This would reduce the nominal value per share from £1 to 50p. In this case the balance sheet immediately after the split would be:

	£000		£000
1,200,000 ordinary shares of 50p each	600	Net assets	1,200
Share premium	60		
Reserves	540		
	1,200		1,200

With a share split the share price would be expected to fall in line with the reduction in the nominal value. The expected share price would fall to 150p, however increased marketability and market forces in general would also affect the price of the new shares.

4.6   Share Consolidation

A share consolidation is the exact reverse of a split, so that in the example above a share consolidation could involve the nominal value per share being increased to £2. In such a case, the ordinary share capital in the balance sheet would remain at £600,000 but would be represented by 300,000 shares of £2 nominal each.

With a share consolidation, the price would be expected to rise in line with the share consolidation. In this case it would be expected to double to 600p, subject to market forces.

Summary of effect of a capitalization issue, share split and share consolidation					
	Nominal Value	Number of shares issued	Share price after issue	Number of shares held after issue	Value of holding after issue
Position prior to issue	£1	600,000	300p	1,000	£3,000
Capitalization issue	Unchanged at £1	1,200,000	150p	2,000	£3,000
Share split	Reduced to 50p	1,200,000	150p	2,000	£3,000
Share consolidation	Increased to £2	300,000	600p	500	£3,000

4.7   Renounceable certificates

When a company makes a capitalization issue it sends every shareholder a new renounceable certificate for the number of shares to which he is entitled. If the shareholder wishes to retain the shares, he need do nothing at all. On the back of the renounceable certificate is stated an 'expiry date', and if the shareholder takes no action by this date the certificate becomes a conventional registered share certificate.

On the other hand, if the form on the reverse of the certificate is signed by the shareholder before the expiry date (the process of signing is called 'renunciation'), then the shares represented by the capitalization issue can be transferred into the name of a third party without the need for a signed stock transfer form.

4.8   Rights issues (also called secondary offerings)

What is a rights issue?

What was formerly called a rights issue was described as a secondary offering under the FSA approved terminology. However, the term rights issue is still commonly used to describe the operation, so rights issue will be used throughout the remainder of the book.

A rights issue is an issue of new shares to existing shareholders in proportion to the number of shares already held by each shareholder. The price at which the new shares are issued is below the current market price of the shares to encourage the shareholders to take up the issue. The new shares rank pari passu (equally) with all other shares of the same category once the issue is completed.

Apart from the need to be below the current market price, the actual price at which the new shares are issued depends on the size of funds needed by the company, the status of the company and market conditions in general.

The shareholder will receive a renounceable letter detailing information, number of shares provisionally allotted and due date for payment. This renounceable letter is also called a provisional allotment letter.

The reasons for a company to make a rights issue

The purpose of a rights issue will differ from company to company, but there are three main reasons why a company may need to make a rights issue, and one reason why a company may wish to make a rights issue.

The main reasons for making a rights issue are:

● When a company wishes to expand it may well request extra cash from its shareholders by way of a rights issue to finance that expansion.

● Extra fixed assets may be acquired and current assets will no doubt increase. However, while additional credit may finance some of these extra demands, an increased capital base by way of a rights issue may also be required. Another method of expansion is by means of takeovers, which will need additional equity finance.

- A company may need to strengthen its balance sheet by obtaining extra share capital. When a company has too high a ratio of interest-bearing loan capital compared with its shareholders' funds, it is said to be highly geared. Highly-geared companies can suffer if there is a squeeze on profits, because the interest on the borrowing is a debt that is payable whether or not profits are made. In 2001 BT made a widely publicized rights issue to strengthen its balance sheet and to improve its credit rating, which had been downgraded.

- One final reason a company may wish to make a rights issue, as opposed to needing to make one, is simple opportunism. In some cases rights issues have been used to finance takeovers.

When share prices are relatively high shareholders are generally quite happy to subscribe for further shares by way of a rights issue. Some companies then put the money so raised on deposit in the money markets, while searching for a suitable business to take over.

Advantages of a rights issue to a company

Subject to the Articles of Association, a rights issue may be made at the discretion of the directors, whereas under the 1985 Companies Act and the Rules of the Stock Exchange, all issues of shares for cash, apart from rights issues, must be approved by shareholders in general meeting.

The administrative costs are less than for a new issue of shares because there is no need to publish listing particulars provided the rights issue will increase the class of capital to which it relates (usually ordinary capital) by less than 10%. However, even where the publication of listing particulars is waived, information must still be published in the form of a brochure available to the public.

Shareholders who take up their rights will retain the same percentage of the company's share capital, and hence will retain the same voting powers.

Disadvantages of a rights issue for a company

Most rights issues are underwritten, because there is no legal obligation on the part of shareholders to subscribe (although the shares must first be offered to existing shareholders). However, should the issue be left with the underwriters, this is in effect a vote of no confidence in the directors by shareholders and the Stock Market in general.

The timetable for a rights issue

Each company will lay out a timetable for the rights issue in the information provided to the shareholder. The shareholder needs to take note of this so that he does not omit to take any necessary action with regards to the rights issue. The following information shows how the timetable operates:

Expected timetable for the rights issue (all dates are in the same year)

Latest time for receipt of proxies	9 am on Saturday 1 June
Extraordinary general meeting	9 am on Monday 3 June
Provisional allotment letter despatched	Monday 3 June
Dealings in new shares commence, nil paid	Tuesday 4 June
Latest time for splitting, nil paid	3 pm on Thursday 20 June
Latest time for acceptance and payment in full	3 pm on Monday 24 June
Dealings in new shares commence, fully paid	Tuesday 25 June
Latest time for splitting, fully paid	3 pm on Friday 12 July
Latest time for registration of renunciation	3 pm on Tuesday 16 July
Definitive certificates for new shares despatched	Tuesday 30 July

With this issue, as with many rights issues, the company first requires a resolution to be passed. Voting can be done in person or by arranging for someone else to vote on your behalf (a proxy). The first two dates of 1 and 3 June relate to the extraordinary general meeting. Once the resolution is passed provisional allotment letters will be sent to shareholders on 3 June. The rest of the timetable gives the cut-off dates and times for each of the stages subsequent to the rights issue being completed. The whole process will be completed on 30 July when the new share certificates are sent out to the shareholders.

4.9 Choices of the shareholder when a rights issue is made

- **Subscribe for the new shares** (this is sometimes called taking up the rights). If the shareholder has sufficient cash resources to buy the new shares, and if he feels the company will use the money so raised in a profitable way, then he should take up the rights.

  If the shareholder feels the new shares are worth having, but he lacks the cash to pay for them, he can sell sufficient of the rights to enable him to take up the balance. The detailed calculations appear in section 10.

- **Sell the rights.** The new shares are cheaper than the current market price, and both new and old shares will rank pari passu (on equal footing) when the formalities have been completed. Thus the new nil paid shares have a value for which a third party would be willing to pay. If the shareholder is not happy about the rights issue or requires some extra cash he should sell the rights. Usually the rights are sold via a broker who will charge commission.

- **Do nothing at all** is an alternative to selling the rights. Under the terms of all UK quoted company rights issues, if the amount payable for the new shares has not been received by a stipulated deadline the company will sell the new shares in the market. This may be advantageous if the shareholding and hence the rights in respect of it are very small. The shareholder will then receive the sale proceeds of the new shares, less the rights price (the amount due to the company for the new shares) and any expenses, except where the proceeds do not exceed £3, in which case the proceeds may be kept for the company's benefit.

Before pursuing this course of action the shareholder must check the terms of the issue, because in a minority of cases the rights simply lapse, i.e. the rights become worthless to the shareholder, if no action is taken by the stated deadline. This applies quite commonly to shares of overseas companies. Although most UK shareholders will not hold such shares, those who do need to be aware of the dangers.

In deciding on his course of action the shareholder should simply ask himself two questions:

● Do I wish to invest more money in the company?

● If so, have I the cash to meet the necessary subscription?

If the answer to the first question is 'yes', then he will consider the second. If he has enough cash, then he will take up the rights. If he has insufficient cash he can sell enough of the rights to purchase the remainder. If the answer to the first question is 'no', then he will either sell the rights or let them lapse.

Deep-discounted rights issues

These differ from ordinary rights issues in that the issue is not underwritten because new shares are priced substantially below the current share price. This is done virtually to ensure that the issue is taken up in full. Stock Exchange rules state that the subscription price of a deep discounted rights issue is 20% or more below the current market price.

A deep-discounted rights issue also reduces the price per share considerably which makes the shares more marketable. This is similar to the effect of a capitalization issue, but with the added bonus that the company raises fresh capital at the same time.

Problems do arise for the individual shareholder with a deep-discounted issue if he wishes to sell enough of the rights to purchase the remainder at no cost. Because shares are sold there is a potential capital gains tax liability. With a conventional rights issue this is unlikely to happen, but with a deep-discounted issue this is a common problem.

4.10　Rights issue calculations

Introduction

Ultimately the ex rights price (the price of the shares after the rights issue has been completed) will be decided by market forces in just the same way as is the ex cap price in a bonus issue.

Rights issues are often accompanied by a forecast of the rate of dividend on the enlarged capital. Nevertheless, it is possible to calculate the theoretical ex rights price, together with other relevant calculations which will be explained below.

The ex rights price

This is the price that all shares, both old and new, will be expected to reach once the rights issue has been completed and the new shares are fully paid.

Let us look at a typical example. Suppose a company decides to make a rights issue of one new share for every three held, and the amount payable to the company for each new share is 80p (subscription price). Let us suppose that the price of the shares immediately prior to the rights issue is 100p. The ex rights price is calculated as follows:

3 old shares prior to the rights issue are worth	300p
+ 1 new share for which 80p is payable	80p
4 shares ranking pari passu after the issue are worth	380p
Therefore 1 share after the rights issue should be worth	95p

Thus the ex rights price is 95p.

This is the price that the shares will be expected to trade at on the stock market when the issue is complete. Ex rights means that the purchaser of these shares will have no right to the new shares (ex meaning 'without').

Price of the new shares in nil paid form

Since the new shares are expected to be worth the ex rights price of 95p, and since a payment of 80p must at some time be made to the company, the price of the new shares in nil paid form, i.e. nothing yet paid to the company, can be expected to be 15p (95p - 80p).

The formula for calculating the price of new shares in nil paid form is ex rights price minus subscription price. This price is the amount a third party would theoretically be willing to pay for each new share in nil paid form.

Value of the rights

This is the difference between the price of the shares prior to the rights issue commencing and the expected ex rights price. In our example the value of the rights would be 5p (100p - 95p).

This value of the rights is the amount (excluding deductions for costs) that a shareholder would expect to receive if he sold the rights attaching to a single share.

Note that the ratio of the value of the rights to the price of the new shares in nil paid form is in the same proportions as the terms of the issue (1:3 in this example). This is a useful check on arithmetical accuracy.

How to calculate the number of new shares to be sold to enable a shareholder to finance the purchase of the balance of the new shares to which he is due

We start with the formula:

$$\text{number of nil paid shares sold} = \frac{\text{subscription price x number of new shares allotted}}{\text{ex rights price}}$$

In our example, a shareholder who owned 3,000 shares immediately prior to the rights issue would have the right to subscribe to 1,000 new shares at 80p per share (i.e. one new share for every three old shares held). Using the formula we see:

$$\frac{\text{subscription price x number of new shares allotted}}{\text{ex rights price}} = \frac{80 \times 1,000}{95} = 842.1$$

As you can only sell full shares, the number taken up is rounded down to 157 shares (1,000 - 843).

Check: 157 new shares with a payment of 80p per share = £125.60 to pay.

Cash received from sale of 843 new shares at 15p each = £126.45.

Notes:

1. Always round down the number of new shares to be retained, because you cannot sell a fraction of a share. If you round up the number, then there will be a small extra amount to be paid.

2. If the sale of the nil paid shares raises more than 5% of the current market value of the investment, there is a potential capital gains tax liability.

Summary of rights issue calculations

Let us now sum up the position of our shareholder who owned 3,000 shares prior to the commencement of the one-for-three rights issue already described.

When the shareholder has decided to take up the rights:

●   prior to the issue the value of his holding was £3,000 (3,000 x 100p);

●   after the issue has been completed he will own 4,000 shares expected to be worth £3,800 (4,000 x 95p), and the amount paid for the new shares to the company will be £800 (1,000 x 80p).

The net result is that our shareholder has paid £800 and the value of his shareholding is expected to increase by the same amount.

When the shareholder has decided to sell his rights:

●   prior to the commencement of the rights issue his shareholding was worth £3,000;

●   after the issue has been completed his 3,000 shares should be worth £2,850. However, the expected loss in value of £150 has been compensated for by the sale proceeds of £150.

The sale proceeds can be calculated in one of two ways:

3,000 x value of rights, i.e. 5p = £150

or

1,000 new shares sold in nil paid form for 15p each = £150

When he sells sufficient new shares to enable him to purchase the balance:

- prior to the rights issue his holding was worth £3,000;

- after completion of the formalities he now owns 3,157 shares expected to be worth £2,999.15 (3,157 x 95p).

Note: the 85p difference is caused by the rounding down.

It will be seen that a net 85p will be left in the shareholder's hands, representing the difference between the amount of the sale proceeds and the amount due to the company on the subscription for the new shares and allowing for the fraction of a share that is rounded down.

We can see from the calculations that the shareholder in a rights issue does not receive something for nothing. This reinforces the fact that the amount of the discount is immaterial, and that the investor's decision depends on the answers to the two questions:

- do I wish to invest more money in this company?

- if so do I have the cash to meet the necessary subscription?

4.11 Vendor placings as an alternative to a rights issue

As we already know, one reason for a rights issue is to help to finance takeovers or acquisitions. An alternative method of raising finance for this purpose is a vendor placing.

For example, if Company A wanted to purchase a subsidiary from Company B for, say, £100 million in cash, a vendor placing would work as follows. A issues new shares to B, and simultaneously A's merchant bank buys these new shares from B for £100 million. The merchant bank will then place the shares with its own clients; usually institutional clients. A common refinement is to introduce a 'claw back' provision whereby the shareholders in A have the right to acquire the shares from the merchant bank on the same terms as are offered to the placees, and in priority to the placees.

Vendor placings cannot be made without the approval of the shareholders.

A variation on a vendor placing is a vendor rights issue. This is where the shares issued are purchased by a single buyer (usually an issuing house). The shares are then offered to the shareholders of the issuing company as in a rights issue. This avoids the dilution that takes place with a vendor placing.

4.12 Comparison of capitalization and rights issues

We can now summarize the similarities and differences in the following table:

Capitalization issue	Rights issue
1. A mere book-keeping exercise which does not raise any cash.	A means of raising cash for the company.
2. The new shares are issued free to existing shareholders on a pro rata basis.	The new shares are issued at a price below the current market price to existing shareholders on a pro rate basis.
3. The ex cap price will fall in proportion to the amount of new shares issued, in theory. In practice the ex cap price will be determined by market forces.	In theory the ex rights price will fall in proportion to the new shares issued, but fall will be offset by the amount of cash payable to the company on the new shares. In practice the ex rights price will be determined by market forces.
4. The administration is by renounceable certificate.	Administration is by way of allotment letter.
5. The shareholder need not make any decisions.	The shareholder must decide whether to: (a) take up the rights; (b) sell sufficient new shares to finance purchase of the balance; (c) sell the rights; (d) do nothing.

4.13 Open offer

An open offer is an invitation to existing shareholders to purchase shares in proportion to their holdings. It is often made in conjunction with a placing (see Chapter 3), which is made with the City institutions rather than to the private shareholders of the company. The open offer is usually made to the existing private investors who 'would find their stakes in the company watered down by this, so the company will usually make an open offer at the same time'. (Source: *Investors Chronicle*, 25 February 2000, page 82).

The offer price is nearly always at a discount to the current share price; however there are some offers where the price is at a premium. A premium price can occur when the company is in urgent need of capital due to financial difficulties and needs a refinancing or capital re-organization to survive.

The shareholder will receive an assignable or transferable application form with an open offer, which has the facility to be split. He must pay for the shares straight away.

An open offer is basically similar to a rights issue. The main differences for our purposes are as follows:

● With a rights issue the shareholder receives a renounceable letter and with an open offer receives an assignable or transferable application form;

● With a rights issue there is a period of time, usually around 21 days, when the rights can be sold 'nil paid'. With an open offer the investor has to pay the full amount by the acceptance date – there is no concept of 'nil paid' with an open offer;

● Investors can sell the shares acquired via an open offer only once the new shares are issued;

● With a rights issue if the investor does nothing, the rights will be sold and the proceeds remitted to him (unless these are less than £3). With an open offer, if the investor does nothing he will receive no cash from the sale of the shares not taken up, thus diluting his equity stake in the company.

Companies may prefer to use an open offer to raise funds because they receive their money more quickly than in a rights issue. It can also be cheaper to the company to underwrite an open offer than a rights issue because of the timing of the cash received from investors.

4.14 Allotment letters and letters of acceptance

The functions of these documents

Letters of allotment or letters of acceptance are used in connection with a new issue by way of an offer for sale or an offer for subscription. With a rights issue a provisional allotment letter is issued. There is no practical difference between any of these documents and we can consider the terms to be synonymous.

When a new issue or a rights issue is made the published details, whether contained in listing particulars or in a prospectus, will state how and in what instalments the subscription is to be paid.

Having sent a cheque for the initial amount required on application, the successful investor will receive an allotment letter. This is a legal document which:

● Acts as a receipt for money paid to the company for shares;

● Gives details of the remaining instalments (if any) required;

● Can be exchanged for a share certificate when fully paid, on the terms set out in the allotment letter itself;

●   Acts as a document of title to the shares prior to the issue of the definitive certificate.

To transfer ownership, the holder signs renunciation form X. He then hands the allotment letter to the purchaser, who completes forms Y and Z. (Note some allotment letters have only a form Y.)

Specimen provisional allotment letter (see opposite page)

As previously stated, letters of acceptance and allotment letters are for all intents and purposes the same. The specimen British Aerospace provisional allotment letter was in connection with a new issue by way of a rights issue.

4.15   Further points on allotment letters

Oversubscription

Sometimes the terms of the issue, as shown in the listing particulars or prospectus, ask for an initial payment on application, and a second payment on allotment. In such cases, the successful allottee must immediately return the allotment letter to the relevant authority, together with payment of the sum due on allotment.

When an issue is oversubscribed, and the allottee receives less stock than he requested, any surplus proceeds will be applied towards the allotment monies.

When the terms of the issue prescribe a long time lag between the payment on application and the next due payment, any surplus proceeds are returned to the allottee.

Splitting

This occurs when an allottee wishes to:

●   Sell only part of his allotment, possibly with a view to using the proceeds to pay for the balance of a rights issue;

●   Give away his allotment to two or more people, thus requiring the original to be split into two or more allotment letters.

Consolidation

It can happen that a purchaser acquires a number of allotment letters which he would prefer to consolidate into a single document.

The purchaser will complete the consolidation listing form on one allotment letter and send all the allotment letters to the issuing authority to be replaced by one new allotment letter.

Figure 4.1: Speciment Allotment Letter

CAPITALISATION ISSUES, RIGHTS ISSUES AND
ALLOTMENT LETTERS

SPLIT FROM No.	REFERENCE No.	ALLOTMENT No.
	04364667	00312502

THIS DOCUMENT IS OF VALUE AND IS NEGOTIABLE. IF YOU ARE IN ANY DOUBT AS TO THE ACTION YOU SHOULD TAKE, PLEASE SEEK PERSONAL FINANCIAL ADVICE FROM YOUR STOCKBROKER, SOLICITOR, ACCOUNTANT OR OTHER PROFESSIONAL ADVISER AUTHORISED UNDER THE FINANCIAL SERVICES ACT 1986 IMMEDIATELY.
IF YOU HAVE DISPOSED OF ALL YOUR ORDINARY SHARES AND/OR PREFERENCE SHARES (OTHER THAN EX-RIGHTS), PLEASE HAND THIS DOCUMENT TO THE PERSON THROUGH WHOM YOU MADE THE DISPOSAL FOR ONWARD TRANSMISSION TO THE TRANSFEREE.

Application has been made to the Council of the London Stock Exchange for the new Ordinary Shares which have been provisionally allotted nil paid to be admitted to the Official List. It is expected that such listing will become effective on 8th October, 1991. In the event that such listing does not become effective on or before 10.00 a.m. on 8th October 1991 or such later time and date (not being later than 10.00 a.m. on 15th October 1991) as Kleinwort Benson Limited and the Company may agree, this document will not be of any value and will have no effect. The Listing Particulars relating to the Company, copies of which have been delivered for registration to the Registrar of Companies as required by Section 149 of the Financial Services Act 1986, are contained in the Circular from the Company dated 11th September 1991 (the "Circular"). The definitions in the Circular apply in this provisional allotment letter.
The new Ordinary Shares and the provisional allotment letters have not been registered under the United States Securities Act of 1933, as amended (the "Securities Act") or under the securities laws of any state of the United States or of any province or territory of Canada and accordingly the new Ordinary Shares, this provisional allotment letter and the rights with respect to new Ordinary Shares arising hereunder may not be offered or sold, directly or indirectly, in the United States or Canada except pursuant to an exemption from, or in a transaction not subject to, the registration requirements under the Securities Act and in accordance with any applicable securities laws of any state of the United States or, in the case of an offer or sale in Canada, in accordance with any applicable securities laws of any province or territory of Canada.

BRITISH AEROSPACE Public Limited Company ⌘

Registered in England: No. 1470151   Registered Office: 11 Strand, London WC2N 5JT

RIGHTS ISSUE OF 117,398,242 NEW ORDINARY SHARES OF 50p EACH AT 380p PER SHARE PAYABLE IN FULL ON ACCEPTANCE NOT LATER THAN 3.00 pm ON 28th OCTOBER, 1991

THIS ENTIRE DOCUMENT MUST BE PRESENTED WHEN PAYMENT IS MADE

PROVISIONAL ALLOTMENT LETTER

At the office of the Registrar,
Lloyds Bank Plc, Registrar's Department,
Goring-by-Sea, Worthing, West Sussex BN12 6DA
Telephone: Worthing (0903) 502541

Latest time for:
Acceptance and payment in full
(See paragraph 2 below)   3.00 p.m. on 28th October, 1991
Registration of renunciation   3.00 p.m. on 21st November, 1991
Despatch of certificates   12th December, 1991

0084676
UNITED REFORMED
CHURCH EAST MIDLANDS PROVINCE INC
57 CHATSWORTH ROAD
WORKSOP
NOTTINGHAMSHIRE   S81 0LD

At the office of the Registrar,
Lloyds Bank Plc, Registrar's Department,
Issue Section. P.O. Box 1000, 2nd Floor.
Bolsa House. 80 Cheapside, London EC2V 6EE
Telephone: London (071) 248 9822

Latest time for:
Splitting – Nil paid   3.00 p.m. on 24th October, 1991
Acceptance and payment in full
(See paragraph 2 below)   3.00 p.m. on 28th October, 1991
Splitting – Fully paid   3.00 p.m. on 19th November, 1991

(1) Holdings of Ordinary and Preference Shares at close of business on 27th September, 1991
(2) Number of new Ordinary Shares provisionally allotted to you
(3) Amount payable on acceptance in full at 380p per share

ORDINARY   **0**   **766**   **£2910.50**
PREFERENCE   **16000**

DEAR SIR OR MADAM,   7th October, 1991

1. Subject to and in accordance with the provisions of the Circular and this provisional allotment letter, you have been provisionally allotted, subject to the Memorandum and Articles of Association of the Company, the number of new Ordinary Shares set out in column 2 above, at a price of 380p per new Ordinary Share. New Ordinary Shares have been allotted to holders of Ordinary Shares (other than certain overseas holders of Ordinary Shares) on the basis of 2 new Ordinary Shares for every 5 Ordinary Shares and to the holders of the Preference Shares (other than certain overseas holders of Preference Shares) on the basis of 1 new Ordinary Share for every 20.87508 Preference Shares held, in each case at the close of business on 27th September, 1991. Entitlements to new Ordinary Shares have been rounded down to the nearest whole number. New Ordinary Shares representing fractional entitlements have not been allotted to shareholders but will be aggregated and sold in the market for the benefit of the Company.

2. If you wish to take up the new Ordinary Shares provisionally allotted to you, YOU MUST COMPLETE THE NATIONALITY DECLARATION SET OUT IN BOX A ON PAGE 2 and send this entire provisional allotment letter accompanied by a remittance for the full amount payable on acceptance shown in column 3 above to Lloyds Bank Plc, Registrar's Department, Goring-by-Sea, Worthing, West Sussex BN12 6DA, so as to arrive by not later than 3.00 p.m. on 28th October, 1991. Provisional allotment letters may also be lodged for acceptance by that time, by hand, at Lloyds Bank Plc, Registrar's Department, Issue Section. PO. Box 1000. 2nd Floor, Bolsa House, 80 Cheapside, London EC2V 6EE. This provisional allotment letter will then be returned to the person lodging it, duly receipted. Payment will constitute acceptance of the provisional allotment. Cheques should be made payable to Lloyds Bank Plc and crossed "Not negotiable – A/c British Aerospace". All payments must be made by cheque or banker's draft in pounds sterling drawn on a bank in the United Kingdom which is either a member of the Clearing Houses Association or which has arranged for cheques and banker's drafts to be cleared through the facilities provided for the members of that Association. No interest will accrue on payments made before the due date. The Company reserves the right, but shall not be obliged, to accept (i) provisional allotment letters and accompanying remittances which are received through the post not later than 10.00 a.m. on 29th October, 1991, the cover bearing a legible postmark with a date no later than 28th October, 1991 and (ii) acceptances in respect of which remittances are received prior to 3.00 p.m. on 28th October, 1991 from an authorised person (as defined in the Financial Services Act 1986) specifying the new Ordinary Shares concerned and undertaking to lodge the relevant provisional allotment letter duly completed in due course.

3. Procedure in respect of rights not taken up: In certain circumstances, as outlined above, acceptances received after 3.00 p.m. on 28th October, 1991 may be treated as valid. Subject thereto, if payment in full is not received by 3.00 p.m. on 28th October, 1991, the provisional allotment will be deemed to have been declined and will be cancelled. Any new Ordinary Shares not taken up will be sold in the market by not later than 3.00 p.m. on 31st October, 1991 if they can be sold at a price at least equal to the subscription price and expenses of sale. Any net proceeds after deduction of the subscription price and the sale expenses will be distributed pro rata, by cheque, to the provisional allottees originally entitled thereto, except that individual amounts of less than £3.00 will be retained for the benefit of the Company.

4. Further instructions as to how to deal with this provisional allotment letter are set out on pages 2 and 3 and should be studied carefully. These instructions are an integral part of this provisional allotment letter.

5. The new Ordinary Shares will, when issued and fully paid, rank pari passu in all respects with the Ordinary Shares now in issue, save that they will not rank for the proposed interim dividend in respect of the year ending 31st December, 1991 nor entitle holders to participate in the Interim Scrip Dividend Scheme.

6. Entire provisional allotment letters with the stamp of Lloyds Bank Plc duly impressed on page 1 or, in the case of renunciations, on pages 1 and 2 thereof, may, provided that the nationality declaration set out in Box A on page 2 and, if applicable, the nationality declaration set out in Box B on page 4 have been duly executed, be exchanged for share certificates from 22nd November to 10th December 1991. In such cases, the share certificates will be despatched to the lodging agent on 12th December 1991. After 21st November, 1991 and pending the issue of share certificates, transfers will be certified by the Company's Registrar, Lloyds Bank Plc, Registrar's Department, Goring-by-Sea, Worthing, West Sussex BN12 6DA, against surrender of provisional allotment letters, stamped as aforesaid on pages 1 and 2. After 12th December, 1991, provisional allotment letters will cease to be valid for any purposes whatsoever and Lloyds Bank Plc will, subject to receipt of a duly signed nationality declaration, forward by ordinary post any share certificates remaining in its hands to the registered holder (or in the case of joint holders, to the first-named holder) at his registered address. All share certificates, other documents and cheques will be despatched through the post at the risk of the person(s) entitled thereto.

7. By taking up the rights represented hereby, you represent and warrant that no such rights are being taken up, directly or indirectly, by or for the account or benefit of a person in the United States, except rights being taken up by or for the account or benefit of qualifying U.S. institutional shareholders each of which has executed and delivered an investment letter (the form of which may be obtained from Lloyds Bank Plc, Registrar's Department) which, in the case of rights being taken up by a nominee for the account or benefit of a qualifying U.S. institutional shareholder, is delivered herewith or, in the case of a qualifying U.S. institutional shareholder with a registered address in the United States, was delivered directly to Lloyds Bank Plc prior to 2nd October, 1991.

By Order of the Board.
S. D. Windridge, Secretary.

Lodged for payment by:	Received the amount payable on acceptance	ACCOUNT NUMBER	ALLOTMENT NUMBER
		04364667	00512502
			766
			£2910.80
	Stamp for Lloyds Bank Plc and date	British Aerospace Public Limited Company	
		Rights Issue of	
		117,398,242 new Ordinary Shares	

Choices to be made by the allottee who receives a letter of acceptance or allotment letter

Whether the issue concerned is a new issue or a rights issue the administrative procedures whereby the ultimate buyer obtains the relevant certificate are the same.

The person to whom the allotment letter is sent, the allottee, has the following choices, as have already been described, for a rights issue:

- Retention – take up the shares represented by the allotment letter, and pay any calls due. The fully paid allotment letter will be replaced by a share certificate.

- Renunciation in whole or part – sell sufficient to finance the purchase of the balance, or sell all the shares represented by the allotment letter. In either case the allottee will sign form X, the form of renunciation, and send the allotment letter to his broker (preferably by registered post because it is effectively bearer in nature because it is signed in blank).

- Consolidation – the exchange of several allotment letters for a single one.

- Splitting – where the allottee wishes to sell or give some of the shares to two or more people. He will sign form X and send the allotment letter to the issuing authority with details of the desired split.

Lost allotment letters

If an investor loses an allotment letter, he must apply to the organization handling the issue to ask for a duplicate.

Before a duplicate can be issued, the investor will have to complete a letter of indemnity which basically promises to reimburse the issuing organization for any loss it may incur from issuing the duplicate document.

The letter of indemnity will require countersignature from a bank or insurance company, and it will countersign only if the investor is creditworthy for the value of the underlying securities. Banks will ask the investor to sign an authority, known as a counterindemnity, to authorize the debiting of the customer's account if the bank has to pay up under the letter of indemnity. Banks and insurance companies make a charge for joining in letters of indemnity.

Worked example of allotment letter calculations and procedures

Mr A has made an application for £5,000 (nominal) in a new public offer for sale of a 15% debenture stock. The issue price of this stock is 98.5%: payment is 10% on application, 15% on allotment, and the balance in four months' time. The issue is oversubscribed and he receives an allotment of £2,000 (nominal) of stock. He wishes to transfer this allotment equally to his wife and his daughter (aged 30).

Indicate the procedure necessary from the time of completing the application form to the issue of the individual certificates in the names of Mrs A and of Miss A.

Suggested answer

Mr A will have sent a cheque for £500 (10% of nominal amount applied for).

He receives an allotment letter for £2,000 nominal which will indicate that the amounts due on application and allotment have been paid. The total due after application and allotment is 25% of the nominal amount of stock (2,000 x 25% = £500). The excess £300 submitted with the application will be used to pay the allotment monies.

Mr A will require the allotment letter to be split. He therefore signs the form of renunciation (form X) and completes the detail of the required split. The allotment letter is then sent to the issuing house indicated thereon.

The issuing house will return two 25% paid allotment letters for £1,000 nominal each, and the form of renunciation will be stamped 'original duly renounced'.

Mr A will give the new allotment letters to his wife and daughter who will each complete their names on the respective registration application forms, form Y and form Z (if there is a form Z).

The wife and daughter will pay the balance due on the stipulated date. This amount is computed for each allotment letter as follows:

Full issue price 98.5% of £1,000	= £985
Less: 25% of nominal already paid	= £250
Balance due in four months' time	= £735

There will be no brokers' commissions to pay.

Once the allotment letters are fully paid, the certificates will be sent in accordance with the procedures laid down in the allotment letter.

5

THE STOCK EXCHANGE DEALING PROCESS

Objectives

After studying this Chapter, you should be able to:

- describe rolling settlement; CREST; and how registered securities are transferred;

- assess the issues that apply to lost share certificates;

- explain the Stock Exchange dealing costs;

- understand the purpose of contract notes;

- evaluate the effects of the actions of bulls and bears on the market;

- describe the dealing process;

- understand SEAQ;

- explain Normal Market Size, and the role of the Order Book (SETS).

5.1   Rolling settlement

On 18 July 1994 the Stock Exchange introduced rolling settlement. With rolling settlement a stock exchange transaction becomes due for settlement a set number of working days after the deal was made.

Rolling settlement for equities

Initially settlement for purchases or sales of equities (ordinary shares) was made 10 working days after the deal made (T+10). It was reduced to five days (T+5) in 1995 and moved to 3 days (T+3) in February 2001. The future target settlement period is 2 days (T+2). This will bring the UK into line with European stock exchanges which settle between two and seven days after the deal is done.

Settlement for deals can be done by CHAPS transfer, cheque, or debit card.

Rolling settlement for company loan stocks

Company loan stocks have been on rolling settlement for a number of years and settlement is three working days (T+3).

Cash settlement

Not all deals are settled on a rolling settlement basis. Certain deals are done on cash settlement when payment is due on the next working day after the deal has been arranged. In practice payment is due as and when stated on the contract note and periods of up to seven days from the date of the deal to the cash settlement date can be seen.

Cash settlement normally applies to transactions in the following securities:

- British government stocks (gilts);
- Commonwealth and foreign government securities;
- UK corporation and county stocks;
- New issues in allotment letter or renounceable certificate form;
- Bearer bonds;
- Foreign currency securities;
- Unit trusts.

5.2   CREST and stock and share certificates

Description and purpose of stock and share certificates

All owners of registered stocks and shares are legally entitled to share certificates showing the details recorded by the company registrar in the register of owners. There is no obligation to use CREST. However, the trend is towards dematerialization of stock and share certificates, where holdings only exist in electronic (uncertificated) form in CREST. The details which can be expected to appear on the certificate are:

- Name of the company or issuing authority;
- The type of stock or share;
- The holder's name (with or without the address);
- The number of shares or amount of stock represented by the certificate;
- Certificate number.

A certificate is merely a record of an entry in the register of shareholders, but the shareholder should take care not to lose it because missing share certificates can cause problems when ownership is to be transferred.

CREST is a book-entry transfer system with electronic messages passing between CREST and company registrars relating to changes in ownership of UK stocks and shares against payment. No certificates are issued for stocks and shares held on CREST.

The CREST system gives the shareholder one of three options to:

- to hold share certificates in their own name. CREST provides facilities for investors holding certificates to sell their shares or for buyers to receive certificates if they wish to;

- to hold shares through a nominee account operated by a bank or stockbroker, which is likely to be held electronically in CREST, but does not have to be;

- to become a 'sponsored member' of CREST, meaning that shares are held electronically in the name of the individual investor, but the operation of the electronic interface with CREST is carried out by a bank or stockbroker appointed by the investor.

Note: CREST is the name of the system, the letters are not an acronym (i.e. an abbreviation of words to make a single word).

Lost share certificates (for non-CREST holdings)

When a shareholder loses a certificate, he can apply to the company registrar for a duplicate certificate. However, before such a document can be issued, the registrar will require an indemnity to which a bank, insurance company or stockbroker is a party.

The bank, insurance company or broker will agree to compensate the company registrar for any loss he may incur by issuing a duplicate certificate. This indemnity will therefore involve these financial bodies in a contingent liability, since in theory a claim, based on the original certificate, could arise at any time for the value of the shares represented by that document. Thus there is usually a charge levied for issuing indemnities, and the investor is asked to sign a counterindemnity agreeing to reimburse the financial institution for any claims it is required to meet. Most banks delete all reference to indemnities for lost share certificates 10 years after issue.

When the investor wishes to sell the securities, and only then discovers that his certificate is lost, he can save time by forwarding the indemnity to the selling broker along with a signed stock transfer form. There is no need to wait for the duplicate certificate in this case.

The moral of this story is to keep share certificates in safe custody at a bank, or in a nominee name, or hold in uncertificated form in CREST. By choosing one of these options there is less likelihood of losing the certificate.

Balance certificates

It is perfectly in order to sell only part of a share holding. In such cases the seller will surrender the original certificate and receive a new certificate for the unsold balance in due course. The stock transfer form signed by the seller will specify the number of shares he actually wishes to sell. If the shares are on the CREST system an entry relating to the balance will be made.

4.3   Transfer of registered shares

A registered share is a share where the company concerned keeps a record of shareholders. This record, or register, is maintained by the company registrar, who records all changes of ownership. However, before he will record a change of ownership, the company registrar will require the share certificate and a stock transfer form (if held in certificated form) signed by the seller. Once these documents have been received, the company registrar will issue a new certificate to the buyer, having cancelled the old one.

Simple transfer of shares between two parties

It is not legally necessary for quoted shares to be sold on the Stock Exchange. A privately negotiated deal can be arranged, and in such cases the company registrar will change the registration details on receipt of the old certificate and signed standard stock transfer form.

4.4   Stock Exchange dealing costs

Broker's commission

The rates of commission are quoted as a percentage of the consideration, which is the number of shares multiplied by the dealing price per share or the amount of stock multiplied by the dealing price of the stock.

Broker's commission is, technically, negotiable, but brokers have their own set of commissions for private clients. Then rates will vary between then traditional brokers and the cheaper dealing-only services such as telephone or Internet brokers whose fees are lower due to their lower cost base and 'no-frills service'. Commission is charged on the consideration (i.e. the number of shares multiplied by the price). Examples of the calculation of commission and other costs are shown below.

If the deal is done via an agent, e.g. a bank, then the broker's commission will be divisible with the agent. This fact will be shown on the contract note.

If the investor is purchasing gilts or other fixed-interest stocks, the consideration has added to it, or subtracted from it, accrued interest. The brokers' commission is calculated on the combined figures.

PTM levy

This is a levy to fund the Panel for Takeovers and Mergers. It applies to all deals (except gilts) of over £10,000 consideration, on either purchase or sale. Gilts are exempt from the PTM levy. On all other deals it is a flat rate of 25p on deals over £10,000 consideration.

Stamp duty

Stamp duty (also called transfer stamp duty) is levied on all purchases of equities at the rate of 0.5% of the consideration on shares. The minimum amount to be paid is £5, rising in £5 stages.

Examples of the effect of dealing costs

On Monday 12 March 2001 an investor purchases 5,000 shares in Alpha plc at 125p. Broker's commission is 1.65% on the first £7,000, and 1.2% on the next £3,000. The total payable would be:

	£
Consideration (5,000 x 125p)	6,250.00
Broker's commission (£6,250 @ 1.65%)	103.12
* Stamp duty (£6,250 @ 0.5%)	35.00
PTM levy	Nil
Total payable	6,388.12

Stamp duty £6,250 @ 0.5% = £31.25 – this is rounded up to the nearest £5, thus is £35.00. The settlement day will be 15 March 2001 (T+3 **working** days after the deal was done).

On the following day, 13 March 2001, the investor sees that the share price of Alpha plc has risen to 150p. He decides to sell the 5,000 shares he purchased the previous day. Explain how the settlement procedure will operate and the net profit he will make.

		£
Consideration (5,000 x 150p)		7,500.00
Less: broker's commission		
£7,000 at 1.65%	115.50	
£ 500 at 1.2%	6.00	
PTM levy	Nil	121.50
Total receivable		7,378.50

NB: Stamp duty is only charged on purchases; PTM levy does not apply because the consideration is below £10,000.

The settlement day will be 16 March 2001 (T+3 **working** days after the deal was done).

Even though the investor has bought and sold the same shares on consecutive days, he will have to send his cheque for £6,388.12 for settlement on 15 March, and will receive a cheque for £7,378.50 on 16 March. His net profit is £990.38 (£7,378.50 - £6,388.12).

Contract notes

A contract note is issued by a broker to a client as evidence of a deal that has been made on his behalf. The contract note includes the following details:

- Name and address of the broker;
- Whether the transaction is a purchase (bought) or a sale (sold);
- The full details of the security dealt in;
- The price, consideration and all charges, so as to show a total payment due to or from the broker;
- The bargain number;
- The date of the bargain and the time the bargain was effected;
- Settlement date;
- Client's name and address;
- The Daily Official List (commonly called SEDOL – the Stock Exchange Daily Official List) code;
- Whether the deal was certificated or uncertificated;
- With a CREST deal, the CREST account number will be shown;
- Whether the broker/dealer acted as an agency broker or as a principal.

The letters 'IF' indicate that the deal was done 'intra firm'; in other words the broker/dealer in effect acted as a principal and acquired the shares from the market making arm of the same organization.

The precise layout of the contract note will vary from broker to broker.

Points for the investor to bear in mind on receipt of the contract note

The most important step is for the investor to check the details to ensure that they represent the instructions that he actually gave the broker. In practice the few discrepancies which do occur can be sorted out with a minimum of fuss, provided the broker is notified immediately.

There may well be a difference between the price at which the shares were dealt in by the broker and the price at which the shares were quoted in the *Financial Times* of that day. The price shown in the *Financial Times* is the middle price of the shares the previous day at the close of business.

The contract note gives the time the deal was done in order that in the event of a dispute over the price the Stock Exchange can check the price ruling at the time stated on the contract note. All deals and all prices are recorded constantly for monitoring purposes.

The price will be different from the mid-price, even if the deal were done at the exact close of business because of the market makers' 'turn', which is the difference between the price at which they will buy (bid) and the price at which they will sell (offer). The bid price is always lower than the offer price, because the market maker would wish to profit on the deal. Thus if the shares were purchased the price would be above the mid-price, and if they were sold the price would be below mid-price.

A 'turn' of 2p would be quite common on an actively-traded share. For shares in which there are relatively few dealings the market makers' turn could be wider. The term 'narrow market' describes the situation where there are few transactions in a particular share.

Contract notes should always be retained. Purchases and disposals of securities must always be declared on the tax return for the year, and the necessary details will be shown on the contract note.

Ownership of the relevant securities vests in the purchaser from the moment the broker, acting as the purchaser's agent, makes a deal with the market maker. The 'bought' contract note is evidence of the date of ownership, and this can be important if there are any rights issues or bonus issues made around the time of the deal. The contract note also shows whether the purchaser is entitled to the next dividend or interest payment. The purchaser is so entitled unless the contract note specifically states 'ex div'. In cases where the contract note shows the transaction to be 'ex div' the next dividend will be the property of the seller of the shares.

5.5 The various abbreviations used with stock/share prices

These abbreviations are found on contract notes, in the *Financial Times* and the Daily Official List. 'x' is an abbreviation for 'ex', meaning 'without'.

- ***xd or ex div = ex dividend***. This means that the seller will retain the next dividend (or interest payment in the case of fixed-interest stocks). With shares the company will specify a date just before the due date of the dividends. All deals between that date and the date the next dividend is due will be ex div.

  xd applies to both stocks and shares.

- ***xr = ex rights***. When a rights issue is made, the original shares are marked xr, to show that any rights made remain with the seller.

  If someone sold the shares 'xr' it would mean that he (the seller) would subsequently receive and be entitled to the provisional allotment letter for the rights. The ex rights price is the price at which all the shares are expected to settle once the rights issue has been completed.

  xr applies only to shares.

- ***xc = ex capitalization***. When a capitalization issue is made, the original shares are marked 'xc'. The capitalization issue will be received by the seller of the shares, not the buyer, and the price of the sale will be the expected ex capitalization price.

xc applies only to shares.

● ***xa = ex all.*** Sometimes a capitalization issue, rights issue and a dividend payment are made simultaneously. Ex all means that all capitalization shares, all rights and the next dividend vest in the seller.

xa applies only to shares.

● ***cd or cum div = cum dividend***. This abbreviation is not found against a stock or share price, but if the stock or share is not xd then it will be cd. Cum dividend means that the purchaser will receive the next dividend or interest payment due.

xd, xr, xc and xa are all abbreviations found in the *Financial Times*. However, xa does not appear in the Daily Official List and xd is shown simply as 'x' in the Daily Official List.

5.6   Bulls and bears

Bulls

A bull is a general term for someone who expects share prices to rise. He will buy shares in the hope of selling them for a higher price within a few days. When a bull buys shares in anticipation of a short-term price rise that does not occur he is called a 'stale bull'.

With the advent of rolling settlement a bull will have to pay for the shares prior to receiving the sale proceeds. He may be able to come to some agreement with his broker to net the proceeds and pay interest or a fee for this service, but this is entirely up to the broker.

Bears

A bear is the opposite of a bull because he sells shares he does not own, hoping to buy the shares very quickly at a lower price. This process is known as 'selling short'. If the bear has correctly anticipated the price movement he will settle in the same way as described for a bull, except he will receive the cheque first and pay the purchase costs later. When the bear already owns the shares and sells because he expects their price to fall, he is called a 'covered bear'. The theoretical potential loss for an uncovered bear is unlimited, since the price of the shares could rise to infinity.

Bulls and bears will be seriously affected by the move to rolling settlement. Previously they were heavy account dealers, taking their profits (or losses) on settlement day. Rolling settlement will probably see a reduction in bull and bear activity, although some stockbrokers may offer a service for good clients along the old account lines – but at a fee. In addition, pure speculators can now use spread betting instead of dealing in the real market. Spread betting is a very useful alternative for a bear who wishes to sell short. (See Chapter 9 for details of spread betting.)

Bull and bear markets

The terms 'bull' and 'bear' are also used to describe the mood of the stock market in general. If share prices in general are rising, the market is said to be 'bullish', and when prices in general are falling, the market is said to be 'bearish'. The Stock Exchange defines a bear market as one where the FTSE 100 index falls 20% below its all-time high. When there is a sudden turn in market sentiment, and prices which had been falling suddenly rise, uncovered bears are said to be 'squeezed'.

5.7 An outline of the dealing process

The investor and the stockbroker

A stockbroker acts as an agent between the investor and the market maker.

It is now possible for an investor to approach a market maker direct. However, the majority of small, private investors will still use the traditional intermediary system because market makers will deal only with high-value, i.e. institutional, investors. Information required by the broker in all cases will be:

- Whether to buy or sell;

- Full details of the security;

- The amount of stock or number of shares to be dealt in;

- Whether the deal is at 'best' (i.e. the best price that can be obtained at the time) or whether there is a limit on the price of the security above which a purchase must not be effected and below which a sale must not be carried out.

Once the deal is agreed the investor becomes the owner of the shares. The broker will send out a contract note with full details of the deal. This acts as evidence of ownership, pending receipt of the certificate or CREST statement. Details of the transaction are input into SEAQ. On settlement the investor pays the broker.

5.8 Points that may require clarification when dealing in stocks and shares

Because the Stock Exchange works on the basis of 'dictum meum pactum' or 'my word is my bond', it is essential that all instructions to the broker are clear and precise.

Two major complications can arise: first, the need to distinguish between 'buy' and 'invest'. The problem regarding 'buy' or 'invest' occurs when the security being purchased is denominated in stock units.

Take 9% Treasury 2008 with a price of £119.52 as an example. For this stock the price of every nominal £100 is £119.52. Thus the instruction 'buy £4,000 9% Treasury 2008' would involve a basic cost, excluding charges, of £4,780.80, whereas 'invest £4,000 in 9% Treasury 2008' would mean the purchaser was to pay a basic £4,000 excluding charges. (See Chapter 7 for calculations relating to British government securities)

Secondly, the need to ascertain whether a buy and sell order are contingent upon each other. Sometimes an investor may simultaneously instruct a broker to buy one security and sell another. If both orders are 'at best', there is no problem, but when one or both orders has a limit, then complications can arise. Should the order with a limit prove incapable of being transacted, ought the other order to be executed? If the unexecuted order is a 'sell', then the client may have been looking to the sale proceeds to finance the purchase. If the unexecuted order is a 'buy', the client may not wish to go liquid (i.e. hold cash).

Thus clear instructions as to whether the execution of one order is contingent on another must be given at the time the client instructs the broker.

5.9   SEAQ and SEAQ International

SEAQ is the Stock Exchange Automated Quotation system. It is a continuously updated system which distributes market makers bid and offer prices to the market. Market makers must maintain their prices during the mandatory quote period (MQP) which is 08.00 to 16.30, Monday to Friday when market makers on SEAQ and SEAQ International are obliged to make firm two-way quotes for the securities in which they are registered.

The main functions of SEAQ are:

- To convey prices and other information to dealers via terminals to enable brokers to obtain quickly the 'best prices' available for their clients;

- To provide an 'audit trail' to check suspicious price movements, e.g. because of insider dealings. This is why all equity contract notes must show the time as well as the date of dealing.

SEAQ International

SEAQ International provides market-price information for the leading international stocks. It provides a firm dealing price in a large number of securities from many countries.

Spread and touch

Shares have two prices – the bid price (the price at which the market maker will buy shares) and the offer price (the price at which the market maker will sell shares). The difference between these two prices is called the spread.

Different market makers will quote different bid and offer prices for the same shares. The touch is the closest price between the different prices quoted by the different market makers. For example: the following bid/offer prices are quoted on SEAQ for Alpha plc:

198-203

197-201

199-204

The touch on these shares is 199-201 (i.e. the highest bid price and the lowest offer price). An investor who wished to sell shares in Alpha would go to the market maker offering the bid price of 199p, and an investor who wished to buy Alpha shares would go to the market maker quoting 201p.

The wider the touch, the less liquid the shares. The average touch is around 1.1%, but for shares in smaller companies that are infrequently traded the touch will be much wider.

5.10   The order book – also called SETS

The order book is based on an order-matching system in which firms display their bid (buying) and offer (selling) orders to the market on an electronic order book. When bid and offer prices match, orders are automatically executed against one another on screen. The book is open from 09.00 to 16.30, Monday to Friday. It provides fully automated electronic trading for FTSE 100 securities, stocks in many shares in the FTSE 250 index and securities with traded options on LIFFE.

There are four types of order:

● **limit** – which specifies the size and price at which an investor wishes to deal. If matches can be found, the order is immediately executed, in whole or part. If not, it remains on the order book until a suitable match comes along within the expiry date or it is deleted;

● **at best** – buy or sell orders are entered on the system, and are executed immediately at the best price available in the system;

● **fill or kill** – these are either executed immediately in full or rejected. They may include a limit price;

● **execute and eliminate** – similar to 'at best' but with a specified limit price, so that it is matched immediately down to the specified price. Any unexecuted part of the order will be rejected.

5.11   Dealing in non-SETS securities

For non-SETS securities, market makers are obliged to display their prices to the market throughout the trading day for all of their registered stocks. They must also display their bid and offer prices and the maximum transaction size to which these prices relate.

Market makers compete to offer the best quote – and make their income by buying and selling stocks at a profit. The competing quote system is supported by the SEAQ service.

Market makers' bid and offer prices and sizes are shown, and these are used to create the SEAQ 'yellow strip'. The yellow strip identifies at any moment in the trading day, from an investor's point of view, the best bid and offer price for every SEAQ security, and the identities of up to four market makers quoting this price. Other market makers' names and quotes can also be viewed.

5.12   SEATS PLUS

SEATS PLUS is the Stock Exchange Alternative Trading System. SEATS PLUS mainly supports the trading of AIM stocks. SEATS PLUS is a combination of competing quotes and/or firm offers. These quotes are often from one market maker, or two or more in the case of AIM shares. The SEATS PLUS system aims to make it easier to trade in smaller company shares, including shares quoted on AIM.

Normal market size and marketability

Normal market size for the UK equity market is calculated for each security and is based on the average size of deals made in a share over the past 12 months. It is the maximum size a market maker is obliged to deal in at the price he is quoting. The percentage is intended to represent the normal institutional bargain. The percentage is set at 2.5 per cent. The NMS values range from 100 shares to 200,000 shares and the values are recalculated and amended every quarter. NMS is the minimum quantity of securities for which a market maker is obliged to quote a firm two-way price on SEAQ or SEAQ International.

Although it might be expected that the largest, most actively traded companies would have an NMS of 200,000, this is not necessarily the case. For example on 30 March 2001, HSBC (a FTSE 100 share) had an NMS of 200,000, while MV Sports (an AIM listed share) also had an NMS of 200,000. The price of HSBC shares on that date was 844p and MV sports price 0.75p. This means that the market considers a normal transaction in HSBC to be worth £1,688,000, whereas for MV Sports a normal transaction would be worth £1,500. Thus NMS is clearly not a guide to the size of the company, but is a guide to the value of a normal institutional deal. It is clear from the NMS for MV Sports that the company is not really seen as a stock that would be found in an institutional portfolio because institutions would not deal in such small amounts.

On the SEAQ (Stock Exchange Automated Quotation System) screen the NMS of a share is shown in thousands. All shares with an NMS of 2,000 or more have the price of the trades shown immediately up to a maximum trade of 3 x NMS. Trades in excess of this size will be reported 90 minutes afterwards. Trades in the less liquid securities will not be published on SEAQ, except where such trades are either agency crosses (i.e. one market maker selling to another market maker), or when the company is involved in a takeover bid. In such cases these trades will be published immediately.

To increase marketability of shares the London Stock Exchange requires at least two market makers to display firm quotations on SEAQ for stocks with an NMS below 1,000 shares. (Poor marketability does not mean that shares cannot be bought or sold, but that the difference between buying and selling price is larger.) To increase the number of deals done automatically, the order book (SETS) can be used to match deals, which is particularly useful for shares with an small NMS.

6

PERSONAL TAXATION

Objectives

After studying this chapter, the reader should be able to:

● apply the principles of income tax, capital gains tax, inheritance tax and National Insurance to practical situations;

● calculate tax liabilities in respect of the above, given a description of an individual's or family's circumstances.

6.1   Introduction

Taxation is a very complex subject on which whole books have been written. In this chapter we look at three taxes:

● Income tax;

● Capital gains tax (CGT);

● Inheritance tax (IhT);

● National Insurance that specifically affects individuals.

(National Insurance is not specifically classed as a tax, but is levied on certain earned income. Many investors who are liable to National Insurance have little understanding of the impact of this on their disposable income or on the pension they will receive upon retirement.)

Income, capital gains and inheritance taxes that affect the investment strategy of private individuals are examined in this chapter so as to give an overview of tax in general. This chapter will form a useful background to help in understanding the detailed yield calculations in the gilts chapter, Chapter 7. Likewise, an understanding of the general taxation scene will be essential when considering portfolio planning.

Briefly, income tax applies, as would be expected, to income, whereas capital gains tax applies when assets are bought and subsequently sold at a profit. CGT applies when an asset has actually been sold at a profit or otherwise disposed of, although as we shall see, there are many exemptions and allowances. An IhT liability can arise in two major situations

Investment Management

– when a person dies leaving a large estate, or on lifetime transfers that occur when assets are passed between individuals who are not husband and wife.

If an individual holds shares, income tax could apply in the case of dividends, capital gains tax could apply to any profit on a subsequent sale, whereas IhT could apply after the death of the holder when the shares were transferred to a beneficiary under the will, or if the shares were given to a party other than the spouse during the life of the donor.

Tax is calculated on a period called the 'tax year' which runs from 6 April to 5 April the following year.

6.2 Income tax

Persons liable and income assessable to income tax

As stated above, the tax year begins on 6 April each year. With a few exceptions, all income received by an individual is assessable to income tax including the following:

- Pensions. It does not matter whether the pension is received from an ex-employer, or whether it is a state pension or regular payments from a private pension plan. All are taxable. A common error in examinations is for students to say that a person aged over 65 is a pensioner and therefore pays no tax. This is not true. A pension is taxable income and once this amount, together with any other income such as interest, exceeds the tax-free allowances figure income tax will be payable.

- Salaries, wages, bonuses and commission.

- Interest from any source, dividends and the 'income' element of an annuity.

- Benefits in kind are, generally speaking, taxable only where the recipient earns £8,500 per annum or more or is a director of the company giving the benefits. These benefits include rent-free accommodation occupied by some employees, and company cars (calculated on car value and engine capacity).

- Tips.

- Lump-sum redundancy payments, but only on amounts in excess of £30,000; the first £30,000 is tax free.

- Rents received and other income from land and property.

- Profits from business and professions.

- Certain Social Security benefits are taxable (knowledge of these is outside the scope of the syllabus).

Income that is not taxable

The main exceptions that constitute non-taxable income are:

- Interest on National Savings Certificates, Children's Bonus Bonds, TESSAs and cash ISAs.

- The first £70 of interest received on a National Savings Bank Ordinary Account. Any additional interest over the £70 is taxable.

- Interest on contractual savings under any SAYE scheme.

- Dividends received under personal equity plans (PEPs) and individual savings accounts (ISAs).

The meaning of the term 'allowance'

Not every penny of income is taxable. Everyone is entitled to an 'allowance' which is a monetary amount below which no tax is payable. The allowance to which you are entitled depends on whether you are married, divorced, single or widowed, or whether you are a one-parent family. Pensioners, or to be more precise, single people aged 65 or over and married couples where at least one partner is of that age, are also entitled to a special 'age allowance'. There is also an allowance available to a person registered as blind, called the blind person's allowance.

Rates of tax allowance

The allowances given relate to the tax year 2001-02. The rates to be used in the examination are given on the paper itself, thus the rates do not need to be memorized.

	Personal allowances	Married couple's allowances
	£	£
Basic personal allowance	4,535	nil
Age allowance 65-74*	5,990	5,365
75 and over*	6,260	5,435
Blind person's allowance	1,450	nil

If income is in excess of £17,600, the age allowance is reduced by £1 for every £2 of additional income. When scaling affects the married couple's allowance, the minimum allowance granted is £2,070 irrespective of age over 65.

Other allowances are available to offset against income tax. These relate to mortgage interest, pension contributions, and any sum expended wholly, exclusively and necessarily in the performance of duties. This final allowance is wide-ranging and includes items such as subscriptions to professional bodies and safety clothing necessary for the performance of duties.

Personal allowances

- Basic personal allowance;

- Married couple's allowance – but only for couples where one person was born before 6 April 1935;

- Children's Tax Credit;

- Age allowance;

- Blind person's allowance;

- Pension contributions;

- Professional and union subscriptions.

Basic personal allowance. This is available to everyone. The moment a child is born he or she is entitled to a basic personal allowance of £4,535 to offset against any income he or she receives. The basic personal allowance is given to single people and to husbands and wives separately. The unused basic personal allowance or any unused part cannot be transferred to another person. Persons over the age of 65 receive a higher allowance.

Married couple's allowance. This allowance is only available for couples where one person was born before 6 April 1935. Persons over the age of 65 receive a higher allowance. The married couple's allowance is automatically given to the husband, but if his income is insufficient to utilize fully the married couple's allowance, the unused allowance, or part of the allowance, can be transferred to the wife. In order to transfer the allowance, the husband must give written notice to the Inland Revenue. This allowance is restricted to 10%.

Children's Tax Credit This allowance is paid to single parents, married couples and unmarried couples living together as husband and wife, with one or more children under 16 resident with them. Only one allowance of £5,220, restricted to 10% (i.e. it is worth £522 per year) is paid, irrespective of the number of children qualifying. The allowance is scaled down for 40% tax payers by £2 for every £3 of income above the £29,400 basic-rate band ceiling. This means that there will be no Children's Tax Credit when income exceeds £37230. (Calculated £29,400 + (5220 x 3/2) = £7,830.)

Age allowance. There are two bands of age allowance: 65-74 and over 75. The age allowance is not available in full to every person in those age bands, but is scaled down if the income before deducting allowances exceeds £17,600. The scaling down is done by reducing the allowance by £1 for every £2 of additional income. The formula is:

$$\text{Age allowance} - \frac{\text{Total income (before allowances) of £17,600}}{2}$$

If the resultant figure is below the basic personal allowance then the basic personal allowance is given in place of the age allowance. Note: the scaling-down calculation is done only if income exceeds £17,600. In the case of a married couple where the age allowance is reduced below the basic personal allowance, the married couple's allowance is scaled down by the excess, but will not be less than £2,070.

Blind person's allowance This is available to anyone registered blind, and it can be transferred between husband and wife. The allowance is £1,450 and is given in addition to any other allowances.

Pension contributions. Contributions to pension plans are eligible for tax relief at the investor's highest rate of income tax. Most pension contributions are made to an occupational scheme, and the maximum percentage of salary that is allowable for tax relief is 10%. If an individual has a personal pension plan, the percentage of his salary he can pay into the plan is set by his age as follows:

Age	Personal Pension plan: maximum %
Up to 35	17.5
36 to 45	20
46 to 50	25
51 to 55	30
56 to 60	35
61 and above	40

Notes
1. The percentages for personal pension plans are given on the exam paper.
2. Pensions are covered in Chapter 16.

Professional and union subscriptions The Inland Revenue allows individuals who are members of professional bodies and/or members of unions to receive tax relief at their highest rate of tax on those subscriptions.

Independent taxation When calculating tax payable for a married couple, each person is treated entirely separately.

Once an individual's taxable income has been calculated by deducting the relevant allowances from the gross income, he or she pays tax as follows:

Taxable income	Rate of tax (%)
Up to £1,880	10 (lower rate)
£1,881 to £29,400	22 (basic rate)
On the remainder	40

The 10% band is called lower rate tax, the 22% rate is called basic rate tax, and the 40% rate higher rate tax.

Note: Where basic rate tax is referred to within the text, the basic rate is the 22% rate.

The Income tax position of dividends and interest

Tax position of dividends.

Dividends are paid net of 10% tax, and all recipients must declare such dividends on their income tax return. The company that pays the dividend has already deducted 10% tax at source, thus having already borne tax the dividend has a tax credit of 10%. In order to calculate the tax implications we must first of all 'gross up' the net dividend. This means that the amount of the dividend is multiplied by 100 and divided by 100 less 10%. Thus the dividend is grossed up by 100/90.

'Gross' means before tax, and if I receive a dividend of £90 net of basic tax, it is the equivalent of £100 of taxable income, assuming I am a basic-rate taxpayer. In this case, ignoring the timing implications, £100 gross would only be worth £90 after deduction of basic-rate tax, therefore £90 net of basic tax is the equivalent of £100 gross.

Basic-rate taxpayers, when they receive their net dividend, will be deemed to have met their tax liability in full because the income tax due on the dividend at the rate of 10% will already have been deducted at source.

Non-taxpayers and most institutional investors cannot reclaim the 10% tax credit. However special rules apply to shares held in a PEP or an ISA, which will have the tax credit paid into the account up to 5 April 2004. Registered charities will receive a reducing proportion of the tax credit up to 5 April 2004.

Higher-rate taxpayers will have to pay a total of 32.5% tax on the gross dividend, which will satisfy the 40% tax liability. Schedule F of the Finance Act 2000 specifies that the 32.5% is made up of 10% Schedule F ordinary rate and 22.5% Schedule F upper rate, totalling 32.5%. The 10% is deducted at source. The remaining 22.5% must be declared on the next tax return and the tax due is payable after the Inland Revenue has processed the tax return.

6.3   Numerical example of taxation as applied to dividends

Suppose a shareholder received a dividend cheque for £168.75. What are the tax implications?

First of all we gross up the £168.75 to obtain a gross equivalent of £187.50, i.e.

$$\frac{168.75 \times 100}{(100 - 10)} = £187.50$$

We shall then study the effects, which will depend on the tax position of the shareholder.

If the shareholder is a non-taxpayer

	£
Gross equivalent	187.50
Less amount of tax deducted at source (10%), i.e., tax credit	18.75
Net paid by company	168.75

8

The Inland Revenue will NOT refund £18.75 to the non-taxpayer. Thus the dividend is worth £168.75 to the non-taxpayer.

If the shareholder is a 10% taxpayer

The gross equivalent of the dividend is £187.50. The shareholder has no further liability to income tax, but cannot reclaim the tax deducted at source. Thus the dividend is worth £168.75 to the 10% taxpayer.

If the shareholder is a basic-rate taxpayer

As far as the Inland Revenue is concerned the 10% tax credit satisfies the basic rate taxpayer's liability to any further tax on the dividend. Thus the dividend is worth £168.75 to the 22% taxpayer.

If the shareholder pays tax at the top rate of 40%

	£
Gross equivalent	187.50
Less amount deducted at source	18.75
Net paid by company	168.75

In this case there is a further tax liability of £42.19 calculated thus:

	£
Gross equivalent	187.50
Tax due at 32.5%	60.94
Less tax already paid by company	18.75
Tax due to Inland Revenue	42.19

Another way of looking at this is to say that he must pay a further 22.5% (32.5% - 10%) on the gross amount (£42.19). Thus the dividend is worth £126.56 to the 40% taxpayer.

6.4 Tax position of interest

If interest is paid by a company on a loan stock, by a bank or building society, or on a British government security, the position is that 20% tax (the savings rate) is deducted at source. The tax deducted at 20% satisfies a lower and basic rate taxpayers' liability to tax. Thus, interest and dividends are treated differently for tax purposes.

Interest paid on British government securities can be paid gross. Interest paid on National Savings Bank accounts is automatically paid gross (i.e. without the deduction of tax). In such a case the non-taxpayer will simply declare the interest, but have no further liability for tax. The 10% and 22% tax payers will have to pay tax at the savings rate of 20% and the 40% taxpayer will have to pay tax at 40% on the gross interest. If interest is paid by a bank or building society, it is paid with 20% tax deducted. However non-taxpayers can have the interest paid gross upon signing a declaration that they are non-taxpayers. Thus dividends and interest are treated differently for income tax purposes.

Numerical example of taxation as applied to bank, building society or loan stock interest

Taking the amount of interest paid as being £150 from any of the above holdings, the tax implications are as follows:

If the investor is a non-taxpayer

	£
Gross equivalent	187.50
Less tax deducted at source (20%)	37.50
Net interest paid	150.00

The Inland Revenue will refund the tax deducted of £37.50 to the non-taxpayer. Thus the interest is worth £187.50 after the tax refund.

If the investor is a 10% taxpayer

	£
Gross equivalent	187.50
Less tax deducted at source	37.50
Net interest paid	150.00

This satisfies the 10% tax payers tax liability, thus the interest is worth £150 after tax.

If the investor is a basic rate taxpayer

As far as the Inland Revenue is concerned, the 20% tax deducted at source satisfies the investor's tax liability. Thus the interest is worth £150.

If the investor is a 40% taxpayer

	£
Gross equivalent	187.50
Less tax deducted at source	37.50
Net interest paid	150.00
Additional tax liability at 20%	37.50
Interest after tax	112.50

The 40% taxpayer is liable to a further 20% (40% - 20%) tax on the gross equivalent interest, i.e. £37.50. He therefore receives £112.50 after his tax liability has been met.

Summary of tax position re dividends and interest

	Interest	Dividends
Rate of tax deducted	20%	10%
Satisfies basic-rate liability?	Yes	Yes
Reclaimable by non-taxpayer?	Yes	No
Higher rate of tax charged	20% (40-20) if the interest is paid with tax deducted at source. If the interest is paid gross e.g. on gilts, then 40% is payable.	32.5% (but the 10% tax deducted at source is offset against this amount)
Net interest/dividend grossing up	100 / 80	100 / 90

6.5   National Insurance

The impact on investment decisions of National Insurance contributions must be assessed. In effect, this means that the calculations of an investor's marginal rate of income tax will now have to include the effect of National Insurance contributions where they are applicable.

Who pays National Insurance contributions?
Class 1 contributions
You must pay National Insurance (Class 1 contributions) if you are:

● Employed in Great Britain or Northern Ireland;

● Aged between 16 and 60 (women), or 16 and 65 (men);

● Earning above the lower earnings limit which is £72 per week (£3,744 per annum).

The earnings ceiling for National Insurance is £575 per week – £29,900 per annum. The amount paid then depends upon whether your pension is contracted in to SERPS (State Earnings-Related Pension Scheme) or contracted out of SERPS. Employees who are contracted out of SERPS will be making payments into an occupational (employer's 'approved') pension scheme which is contracted out of SERPS. An employee who is contracted out will receive the basic state pension on retirement, but not the additional pension from the state, i.e. the SERPS pension.

The 2001-2002 Class 1 contribution rates are:

Employee

Weekly earnings	On the first £72	On the remainder	
		Contracted out	Not contracted out
Up to £71.99	Nil	Nil	Nil
£72 to £575	2%	8.4%	10%
Over £575	Nil	Nil	Nil

Note: if earnings are £72 per week or more, then all the earnings are subject to National Insurance, not just the excess over £72. All rates necessary for tax calculations in the examination will be given on the question paper; none of the above rates needs to be memorized.

6.6 Examples of income tax and National Insurance calculations

The allowances and tax rates used are given above.

(a) A married man aged 50 whose wife does not work earns £42,000 gross during 2001-2002 and makes pension contributions to a contracted-out pension scheme of £2,000. The amount of income tax and National Insurance he would pay would be:

		£	£
(i) Gross income			42,000
Less: basic personal allowance		4,535	
Pension contributions		2,000	6,535
Taxable income			35,465
Tax payable:			£
On first	1,880 at 10% =		188.00
On next	£27,520 at 22% =		6,054.40
On remaining	$\frac{£6,065}{35,465}$ at 40% =		2,426.00
Income tax payable			8,668.40
(ii) National Insurance			
£3,744 * at 2%			74.88
£26,156 ** at 8.4%			2,197.10
£29,900 ***			2,271.98

* Calculated. £72 x 52 = £3,744

** Calculated (£575 - £72) x 52 = £26,156

*** Calculated (£575 x 52) = £29,900

Thus he pays a total of £10,940.38 income tax and National Insurance

(b)   John Smith is a widower aged 69, and has a gross income of £12,960.

Tax position

Gross income	12,960.00
Less: age allowance (65-74)	5,990.00
Taxable income	6,970.00
Tax payable: £1,880 at 10% =	188.00
£5,090 at 22% =	1,119.80
Tax payable	1,307.80

No liability to National Insurance because he is over 65.

(c)   Martin Jones is aged 77, married and has a gross income of £18,000. His wife does not have any income in her own right.

Tax position

As his gross income exceeds £17,600, the age allowance will have to be scaled down thus:

$$£6260 - \frac{£18,000 - £17600}{2} = £6,260 - £200$$

Reduced age allowance   = £6,060

As £6,060 is above the basic personal allowance, the age allowance is reduced by £200 to £6,060. The married couple's age allowance is unchanged at £5,435.

	£	£
Gross income		18,000
Less: reduced age allowance		6,060
Taxable income		11,940
Tax payable: 1,880 at 10% =		188.00
10,060 at 22% =		2,213.20
11,940 Tax payable =		2,401.20
Less married couple's age allowance (£5,435 at 10%)		543.50
		1,857.70

d) Judy Pearson is a single, aged 38 and earns £45,000 p.a. She makes contributions to a personal pension plan of £10,000 p.a.

Tax position

Maximum eligible pension contributions into her personal pension plan are 20% of £45,000 = £9,000 (20% is for age 36-45). Thus £1,000 of the pension payments are not eligible for tax relief. Personal pensions are not part of SERPS, thus she will pay the contracted-out rate of National Insurance.

	£	£
Gross income		45,000
Less: basic personal allowance	4,535	
Pension contributions	9,000	13,535
Taxable income		31,465

Tax payable:		£
10% on £1,880	=	188.00
22% on £27,520	=	6,054.40
40% on £2,065	=	826.00
31,465		
Income tax payable		7,068.40
National Insurance payable		
£3,744 at 2%		74.88
£26,156 at 8.4%		2,197.10
£29,900		2,271.98

Thus she pays a total of £9,340.38 income tax and National Insurance.

(e) Peter Henderson is aged 23, married, with a gross unearned income of £4,500 p.a. as a student. His wife Susan is aged 24 and earns £19,500 p.a. gross. She pays pension contributions of 5% of her salary into a SERPS scheme.

Peter's tax position	£
Gross income	4,500
Less: basic personal allowance	4,535
Taxable income	Nil

Peter is a non-taxpayer. (There is no refund of unused allowances.)

Peter is not liable to National Insurance because his income is unearned.

Susan's tax position	£	£
Gross income		19,500
Less: basic personal allowance	4,535	
Pension contributions	975	5,510
		13,990

Tax payable		£
£1,880 at 10% =		188.00
£12,110 at 22% =		2,664.20
£13,990		2,852.20

National Insurance

	£
£3,744 at 2%	74.88
£15,756 at 10%	1,575.60
£19,500	1,650.48

Note: Married Couple's allowance does not apply because neither of them was born before 6 April 1935.

6.7   Capital gains tax

Introduction

Capital gains tax is levied when assets are purchased and subsequently sold at a profit. All 'disposals' or sales of assets subject to CGT are to be declared on the tax return so that the Inland Revenue can calculate the total taxable capital gains for the tax year. When a disposal of an asset is made not by sale but by disposing of it in some other way, (e.g. by way of gift, by total destruction or, in the case of shares if the company is declared insolvent), the loss is treated as a disposal. If, at the end of the tax year, there are net capital losses, these can be carried forward to a future year and offset against future gains. There is an annual exemption of £7,500 (2001-2002) per person which means that an investor with total chargeable gains of £7,500 or less in 2001-2002 will not pay CGT. Any chargeable gains in excess of £7,500 are taxable at the investor's marginal rate of income tax, although it is still called capital gains tax. The chargeable gains in excess of the £7,500 allowance are added to the taxable income to establish the investor's marginal rate of tax. Any unused part of the £7,500 exemption cannot be carried forward. Husbands and wives each have their own

CGT allowance. Any unused allowance is not transferable between husband and wife. Any purchases or sales of assets (basically stocks and shares for our purposes) must be recorded on the investor's tax return.

The basic rate of CGT is 20% (i.e. the savings rate) NOT 22%. A top-rate taxpayer pays CGT at 40% (see pages 93-95 for calculation).

Investors who are subject to CGT and assets that may incur CGT on disposal

In the terms of the Inland Revenue a 'chargeable person' is either UK resident or ordinarily resident for the year in which the relevant disposal occurs, and has disposed of a 'chargeable asset' during the tax year. Any form of property in the widest sense is a chargeable asset, even if the property is situated outside the UK.

Any losses incurred on disposal of chargeable assets are termed an 'allowable loss'. Allowable losses are set off against chargeable gains to establish the net taxable gain. However, not every asset will incur a chargeable gain or establish an allowable loss on disposal.

Assets that are outside the scope of CGT

The main exceptions that are outside the scope of CGT are gains or losses in connection with:

- British coins, including post-1836 gold sovereigns;
- British government securities (more commonly called gilts), and stocks issued by public corporations and local authorities;
- Chattels where the sale proceeds of an individual item are below £6,000;
- Company fixed-interest loans or debentures (but not convertible loan stocks);
- Foreign currency or sterling acquired for family or personal expenditure;
- Gambling winnings, including prizes from premium bonds;
- Life insurance policy proceeds in the hands of the policyholder or his beneficiary;
- Medals and decorations for valour so long as they have been sold by the original recipient or by the recipient of these medals by way of a legacy;
- National Savings certificates, yearly plan, premium bonds, SAYE schemes, personal equity plans (PEPs) and individual savings accounts (ISAs);
- Sale of a dwelling house that was the vendor's only or principal residence prior to such disposal;
- Sale of a property occupied rent free by a dependent relative as his or her main residence, provided the property was so occupied before 6 April 1988;
- Wasting assets, i.e. items that have a predictable life of less than 50 years, e.g. motor cars.

Bodies that are exempt from CGT

These are:

● Registered charities;

● Pension funds;

● Friendly societies;

● Non-residents.

Indexation allowance on capital gains

The indexation allowance was first introduced by the Finance Act 1985 and amended by the Finance Acts 1988, 1994 and 1998. It takes into account the fact that many capital gains are created or increased by inflation. All gains are subject to indexation relief on the value at 31 March 1982 or cost if acquired after this date. The Finance Act 1998 froze the indexation allowance as at 5 April 1998 when the RPI was 162.6.

The Finance Act 1994 altered the manner by which the indexation allowance can reduce the taxable capital gain in real terms, but cannot be used to turn a monetary gain into an indexed capital loss nor to increase a monetary capital loss by application of the indexation allowance. This ruling came into force for disposals made on or after 30 November 1993.

Effect of the indexation allowances and taper relief on capital gains

Indexation allowance enabled gains to be identified on a 'real gain' basis, i.e. removing the effect of inflation. Taper relief was introduced in the Finance Act 1998 and it altered the way capital gains are calculated.

Taper relief

Taper relief reduces gains on a sliding sale according to the COMPLETE number of years, up to a maximum of 10, that an asset has been held from purchase or 6 April 1998. For assets held prior to 6 April 1998, indexation relief is applied to the cost up to that date and taper relief applied to that indexed cost according to the number of years held subject to a maximum of 10 years.

For assets subject to CGT and purchased after 6 April 1998, taper relief did not apply until year 3 of ownership.

For assets purchased prior to 17 March 1998 an extra year is added, e.g. an asset purchased in February 1998 and sold in June 2002 receives 5 years taper relief (4 complete years plus the extra year because it was purchased prior to 17 March 1998).

Taper relief and gains on sale of assets

Number of whole years in qualifying holding period	Percentage reduction available %	Percentage of gain chargeable
1	0	100
2	0	100
3	5	95
4	10	90
5	15	85
6	20	80
7	25	75
8	30	70
9	35	65
10 or more	40 maximum	60 maximum

How to calculate the CGT payable on disposal of shares

Calculation of indexation factor

Calculate the indexation factor using the formula

$$\frac{RD - RI}{RI}$$ worked to 3 decimal places.

RD is the Retail Price Index (RPI) in the month the sale took place (disposal) up to April 1998. RI is the RPI in the month the shares were purchased, or the RPI for March 1982 if the shares were bought before this date.

Apply the indexation factor to the cost of the shares or the March 1982 value if held at that date. The factor is applied by first multiplying it to the cost/March 1982 value, then adding it to the cost/March 1982 value.

If the shares were purchased before March 1982 the indexation factor (calculated on the March 1982 RPI) can be applied to the purchase cost, however this would be of use only if the purchase cost were higher than the March 1982 value.

Calculate the taxable gain as follows (**taper relief not applicable**):

	£
Net sale proceeds	
Less purchase cost adjusted by indexation allowance	_____
Taxable gain	═══════════

Taper relief applicable:

	£
Net sale proceeds	
Less purchase cost adjusted by indexation allowance	_____
Gain before taper relief	
Number of years taper relief %	_____
Taxable gain	═══════════

The cost of shares includes all dealing costs, and the sale proceeds are the net proceeds after dealing costs. If the resultant figure shows an indexed loss, the actual taxable gain/loss will be NIL.

Work out the tax.

Note: the Inland Revenue can provide a free leaflet giving the market prices of all quoted shares on 31 March 1982. This will enable the investor to establish the amount to which he should apply the indexation allowance for shares bought before March 1982.

Numerical example

An investor invested £10,000, including all costs, in Z plc in February 1987. In May 2001 he sold the shares for £35,000. This is his only disposal for CGT purposes in the current tax year.

● The RPI in February 1987 was 100.4.
● The RPI in April 1998 was 162.6.
● The RPI in May 2001 was 172.8

Calculate his liability to CGT assuming:

(a) His taxable income was £12,000;

(b) His taxable income was £28,500;

(c) His taxable income was £30,000.

Solution

Before calculating the CGT liability it is necessary to calculate his taxable capital gain.

Note: he has not made any other disposals for CGT purposes in the current tax year, thus the £7,500 allowance is offset against the gain.

Firstly calculate the element of the gain which is subject to indexation:

(i)   Indexation factor $= \dfrac{162.6 - 100.4}{100.4}$ $= 0.620$

(ii)   Indexation allowance   = cost x factor

   = £10,000 x 0.620

   = £6,200

		£	£
(iii)	Sale proceeds		35,000
	Less: cost	10,000	
	Add: indexation allowance	6,200	16,200
	Gain before taper relief		18,800
	Taper relief – 4 years taper relief at 10% of £18,800		1,880
			16,920
	Less: CGT allowance		7,500
	Taxable gain		9,420

(a) Taxable income £12,000 + taxable capital gain £9,420 means the total of £21,420 leaves him in the basic-rate tax band.

   CGT payable=   £9,420 at 20%

   =   £1,884

	£
(b) Taxable income	28,500
Taxable capital gain	9,420
	37,920

This makes his marginal rate of tax 40%, however tax is not applied to the whole of the gain at 40% but first the unused part of the basic rate band is utilized as shown opposite:

CGT payable:	£
On £900 (£29,400 - £28,500) at 20% =	180.00
On balance of £8,520 (£9,420 - £900) at 40% =	3,408.00
CGT payable	3,588.00

(c) As his marginal rate of tax is already 40%, the whole of the capital gain is taxed at 40%.

CGT payable   =   £9,420   x 40%

              =   £3,768

6.8 Taxation of children's investment income and capital gains

Every child is entitled to a single person's income tax allowance of £4,535. However, where the money for the investment has been provided by a parent, the investment income and capital gain will be treated as the donor parent's for tax purposes. However, if the income is less than £100 p.a. it is disregarded for the parental tax position. If the income exceeds £100, the whole of the income is taxed at the donor parent's marginal rate of income tax. The main exception is for money invested in Children's Bonus Bonds (see Chapter 17), which do not attract a tax liability for the parent.

On the other hand, where the money for the investment has been provided by someone other than a parent, for instance a grandparent, then the income from that investment is treated as the child's for tax purposes. Provided the child's total income in these circumstances is below £4,535, he will not have to pay tax.

6.9 Inheritance tax

Introduction

Basically Inheritance Tax (IhT) is a tax on the estate of a deceased person, but the tax is also payable on lifetime gifts when these exceed £242,000.

Rates of IhT
Death rate

These are:

- First £242,000   Nil
- £242,001 and above   40%

Lifetime gifts rate

These are:

Years before death	% of death rate
Not more than three	100
More than three but not more than four	80
More than four but not more than five	60
More than five but not more than six	40
More than six but not more than seven	20
Over seven years	Nil

Lifetime gifts that are not taxable

These include:

- Any amount transferred between husband and wife provided both are domiciled in the UK, and that the transfer is for the total use, and totally at the disposal of, the spouse to whom the assets are transferred. If one spouse is a foreign domiciled spouse, transfers are exempt only up to £55,000.

- £3,000 in any tax year. Husband and wife each have a £3,000 tax-free allowance, and any unused balance can be carried forward into the next year only. Thus if neither husband nor wife have made any gifts within the previous tax year their combined allowance would be £12,000 in the following fiscal year.

- Wedding gifts of up to £5,000 by each parent, £2,500 by the bride or groom and each grandparent and up to £1,000 by any other person.

- Gifts that are from normal taxed income; in other words, any gifts that are paid from your income rather than from your capital.

- Small gifts up to a maximum of £250 to any one individual. It is therefore possible to make gifts up to £250 per person to any number of people without incurring IhT.

- Transfers to a charity where the gift becomes an asset of the charity.

- Transfers of heritage property and other assets of value to the nation or bodies such as the National Trust.

- Gifts to political parties.

Potentially exempt transfers (PETs)

If a transfer does not fall within the exempt transfers listed above, it does not mean that there is an automatic liability to IhT.

Lifetime gifts that could be subject to IhT are ones made during the donor's life. If the donor survives for seven years there will be no liability to IhT. The potential liability arises if the donor dies within seven years of making the gift. Lifetime gifts made within seven years of death are added back to establish the size of the estate on death. If the total exceeds the annual exemption allowance at time of death, the IhT will be payable. However, the transfer may not be subject to 100% of the tax; there is a sliding scale whereby the tax is mitigated if death occurs after three years.

One way of protecting the beneficiary of a lifetime transfer should death occur within the seven-year period is to take out a life policy that pays out only if death occurs before a set date. Provided the policy is written in trust for the beneficiary of the transfer, the proceeds themselves will not attract IhT but should supply the cash to pay any such liability on the PET.

Transfers that are not taxable

The 1992 Finance Act removed two major assets from the Inheritance Act net. Transfers of family companies and working farms owned or tenanted by the farmer are no longer subject to IhT. Whether the transfer is made as a lifetime gift or upon death does not affect the position – there is no liability to IhT.

Example of IhT liability and a PET

Mr R made a gift of domestic property worth £300,000 to his son on 20 July 1996. He had already made gifts that absorbed the annual exemption that year. On 3 January 2001 Mr R died. His estate was valued at £325,000 after subtracting all reliefs and exemptions. The total IhT bill is calculated thus.

(a) On the PET of £300,000

Mr R died more than four but not more than five years after making the gift. IhT will therefore be charged at 60% of the death rate of 40%

			£
Value of gift	£300,000		
Tax payable on first	£242,000		Nil
On balance of	£58,000	at 24%*	13,920
IhT payable			13,920

* calculated 60% of 40% = 24%

(b) On the estate

Value at death	£325,000
IhT on £325,000 at 40% =	£130,000

Note: the £242,000 is offset against the lifetime gift first, and any unused portion carried over to the remainder of the estate. The death rate of 40% applies in full to the value of the estate on death.

Tax and the examination

In the examination you will find the various rates of tax and allowances required to answer the questions given on the paper. These are the rates you must use. However, you will still have to be able to produce the tax computations given in this chapter.

Conclusion

We have studied income tax, national insurance, CGT and IhT in this chapter in general terms. The unique tax aspects of certain investments, such as unit trusts, investment trusts, offshore funds and insurance products will be examined in detail in the relevant chapters covering those investments.

7

GILT-EDGED SECURITIES

Objectives

After studying this chapter, the reader should be able to:

- assess the significance of British government securities (gilts) in funding the government's borrowing requirements;
- differentiate between the categories of gilt;
- explain how gilts are issued, including the use of auctions, switch auctions, conversion offers and gilt strips;
- understand the basics of the gilt repo market;
- apply the principles of taxation to calculate after-tax yields for different types of investor;
- apply the information from the *Financial Times* to the needs of different types of investor;
- appreciate the significance of 'cum div' and 'ex div' for gilt prices;
- evaluate the significance of gilt-edged switching and its implications for the yield curve;
- explain the dealing process for the Bank of England Brokerage Service.

7.1   The government as a borrower

The government has several ways available to raise capital. One major source of funds is the issue of British government securities, which are more commonly called 'gilt-edged securities' or 'gilts'.

Gilts are quoted on the Stock Exchange and are the safest form of quoted investment because the capital and interest is guaranteed by the UK government. There are stocks issued by other bodies that are virtually as safe as gilts, such as corporation loan stocks and public board securities. However, there is still a slightly higher chance of default with these stocks than with the gilts issued by the government. These other non-gilt stocks are classed as near- or quasi-gilts.

The government uses the funds raised by issuing gilts to help finance the Public Sector Net Cash Requirement (PSNCR), which was previously called the Public Sector Borrowing Requirement (the PSBR).

The Bank of England uses sales and repurchases of gilts to the banking sector as a means of influencing short-term levels of interest rates for monetary policy purposes. This is done via the gilt repo market (see section 4).

Gilts can be classified as either conventional or index-linked. Conventional gilts issued carry a fixed rate of interest (called a coupon) per nominal £100 stock held whereas for index-linked gilts both the coupon and nominal value are linked to the RPI (retail price index).

The price that the government fixes on a new issue of gilts, or the price that is paid by the investor on the stock market, determines the actual rate of interest the investor will receive. Virtually all stocks carry a date on which they must be redeemed (repaid) by the government.

Whatever the reason for issuing gilts, these securities are of major importance, not only to the government, but also to the investor. Although there are only around 66 gilts, compared with around 2,400 shares in UK companies quoted on the Stock Exchange, the value of the average deal relating to gilts is over £3 million, whereas the value of the average deal relating to equities is around £64,400 (figures to year end 2000). Source: London Stock Exchange Web Site, Statistics section. http://www.londonstockexchange.com/historic.asp.

The amount of gilts in issue is enormous, and they play a significant part in the asset portfolios of institutions and of individuals. Table 7.1 represents the latest available figures at the time of writing:

Table 7.1: Holdings of UK national debt at 31 March 1999

Sterling national debt	£BN	Holders of national debt	£BN
British government stock:		Insurance companies	103
Up to 5 years	95	Pension funds	76
5-15 years	125	Investment/unit trusts	4
Over 15 years	72	Banks and building societies	27
		Public sector	6
Treasury bills	9	Individuals	85
Non-marketable*	105	Non-residents	62
		Other	42
Total	**406**	**Total**	**406**

* includes National Savings/Bank of England holdings

Source: Bank of England, quoted in Financial Times, "Markets 2000: A Millenium Guide", January 2000

7.2   Categories of gilts

Gilts are divided into five categories: shorts, mediums, longs, undated and index-linked. When you purchase any gilt you will always see figures in the title, e.g. 5% Treasury 2004. The 5% is called the 'coupon' and it means that for conventional gilts an investor will receive £5 interest per annum for every nominal £100 of stock he holds. The 2004 in the title is the date on which the conventional gilt will be redeemed (repaid) at par. For index-linked gilts, the redemption value will depend on the RPI (see section 7).

Shorts

These are gilts that have less than five years to run until redemption.

Mediums

These stocks have between 5 and 15 years to run to redemption. The *Financial Times* no longer calls these stocks 'mediums', but categorizes them as 5 to 10 years and 10 to 15 years.

Longs

These stocks have over 15 years to run to redemption, but they will always carry a redemption date. In April 2001 the longest-dated of these stocks was 4¼% Treasury 2032. The date means that the stock will be redeemed by the government in 2032.

Undated

The government is under no obligation ever to redeem undated stocks. However, there is just one undated stock that will eventually be redeemed, and that is 3½% Conversion 1961 aft. The reason for this is that a sinking fund exists whereby each year the government redeems 1% of this stock, either by purchasing it in the open market, or if insufficient stock is available in the market, by a ballot.

Another point about undated gilts is that some of them carry a date followed by the abbreviation 'aft', for example, 3½% Conversion 1961 aft and 3% Treasury 1966 aft. 'Aft' is an abbreviation of 'after' and means that when the stock was issued it would be redeemable in 1961 or 1966 (depending on the stock) or at some time after. The option to redeem lies with the government and the decision to redeem or not depends on the general level of interest rates and the coupon of the stock. As the coupons of these stocks are low at 3% and 3½%, the government is borrowing the money far more cheaply then it could do elsewhere. It is obviously better for the government not to redeem these stocks unless the general level of interest rates falls below 3 or 3½% (an occurrence not seen since before World War II, but one which could conceivably arise again given the current macroeconomic low-interest low-inflation situation). All undated gilts carry coupons of 4% or less.

Only three gilts pay interest quarterly, all undated. They are 2½% Consolidated (Consols), 2½% Annuities and 2¾% Annuities.

Note: the two annuity stocks mentioned above are not shown in the *Financial Times*, thus there is a common misconception that there are only six, not eight, undated gilts.

Index-linked

These gilts are unique in two ways. First, the coupon is index-linked to the retail price index, so that each half-year when the interest is paid, the investor will receive coupon rate plus index linking. For the investor this means that the purchasing power of the interest received will remain constant in real terms, unlike all other fixed-interest stock where inflation erodes the purchasing power of fixed-interest payments. Secondly, the capital is also index-linked. The index linking of the capital is calculated by using the RPI eight months prior to the issue date, and the RPI eight months prior to redemption date. With an index-linked gilt the nominal £100 is index-linked on redemption, so the investor will receive more than £100 actual cash. The index linking of the capital applies only on redemption, but the price of index-linked gilts at any time reflects the element of index linking that is occurring and is likely to occur in the future.

The *Financial Times* shows the RPI eight months prior to the issue date against each of the index-linked gilts.

Convertible gilts

There are several gilts that are convertible into longer-dated gilts. In the *Financial Times* their title is 'Conversion' or 'Conv'.

The stock allows an investor to take a view on future interest rates. He knows when he purchases these gilts, exactly what the interest and redemption yields on the stocks will be if he does not convert. He also knows the terms of conversion and the details applicable to the stock into which he can convert. This conversion option allows him to take a view on future interest-rate movements. Full details of the conversion terms and the gilt into which the conversion can take place should be obtained from a broker.

The conversion takes place at the holder's option. If he feels that the stock into which he can convert is unattractive then he will retain the original and it will be redeemed at the earlier date. The gross redemption yields of convertible gilts are lower than for comparable non-convertible gilts. This takes into account the attraction of the conversion option.

7.3   Issuing of gilts

Gilts are issued to fund the Public Sector Net Cash Requirement (PSNCR). When there is a requirement for more money for the PSNCR, gilts are used to fund it. When the PSNCR is negative gilts are purchased by the government either on the Stock Market or by a reverse auction In 1993 the net amount (new issues minus redemptions) raised was £50,965.2 million, compared to a net repayment (redemptions minus new issues) of £9,047.8m in 2000. This indicates a major fall in the PSNCR.

Issuing gilts via the auction method

All scheduled new issues of gilts are now made by auctions and details are announced in advance. (Investing in Gilts, February 2001, http://www.bankofengland.co.uk). There is no minimum price set, and investors bid the price they are willing to pay. Stock is allotted starting with the highest bid and working down until all bids are satisfied, or the stock available has been sold. Each bidder pays the price he bid. The government may decide to issue the stock in partly-paid form. The balance will be due at a later date, set by the government at the time of issue.

A private individual can avoid the difficulty of buying gilts by auction by applying via a 'non-competitive bid'. The price paid is the weighted average price paid by succesful competitive bidders. The minimum amount on a non-competitive bid is £1,000 nominal of the gilt and the maximum amount is £500,000. The exception to this maximum is when the gilt being auctioned is an index-linked gilt, where the maximum non-competitive bid is £250,000.

Switch Auctions

Switch auctions were introduced in 1999 by the Debt Management Office (DMO). These auctions are not open to private investors, but only to gilt-edged market makers (GEMMs). A switch auction has some similarity to conversion offers (see below). The DMO offers to switch a nominal amount of a gilt for another gilt. Switch auctions are run on a competitive bid basis only, there is no non-competitive bidding allowed. The DMO publishes an indicative clean price for the gilt that it wishes to buy (i.e. the gilt out of which the holders – GEMMs – will switch). GEMMs then bid a quantity of the stock they are willing to sell and also a price for the new stock being offered to them. The DMO transacts the switch with the highest bidders.

Conversion offers

In addition to convertible gilts and switch auctions, the DMO does from time to time offer the holders of a particular gilt the right to exchange or convert their holdings to another specified gilt at a set rate called the 'conversion rate', which is based on market price. There is no requirement for the holder to accept this offer, but if the majority of holders accept the offer, the remaining holders may find that their holding is less liquid (i.e. it is not traded as frequently, thus the price on the market for the unconverted gilt may be less favourable to the holder). Such stocks are known as 'rump stocks'.

The reason for the development of switch auctions and conversion offers is to increase the number of strippable gilts, also known as gilt strips.

7.4   Gilt strips

Gilt strips were introduced in December 1997. The Bank of England specifies which gilts are 'strippable'. Not all gilts are 'strippable'. Stripping is the process of separating a fixed-rate interest-bearing gilt into its individual interest (coupon) and redemption payments. These can be held separately and traded in their own right as non-interest bearing or zero-coupon bonds.

Example:

7¼% Treasury 2007 (a strippable gilt) with dividends paid on 7 June and 7 December each year until redemption. This stock is due for redemption on 7 December 2007.

Taking today as 21 April 2001, this gilt could be divided into 15 strips. One strip would be for the repayment of the principal on 7 December 2007. This would be called a zero-coupon strip because no interest is payable on the maturity of the gilt. The holder would receive a payment for the strip's nominal value. Zero strips would trade at a discount to the nominal value in the period prior to maturity. The zero strip would not be subject to capital gains tax because gilts are exempt from CGT.

The remaining 14 strips would relate to each of the half yearly interest payments due each 7 June and December up to and including 7 December 2007. The interest received would be treated as any other interest payment – paid gross, but subject to tax at the investor's marginal rate of income tax.

7.5   Gilt repo market

The gilt repo market was opened on 2 January 1996. A gilt 'repo' is a sale and repurchase agreement under which party A sells gilts to party B with a legally binding agreement to purchase equivalent gilts from part B at an agreed price at a specified future date. The market effectively allows stock (gilts) to be lent. The main participants in the repo market are clearing banks, building societies, major European banks, discount houses, gilt-edged market makers (GEMMs) and international security houses.

The gilt repo market is used by the UK monetary authorities to influence interest rates. The larger the difference between the original price and the repo price for a given time period and underlying transaction amount, the more likely it is that the operation will exert upward pressure on interest rates. Prior to the inception of the gilt repo market, Treasury bills were the most common financial instrument used by the monetary authorities as a means of influencing interest rates.

7.6   Taxation of gilt-edged stocks

All interest paid on gilts is subject to income tax in the hands of a private investor or corporation tax in the case of a limited company investor. Gilts are held on the Bank of England Register and the interest received is paid gross. This interest must be declared to the Inland Revenue and it is taxable at the investor's marginal rate of income tax. A basic-rate taxpayer pays the savings rate of tax of 20%. The investor can opt to have the 20% tax deducted at source on application to the Bank of England Registrars department.

All gilts are totally free of capital gains tax in the hands of the investor, but the full effect of the taxation of gilt-edged stocks will be seen below where the yield calculations show the effect of taxation on gilts for various classes of investor.

7.7 Yield calculations

Yield can be defined as the rate of return from an investment, expressed in percentage terms. The yield calculations are important to investors when deciding on the gilt to purchase. Gilts not only have a variety of maturity dates, but also a wide variety of coupons. The coupon of a gilt is the first figure found in the title of a stock and it is the rate of interest an investor will receive per nominal £100 of stock held. The price of the gilt is the price per nominal £100 of stock. If a gilt is quoted at 75.84 this means that (ignoring all dealing costs), the investor will have to pay £75.84 to purchase £100 nominal. A gilt that is priced below £100 per £100 nominal of stock is said to be 'under par'. If a gilt is priced at 113.73 it means the investor will have to pay £113.73 for £100 nominal of stock. In this case the stock is said to be 'over par' par because the market price of £100 nominal is higher than £100. Gilts are priced in decimals down to two decimal places.

Interest yield (also 'flat' or 'running' yield)

You may see all three of the above terms used; thus you should be familiar with them. The interest yield expresses the annual interest payments produced by a fixed-interest investment, such as a gilt, in percentage terms. The formula used to calculate interest yield is:

$$\frac{\text{Coupon x 100}}{\text{Market price}}$$

To start with a simple example, if there was a gilt called 10% Exchequer Stock 2010 which had a market price of 50 then the interest yield would be:

$$\frac{10 \times 100}{50} = 20\%$$

In other words, £100 invested in this stock would produce gross interest of £20 per annum. Because this is a fixed-interest stock the investor will continue to receive £20 per annum until the stock is redeemed in 2010, or until he decided to sell the stock.

The interest yield calculated here of 20% is the gross interest yield, i.e. no reduction is made for the effect of the investor's marginal rate of tax. To arrive at the net interest yield, which is the after-tax return to the investor, his marginal rate of tax must be deducted from the gross interest yield.

Taking the example given of a gross interest yield of 20%, then arriving at the after-tax figure for two different investors, one paying a marginal rate of tax of 22% and the other a marginal rate of 40%, the formula used is:

$$\text{Gross interest yield} = \frac{(100 - \text{marginal rate of tax})}{100}$$

For the 22% taxpayer this gives:

$$\text{Net interest yield} = 20 \times \frac{(100 - 20)}{100}$$

$$= \frac{20 \times 80}{100}$$

$$= \underline{16.0\%}$$

(NB: For a basic-rate taxpayer fixed interest is only taxed at 20%.)

For the 40% taxpayer this gives:

$$\text{Net interest yield} = 20 \times \frac{(100 - 40)}{100}$$

$$= \frac{20 \times 60}{100}$$

$$= \underline{12\%}$$

So for the 22% taxpayer the actual after-tax interest received is £16.00 per £100 invested, and for the 40% taxpayer the figure is £12. Only a non-taxpayer would actually receive and retain without future deduction the full £20 per £100 invested.

Redemption yields

For all fixed-interest stocks that carry a date upon which they must be redeemed it is possible to calculate a redemption yield. The situation is slightly different for index-linked gilts. The redemption yield takes into account any capital gain made (if the stock was standing under par when purchased) or capital loss (if the stock was standing over par when purchased).

The redemption yield assumes that the stock is held until maturity, and calculates the gain on an annual basis. Because gains on gilts are free of capital gains tax, the calculation of redemption yields starts after the interest yield has been calculated.

Gross redemption yield

Going back to the example above of the 10% Exchequer Stock 2010 priced at 50, assuming that it is purchased in 2000, there are 10 years to go to maturity. Thus there is an annual capital gain of $50 \div 10 = 5$ points per annum.

To arrive at the gross redemption yield the formula used is:

Gross interest yield ± annual capital gain/loss.

So for this stock the gross redemption yield = 20 + 5 = 25%. Obviously this calculation is somewhat inaccurate regarding the capital gain element because the stock is assumed to be purchased and redeemed on the same dates in 2000 and 2010 whereas the dates will almost certainly be different. The other factor ignored is the effect of compounding the 10-year period. The fact that calculations as shown are somewhat inaccurate must be appreciated. In the examination the question will usually state 'calculate the approximate redemption yield for this stock', to take account of this fact.

Net redemption yield

This is calculated using the formula:

Net interest yield ± annual capital gain/loss.

This calculation takes into account the differing tax treatment of income and capital gain, and is used to assess which stock is most suitable for a particular taxpayer.

Going back to our 22% and 40% taxpayers, the net redemption yield is:

22% taxpayer = 16 + 5 = 21%

40% taxpayer = 12 + 5 = 17%

Grossed-up net redemption yield (also called gross equivalent yield)

This calculation is used to compare the grossed-up return on a fixed-interest stock, such as a gilt, with the gross return on a fixed-interest, fixed-capital investment such as a bank money-market term deposit. It takes the net redemption yield of the stock and grosses it up at the investor's marginal rate of tax. The resultant figure shows the return the fixed-capital investment would have to give to equal the return on the gilt. The formula is:

$$\frac{\text{Net redemption yield x 100}}{(100 - \text{marginal rate of tax})}$$

Again, taking the two taxpayers in the previous example, the figures for grossed-up net redemption yield would be:

22% taxpayer $= 21 \times \frac{(100)}{100 - 20)}$

$= \frac{21 \times 100}{80}$

= 26.25%

40% taxpayer $= 17 \times \frac{100)}{(100 - 40)}$

$= \frac{17 \times 100}{60}$

= 28.33%

In this case a 22% taxpayer would need to find a fixed-interest, fixed-capital investment paying in excess of 26.25% gross whereas the 40% taxpayer would need one paying in excess of 28.33% gross, in order to receive a higher return than the gilt.

Obviously the examples here are hypothetical because no gilt with a coupon of 10% would be priced as low as 50, but they serve to give a simple introduction to the method of calculation.

7.8   Example of gilt calculations

From the following information:

- name of stock – 8% Treasury 2013
- market price – 129.51
- nominal stock – £1,544.28
- market cost – £2,000 (ignoring all dealing costs)

Calculate:

(a)   How the market cost of £2,000 gives a nominal holding of £1,544.28;

(b)   The gross interest yield;

(c)   The net interest yield assuming the investor pays tax at 22%;

(d)   The gross redemption yield (assuming it is now 2002);

(e)   The net redemption yield for a 22% tax payer (assuming it is 2002);

(f)   The gross amount of interest received per annum;

(g)   The grossed-up net redemption yield for a 22% taxpayer.

(h)   What is the purpose of the grossed-up net redemption yield calculation?

Answer

(a)   Nominal $= \dfrac{\text{Market cost} \times 100}{\text{Market price}}$

$= \dfrac{2{,}000 \times 100}{129.51}$

$= £1{,}544.28$

(b)   Gross interest yield $= \dfrac{\text{Coupon} \times 100}{\text{Price}}$

$= \dfrac{8 \times 100}{129.51}$

$= 6.18\%$ (Note: always work to two decimal points)

(c)   Net interest yield $= \text{gross interest yield} \times \dfrac{(100 - \text{marginal rate of tax})}{100}$

$$= 6.18 \times \dfrac{(100 - 20)}{100}$$

$$= \dfrac{6.18 \times 80}{100}$$

$$= \underline{4.94\%}$$

(d)   Gross redemption yield = gross interest yield ± annual capital gain/loss.

Annual capital gain/loss $= \dfrac{(\text{par - price})}{\text{number of years to maturity}}$

$$= \dfrac{(100 - 129.51)}{(2013 - 2002)}$$

$$= \dfrac{-29.51}{11}$$

$$= \underline{-2.68} \ (\text{capital loss})$$

Therefore gross redemption yield = 6.18 - 2.68

$$= \underline{3.5\%}$$

(e)   Net redemption yield = net interest yield ± annual capital gain/loss.

$$= 4.94 - 2.68$$

$$= \underline{2.26\%}$$

(f)   The gross amount of interest received p.a.

$$= \dfrac{\text{coupon} \times \text{nominal}}{100}$$

$$= \dfrac{8 \times 1{,}544.28}{100}$$

$$= \underline{£123.54}$$

(g)   Grossed-up net redemption yield

$$= \text{net redemption yield} \times \dfrac{100}{(100 - \text{marginal rate of tax})}$$

$$= \dfrac{2.26 \times 100}{(100 - 20)}$$

$$= \dfrac{2.26 \times 100}{80}$$

$$= \underline{2.83\%}$$

(h) The purpose of the grossed-up net redemption yield calculation is to find the required gross return from a fixed-interest, fixed-capital investment such as a money-market deposit that will give an equivalent return for a particular taxpayer. It takes into account the differing tax treatment of income and capital gains on gilts.

7.9 Gilt prices in the *Financial Times*

The *Financial Times* lists the prices, yields and other details of gilts under 'UK Gilts – Cash Market' in the 'Companies and Markets' section of the paper and are listed as:

- Shorts (lives up to five years)
- 5 to 10 years
- 10 to 15 years
- Longs (over 15 years)
- Undated
- Index-linked.

For the first five categories the information printed is the same. However, for the index-linked gilt it is not possible to print exact yields because the rate of inflation between now and redemption is unknown. To give investors an approximate guide as to the yield of index-linked gilts, the *Financial Times* assumes two different rates of inflation, one being 5%, the other 3%. They also print next to the title of the gilt the RPI base month for indexing, i.e. eight months prior to issue.

Calculations based on the *Financial Times* yields

Dated gilts

Monday's edition of the *Financial Times* provides slightly different information about these stocks. It gives the dates upon which the interest is due and the date the stock last went ex dividend. Shown below are the details of a gilt as shown in the Tuesday-Saturday editions of the FT.

Tuesday-Saturday edition						
	Notes	Yield		Price	+ or -	52 Week
		Int	Red	£		High	Low
Treas 8pc 2009		6.56	4.82	121.87	+.17	123.12	116.63

The example shows that the highest price the stock reached during the past 52 weeks was £123.12 and the lowest £116.63 per nominal £100 of stock. The current price is £121.87

per nominal £100 stock and the stock price rose 0.17 from the previous day's close of business.

If you then calculate the gross interest and redemption yields using the formulae given in section 7 you will find that the interest yield you calculate is virtually identical to that in the *Financial Times*, but the redemption yield differs from the one quoted in the *Financial Times*.

Using the information above:

$$\text{Gross interest yield} = \frac{8 \times 100}{121.87}$$

$$= \underline{6.56\%}$$

(Assuming it is 2001)

$$\text{Annual capital loss} = \frac{(100 - 121.87)}{(2009 - 2001)}$$

$$= \frac{21.87}{8}$$

$$= \underline{-2.73}$$

$$\text{Gross redemption yield} = 6.56 - 2.73$$

$$= \underline{3.83\%}$$

The gross interest yields in the *Financial Times* are easy to reconcile, because the price of gilts is quoted clean, i.e. accrued earned interest is accounted for by means of a separate transaction. Thus the formula shown will agree.

With the gross redemption yield there is a difference. If you take the *Financial Times* gross interest yield of 6.56% and deduct the annual capital loss calculated by the method shown above, the result is 6.56 - 2.73 = 3.83% whereas the *Financial Times* gross redemption figure is 4.82%. The *Financial Times* capital gain/loss is calculated by adding/subtracting the gross redemption yield from the gross interest yield. Thus in the above example the capital loss = 4.82 - 6.56 = -1.74. This differs from the one calculated above because of two factors. The first is that the *Financial Times* uses the actual date the stock will be redeemed so, instead of the arbitrary eight years, the exact time to redemption is applied in the calculation. The second is the effect of compounding of interest. The principles are similar to those applied in calculating an IRR (internal rate of return) for a set of cash flow forecasts in investment appraisal.

Index-linked gilts

In the *Financial Times* the details of index-linked gilts are as follows:

Tuesday-Saturday edition						
	Notes	Yield		Price	+ or -	52 Week
		(1)	(2)	£		High	Low
4¹/₈% I.L. Treas '30	(135.1) 2.01		2.06	181.76	−0.22	198.66	181.76

The information shows that 4¹/₈% Treasury Stock 2030 is priced at £181.76 per nominal £100 of stock. The '+ or -' column indicates that the price has fallen by 0.22. The first yield column shown as (1) shows the prospective real redemption rate on a projected inflation rate of 5% and column (2) on a projected inflation rate of 3%. The figure in brackets after the name of the stock under 'Notes' (135.1) is the RPI base month for indexing, i.e. eight months prior to issue.

In order to compare the gross yield figures to conventional gilt yields, you simply add the figure given for the gross prospective real return to the rate of inflation assumed by the *Financial Times* for the purposes of the calculation. Thus for the 4¹/₈% Treasury 2030, an equivalent conventional gilt would need to give a return of (5 + 2.01) 7.01% assuming inflation stays constant over the period at 5%, and a rate of (3 + 2.06) 5.06% if inflation is constant at 3%.

To produce the inflation-adjusted coupon, you multiply the coupon by the current RPI and divide by the RPI given by the date of the stock. In the above example, assuming the current RPI is 172.6, the inflation-adjusted coupon is:

$$= \frac{4.125 \times 172.6}{135.1}$$

$$= \underline{5.27\%}$$

To calculate the current redemption value, the same calculation is done, using the £100 nominal value.

$$\text{Current redemption value} = \frac{100 \times 172.6}{135.1}$$

$$= \underline{£127.76}$$

This would be the current redemption value of the stock, assuming it was redeemed in eight months' time. The nearer the stock gets to maturity, the closer the price will move towards the redemption value. The current price is £181.76, thus the gilt is over par because it is above its redemption value.

It is possible to estimate a redemption value of the gilt assuming different rates of inflation. If inflation were assumed to run at 3% p.a. until the stock were redeemed, and assuming that it is now 2001, the Treasury stock will be redeemed in 29 years' time. To calculate the redemption value in 29 years' time, you multiply the current redemption value of £127.76

by $(1.03)^{29}$ which comes to £301.07. Note: if your calculator cannot multiply to the power of 29, simply multiply £127.76 x 1.03, and repeat the process 28 more times.

Redemption value at 3% inflation $\quad = £127.76 \times (1.03)^{29}$

$$= £301.07$$

(The longer method starts off:

$127.76 \times 1.03 = 131.59$

$131.59 \times 1.03 = 135.54$

$135.54 \times 1.03 = 139.61$

and so on.)

The only danger an investor runs with an index-linked gilt is when inflation rises rapidly in the eight months prior to redemption. The base month and redemption month RPIs are both the RPI figures for eight months prior to issue/redemption. A rapid rise in the RPI in the eight months before redemption will not be reflected in the proceeds paid at maturity.

7.10   Ex div and cum div

Gilt prices are said to be either ex div (or xd) or cum div (or cd), 'div' being the abbreviation for dividend. Stocks are quoted ex div about five weeks before interest is due to be paid. The government pays interest only to the holders of stock on its books at the date they are closed. Once the books are closed the stock is shown in the *Financial Times* with 'xd' immediately after the price. The next interest instalment on an ex div stock is paid to the seller of the stock, as opposed to the buyer. If the stock is not shown in the *Financial Times* as 'xd' then it is always cum div, in which case the purchaser will receive the next interest payment due. When a gilt moves from 'cum div' to 'ex div', its price would normally fall to reflect the fact that the seller, not the buyer, will receive the next interest payment.

Interest on gilts is payable half-yearly, with the exception of three undated gilts, 2½% Consols, 2½ % Annuities and 2¾% Annuities, where the interest is paid quarterly on 5 January, April, July and October for all these stocks. The two annuity stocks are infrequently traded on the market, and thus are not readily available for purchase. The reason these two stocks are infrequently traded is that they are 'rump stocks', which are infrequently dealt in and their holding is less liquid (i.e. it is not traded as frequently, thus the price on the market may be less favourable to the holder).

7.11   Gilt-edged switching

This is an operation that is generally carried out by institutional investors to maximize returns on their gilt portfolios. While a 0.06 or 0.03 price movement is virtually of no interest to the small private investor, to the institutional investor with multi-million pound gilt portfolios, such movements are of vital importance. There are three forms of gilt-edged switching: anomaly, policy and taxation switching.

Anomaly switching

Institutional investors deal in huge amounts of stocks at a time, the result of which can mean that the price of two comparable gilts can get out of line with each other. If only one of the gilts is dealt in, that gilt's price will appear high compared to the other one if that gilt has been purchased, and low if it has been sold. These price movements would be picked up by other institutional investors through their usage of computers or graphs to plot movements. Some institutions plot graphs of all gross redemption yields of gilts compared with the number of years to redemption, and any price movement obviously affects the gross redemption yield. Once a stock has got out of line then another institution will take the opposite action and bring the gilt back into line. Normally the gilt yield curve slopes gently to the right, and any stocks that are out of line are easily spotted.

Figure 7.1: The yield curve of an anomaly stock

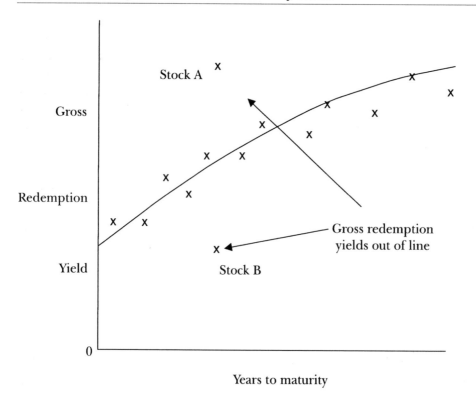

Years to maturity

In Fig. 7.1 the crosses represent the gross redemption yields of comparable gilts. Stocks 'A' and 'B' are out of line with the others and are thus 'anomaly' stocks. Stock 'A' has a higher-than-average gross redemption yield and the investors who plotted this graph would purchase this stock because the price is 'artificially' low in relation to the average, thus pushing up the gross redemption yield. On the other hand, Stock B's gross redemption yield is below average, and the holders of such stock would sell it and benefit from the 'artificially' high price that exists.

As a result of those actions the price of Stock A will rise and Stock B fall as the law of supply and demand works to readjust the prices and yields back into line.

Policy switching

When an investor takes a view on the way that the general levels of interest rates are going to move, he may take action within his portfolio to switch the gilts to match his view. If the investor expects the current levels of interest rates to fall in the future, he could sell his short-dated gilts and purchase long (over 15 years) or undated gilts. This would enable him to lock into the current high yields available on the long and undated gilts. If investors do purchase long and undated gilts the gross interest and hence gross redemption yields of these gilts will fall because their prices will rise. In contrast the price of the shorts (and medium-dated – 5 to 10 years and 10 to 15 years – if the same action is taken) will tend to fall and the gross redemption yields of these short- and medium-dated stocks will tend to rise.

When the investor feels that future interest rates are going to rise he may shorten the maturity of his portfolio. Short-dated gilts are virtually unaffected by market forces; they will always approach par (£100) as redemption draws near (i.e. they have a 'pull to maturity'). If investors as a whole do switch from longs (over 15 years) to shorts, the price of long-dated stocks will fall, and their yields will rise. The investor who has shortened the life of his portfolio by selling his longer-dated and undated stocks will be unaffected by the interest rate rise because he holds shorts, and once he feels that interest rates have risen as far as they will go, he could sell his shorts and reinvest in longer-dated or undated gilts.

If an investor feels that inflation will rise, he can still take effective action within the gilt market by switching his holdings into index-linked gilts. This will give him an annual interest payment revalued in line with the retail price index and on redemption his capital will be revalued in line with the retail price index also. This action will protect the purchasing power of both his interest and capital.

7.12 Yield curves and the effect of policy switching

It is possible to plot yield curves relating to both rising and falling interest rates and their effect on the gross redemption yields of gilts over the number of years to maturity. The 'normal' yield curve, where there is an uncertain financial environment, but no specific expectation of a change in interest rates, will show higher yields on longs than on shorts. This reflects the greater risk involved in long-term lending of any sort as opposed to short-term lending.

According to the expectations theory, the changes in shape of a yield curve will reflect the market's expectations of future movements in interest rates (see Fig. 7.2 (a) and (b)). However, other theories contradict this. According to the segmentation theory, future interest rate expectations have no effect on the shape of the yield curve, because the major investors are locked into their own segment of the market and will not switch whatever the likely forecast of interest rates. Banks, building societies and general insurance companies invest mainly in the short end of the market, whereas life assurance and pension funds invest mainly at the long end. The truth must lie somewhere between these two extremes, but it is a fact that yield curves are studied by some as a means of predicting interest-rate movements.

The yield curves that follow are not actual examples, and in the examination you would not be expected to plot accurate yield curves, but you must be able to show thorough understanding of the effect that an expected change in interest rates could have on the gross redemption yields of gilts in relation to the number of years to redemption. Thus a small freehand drawing indicating these trends would be adequate.

Figure 7.2 (a) Yield curve and the expectation of rising interest rates

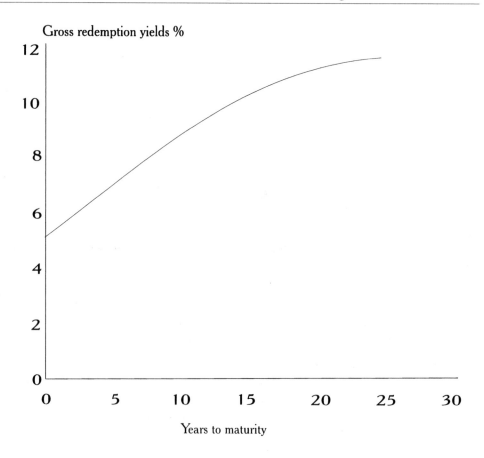

Figure 7.2 (b) Yield curve and the expectation of falling interest rates

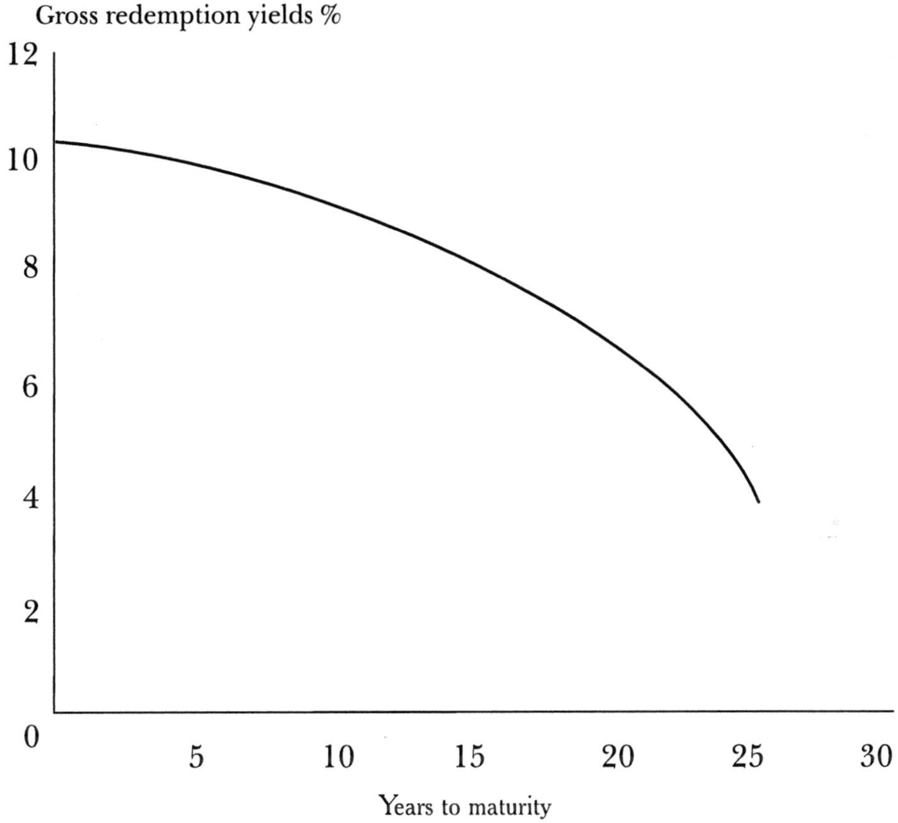

Gross redemption yields %

Years to maturity

7.13   Taxation switching

Two gilts may have similar redemption yields, but one may be a high-yielding gilt with little if any capital gain, whereas the other may be low-yielding with a large capital gain element. However, a taxpayer would firstly calculate the net redemption yields of the stocks to ascertain the most appropriate one for his needs. As the highest rate of tax is now just 40%, low-coupon gilts do not necessarily give the best return to a high (i.e. 40%) taxpayer.

Taxation switching is of less interest to most institutional investors who are, in the main, more concerned with the figure for the gross redemption yield, as opposed to the proportion of that return which consists of interest yield and the proportion which consists of capital gain. The private investor, however, could well be more concerned with taxation switching, because CGT is tax-free on gilts, whereas the interest is taxable.

7.14 Dealings on the Bank of England Brokerage Service

Gilts that are already in issue can be purchased one of two ways, either via a stockbroker or via the Bank of England Brokerage Service. New issues of gilts can be purchased from the Debt Management Office (DMO) or via an Auction.

Advantages of dealing on the Bank of England Brokerage Service

These are that:

- This is a simple process using clear forms that are available at any Post Office, from the Bank of England itself or from the Bank of England's web site.

- The costs of purchasing and selling stock on this register are low.

Disadvantages of dealing on the Bank of England Brokerage Service

These are that:

- It is not possible to know the price of the stock prior to sale or purchase, because the price ruling is the one when the Bank of England's Registrars Department receives the buy or sell form.

- Even with first-class post there is a minimum of one day's delay between the order being posted and acted upon by the Registrars Department.

- It is not possible either to deal via telephone or to place a 'limit' as it is with a stockbroker. All deals must be conducted by post.

- The maximum amount that can be invested in a single stock in any one day is £25,000. This will not affect small investors, but for anyone investing well in excess of £25,000 in one stock it would be quicker and cheaper to use a broker.

- There is no limit to the amount of stock that can be sold in any one day, provided the stock was registered on the Bank of England Register.

- The Registrars Department is not able to give any advice regarding suitability of an investment, whereas a stockbroker will give detailed advice.

As a conclusion, the Bank of England Brokerage Service is suitable for small investors. However, for investors with larger amounts to invest, it could be cheaper to use a stockbroker, because dealing costs are usually on a greater downward sliding scale than the Bank of England rates the larger the deal with the broker.

7.15 The future prospects of gilts

At the time of writing, there is considerable debate about the future prospects for gilts. Some analysts predict that gilt prices will drop because:

- The Myners report of March 2001 called for the abolition of the minimum funding requirement (MFR) for pension funds. Under the MFR, pension funds had been obliged to maintain a minimum proportion of their financial investments in gilts. Freedom from this constraint could mean that pension funds would switch from gilts to, say, corporate bonds of good quality which would have a higher yield. Reduced demand for gilts could depress their price.

- If the UK were to ever join EMU, then the currency in which gilts were denominated would obviously become the euro. Currently long-term interest rates on the euro are above sterling long-term interest rates (presumably because sterling is perceived as a stronger currency) . Inevitably, as the single currency has to have a single interest rate, UK gilt rates would rise. As we know, if yields rise, the prices of gilts fall.

Other analysts predict that the prospects for gilt prices are good because:

- The outlook for inflation worldwide is that it is expected to remain low and stable. In that case interest rates should also remain low and stable, hovering around 2 percentage points above inflation. Other things being equal, low interest rates are supportive of gilt prices.

- If we are indeed moving into a low-inflation, low-interest rate, stable but low economic growth era, then the returns on equities will also fall in money terms. This could make gilts attractive and increase demand.

- Financial Reporting standard 17 requires companies to discount the future liabilities of their defined benefit pension schemes by the yield on low-risk bonds. Gilts are the obvious choice of low-risk bond, so FRS 17 may offset the effects of the withdrawal of MFR as regards the demand from pension funds for gilts.

- If we are indeed approaching an era of balanced budgets, then the government will not need to issue new gilts to replace maturing issues of existing gilts. This will reduce the supply of gilts and hence raise their prices. At the time of writing (April 2001), it is predicted that the amount in money terms outstanding on gilts will be exceeded by that outstanding on sterling corporate loan stocks. Watch this space!!

Nobody can predict the future with any certainty. For example, a recession coupled with relatively high government spending could result in a deficit on the Public Sector Net cash Requirement. This would result in extra government borrowing which could increase the supply of gilts and lower their prices. Readers should follow the fortunes of gilts with interest.

8

COMPANY AND OTHER SECURITIES

Objectives

After studying this chapter, the reader should be able to:

- differentiate between the different types of stocks and shares issued by companies;

- analyse the distribution of company assets on liquidation;

- describe the constitutional rights of shareholders, particularly in respect of meetings and voting;

- assess the problems of investing in unquoted companies;

- understand how companies and local authorities raise debt and describe the instruments used;

- describe the main features of permanent interest-bearing shares issued by building societies.

Introduction

This chapter sets out to examine some of the various types of investment other than gilts that are available as direct investments to the private investor.

8.1   Ordinary shares (equities)

By law, the only class of capital a company must have is ordinary shares. These are more commonly called 'equities'. Some companies' ordinary shares are issued as ordinary or deferred stock – but there is no difference for our purposes. (One major company that has deferred stock instead of shares is P&O.)

Is a shareholder personally liable for company debts?

A shareholder is a member, or part owner, of a limited company. Legally, a shareholder is a separate legal entity from his company and owners of fully-paid shares do not have any legal responsibility for the company's debts. Obviously shareholders may undertake such liability if they sign a guarantee, but mere ownership of fully-paid shares in itself cannot make the shareholder personally liable.

With partly-paid shares the position is different, because in the event of liquidation the shareholder could be liable for the amount of uncalled capital on his shares. For example if the issue price of a company's shares were 50p, and the shares were only 20p paid, then in liquidation the shareholders could be personally liable to pay over the 'uncalled' 30p per share to the liquidator. This payment would be required only if the company's funds were insufficient to meet its external liabilities.

Finally, a holder of partly-paid shares could still find himself personally liable for the debts of his company even if he had sold the shares prior to liquidation. A liquidator will call upon the registered owners of partly-paid shares at the time of the liquidation, if he needs the uncalled capital. If it proves impossible to obtain the money from this source, the liquidator has the right to claim from any previous owner of the partly-paid shares who had sold the shares within 12 months of liquidation. This liability on the part of partly-paid shareholders explains why banks are reluctant to take a full legal mortgage of such shares as security. Legal mortgagees of shares are the registered shareholders, and as such could become liable in the event of liquidation.

Most quoted shares are fully paid, apart from a few that have only just been issued and on which the various calls are not yet due.

8.2   Distribution of a company's assets in liquidation

If a company goes into liquidation all its assets are sold and the resultant pool of cash is distributed by the liquidator to the various parties so entitled. The order of repayment is:

- Secured creditors to the extent of money realized from their security;
- Liquidator's expenses;
- Preferential creditors;
- Creditors who hold a floating charge;
- Unsecured creditors;
- Subordinated loan stockholders;
- Preference shareholders;
- Ordinary shareholders.

Ordinary shareholders are entitled to receive any surplus only after payment of all external liabilities. When there are insufficient funds to pay off all the external liabilities, the ordinary shareholder has no personal liability, provided his shares are fully paid.

8.3   Types of ordinary share

So far we have considered ordinary shares (equities) as a single entity. However, within this single class of shareholding there can be various subdivisions.

Preferred ordinary shares

Such shares may carry restricted rights to dividends, and in liquidation shareholders of preferred ordinary shares may not be entitled to as much of any surplus as would be the ordinary shareholders. However, they are repaid before other ordinary shareholders.

Redeemable ordinary shares

Companies can issue ordinary shares that carry a set date for redemption. The shares will be redeemed either by the proceeds of a new issue of shares or by making transfers from profits into a specific capital redemption reserve. Where non-voting preferred shares or redeemable ordinary shares exist, there must also be some conventional ordinary shares that do not suffer from the restrictions.

Deferred ordinary shares

These shares are essentially founders' shares. Sometimes the original owners of the share capital of a company that is about to obtain a Stock Exchange quotation will try and encourage the new issue by agreeing to waive all dividends on their own shares until the rest of the shares have received a minimum stated dividend (say 10%).

Note that in all cases the precise rights of the holders of various classes of ordinary shares will be set out in the company's articles of association.

Dividend payments

Dividends can be looked upon as cash payments to shareholders out of the profits of a company. Usually there are two dividends per year, an interim dividend and a final dividend. Interim dividends may be declared by the directors and are usually paid at the start of the second half of a company's accounting year. Final dividends are proposed by the directors and are usually paid after the company's annual general meeting (AGM). Shareholders at the AGM have the power to reduce or prevent payment of any final dividend, but they may not vote to increase the dividend that has been proposed.

Dividends can be paid only from available profits, thus the maximum dividend which the directors could propose is limited by the profits available. However, retained profits and revenue reserves from previous years can be used to maintain a dividend if the current year has seen low profits.

8.4   The rights of ordinary shareholders

Ordinary shareholders are the owners of a company, but day-to-day control is in the hands of the directors; this is often referred to as being 'ownership is divorced from control'. A moment's thought will soon make it clear why day-to-day control must be in the hands of directors. Imagine, in the case of a UK clearing bank, the chaos which would ensue if every loan application from a prospective borrower had to have the approval of the shareholders!

However, the Companies Acts 1985 and 1989 and the Stock Exchange have laid down clear rules to protect the shareholders from being exploited by not being involved in day-to-day affairs.

The main rights of ordinary shareholders are as follows

- To receive notices of all meetings of the company and to attend, speak and vote at such meetings.

- To appoint a proxy to attend and vote at a meeting on their behalf.

- To share in the profits of a company on a pro rata basis. Thus every single ordinary share will receive the same dividend unless the shares are preferred or deferred shares. Profits can be shared both by paying out a dividend, and by retaining them for future use by the company.

- To receive bonus issues on a pro rata basis.

- To be given the opportunity to subscribe for rights and convertible issues on a pro rata basis. (If this were not so it would be easy for new shares to be issued to certain shareholders only, thus giving them effective control of the company.) This is called the 'pre-emptive right'. However, in certain circumstances there are exceptions to this 'pre-emptive right'. Provided the shareholders pass a special resolution to disapply pre-emptive rights, then new issues of shares can be made without first being offered to existing shareholders.

- To sell their shares or transfer them without restriction. The Stock Exchange insists on free transferability, although the articles of association of some private companies may restrict the transfer of shares.

- To vote to remove directors and to appoint new ones in their place. With quoted companies this sometimes happens when the company is the 'victim' of a successful takeover bid when the new controlling shareholders prefer to appoint their own directors. The removal and appointment of new directors has also been seen when a company has had a poor trading record, and the shareholders feel that new leadership is required.

    - In general, voting at most meetings of shareholders is by show of hands where each member has one vote irrespective of how many shares he owns. However, on important matters a poll will be held, and indeed, a poll can be demanded by five or more members or by members representing one tenth of the voting capital. In a poll, the usual procedure is to allow one vote for each share.

- For a vote to be valid, there must be a quorum, i.e. a set minimum number of shareholders present at the meeting. The Companies Act 1985 set the minimum at two for a quoted company, but the company can specify a higher minimum in its articles of association.

- When a shareholder cannot attend a meeting in person he can appoint someone else, known as a proxy, to act on his behalf. A proxy need not be a shareholder, he cannot vote except on a poll, and he can only speak to demand, or join in the demand for, a poll.

- Where a corporate body, usually an institution or a limited company, owns shares in another company, then the corporate shareholder can either appoint a proxy to attend the meetings, or it can appoint a 'representative'. Under the Companies Act 1985, a representative has all the rights of a shareholder.

- To receive the annual report and accounts (including the auditor's report) at least 21 days before the annual general meeting.

- To receive 14 days' notice of an extraordinary general meeting.

- Under the Companies Act 1985 an auditor who resigns must state whether or not there are circumstances that should be reported to the shareholders. If necessary, a resigning auditor could demand that an extraordinary general meeting be held so that shareholders may be informed of such circumstances.

- The Stock Exchange insists that quoted companies provide information over and above that required by the Companies Act. This extra information consists of:

  - An explanation by the directors of failure to meet any published forecast;

  - An interim unaudited set of accounts covering the first six months of the company's financial year must be sent to shareholders;

  - Where the audited accounts are qualified by the auditors because they do not conform to Financial Reporting Standards (FRS), the directors must explain why this has arisen.

8.5   Company meetings and resolutions

A company must hold an annual general meeting at the end of each financial year. The maximum time period allowed between AGMs is 15 months. A company can hold meetings at other times, as and when it is necessary for the shareholders to vote on various matters. Such a meeting is called an extraordinary general meeting.

AGM (annual general meeting)
The items dealt with at the AGM are usually items that would be classed as ordinary

business as defined by the company's articles of association. Such items are the:

- Consideration of the director's report and accounts;
- Declaration of the final dividend;
- Election (but not the removal) of directors;
- Appointment (but not the removal) of the auditors, and the fixing of the auditor's fee.

Twenty-one days' notice of the AGM must be given to shareholders.

EGMs (extraordinary general meetings)

These can be called at any time to deal with business that is classed as 'special business'. Items that would be classed as ordinary business can be dealt with at the AGM, but often these items arise, and have to be dealt with, more quickly than once a year. Such ordinary business can be dealt with at an EGM.

Fourteen days' notice of an EGM must be given to shareholders.

Resolutions

There are three types of resolution: ordinary, special and extraordinary.

- Ordinary resolutions deal with normal business matters such as declaring a dividend, increasing share capital, or the election of directors. An ordinary resolution requires 51% of votes cast in favour for it to be passed.

- Special resolutions cover such items as changing the name of the company, changing the objects clause or reducing the share capital. A special resolution requires 75% of votes cast to be in favour for it to be passed.

- Extraordinary resolutions deal with major items, for example winding up the company. An extraordinary resolution requires 75% of votes cast to be in favour for it to be passed.

8.6   Companies buying back their own shares

Section 166, Companies Act 1985 gave companies the right to purchase their own shares provided the articles of association allow it to do so. The company must always have some irredeemable ordinary shares remaining in issue.

In theory if a company buys back its own shares when their market price is below net asset value, the supply of ordinary shares is reduced with the remaining shares having a greater earning capacity and net asset backing per share. (Net asset value is the theoretical surplus available to ordinary shareholders in a possible liquidation, divided by the number of shares. The resultant figure is the theoretical amount per share which a shareholder would receive in liquidation.)

There are tax benefits provided the correct procedures are followed. Any rise in the share price of the remaining shares will incur CGT to shareholders only on disposal, as opposed to the normal income tax liability when dividends are declared. The company can purchase its shares either on-market or off-market.

- *On-market purchase:* An ordinary resolution must first be passed at an AGM or EGM. This resolution will specify the maximum number of shares to be purchased and the maximum and minimum price to be paid. The company will then instruct its brokers to purchase the shares on the London Stock Exchange.

- *Off market purchase:* A special resolution must first be passed at an AGM or EGM. The owners of the shares to be purchased cannot vote on this matter. The company will then buy the shares.

8.7   Nominal values of ordinary shares

Under UK law, shares in UK companies must have a nominal value. The nominal value of most company shares is 25p, and all shares quoted in the *Financial Times* have a nominal value of 25p unless otherwise stated. Nominal value is of very little significance to a shareholder, since what matters to him is the market price of the shares. Even in liquidation, nominal value is immaterial, because any surplus will simply be divided up between the ordinary shareholders on a pro rata basis. The only time nominal value does matter is if the dividend is declared as a percentage of a share's nominal value. A holder of a share with a 25p nominal value would receive a net dividend of 2.5p per share if a 10% dividend had been declared. Obviously the total dividend a company pays is influenced by available profits and the policy of the directors. Nominal value plays no part in influencing the total dividend that can be paid out.

Some overseas countries have recognized the irrelevance of nominal value, and issue shares of no par value, for example in the USA shares are issued with no par value. In this case dividends are declared as so much (e.g. 2.5c) per share.

8.8   Concessions

Concessions arise when a company allows its shareholders to use the company's products on preferential terms. Most concessions take the from of discounts on certain company products and are designed to encourage shareholder interest and loyalty. There are advantages to the company in that:

- The share price could rise because the shares are more attractive;
- The concessions may help to increase turnover and profits and may provide useful publicity.

Points to check when considering an investment in companies offering concessions are:

- The company may have the right to withdraw the concessions at any time, so it is essential to check the terms and conditions of the concession to see exactly what the position is.

- Some companies insist that the shareholder holds a minimum number of shares and that the holding has been registered in the shareholder's name for a minimum period of time before the concession can be used.

- Some concessions are limited to shareholders who have actual share certificates and may not be available for shareholders using nominees or CREST.

- The potential investor should consider the merits of the shares themselves as an investment at the same time as assessing the value of any concession.

Shareholders benefit because there is no tax on these 'perks'. Institutional shareholders are not overly keen on concessions because often they cannot use them. Some companies do allow their concessions to be transferred to someone other than the named shareholder, and in this way institutions can use the concessions by giving them to their directors or staff. Examples of concessions currently available are:

Company	Concession	Qualifying holding
Moss Bros Group	10% discount on purchase or hire of goods	1250 Ordinary shares to be held for 6 months
Eurotunnel	30% discount on 6 single or 3 return journeys on Le Shuttle every 12 months	1000 stock units held for 3 months

8.9 The difference between stocks and shares

Although stock is a colloquial term for equities, it is more accurately defined as paper debt issued by the government or companies in consolidated form, tradable in any amount. Shares can only be bought and sold in whole units.

Gilts

Gilts and corporation stocks are generally priced at so much per nominal £100 of stock. Thus if 3½% War Loan is quoted at 72.96, it means that £100 nominal can be purchased for £72.96. (Incidentally, gilts are transferable in units of one penny, so investors are not restricted to buying round £100s of nominal value.)

Company loan stocks

Company fixed-interest loan stocks are generally priced in the same way as gilts, but they are usually transferable in units of 25p, 50p, or £1. When they are transferable in units of less than £1, the units are usually specified on the certificate. Thus a company loan-stock certificate may show £100 on the nominal value, but that it is transferable in units of 50p. If the price in the *Financial Times* appears as 80, then that certificate represents stock worth £80.

Ordinary or deferred stocks of limited companies

When a company issues ordinary stock as opposed to ordinary shares, the certificate will once again show the units in which stock can be transferred.

In the case of ordinary stock, the price quoted in the *Financial Times* is that of a single stock unit as opposed to that of £100 nominal of the stock. Thus a certificate of ordinary stock which shows £100 nominal represented by 400 units of 25p each would be worth £320 if it were quoted as 80 in the *Financial Times*. In this example '80' represents the price in pence of a single ordinary stock unit.

8.10   Preference shares

The difference between preference shares and ordinary shares in liquidation

All companies that are quoted on the Stock Exchange must have ordinary shares, but they need not have preference shares. Where preference shares exist, they are classed as part of the share capital, but usually rank before ordinary shares in liquidation. The precise position would depend on the company's articles of association, but generally speaking any surplus after repayment of all external liabilities will be split as follows:

- To the preference shareholder up to the nominal value of such shares (thus in liquidation the nominal value of preference shares can be important, whereas for ordinary shares nominal value is immaterial);

- Any residue after satisfaction of preference share claims then vests in the ordinary shareholders.

Preference dividends

Dividends on preference shares are said to be fixed, in that the maximum possible dividend is limited to an amount which is shown in the title of the share. A preference share entitled '7% Preference Share' will pay the registered holder a maximum dividend of 7%. The tax implications for the shareholder are the same as for ordinary shares, and the position has already been set out in detail in Chapter 6.

Although there is a maximum dividend payable on preference shares, this is not guaranteed. Preference dividends can be paid only from available profits and at the discretion of the directors. Thus even when profits are available to cover it, the preference dividend may not be paid. However, no dividend can be paid on other, lower-ranking capital while the preference dividend is in arrears. This precedence as to dividend and as to capital rights in liquidation shows why the term 'preference' is used to describe this class of capital.

Types of preference share
Cumulative preference shares

Most preference shares are cumulative, and indeed a preference share will be cumulative unless it is expressly stated to be non-cumulative. The right to any unpaid dividend continues indefinitely, in that no dividend can ever be paid on lower-ranking capital, such as ordinary shares, until the preference shareholders have received their full arrears of dividend. There is no time limit with cumulative preference shares and for some unsuccessful companies there are many years of overdue preference dividend to be paid before the ordinary shareholders can receive any dividend payment at all.

For non-cumulative preference shares once the dividend is not paid for a particular period, it is lost forever. In the following year the preference shareholder would be entitled to one year's dividend only, and the ordinary shareholders could receive a dividend that year provided that the current year's preference dividend had been paid in full.

Participating preference shares

These shares carry the right to an 'extra' dividend when the available profits exceed a stated amount. While the terms of the issue of such shares differ widely, there is generally an upper maximum dividend per share.

Redeemable preference shares

As the title implies, these shares are redeemable, but only subject to certain conditions. While there may be a set date for redemption, or redemption may be at the company's discretion, it may take place only if there are sufficient available profits or if the necessary cash can be raised from the proceeds of a new issue.

Thus there is no guaranteed capital gain from the purchase of a redeemable preference share at less than its nominal value. The position is by no means the same as occurs from the purchase of a dated gilt at a price below par.

Convertible preference shares

Convertible preference shares are preference shares that carry the right to be exchanged into ordinary shares on the terms set out in the issue. As with all preference shares, the rate of dividend is as stated in the title.

Zero-dividend preference shares

These preference shares are issued by investment trusts as one of the types of share issued by a split-level investment trust. (See Chapter 15 for details of investment trusts.) The zero-dividend shares (commonly called 'capital shares') set a redemption date and do not pay any dividend during their life. When the trust is wound up, the zero dividend preference shareholders receive the remaining capital after all other claims have been paid.

Voting by preference shareholders

The precise voting rights will be set out in the articles of association, but generally speaking preference shareholders have the right to vote only if their dividend is in arrears, or if there are any other matters that directly affect them. Whenever a company wishes to vary the rights of any particular class of share, such as a preference share, it must call a separate class meeting. Only holders of the relevant class of share will be eligible to vote at that class meeting.

Are preference shares an attractive investment?

From the point of view of the private investor, the answer is usually 'no'. In liquidation there are all the disadvantages of ranking as a shareholder, and thus being entitled to capital repayment only when all outside creditors have been paid off.

As regards income, there is no obligation on the directors to pay the preference dividend, and yet in times of vast profit increases, only the ordinary shareholders or, to a limited amount, holders of participating preference shares will receive the benefit of increasing dividends. All capital gains on preference shares will count for CGT purposes, whereas gilts and other fixed income stocks are free of all CGT. The interest on a loan stock is a debt that is legally payable, and, in the case of a gilt, is guaranteed by the government. The right to a preference dividend is not an enforceable one, and the preference share is only as secure as the company.

Despite these drawbacks, preference shares in sound companies are attractive to institutional investors. The market price of preference shares will fall to reflect their disadvantages. This means that the dividend yield will be enhanced to reflect the usual risk/reward trade off.

8.11　Company loan stocks and debentures

The difference between a loan stock and a debenture

Quoted loan stocks and debentures usually carry a fixed coupon and have a redemption date. Technically speaking, there is no difference between the two stocks because a debenture is strictly a 'written acknowledgement of debt'. However, debentures are commonly so called because there is some security available to the stockholders to enforce their rights against the company. Loan stock is normally so called because it is unsecured. In practice, this generalization is too sweeping, and the precise position can be determined only by examining the terms of each individual issue.

Sinking funds

A company may decide to set a sum aside from profits each year in order to facilitate redemption of a loan stock. Such arrangements are known as sinking funds.

Non-cumulative sinking fund

A non-cumulative sinking fund arises when funds are set aside each year to purchase other investments (for instance gilts with redemption dates around the same time as the loan stock). When the loan stock is due to be redeemed, there are adequate funds available for redemption.

Cumulative sinking fund

With a cumulative sinking fund, a set sum is generally put aside to cover repayment of loan interest and redemption of part of the capital. As time goes by, the fixed sum will redeem more and more capital, since the interest will diminish in line with the diminishing principal.

Example

Suppose a company issues £10,000,000 of loan stock with a 10% coupon, repayable in 10 years, and suppose there is a cumulative sinking fund of £1,500,000 per annum. In the first year, £1,000,000 will be required to meet the interest and £500,000 will go towards capital redemption. In the second year £950,000 will be required to cover interest and £550,000 will be available towards loan repayment.

Sometimes the company purchases its own loan stock on the open market, whereas in other cases a proportion of the loan stock may be redeemed at par each year. When part is redeemed at par, the decision as to which loan stockholder is to be repaid will be made by ballot. When the market price is under par, the 'lucky' stockholders will benefit, whereas when the market price is over par the stockholder whose stock is redeemed will lose out. The precise terms of a cumulative sinking fund must be carefully studied, but companies will prefer open-market purchase when stock is currently priced under par, and will prefer redemption at par when the market price exceeds nominal value.

Sinking funds make a loan stock more attractive because they provide an assurance that positive steps are being taken to ensure the obligations of the company will be honoured.

8.12 The functions of trustees (in connection with company loan stocks)

Quoted companies that issue debentures or loan stocks appoint a trustee to look after the interests of the loan stockholders. The trustee is usually a bank or insurance company and must be independent of the company. A trust deed governing the terms of the issue will be drawn up.

The trustee will ensure that the terms of the trust deed are complied with. Matters covered by the trust deed will be:

● Rate of interest and dates of payment;

● Redemption date;

● Details of any sinking fund arrangement;

● Details of security for the loan. This may be a fixed charge over a specific asset. In this case the company cannot deal with it in any way without the trustees' consent. Alternatively, the charge may be a floating charge covering all assets. With a floating charge the company may deal with the assets without restriction in the ordinary course of business. A combination of a fixed charge over the land, buildings and book debts with a floating charge over other assets could be taken;

●   Details of the rights of the trustee if the company is in default of the terms of the issue.

The security can be realized by the trustees only on behalf of the loan stockholders. An individual loan stockholder cannot do this.

The advantages of appointing a trustee are that:

●   It would be difficult for the company to make arrangements with each individual loan stockholder regarding the creation of security;

●   A trustee is better placed to act in the interests of the loan stockholders. The trustee has professional expertise;

●   When decisive action is called for, the various loan stockholders probably would not be able to agree among themselves.

8.13   Comparison of ordinary shares and company loan stocks from the point of view of an investor

	Ordinary shares	Company loan stocks
1.	Ordinary shareholders are members of the company. They own the company and can vote at meetings. The value of a vote is more apparent than real, since a private individual will probably own insufficient shares to exert a decisive vote. Day-to-day control is in the hands of the directors.	Holders of loan stocks are creditors who cannot normally vote at meetings. However, the terms of the issue will sometimes allow loan stockholders a vote if the payment of interest or capital is in arrears. Loan stocks are normally held by institutions not private investors.
2.	Ordinary shares are never secured.	Loans can be secured (debentures always are) or unsecured, depending on the terms of issue.
3.	Ordinary shares are not normally redeemed except by special court order. They are automatically redeemed only if they were issued as redeemable ordinary shares.	Loan stocks normally carry a redemption date.

Ordinary shares	Company loan stocks
4. Dividends are paid only from available profits. However, when profits are available a dividend need not be paid. It is for the directors to recommend whether to pay out profits by way of dividend or to retain the profits in the company to finance expansion or to reduce borrowing. Shareholders can vote to reduce the directors' dividend recommendation, but they cannot vote to increase it.	Interest is a debt and is payable irrespective of whether profits are available.
5. In inflationary times companies can sometimes increase prices, and hence profits and turnover. Thus the share price may increase with inflation and dividends may also grow. Much depends on the choice of the company and timing of purchase of shares but the possibility of growth exists.	(a) The interest remains the same irrespective of inflation. Interest therefore declines in purchasing power. (b) The loans are normally redeemed at par at maturity. Thus there is no scope for capital gains unless the stocks are purchased below par. *Note* In the current low-inflation/stable-growth environment, the impact of inflation is very much reduced.
6. Capital gains are subject to CGT.	Capital gains on fixed interest stocks are free of CGT.

8.14 Considerations when contemplating an investment in company loan stock or company debentures, and how these investments compare with gilts

Apart from an investor's own tax position and his own investment aims, the main considerations are as follows:

Is the loan stock formally rated by a credit rating agency such as Moodys or Standard and Poors? Credit ratings are not compulsory for UK listed companies, but where a loan stock is credit rated, this will prove a useful guide to the riskiness of the loan.

- Compare the interest yield and redemption yield with yields on gilts for a similar redemption date. If the loan stock has a comparatively high yield, it may indicate undue risk. Alternatively, a high yield may simply mean that the market has not realized that the loan stock is out of line, thus creating an anomaly situation.

- Does the company appear to be capable of covering interest payments and redemption of the stock on the due date? Consider the prospects of the industry and look at the accounts of the company to assess its financial strength, profit record and future prospects. Ideally, the company should have a stable record in an industry with consistent, if steady, growth prospects. Security of earnings is more important than growth.

- Is the loan or debenture secured? Are there any other loans that take priority?

- Check the articles of association for the terms of the issue.

- Check the trust deed for details of any sinking fund that may exist.

- Compare the rates of interest on bank deposits and other fixed-rate investments.

- Are there any conversion rights to the loan stock?

- Calculate capital and income priority percentages and overall cover.

8.15 Comparison of company loan stocks with gilts

These are that:

- Company loans are only as secure as the company, whereas gilts are guaranteed by the government. Obviously, loan stocks in companies such as banks are virtually as secure as gilts, but this is not the case with all company loans.

- Gilts are all easily marketable, but very 'thin' markets exist in some company loan stocks.

The conclusion from all this is that a private investor should only contemplate an investment in a company loan or debenture that has a redemption yield above that of a gilt with a similar redemption date. Even then the company must be 'sound' and the investor should not be intending to sell the stock, but hold it until redemption, because the dealing costs of selling along with the wider bid-offer spread will reduce the return to the investor.

It is possible that in future companies will issue index-linked loans. These would be particularly appropriate for any utility whose prices are regulated and linked to RPI. Such index-linked loan stocks should be compared to index-linked gilts.

8.16 Convertibles – Convertible loan stock

A convertible loan stock is a fixed-interest loan stock that carries the right to convert into ordinary shares on the terms and conditions set out in the articles of association. The stockholder has the right, but not the obligation, to convert within the stated time. If conversion rights are not exercised by the expiry date, the stock will then revert to a conventional dated loan stock. The conversion rights embedded in the convertible loan stock are effectively a call option on the underlying shares. Call options are analysed under derivatives in Chapter 9.

Convertible preference shares

A convertible preference share is similar to a convertible loan stock, in that it carries the right to convert into a preset number of ordinary shares at, or between, a set future date or dates. If the conversion rights expire, then the shares revert to straightforward preference shares. Again, the convertible rights amount to a call option, this time on the underlying preference shares.

With convertible preference shares, the holder receives a fixed rate of dividend payable out of post-tax profits. With a convertible loan stock, the holder receives a fixed rate of interest payable out of pre-tax profits. In both cases, once the conversion rights are exercised, the holder receives the dividend paid to all ordinary shareholders.

The 'best of both worlds'

The holder of a convertible loan stock has a legal right to receive his fixed interest in the same way as any other creditor is entitled to money owing. In addition, the loan stock is of course an external liability which must be met in full in any liquidation before the shareholders receive a penny. Thus income and capital of a convertible loan are more secure than those for ordinary shares. However, should the company prosper, the loan stockholder can obtain an equity stake by converting at what will be a 'cheap' conversion price.

(Note: if the convertible is not a loan stock, but a preference share, then there is no legal right to the dividend, thus the income and capital are not as secure as with a convertible loan stock.)

The classic example of 'having your cake and eating it' occurs when the trustee of a will trust buys convertibles to help to maintain the income of the life tenant, while retaining the possibility of capital growth through exercise of the conversion rights on behalf of the reversionary interest after the life tenant's death.

Usually a convertible loan stock will be priced above a comparable 'straight' loan stock because of the attraction of the conversion option. However, if the prospects for the shares seem to be poor, the convertible loan stock price should be supported at the level of a comparable fixed-interest stock. This support level is known as the 'bond support price'. A similar situation occurs with convertible preference shares.

To sum up, income from a fixed-interest stock will generally exceed the dividend income from shares in the short term, but in the longer term there is scope for growth in the dividend income and market price of shares.

A convertible enables the investor to take advantage of the higher fixed income in the short term, while retaining the option to benefit from growth of capital and income from the shares in the long term. If the shares do not perform very well he will simply retain the convertible as a straight fixed-interest stock or a straight preference share depending on the type of convertible purchased.

Example of a convertible

Land Securities plc have a 7% Convertible Bond 2008 which gives the holder the right to convert at the rate of 15.63 ordinary shares per £100 nominal of the convertible. The conversion right can be exercised on 31 August in each year up to and including 2008. If the final date for conversion passes and holders have not exercised their conversion rights, the convertible bond will become a loan stock redeemable in 2008. Until the conversion, the holder will receive gross interest of £7 per 100 nominal held. This interest is subject to tax in the normal way.

Compulsory conversion

Many convertible issues state that if 75% (or other preset percentage) or more of the originally issued convertible is converted, the company has the right to convert the remaining convertible preference shares or convertible bonds upon giving 28 days' notice in writing to the holders of these stocks or shares.

8.17 Evaluating the merits of convertibles

Choice of company

The golden rule is choose a convertible only in a company that is likely to be successful. If the company is unsuccessful, the share price will fall and the conversion rights will become worthless. If matters become even more desperate, the value of the convertible could even fall below the bond support price because of fears of default.

Length of option period

If consideration of the company's prospects are favourable, the next consideration is the length of the conversion option. The longer the conversion period the more chance there is for the investor to benefit, because there is a greater time during which the share price could increase.

Conversion premium (or discount)

The conversion premium represents an amount or percentage by which the 'conversion price' exceeds the current market price of the shares at the time the convertible is purchased.

Sometimes the market price of the shares can rise very quickly, and there can be a time lag before the convertible follows suit. In such cases, purchase of the convertible can be a cheap way of obtaining the shares because the conversion price is at a discount to current market price of the shares.

Taxation

Tax considerations also apply, although there are no tax consequences when simply exercising the conversion rights. The return on the shares will consist of dividends and of capital gain, which will be taxed accordingly. The taxable element of the return on the loan stock would be the interest.

Availability of information on convertibles

For the private investor, information is hard to come by. However, some brokers provide 'newsletters' giving details of conversion premiums or discounts, prices, yields, and opinions on whether or not to exercise the conversion option.

Convertible calculations

Assume that today's date is 21 April 2001. A customer has received notification of impending conversion dates in respect of two convertibles that he holds:

- ABC plc 12% convertible unsecured loan stock 2010 is convertible into 25p ordinary shares on 25 May each year from 1996 to 2008 inclusive at the rate of 30 shares for every £100 stock. The market price of the ordinary shares is 280p. The market price of the convertible stock is £105. Net dividends per ordinary share in respect of the year ended 31 March 2001 totalled 9.8p.

- XYZ plc 3.5p convertible preference share 2005 is convertible into 25p ordinary shares on 28 May each year from 1995 to 2001 inclusive at the rate of 38 shares for every 100 preference shares. The market price of the ordinary shares is 370p. The market price of the convertible is 142p. Net dividends per ordinary share in respect of the year ending 31 March 2001 totalled 7.77p.

- Conversion premium/discount

ABC plc

£100 nominal costs £105

£100 nominal converts to 30 shares

Therefore 30 shares cost £105 if obtained via the convertible

Therefore one share obtained via the convertible costs 350p (£105 ÷ 30)

The premium is (350 - 280) = 70p

As a percentage the premium is $\frac{70 \times 100}{280} = 25\%$

XYZ plc

100 preference shares cost (100 x 142p) = £142

100 preference shares convert to 38 ordinary shares

Therefore 38 ordinary shares cost £142 if obtained via the convertible

Therefore 1 share obtained in the convertible costs 374p (to the nearest penny)

The premium is (374 - 370) = 4p

As a percentage the premium is $\dfrac{4 \times 100}{370}$ = 1.08%

Monetary calculations on conversion implications

(i)   ABC plc

	Market value (£)	Gross income (£)
£100 nominal stock	105.00	12.00
30 shares at 280p	84.00	3.27
	21.00	8.73 **

Capital loss on conversion is £21 or $\dfrac{(21 \times 100)}{105}$ = 20%

Income loss on conversion is £8.73 or $\dfrac{(8.73 \times 100)}{12}$ = 72.75%

For ABC there would be a great loss of both income and capital on conversion. Bearing in mind the long time left before expiry of the conversion right, it would be best to retain the convertible for the time being, provided ABC's prospects seem sound.

** To compare like with like, compare the gross dividend (x 100/90) with the gross interest (coupon x nominal).

(ii) XYZ plc

	Market value (£)	Gross income (£)
100 convertible preference shares	142.00	3.89
38 ordinary shares	140.60	3.28
	1.40	0.61

Capital loss on conversion is £1.40 or 0.99%.

Income loss on conversion is £0.61 p or 15.68%.

For XYZ the loss of capital on conversion would be very small, and while gross dividend income is below the fixed dividend rate on the preference share, this could soon be eliminated by dividend increases. As the deadline for the conversion option is fast approaching, action must be taken otherwise the convertible will fall to its bond support level. The investor must therefore convert or sell, depending on the prospects of XYZ.

Note: the 'large' capital loss on conversion for ABC plc and the 'small' loss for XYZ plc are also reflected in the two conversion premiums of 25% and 1.08% respectively.

8.18 Reasons for a company to issue convertibles

Takeovers

When a company wishes to take over another company, it may offer its own convertible loan stock or convertible preference shares in exchange for control of the shares of the company being bid for.

Such a stock can be very attractive to potential vendors of shares in the 'victim', since as we have seen convertibles can give the best of both worlds. In addition, the issue of a convertible defers equity dilution in the bidding company. This enables them to bring the company that has been taken over under the new ownership without problems from possible hostile shareholders of the company that has been taken over. Effectively, this method provides a breathing space.

Lack of security

Sometimes there are insufficient assets available to offer as security for a new issue of a fixed-interest loan stock. The extra benefits from a conversion option may persuade otherwise reluctant investors to subscribe.

Coupon or dividend rate

The convertible can be issued at a lower coupon than that of a comparable 'straight' loan stock. Likewise, the fixed dividend on a convertible preference share can be lower than that on a straightforward preference share.

As an alternative to a rights issue

A convertible can be an alternative to a rights issue. If the current share price is below nominal value, a company cannot make a rights issue because the subscription price must be at least equal to nominal value.

Long-term financing

Convertibles can be used as a means of financing long-term projects. Subscribers would require a guaranteed income in the first few years while the profit levels were likely to be low.

In later years the investor could convert if the project had been as successful as had been anticipated.

Redemption and conversion

If the company prospers, redemption of the convertible will be unnecessary since the stockholders will all exercise their conversion rights.

Note: the disadvantage of convertibles, especially of convertible loan stocks, from the issuer's point of view is that:

- If the company prospers, conversion will dilute the control of current shareholders and the new shareholders will have acquired 'cheap' equity.

- If the company does not prosper, conversion will not take place and the company will probably be seen as 'overborrowed'.

8.19 The problems of investing in unquoted companies

Whereas dealing in quoted shares is regulated by the Stock Exchange, dealings in unquoted shares are unregulated by the Stock Exchange. Unquoted companies are those whose shares are not traded on the Stock Exchange. From the investor's point of view this means any companies whose securities are not dealt in on the Stock Exchange's Main Market or AIM. In most cases deals are done only on a matched bargain basis (i.e. a buyer and seller must have been found who will deal with the same amount of stock).

It is not impossible for an investor who has recently come into a large sum of money to be approached with a view to investing in an unquoted company. This may occur if the company he is employed by sees an opportunity of raising some much needed new finance, or it may just be a friend who makes the suggestion. Whatever the means by which the approach is made, the investor needs to look very carefully at the many disadvantages that apply to this form of investment.

Issues that need to be raised when considering investing in unquoted companies

- *Why is the company wanting to raise new capital?* What is the state of the balance sheet? A full analysis needs to be carried out to ascertain whether the company is a 'sinking ship' or whether it is sound, but in need of a capital injection for, say, some major expansion. See Chapter 12 for balance sheet analysis.

- *What is being offered in return for the investment?* Is it a directorship, debenture stock, loan stock or shares? Does the investor really need what is being offered to complement his position? It is more than likely that the money invested will not produce the right sort of investment for that particular individual.

- *Lack of marketability* – private company shares can be very difficult to sell. The articles of association of the company may restrict the transfer of its shares, and in such a case it may be impossible to find a purchaser who will meet these regulations.

- *Difficulty in valuing unquoted shares* – there is no straightforward valuation available for unquoted shares. For quoted shares valuation is simple, just a matter of obtaining the prices from a stockbroker, but for unquoted shares the price to a large extent is what a prospective investor is willing to pay.

- *Problems in find a buyer for the shares* – because of the two problems mentioned above it may be impossible for the investor to realize his shares when he wishes to, and this is especially difficult if he needs the cash from his investment for a particular purpose.

- *Attractiveness of unquoted shares as security for a bank loan* – unlike quoted shares, private company shares are not attractive to banks as security against a loan. This is because the bank may not be able to sell the shares if it needs to exercise its power of sale in event of the loan being in default. If the articles of association of the company restrict the transfer of the shares then the power of sale is virtually worthless.

- *Impact of liquidation of the company on a shareholder who is also an employee* – in such a situation the loss will be compounded. The shareholder will not only lose his job, but, depending on the class of capital he contributed, he could also lose the cash he invested in the company.

Overall, it is inadvisable for an ordinary investor who does not have an existing, well-balanced portfolio and sufficient cash that he can afford to loose to invest in an unquoted company. The exception would be if, after taking all the potential problems into account, and having had expert, independent advice about the prospects of the company, he wished to invest as a means of becoming an director of the company. In such a case he would be looking at the contribution he could make to the development of the company in the long term.

8.20　Local authority loans

The different types of local authority loan

There are three types of local authority loan:

- Fixed loans;
- Yearlings;
- Local authority stocks.

Fixed loans (also known as local authority bonds or mortgages)

These are fixed-capital investments where the rate of interest is fixed at the outset and the loan cannot usually be repaid early. However, some authorities will allow early encashment against a penalty charge. There is no secondary market. The return therefore consists entirely of interest, which is taxed accordingly.

These fixed loans are really suitable only for basic rate taxpayers who require income and who can afford to tie up their capital for the period of the loan. Higher-rate taxpayers probably prefer capital gains rather than income.

Yearlings (local authority negotiable bonds)

Despite the name 'yearlings', they can have a life of one or two years. The minimum investment is £1,000. There is a secondary market and the yearlings can be bought and sold at any time at the current market price.

If the investor buys a new issue there will not always be any capital gain or loss if he holds the yearling until maturity, because many 'yearlings' are issued at par. However, a capital gain or loss will normally occur if he buys or sells on the secondary market. Interest is paid net after deduction of 20% tax.

Local authority stocks

These are traded on the stock market and prices are quoted in the *Financial Times* under the heading 'Other Fixed Interest'. Interest is paid in the same way as for all local authority stocks with 20% tax deducted at source.

Security of local authority stocks

The assets and rates of the local authority are charged as security for these loans, and the government-backed Public Works Loans Board has a statutory duty to lend to a local authority to enable it to meet its commitments.

8.21   Permanent interest-bearing shares (PIBS)

These are fixed-interest shares that were first issued in June 1991 by building societies. They are issued and traded on the Stock Market to provide capital, which counts towards their capital adequacy ratio. 'Permanent' means that the shares have no set redemption date, i.e. they are undated.

PIBS are not protected by the Deposit Protection Board because they are quoted securities, not accounts with a building society. Settlement for a PIBS transaction is three working days (T+3) after the date of dealing and the price of PIBS is quoted 'clean'. Accrued interest is calculated separately and is added to or subtracted from the settlement total in the same ways as accrued interest is dealt with on gilts.

Unlike other securities quoted on the Stock Exchange, each PIBS specifies a minimum amount that can be purchased. The minimum on the issue varies; for example the minimum on the 13% Britannia PIBS is £1,000 and on the 13% Bradford and Bingley PIBS £10,000.

PIBS holders, subject to the rules of the society, are members of the society and are entitled to attend general meetings. However, voting powers are limited to one vote per holder, regardless of the size of the PIBS holding, in common with the rights of all other building society shareholders.

The interest rate on PIBS can be fixed or as a margin over a specific market rate of interest (although all the early issues carry a fixed rate of interest).

PIBS are non-cumulative and do not participate in the profits of the building society. On winding up, PIBS rank after all other debts and share accounts (other than deferred shares) for repayment of interest and principal. If a building society converts to plc status (i.e. becomes a quoted company), then the PIBS will be changed into subordinated unsecured loan stock of the company.

From an investor's point of view, PIBS are similar to non-cumulative, undated preference shares in a company. PIBS are not identical to unsecured loan stock in a company, because failure to pay the interest on PIBS does not mean the building society would be wound up, whereas failure to pay interest on a loan stock will result in liquidation proceedings starting.

8.22 Risk, the reverse yield gap and the long gilt/equity yield ratio

From a study of this chapter and the earlier chapters, you will readily appreciate that some investments are more risky than others. For the moment, let us simply compare gilts, local authority quoted stocks and the various types of company security. Considering them in order of riskiness would appear give the following ranking:

● Equities (most risky);

● Preference shares;

● Unsecured loan stock;

● Secured loan stocks;

● Local authority stocks;

● Gilts (least risky).

Risk and return

We have suggested that one of the prime rules of investment is that the greater the risk, the greater must be the return. If we were to represent this in the form of a graph we would expect the position to look like Fig. 8.1.

Figure 8.1: Risk and rate of return

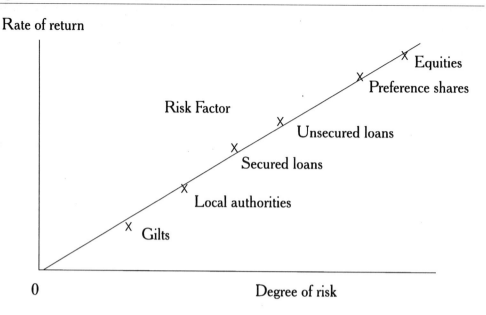

Note: *the graph is for illustration purposes only and is not drawn to scale.*

Obviously a secured loan stock in a speculative company could be more risky than an unsecured loan stock in, say, a bank, but the graph assumes that we are comparing different classes of security in the same company with gilts and local authority stocks.

Why the reverse yield gap makes the above graph seem unrealistic

The graph in Fig. 8.1 illustrates the position accurately except for one major discrepancy – the returns on equities compared with fixed-interest stocks. In theory, the return on equities should be much higher than that on gilts, because gilts have the backing of the government, whereas equities are only as good as the company issuing them. However, since 1959 equities have yielded less than gilts if we use dividend yields and redemption yields to make the comparison. Because this is the 'reverse' of what we would expect, the term 'reverse yield gap' has been coined.

The explanation of this phenomenon is that for conventional fixed-interest gilts, inflation erodes their value in real terms. Both the redemption value and the interest payments of a conventional fixed-interest stock are constant in money terms and so their real values will fall due to the effect of inflation. The exception to this is index-linked gilts, which are insulated against the effects of inflation. Equities, on the other hand, give scope for both growth of dividends and for growth of capital. Indeed, it must be remembered that the return from equities consists of two elements, dividends **and** capital growth. When the growth in share

---

prices is included in the calculation of the return on equities, returns on shares in general have out-performed both gilts and inflation over the long term. This long-established relationship between returns in different asset classes explains why investors are prepared to accept a lower initial dividend yield from equities than from gilts. There are periods when fixed-interest securities show higher total returns than equities, usually when inflation is relatively low and/or falling, but these are exceptions.

The long gilt/equity yield ratio

Nowadays, instead of referring to a yield gap in absolute terms, it is more common for the gap to be expressed in the form of a ratio. The ratio is called the long gilt/equity yield ratio and it is calculated as follows:

$$\frac{\text{The gross redemption yield on the British Government 20-year benchmark gilt}}{\text{The dividend yield on the FTSE Actuaries All Share Indices}}$$

Average yields in the years shown were:

Year	Dividend yield (%) on FTSE All-Share Index	Redemption yield (%) on long-dated (20-Year) gilts	Ratio
1995	3.96	8.26	2.09
1996	3.8	8.1	2.13
1997	3.46	7.09	2.05
1998	2.99	5.45	1.82
1999	2.42	4.7	1.94
2000	2.17	4.7	2.17

Sources: Office for National Statistics, Economic Trends, December 1999, November 2000, Table 6.8, Financial Statistics, January and December 2000 , Table 7.1G

As can be seen from the above, the ratio has consistently hovered around the 2 mark, with a high of 2.17 and a low of 1.82. It has been suggested that shares are cheap compared to gilts when the long gilt/equity ratio falls much below 2: http://www.metronet.co.uk/bigwood/shares/yield.html. This is because the lower the price of a share, the higher its dividend yield, and the higher the dividend yield, the lower the long gilt/equity yield ratio.

The relevant information for this ratio can be found in the *Financial Times* under the heading of 'Long gilt/equity yield ratio' and students must be aware of the current rates at the time of the examination. On 4 April 2001, with 20-year benchmark gilts yielding 4.73% and equities yielding 2.60%, the ratio was shown as 1.82. On 4 April 2001 the FTSE All Share index stood at 2636.55. If we apply the long gilt/equity ratio of 2 as being the expected norm, then the FTSE All Share index would be expected to stand at

2897.31 (calculated as: $\dfrac{2636.55 \times 2}{1.82}$ = 2897.31)

It would be interesting for readers to look at the FTSE All Share indices at the end of 2001 to see what the index stands at, and what the current long gilt/equity ratio is. The FTSE All Share indices are covered in detail in Chapter 19, but for the purposes of this exercise we can simply take this index as a measure of share prices and dividend yields.

9

DERIVATIVES

Objectives

After studying this chapter, the reader should be able to:

- define a derivative and become familiar with the terminology relevant to the derivatives under discussion;

- explain how the FTSE 100 Index Future can be used by fund managers to manage their equity risks;

- explain how the Mini FTSE 100 Index Future can be used by investors to manage their equity risks;

- evaluate the benefits and drawbacks of these two futures in the context of equity risk management;

- assess the benefits and drawbacks of equity swaps as a tool for managing equity risk;

- describe how traded options work (including index options);

- analyse the factors that influence the premium of a traded option;

- evaluate the benefits and drawbacks of traded options as a means of managing equity risk;

- describe how warrants to subscribe operate;

- differentiate between futures and options;

- assess the benefits and drawbacks of spread betting for investors;

- asses the benefits and drawbacks of contracts for difference for investors.

9.1 What is a derivative?

A derivative is an instrument whose price is derived from the price of an underlying asset or from an underlying index. The payoff from a derivative is linked to the payoff from the underlying asset/index, so when the price of the underlying asset or the level of the underlying index changes, then the payoff (gain or loss) for the holder of the derivative will also change.

For our purposes the underlying asset will be a share and the underlying index will be the FTSE 100 Index. The derivatives that will be examined in this chapter are futures, equity swaps, options, and warrants. In addition we shall examine contracts for difference and spread betting, which can be considered as quasi-derivatives.

Derivatives are an alternative means whereby investors can alter their risk exposure in respect of a financial asset. When there is economic news that impacts upon the current and likely future price of a financial asset, the investor will change his position in the market which most efficiently achieves the objective. The factors that apply in deciding whether to use the market in the underlying asset directly or whether to use the relevant derivatives market are:

- Efficiency/price discovery
- Gearing/leverage
- Tax and transaction costs (to be examined later as appropriate)

Let us now examine the concepts of price discovery and gearing in connection with derivatives.

Efficiency/Price discovery

When comparing the derivatives market with the market in the underlying asset, the one that investors consider the most efficient will be the market where prices will first be changed in response to new information. The market that most quickly reflects changes in information by changes in price is called the market of price discovery.

In some instances it is the derivatives market (in particular the futures market) that is the market of price discovery from which investors send messages to show how the new information will impact on the underlying asset or index. In such cases, investors will tend to use the derivatives market, rather than the 'real' market, to change their position (other things being equal).

Gearing/Leverage

For all derivatives, gearing can be defined as the ability to participate fully in any rise or fall in the price of the underlying asset/index, for an initial outlay which is just a small percentage of the cost of buying or selling the underlying asset/index outright. This applies in both directions (to gains or losses). Thus gearing ensures that the payoff for a given investment in a derivative is much greater (either by way of loss or by way of gain) than the gains or losses to be incurred by investing the same amount in the underlying asset or index.

For investors who wish to speculate, the high gearing of derivatives makes them a more suitable method of speculation than sale or purchase of the underlying asset on the cash market, simply because the initial cash outlay on derivatives is relatively low. If a speculator believes that the price of shares will fall, but he does not actually own any shares, then he would like to be able to sell at today's price and buy them back in the near future at a lower price, i.e. 'sell short' to pocket the difference. However, the speculator will find it difficult to sell short shares he does not own, because brokers usually require evidence of ownership or some form of collateral in the absence of such evidence. However, there are derivatives that do enable speculators to effectively 'sell short' and then buy back later at the (hopefully) lower price to make a profit. In addition, we shall see that the relatively low initial outlay for derivatives can make them more attractive than the sale or purchase of the actual shares as a technique for risk management.

The concept of arbitrage as applied to derivatives

When two identical assets simultaneously have different prices in different markets, an arbitrage opportunity occurs whereby the asset can be purchased in the market where it is 'cheap' and sold in the market where it is expensive. If these transactions take place simultaneously, the arbitrageur will make a riskless profit.

The value of a derivative is linked in a logical way to the price of the underlying asset, so if the price of the derivative is 'cheap' then arbitrage activities will force up the price of the derivative and force down the price of the underlying asset. The opposite will apply if the asset is cheap and the derivative is expensive. Thus by its very nature, arbitrage will tend to bring the prices of derivatives and underlying assets back into line because there will be extra demand in the 'cheap' market, forcing the price up, and extra supply in the 'expensive' market which will force prices down.

Exchange-traded and over-the-counter (OTC) derivatives

Exchange-traded derivatives are traded on an organized exchange, such as LIFFE (London International Financial Futures Options Exchange). The terms and conditions are standardized; prices are readily available via open outcry or more often via a computer screen. For exchange-traded derivatives, a clearing house acts as a guarantor that the counterparties will fulfil their obligations.

OTC derivatives are private contracts between two parties without any clearing house involvement. Thus there is a potential risk that one of the parties to an OTC derivative will default on the obligations, because there is no clearing house to act as guarantor. This potential risk is often referred to as 'counterparty risk'. Obviously, when the counterparty is a UK commercial bank regulated by the FSA, counterparty risk should be minimal.

OTC contracts can be tailor-made to meet the needs of both parties. In addition, pricing is done on a deal-by-deal basis, so prices on the OTC markets are less transparent than those for exchange-traded derivatives.

All futures are exchange-traded, and traded options by their very nature are also exchange traded. However, it is possible to set up options that are OTC. Equity swaps are all OTC.

Having had an overview of derivatives, let us now examine the first category of derivative, the future.

9.2 How the FTSE 100 Index future works

The obligations under the futures contract.

This future is an index future that has the FTSE 100 Index as the underlying index. For our purposes, let us simply assume at this stage that the FTSE 100 Index is a measure of the overall price movements of the constituents of the index, which are the biggest 100 companies listed on the London Stock Exchange. A more detailed coverage of this index will be found in Chapter 19.

The contract works as follows:

1. A monetary value is placed on the FTSE 100 Index. The valued is calculated at £10 per index point. Thus if the index number is 6000.0 then the monetary value of one futures contract at that point in time is £60,000.

2. At the time an investor enters into a position on the FTSE 100 Index future, a price will be agreed. This price will be an index number for the FTSE 100 Index.

3. Let us assume that when an investor takes a position in this futures contract the index number is agreed at 6000.0. (The mechanics of pricing are covered later.) This means today the investor has entered into an obligation to buy or sell the index at 6000.0 on the last trading day of the future (when the contract will expire and has to be settled). The last trading day can be in March, June, September, December (the delivery months) and it is normally the third Friday in the delivery month. Futures contracts are only available in the three nearest delivery months, so for a contract taken out in April, there would be a choice of June, September or December as delivery months.

4. If the contract is one entered into on 1 March with a June delivery month, then overall gain or loss on the June expiry date will be based on the difference between the 6000.0 price agreed when the deal was made on 1 March and the Exchange Delivery Settlement Price (EDSP) ruling on the third Friday in June.

5. The EDSP is based on the average values of the FTSE 100 Index every 15 seconds between (and including) 10:10 and 10:30 (London time) on the Last Trading Day. Of the 81 measured values, the highest 12 and lowest 12 will be discarded and the remaining 57 will be averaged to calculate the EDSP. Where necessary, the calculation will be rounded to the nearest half index point. Thus if the EDSP for June was 6500.0, then the monetary value of the future would be £65,000. The minimum EDSP movement that can cause a change in the future's value is 0.5 of an index point and the minimum amount by which the future's value can change is £5.

6. The financial gain or loss on the above contract would depend on whether the holder was a buyer of the index (long) or a seller (short). A buyer of an index future is the person who is committed to buying the index on the expiry date of the future at the price set at the time the futures contract was first entered into. If the underlying index has risen at the expiry date, the buyer will make a gain on the futures position, because

on expiry he will notionally fulfil his obligation to buy the index at the agreed price of 6000.0 and then will immediately notionally sell the index back at the current (higher) price. On the other hand, a seller (short) is the one who gains if the underlying falls in value between the date of entry into the futures position and the expiry of the future.

7. Thus in the above example, a person who had entered the futures market as a buyer (long) when the price of the future stood at 6000.0 would have made an overall gain of £5,000. The buyer in March agreed to notionally buy the index for £60,000 from the clearing house in June, and when the June expiry date arrived the value of the index was £65,000. Thus the buyer was able to 'buy' the index for £60,000 at the expiry of the future and to 'sell' it back to the clearing house for £65,000. On the other hand, the seller (short) would have made an overall loss of £5,000 because he notionally agreed in March to sell the index to the clearing house at £60,000 in June and then had to notionally buy it back at the June expiry date for £65,000.

8. The contractual obligations do not arise directly between the buyer and the seller. The buyer's rights and obligations are with the clearing house, as are the seller's. If the buyer defaults on his obligations this is of no direct concern to the seller, and vice versa. The clearing house takes over any counterparty risk.

9. The simplest way to calculate the overall gain or loss is to say that for a single futures contract the buyer gains £10 for every full point by which price of the index future rises between taking a position in the futures market and leaving it, and the seller gains £10 for every point by which the price of the index future falls during this period. However, for changes in the index of less than one full point, say between 0.5 and less than 1, the monetary gain or loss under the future is £5. For changes of below 0.5, there is no cash settlement required under the future.

Cash flow aspects of the FTSE 100 Index future

While the calculation of the overall gain or loss is as shown above, in practice the overall gain or loss on a future arises incrementally, every working day, through a procedure known as mark to market. In addition, when first entering into a position in the futures market, a buyer or seller has to provide a deposit, known as the initial margin. The amount of this margin is based on the maximum amount estimated to be needed to cover one working day's losses on a futures position. Let us take as an example a future where the price was 6000.0 on entry and 6,500.0 at maturity of the position. Let us make the simplifying assumption that the position was entered into just four 4 working days before the last day of trading. Let us also assume that the initial margin payable to the futures clearing house was £3,000 (5% of the £60,000 notional value of the index). The initial margin is a returnable deposit held by the clearing house to protect LIFFE and its users from fraud or insolvency on the part of one party to a futures contract.

The cash flows for the buyer/long would look like this:

Investment Management

Day	Index price	Initial margin paid at outset & returned at maturity £	Daily gain/loss to be settled by buyer's variation margin £	Cumulative cash flow £
1	6,000.0	(3,000)		(3,000)
2	5,950.0		(500)	(3,500)
3	5,990.0		400	(3,100)
4.	6,500.0	3,000	5,100	5,000

The cash flows for the seller/short would look like this:

Day	Index price	Initial margin paid at outset & returned at maturity £	Daily gain/loss to be settled by seller's variation margin £	Cumulative cash flow £
1	6,000.0	(3,000)		(3,000)
2	5,950.0		500	(2,500)
3	5,990.0		(400)	(2,900)
4	6500.0	3,000	(5,100)	(5,000)

It should be noted that a buyer or seller does not have to hold a position in the futures market until maturity. The buyer or seller can voluntarily close out the position himself at any time prior to maturity. Thus taking the above details as an example, a buyer could have closed out on day three by entering into a sell position for the number of contracts he currently held as a buyer. The buy contract would have been settled by the payment of the variation margin for the day of £400, plus the repayment of the initial margin. There would be no further obligations under the futures contract, because any daily gains on the buy position would be exactly matched by corresponding losses on the sell contract.

To sum up, if a buyer closed out on day three, the position would be:

Day	Index price	Initial margin paid at outset & returned at maturity £	Daily gain/loss to be settled by buyer's variation margin £	Cumulative cash flow £
1	6,000.0	(3,000)		(3,000)
2	5,950.0		(500)	(3,500)
3	5,990.0	3,000	400	(100)

Thus the buyer would have crystallized his loss at £100 on day three, and any further obligations (positive or negative) under the future would be at an end.

Naturally, a seller could have closed out on day three by entering into a matching buy contract. This would have crystallized the seller's gain on the future at £100.

The purpose of the initial margin and variation margin

The purpose of the initial margin, which is paid to the futures clearing house, is to ensure that if the party to a future has incurred a loss on the daily mark to market of the position and does not settle that loss, the funds from the initial margin can be used for this purpose. Provided the daily variation margins are fully settled, the initial margin will be returned in full at the expiry or close out of the position. However, if the variation margin commitments are not honoured, the initial margin can be utilized for that purpose. Thus for example on day 2 above, when the buyer had made a loss of £500, if he defaulted on the variation margin payment, the clearing house would utilise £500 from the initial margin to meet the obligation. In addition, the clearing house would immediately close out the future (by entering into a matching sell contract on the buyer's behalf), so that the futures position would effectively be ended. The remainder of the initial margin, less costs, would then be repaid to the buyer.

The benefits of this system were well illustrated in the Nick Leeson affair when Barings bank made its huge losses in Singapore on the futures markets. Because of the clearing house involvement, the other parties to the futures contracts were not affected, nor was the futures exchange (SIMEX) financially affected by the failure of Barings bank.

9.5　Pricing of FTSE 100 Index futures

Basis or fair value premium

Prior to maturity, a future will normally trade at an index figure above that of the actual index on the day. This difference between the spot rate of the index and the futures price at that time is known as basis or fair value premium.

The only time the two prices (spot index price and FTSE 100 Index future price) are guaranteed to be identical will be on the last trading day of the futures contract, when the future's price must mirror the spot price as set by the formula shown above for ESDP.

Investment Management

The principle of forward pricing

The actual price of the FTSE 100 Index future on any given day will tend to equate to its forward price for the date of the maturity of the futures contract. The nearer the time to maturity, the closer actual price of the index future will be to the spot index value.

The following example illustrates how the price of an index future prior to maturity will be linked to the FTSE 100 Index level for that day. Let us assume the following apply:

> 1. *Today is 15 December.*
>
> 2. *Actual FTSE 100 index level on 15 December (spot level): 6,000.0*
>
> 3. *Expiry date of the future: 15 March*
>
> 4. *Number of days before the maturity date of the FTSE 100 Index Future: 90*
>
> 5. *Interest rates: 6% per annum*
>
> 6. *Annual dividend yield on FTSE 100: 2.5%*
>
> *The so-called fair value of FTSE Index future on 15 December is: Spot level + (cost of carry - carry return). The cost of carry is the interest which would have been foregone by the laying out cash to buy the index on 15 December as opposed to delaying purchase of the index until 15 March. The carry return is represented by the dividends which would have been foregone by waiting until 15 March to acquire ownership of the underlying index, instead of acquiring such an interest on 15 December.*
>
> *The calculation is: $6,000 + (6,000 \times 0.06 \times {}^{90}/_{365}) - (6,000 \times 0.025 \times {}^{90}/_{365}) = 6,052.0$ (to nearest 0.5)*

Explanation

This explanation assumes that it is possible for an investor at any given time to purchase a portfolio of shares that exactly replicates the FTSE 100 Index. As soon as shares are purchased, the purchaser is entitled to the dividends (assuming 'cum div').

Suppose on 15 December an investor has available a sum of £60,000, which is equal to the value of one FTSE 100 index future contract at 6,000.0. He could in theory invest the money in a portfolio of shares representing the FTSE 100 index. In 90 days time, the investor would own shares equivalent to 'the index' and would have received dividends on those shares representing 2.5% per annum of the initial investment, assuming dividends are paid at a constant rate throughout the year.

On 15 March at the maturity of the future in 90 days time, he could sell the shares. Let us assume that the value of the shares had risen by 10% at the maturity date of the future, so the shares would be worth £66,000. The investor should also have received dividends of £369.86 during the 90-day holding period. However, the investor would have foregone interest of £887.67 by purchasing the shares on 15 December instead of waiting until 15 March to acquire an interest in them, assuming interest rates of 6% per annum.

Thus the net gain using the 'real' market would have been £66,000 - 60,000 - 887.67 + £369.86 = £5,482.19.

Now let us examine likely position if the £60,000 had been utilized on the futures market on 15 December. This illustration ignores the complexities of the various margin call payments.

If the FTSE 100 Index had risen by exactly the same 10% between 15 December and 15 March, the spot FTSE 100 expiry day would have been 6,600. Thus the ESDP for the future would have been 6,600.0. Thus a buyer of one FTSE 100 Index future on 15 December would have gained (6,600.0 - 6,052.0) x £10 = £5,480. The difference between the real market gain and the futures market gain is accounted for by the rounding of the futures price.

However, if the price of the future on 15 December had been 6,000.0, the same as the spot index value, then the gain on the index future would have been (6,600.0-6,000.0) x £10 = £6,000. Bearing in mind the principles of arbitrage, had the future traded at 6,000.0 on 15 December, then in theory holders of shares would have been tempted to sell them and take a 'buy' position in the futures market. The demand from buyers would have forced up the price of the future towards the fair value of 6,052.0, or alternatively the price of the shares would have fallen in response to the sales.

Summary of the effect of various economic variables on the fair value of the futures price prior to maturity

Factor	Effect on fair value of future prior to maturity
Interest rates	The higher the interest rates, the greater will be the difference between fair value and spot value.
Dividend yield	The higher the dividend yield the lower the difference between fair value and spot value.
Time to maturity	The longer the time, the greater will be the difference between fair value and spot value, assuming that interest rates are above dividend yields.

Basis analysis

Basis represents the difference between the actual price of a future at any given time and the spot value of the FTSE 100 Index. There are different measures of basis and these will be illustrated using the figures from the previous example.

To recap the details are:

Spot Index value	15 December 6,000.0
Fair value of future	15 December 6,052.0

In addition, let us assume that the actual price of the future on 15 December is 6,075.0

The following table sums up the position:

Simple basis : actual futures price less spot index $\qquad$ $6,075.0 - 6,000.0 = 75.0$

Fair value basis: fair value - spot index $\qquad$ $6,052.0 - 6,000.0 = 52.0$

Value basis: difference between the fair value and the actual price $\qquad$ $6,052.0 - 6,075.0 = -23.0$

Implications of basis value

As has been illustrated already in connection with fair value, arbitrage in the case of the FTSE 100 index future would involve buying or selling a portfolio of stocks which replicated the FTSE 100 index and taking an opposite position in the index future.

Thus when a future price is above its fair value, and has negative value basis as above, investors will be tempted to sell the index future and buy an underlying portfolio of shares. This activity should in theory force the price of the future down towards its fair value level. However, although an operation such as this looks an attractive risk free proposition, in reality there are a number of limitations to this apparently risk-free way of making money. The obvious ones are dealing costs on the shares, the bid offer spread, stamp duty, and commission.

9.6 How a fund manager could use the FTSE 100 Index future to hedge the value of a portfolio of shares

Let us suppose that a UK fund manager wishes to stabilize the performance of his equity portfolio (currently valued at £10m) prior to the date of the next quarterly performance tables. This could be achieved by means of the FTSE 100 Index future. Using the examples previously shown, let us assume that today is 15 December and:

> FTSE 100 Index future price at 15 December stands at 6,075.0

> Spot FTSE 100 Index at 15 December is 6,000.0

> Interest rates 6% per annum

> Dividend yield 2.5% per annum

Let us assume the ESDP of the future on 15 March is 6,600.0 and the spot FTSE 100 index stands at that figure.

Use of Stock Index Futures to stabilize an equity portfolio

The contract value is £10 per point change in the FTSE 100 Index closing rate from one day to another. The person who buys the future is termed a 'long' and he will benefit if the

FTSE 100 rises. The person who sells the future is termed a 'short' and will benefit if the index falls. Settlement is in cash, with the usual initial margin and variation margin procedures.

A fund manager would **sell** the appropriate number of futures contracts to stabilize the performance of the portfolio. The number of contracts sold would be:

Value of fund to be hedged ÷ (futures price x index point value)

$$= \frac{10,000,000}{6,075 \times 10} = 165 \text{ (rounded up)}$$

> *Note: The number of contracts required to hedge an exposure is often referred to as the hedge ratio. You cannot deal in fractions of futures contracts so the number of contracts from the formula calculation will have to be rounded up or down.*

If the underlying FTSE 100 Index future had risen on 15 March, as it has done, then the portfolio manager would have lost out on the future, but would be compensated by a gain on his shares. If the FTSE 100 Index had fallen below the 6,075.0 on 15 March, the manager would have gained on the future, but this would be counterbalanced to a great extent by a fall in the value of the underlying portfolio.

Selling futures to hedge a portfolio. In the above example, using the details shown, the position would have been:

Outcome if no action had been taken	Monetary consequences if no action taken	Outcome when future used (ignores margin calls)
Portfolio will rise by difference between spot Index on 15 Dec & spot on 15 March	Value at 15 Dec £10m Value at 15 March £11m Gain in value £1m	Loss on future on 15 March (6,600.0-6,075.0) x 10 x 165 = £866,250. Thus the future does not exactly hedge the change in underlying values.

Reconciliation

The alternative to using the index would be to sell the shares on 15 December, invest the cash until 15 March, and then compare the value of the cash in hand with the value of the underlying shares and dividends at 15 March.

Financial wealth on 15 March if shares sold on 15 December	**Financial wealth on 15 March if shares retained on 15 December, but futures position as seller taken when futures price was 6,075.0**
Sell shares 15 December £10,000,000 Invest money for 90 days at 6%. Balance at 15 March is £10,147,945.	Make a loss on the future on 15 March of £866,250, but offset by dividends of £61,643. Own shares now valued at £11m. Net wealth is £10,195,393.

Obviously the standardized nature of the futures contracts, coupled with the negative value basis (here of -23 points), means that it will not be possible to construct an exact hedge. In addition the assumption that dividends are paid at a constant rate over the year will not normally apply in practice.

Benefits of the futures method of hedging

- Avoids heavy brokers' fees, stamp duty, bid-offer spreads and possible tax consequences which would have arisen if the underlying shares had been sold on 15 December and the proceeds invested. To some extent the value basis (here -23) should account for this, but the dealing costs will vary from firm to firm and from transaction to transaction.

- The underlying portfolio can be left undisturbed. This is beneficial if the portfolio has been constructed with the aim of achieving the optimal mix of equities.

- If the underlying equities had been sold for cash, the size of the transactions may have moved the prices against the fund manager by driving the share prices downwards. The taking of a position in the futures market avoids this potential diminution in the value of the underlying equities.

- The transaction costs for futures are relatively low.

- The futures position can be closed out at anytime prior to maturity of the futures contract.

Drawbacks

- The hedge will operate effectively only to the extent that the portfolio replicates the FTSE100 Index. (However, currently there are many 'tracker funds' which do this.)

- There may be legal problems if the rules of the fund forbid the use of derivatives.

- If the FTSE 100 has risen during the time the futures position existed (as in this example), it can be difficult to explain the loss on the derivatives position to the trustees of the fund.

- Sophisticated IT systems are required to track the position and ensure that the variation and initial margin payments are made on time.

- The costs of management time can be high because expertise is required for dealings in the futures position.

- Because of the fact that futures are exchange traded and standardized, the hedge cannot exactly match the underlying exposure.

- If the position is closed out prior to maturity, basis risk will arise, in that the futures price will not be the same as the spot value of the index at close out.

9.6   Mini FTSE 100 Index future

Many futures exchanges throughout the world have introduced mini index futures as a response to the development of spread betting (see section 9.16). The Mini FTSE 100 Index future works in the same way as the FTSE 100 Index future already described, but the contract size is £2 per index point, as opposed to £10 on the ordinary future. The minimum price movement is £1 as opposed to £5 on the conventional future. The mini future and the conventional FTSE 100 Index future are fully interchangeable, so that, for example, five Mini FTSE 100 Index futures contracts are exactly the same as one ordinary one.

The mini future is relatively new (started in September 2000) and it is aimed at the private investor, as opposed to the institutional investor. Obviously, the price movements for any given change in the underlying index will be smaller on the mini future, and so the initial margin amount will also be lower than for a conventional future. This should facilitate the use of this future by private investors, but it cannot be stressed too highly that futures should be used only by those who have a full understanding of the risks and who can afford to lose money if the position moves adversely.

Private investors can trade in the FTSE 100 Index futures only by employing a broker to act as an intermediary with LIFFE. The broker will require the investor to open an account with him, and will insist on taking a deposit before agreeing to act on the client's behalf. The size of the deposit will depend on the maximum number of contracts the broker agrees to enter into on behalf of the investor. According to LIFFE's publicity brochure on the Mini FTSE 100 future, dealing costs on this future typically represent only 33% of those which would have been incurred from dealing in the equivalent value of underlying shares.

Although the investor is protected by the initial and variation margin system from counterparty default once the broker has registered a contract with LIFFE, there is no protection if the broker misappropriates the client's funds and does not pay them over to LIFFE in accordance with the client's instructions.

9.7   Summary of futures as a risk management tool and as a speculation

When an investor takes a position in the futures market that is equal and opposite to the investor's position in the equity market, the future will act as a hedge of the investor's risks. Thus in our previous example, a fund manager who holds a diversified portfolio of equities that reflects the performance of the FTSE 100 Index could sell an appropriate number of

FTSE 100 Index futures to hedge the position. Any change in value of the underlying shares would be reflected in an opposite change in the payoff on the futures position (to the extent that the portfolio's performance matched that of the index).

However, anyone taking a position in the futures market that is *not* matched by a position in the equity market itself, is speculating. A buyer will gain if the index rises, whereas a seller will gain if the index falls. Both are gambling that the index will move in their favour, but neither can know what will actually happen over the period of the futures position.

9.8   Equity swaps

Swaps are over-the-counter (OTC) instruments, so their precise nature is not standardized, but is determined by negotiation between the two parties. An equity swap is an agreement between two parties in which at least one party agrees to pay the other a return based on some type of equity index, or a return based on that of a particular share. The payment made by the other party could be based on a floating rate of interest, a fixed rate of interest, or on another equity index. Where appropriate, the swap can be structured to hedge against exchange-rate fluctuations. A key characteristic of equity swaps is that there is no exchange of principal, all that is swapped are the returns based on equity indices, individual equities or interest rates.

Let us now examine some applications of equity swaps.

Equity swaps as a means of international diversification by fund managers

Suppose a UK-based fund manager holds a diversified portfolio of UK-listed shares, valued at around £100m in total, but he wishes to diversify internationally so that, say, 20% of the fund is exposed to the US S&P 500 Index. He could sell £20m of the value of his UK portfolio and invest the money in a diversified portfolio of US shares that was broadly representative of the S&P 500. However the disadvantages of achieving diversification through the 'real' market are:

● This would be very expensive in terms of transaction costs.

● Large sales from the UK portfolio could depress the prices of the shares being sold.

● There could be CGT liabilities if the sales crystallized a gain on the shares.

● Dealing with foreign stock can be extremely burdensome because of different legal systems, lack of information, different accounting conventions and any dividend withholding tax. This tax arises out of the tax regulations that permit the tax authorities of a country to withhold a portion of the dividends of shares owned by overseas investors. In some cases, these withheld dividends can be recovered but that does incur some additional costs.

The equity swap was primarily developed to deal with these problems and it would operate along the following lines.

● The UK Fund manager enters into a swap in which he agrees to make quarterly payments to a swap dealer linked to the FTSE 100 Index's return over the period and applied to a notional principal of £20m.

● The dealer will in return make quarterly payments to the UK fund manager based on the return on the S&P 500 Index (less a margin) as applied to a notional principal of £20m.

Note that the swap dealer will require some compensation by way of bid/offer spread to cover his risk and costs in setting up the swap. In reality, the swap dealer may stipulate that the S&P-linked payment he makes has a deduction of, say, 0.25% from the S&P return and we shall assume this to be the case here.

The UK fund manager has, in effect, sold UK stock for £20m and invested in US stock for the period of the swap contract.

An important feature of equity swaps that the equity return can be negative. Thus if, say, the FTSE 100 Index falls and the S&P 500 rises, the UK fund manager will gain on both sides of the swap and the dealer will lose on both sides of it. In general, equity swap payments will appear to be quite volatile but this reflects only the normal volatility of the markets. The same results would have been obtained by selling the UK shares and buying a set of US shares which represented the S&P Index.

The position can be illustrated by a classic swap diagram as follows:

Figure 9.1: Swap diagram

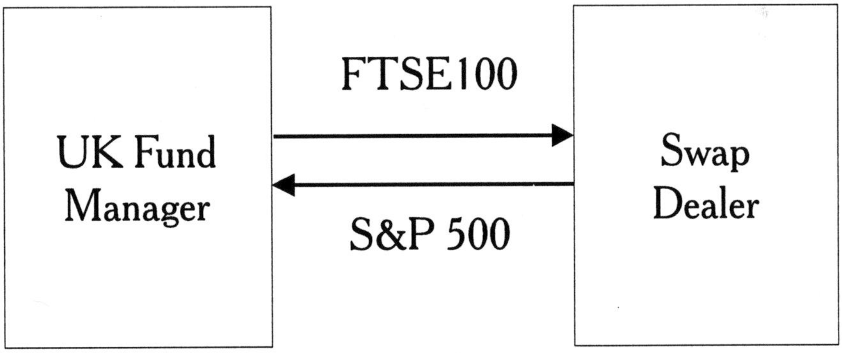

Thus if over a particular quarter the FTSE 100 Index had made a negative return of 5% and the S&P 500 had made a positive return of 6.25%, the payments would have been a net settlement of £2.2m from the swap dealer to the UK fund manager.

As can be seen from Figure 9.2, the return on the FTSE 100 Index is negative, so the swap dealer has to pay the UK fund manager £1m (£20m at 5%). The S&P Index has made a positive return, so the swap dealer has also to pay out £1.2m on the S&P part of the swap (£20m at 6%). Thus the swap dealer has to make a net payment of £2.2m to the UK fund manager on this occasion.

Figure 9.2: Swap diagram

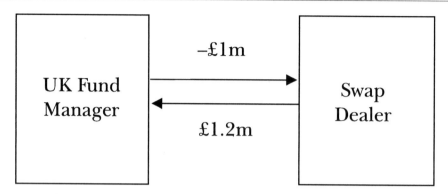

Note

1.   The notional principal of £20m does not change hands at any time. The £20m is simply the amount on which the returns on the two indices are applied to determine the swap payments.

2.   'Return' means the total return on the indices that is calculated from capital gain/loss and dividend payments.

3.   If the UK fund manager had wanted to be exposed to the currency risk as well as to the equity risk from the S&P Index, the swap could have been structured so that the notional principal on which the swap dealer's S&P return was calculated was the US$ equivalent of £20m converted at the spot ruling on commencement of the swap. For example, if the spot rate at the start of the swap had been £1 =US$ 1.50, the notional principal for the swap dealer's obligation would have been US$ 30m. If the spot rate at the end of the quarter had been US$ 1.60, and the returns on the two indices had been as above, the payments would have been as follows:

Figure 9.3: Swap diagram

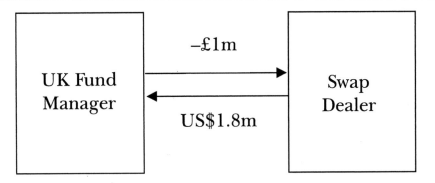

Note the US$1.8m payment is calculated at 6% of US$30m. The sterling payment is calculated as shown in the previous example.

The UK fund manager would then have converted the US$ 1.8m to sterling at the spot rate of US$1.6 to £1.125m, thus obtaining a net return of £2.125m (£1.125m from the S&P Index and £1m from the negative return on the FTSE 100 Index).

Equity swaps and emerging markets

Emerging markets can deliver outstanding returns but they can suffer from low liquidity. A newly constituted UK unit trust with cash of £20m to invest could acquire an exposure to an emerging market by investing that £20m in a portfolio of equities listed on that market's stock exchange. There are once again the problems of transaction costs, lack of information, different legal systems, withholding taxes, as set out for the US stock market exposures described above. However, the other additional problem from emerging markets is that at times of economic difficulty these markets can become very illiquid, with wide bid/offer spreads and few buyers.

An equity swap with a notional principal of £20m could be structured so that the swap dealer pays a return based on performance of the emerging market as measured by the appropriate index, and the UK fund manager pays, say, LIBOR on that notional principal.

If we assume that the swap payments are annual, that the relevant LIBOR for the period is 7.00 % per annum, and that the emerging market gives a positive return of 5% over the period, the payments would look like this:

Figure 9.4: Swap diagram

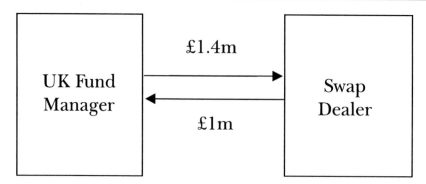

Thus for this particular period, there would be a net payment of £0.4m (£1.4m – £1m) from the fund manager to the swap dealer. In practice, as in the previous example, the swap dealer would require a margin to provide a bid/offer spread to cover his costs and risks.

The benefits for the UK fund manager are:

● Quick, cheap access to a return based on the emerging market.

● The credit risk is limited to the swap dealer, and once the expiry date of the swap is reached, the exposure to the emerging market ceases to exist.

● The swap could be closed out before the expiry date if the fund manager so required, provided he could negotiate a matching swap with opposite payment obligations. Such a swap would then end exposure to the emerging markets, but there would be some loss on a bid/offer spread of the two swaps.

● If the underlying shares in the emerging market had been purchased, the UK fund manager would have been faced with the problems of finding a buyer for the shares when he wished to leave that market.

● The UK fund manager can eliminate his exposure to fluctuations in the currency of the emerging market by having the cash flows for both sides of the swap based on a notional principal denominated in sterling, as in this example.

9.9   Comparison of swaps and futures

Futures are standardized with the only negotiable feature being price. Generally speaking, the available expiry dates for the futures are for only 3, 6, and 9 month periods, whereas a swap can have whatever expiry date is mutually agreeable. It could require many different futures contracts being arranged to cover a period of, say, five years whereas only one single equity swap contract is required.

● Thus the future would be complex to administer with many contracts for different expiry dates, initial margins and margin calls, whereas the swap is a single arrangement and is easily understood.

- The swap can be tailor made, especially as regards settlement dates and underlying amounts, so the hedge could be a better match than the future with its standardized contract terms for expiry dates and notional amounts.

- The swap avoids the possible tax complexities on margin calls for the future.

- There is effectively no counterparty risk with futures once the clearing house has confirmed the contract. However, in practice counterparty risk is minimal with the swap if the swap dealer is part of a major UK bank under FSA supervision.

- Pricing of exchange-traded futures is transparent, whereas pricing of OTC swaps is negotiable.

9.10   Equity swaps and individual shares

Being OTC instruments, there are no formal standardization requirements for equity swaps, so they can also be structured so that they are based on specific industries or market sectors, or even individual stocks.

For example, a director of a listed company may have a contractual obligation as a director to hold a minimum of 500,000 shares in the company. If the director wished to hedge his exposure to the company without selling the shares he could enter into an equity swap as follows:

- He agrees to pay the swap dealer the return based on 500,000 shares in his company. The shares had a market value of about £10 million at the start of the swap.

- The notional principal is £10m.

- The director receives from the swap dealer a return based on LIBOR - 0.25% on notional principal of £10m.

The director has effectively sold the shares to the swap dealer for the period of the swap, yet he still retains title to the shares and hence can still vote as a shareholder and he does not have to pay any CGT which could have arisen if the stock had been sold. There will be tax to pay on the income received from the swap dealer.

Note
The director must be careful not to contravene any of the insider-dealing prohibitions (see Chapter 20, page 419).

9.11   Traded options

Traded options are traded on the London International Financial Futures and Options Exchange (LIFFE). Traded options are a type of derivative (i.e. their value derives from that of another asset) and, as their name implies, can be bought and sold at any time during their lives. At maturity, the holder of an option can exercise it or abandon it.

A 'call' traded option gives the purchaser the right, but not the obligation, to buy the underlying shares. A 'put' traded option gives the purchaser the right, but not the obligation, to sell the underlying shares.

Traded options can only be arranged in certain securities. At present there are traded options available in approximately 90 classes, some of which include index options in FTSE 100 and Eurostyle FTSE 100, as well as shares such as Barclays, Sainsbury and Unilever. Details of the classes available can be found in the *Financial Times*.

Traded options run for three-, six- and nine-month periods and are standardized contracts. Although the price of the option and the exercise price are quoted for a single share, each contract, which is indivisible, relates to 1,000 shares. If a traded option is bought and sold on the market gains or losses are allowed for CGT purposes. If the traded option is actually exercised, the position for CGT is that the cost of a call option is added to the purchase price and the cost of a put is deducted from the sale proceeds.

Note: these rules are applicable only to the private investor. Professionals investors pay income tax or corporation tax.

Traded options can be sold at any time and settlement is for 'cash', thus payment is due on the next working day.

How prices of traded options are quoted

Let us examine details of a traded option in shares of XYZ plc, a listed company.

Note: assume today is 2 November.

		Calls			Puts		
Option	Exercise price	Dec	Mar	June	Dec	Mar	June
XYZ plc	1450	85½	135½	188	47½	81	118
(*1478½)	1500	57	108½	164	71	104½	143

* underlying share price

Explanation of price of the XYZ plc traded option

The exercise price is the price at which the shares can be bought (call option) or sold (put option) if the option is exercised.

The price of a traded option, which strictly speaking is called the option premium, is set by supply and demand. However, the theoretical components of the price of traded options are:

● *Intrinsic value*: Amount by which the share price exceeds the exercise price for a call, or amount by which the exercise price exceeds the share price for a put. This figure can be given an exact value. When an option has a positive intrinsic value, it is said to be 'in the money'. However, an out-of-the-money option can never have a negative intrinsic value, because options do not impose any obligation on the holder who will just abandon it if the option is out of the money at maturity.

● *Time value*: This value is subjective. Generally speaking, the longer the option has to run, and the more volatile the price of the underlying share, the greater the chance of the underlying share price moving in favour of the holder of the option, and the greater the time value component in the premium.

Examples from the above

Prices for options on individual shares are quoted in pence per share. Thus, because one contract relates to 1,000 shares, it is necessary to multiply the quoted price by 1,000. So taking the December 1450 call as an example, the price of one contract would be 85.5p x 1,000 = £855.

The call option premiums are made up as follows:

	December	March	June
Intrinsic	28½	28½	28½
Time	57	107	159½
Option premium (price)	85½	135½	188

(Intrinsic value is calculated: 1478½ – 1450).

If we look at the bottom line of put options (i.e. the 1500 exercise price), we can see that the prices are made up as follows:

	December	March	June
Intrinsic	21½	21½	21½
Time	49½	83	121½
Option premium (price)	71	104½	143

Note: an option contract relates to 1,000 shares. The cost of only one December put traded option contract would be £710 (excluding commission).

Out-of-the-money and 'at-the-money' options

The concept of 'in-the-money' options and 'out-of-the-money' options applies as follows. For example, the December 47½ put is 'out-of-the-money' because the exercise price of 1450p is below the current share price of 1478½p. 'Out-of-the-money' traded options are more speculative than 'in-the-money' ones and thus can be said to be 'higher geared'.

If the exercise price is approximately equal to the underlying share price, the option is said to be 'at the money'.

Traded option terminology

Exercise price

This is the price at which the traded option can be exercised. Statistically, only approximately 5% of traded options are ever exercised. The majority of traded options are either sold in the market or allowed to expire, thus becoming worthless.

Writers

These are the organizations, approved by the Stock Exchange, that will guarantee to honour any traded options which may be exercised.

Premium

The premium is the price of the traded option. The premium is composed of time value and intrinsic value, but the amount is always quoted as a single figure.

Expiry dates and series

The expiry date is the last day on which a traded option can be exercised. Expiry dates are fixed at three-monthly intervals, and there are three possible expiry cycles:

- January, April, July, October
- February, May, August, November
- March, June, September, December

When a traded option is written on the shares of a company it is allocated to one of the above three cycles. It is rare for the allocated cycle to be changed. At any one time only three of the four months specified in the cycle will be quoted.

All options on a particular security that have the same exercise price and exercise date are known as a series.

Option premiums for traded options

The prices are published in various newspapers, such as the *Financial Times*. However, the prices are based on the settlement prices of the previous day, and there is always a spread between 'bid' and 'offer' prices.

Other charges on traded options

Commission rates are negotiable between investor and broker. One example of the rates quoted is 1.5% of the option premium, plus £1 per contract subject to a minimum of £20, although commission is usually charged at half these rates on closing deals.

Index-traded options

Index options are not based on individual shares, but on an index. The underlying index we shall consider is the FTSE 100 Index. LIFFE is constantly developing and refining its range of index options and readers should consult LIFFE's website and the *Financial Times* for an up-to-date list of these index options. A **call** option gives the holder the right but not the obligation at the expiry of that option to take a position in the FTSE 100 Index Future as a **buyer** on the pre-set index number (the exercise price) stated in the option. If the FTSE 100 Index ESDP at maturity is above the exercise price of the call option, the holder will exercise. If the ESDP (Exchange Settlement Delivery Price) is below the exercise price, the call option will be abandoned. The maximum loss to the holder of a call option in this case will be the amount of the premium. A **put** option at expiry gives the holder the right to take up a position in the FTSE 100 Index future as a **seller** on the pre-set index number (exercise price) of the option. If the ESDP at maturity is below the exercise price, the put option will be exercised. If the ESDP is above the exercise price, the put option will be abandoned and the maximum loss will be the premium cost.

If an index option is exercised, the holder will receive cash equal to the difference between the index value on the day of exercise and the exercise price of the series being executed, multiplied by £10.

These options are quoted with a large range of index values, and with four-month, not three-monthly, expiry dates. Thus they expire at monthly intervals.

Taking today as 2 November:

CALLS	5800	5900	6000	6100	6200	6300	6400	6500
Nov	520½	427	340	250½	176	112	62	28½
Dec	568	484	403½	330½	260½	198½	142	99½
Jan	656	577	498	419½	349	284½	220	172½
Feb	715½	636	557	478½	414	350½	288½	239½

PUTS	5800	5900	6000	6100	6200	6300	6400	6500
Nov	15	22	33	43½	70	107	159½	229
Dec	51½	75	83	109	138½	169½	226½	284½
Jan	106½	127	148½	170½	201½	237½	276	329½
Feb	164½	180	196	213½	243	274	308	357

The minimum contract size is 1,000. For options on the FTSE 100 Index, the premium is quoted in index points, and each index point is valued at £10. To purchase a call option expiring later in November with the exercise price of 6500.0 the cost will be £285 excluding dealing costs. If the ESDP at the November expiry is 6716.0, the November call will be exercised. On exercising the option the amount received is £2,160 (calculated 6716.0 – 6500.0 = 216 x £10 = £2,160), thus a net profit of £1,875 (£2,160 - £285) before dealing costs will have been made, assuming only one index contract had been taken up.

There are two distinct types of option with index options, the European option which can be exercised only on its expiry date, and the American option which can be exercised on any normal business day up to the expiry date. There is a formula for calculating the ESDP on a daily basis for the American options. This is a very complex formula and details can be found on the LIFFE website: www.LIFFE.com.

Index options are particularly useful for providing protection for a portfolio against adverse movements in share prices

Hedging a portfolio of equities using index-traded options

If an investor has a portfolio of equities and expects the market to fall in the next few months he can protect the capital value by selling the shares, taking a position as a seller of the FTSE 100 Index future, or he can use a put index-traded option. Selling all the shares will incur heavy dealing costs on a large portfolio and may also give rise to a capital gains tax liability. If he is wrong about the movement of the market and it rises, he has lost out on the rise in value that would have occurred in the portfolio.

The purchase of a put index-traded option protects against a fall in share prices because as the market falls the put index-traded option rises in value. If share prices rise the put index-traded option will fall in value, thus the cost of the option is lost but the rise in the value of the portfolio will compensate for the loss. Any gain on a traded option is liable for CGT, but the gain is likely to be far lower than that from selling the whole equity portfolio.

Provided the fund manager can find an index option that reflects his portfolio, he can provide a hedge against falls in the market while still retaining the opportunity to benefit from the upside movement. Let us take an example of a portfolio, using the FTSE 100 Index put option figures given above.

The investor has a portfolio of blue chip equities valued at £230,000 today. He feels that the market may have reached its peak and will fall back by 10%. He wishes to retain the right to sell the market at 5900 for three months. He will purchase a February 5900 put option at 180 index points. The cost of the February 5900 put at 180 is:

●   Buy 4 x February 5900 at £1,800 each = £7,200 (plus dealing costs)

Calculation

Each index point is worth £10; each put covers £59,000 (5900 x £10).

Thus he will purchase ($\frac{£230,000}{59,000}$ = 3.9) 4 puts to cover his position.

If the market falls in the next three months and the ESDP is 5310.0 (5900 less 10%) the put option will be exercised. He will receive £23,600 {4x (5900-5310) x 10}which, before dealing costs, gives him a net profit of £16,400 (£23,600 – £7,200). The portfolio will have fallen by 10% from £230,000 to £207,000, a loss of £23,000. This is not entirely covered by the net gain on the index option, but hedging the portfolio has protected most of the value. Obviously the greater the fall in the index, the greater the benefit of this option. In reality, the portfolio may fall by more or less than the fall in the market, unless the chosen index and the portfolio exactly mirror each other in weighting and number of holdings of shares.

If, however, the market rises so that the ESDP is above 5900.0, the option will simply be abandonned and the premium of £7,200 will be lost. However, the rise in value of the portfolio could well offset the cost of the premium for buying this particular put index-traded option.

Option pricing (i.e. premium)

Option pricing is based on logical principles, but a detailed analysis of the numerical techniques is beyond the scope of this book. However, we shall examine the concepts that underpin the pricing of options on shares.

Table 9.1: Effect of a rise in the following on the premium of an option

Factor	Effect on a call	Effect on a put
(i) Current price of underlying asset(affects intrinsic value)	Rises	Falls
(ii) Expected price volatility of underlying share	Rises	Rises
(iii Time to maturity of option	Rises	Rises
(iv) Short-term interest rate	Rises	Falls
(v) Anticipated dividends (cash payouts) prior to maturity if underlying asset is a share (affects intrinsic value)	Falls	Rises

Explanation of the above table

(i) Changes in the current price of underlying share.

The intrinsic value of an option is reflected in the difference between the price of the underlying share and its exercise price. Changes in the underlying share price must therefore affect the option premium.

(ii) Changes price volatility

In order to calculate the standard deviation for share-price movements, price changes over a past period are recorded and the mean (average) and standard deviation are calculated to measure past volatility. The method of calculation of standard deviation is outside the scope of this syllabus, but you do need to know the consequences as illustrated below.

For example, if over a past period the mean price of the share is 40p and the standard deviation is 2p, the position is:

- around 68% of prices were between 38-42p (one standard deviation) (34% 40 – 42p, 34% 38 – 40p)

- around 95% of prices were between 36-44p (two standard deviations) (47½% 44 – 40 and 47½% 36 – 40)

- around 99% of prices were between 34-46p (three standard deviations)

- Thus there was only a 2.5% chance that the price at any time over the period rose above 44p and only a 2.5% chance that it fell below 36p during the period.

Thus the greater the standard deviation, the greater the volatility of past price movements. It is generally assumed that past volatility (historic volatility) is a guide to potential future volatility. Thus where two shares have the same mean price from measurements of past period changes, the one with the higher standard deviation will have had the greater past price volatility and will normally have the greater implied future price volatility. Thus an option on a share that exhibits higher volatility will have a higher premium than an option on a share with lower price volatility. This is because a higher volatility implies a higher chance of a larger favourable price movement or a larger adverse price movement. If the movement is favourable, the option will be in the money and the intrinsic value at maturity will increase by the amount of the favourable movement. However, if the price movement is adverse, once the option has moved 'out of the money' the amount of the adverse price movement is irrelevant to the option holder. An option can never have a negative intrinsic value, and if it is out of the money at expiry, it will be abandoned whether the amount by which it is out of the money is large or small.

As regards forecasts of the future share price movements, the convention adopted is that the Random Walk Theory (see Chapter 11) applies to the market in the underlying share. This theory claims that at the start of every day there is a 50% chance that the market price of the share will rise and a 50% chance that it will fall. Thus the convention is that the direction of the price movement cannot be forecast, but the size of the movement (whichever way that might be) can be predicted using standard deviation techniques.

To illustrate this concept, let us examine two call options with the same expiry date, same strike price (40p) but different underlying shares.

- The underlying share for option A has a mean past price of 40p, with a standard deviation of 2p

- The underlying share for option B has a mean price of 40p, but a standard deviation of 3p.

Underlying share price at maturity re option A	Probability of price, based on standard deviation	Intrinsic value of option A at maturity
40p-42p	34%	0-2p
Over 42p	16%	Over 2p
Under 38p	16%	Nil
38-40p	34%	Nil

Underlying share price at maturity re option B	Probability of price based on standard deviation	Intrinsic value of option B at maturity
40-43p	34%	0-3p
Over 43p	16%	Over 3p
Under 37p	16%	Nil
37-40p	34%	Nil

- The convention is to assume that future volatility will reflect past volatility.

- Both options are considered to have an equal (50%) chance of expiring out of the money.

- There is a 34% chance of option A expiring with an intrinsic value of between 0p and 2p and a 16% chance that its intrinsic value will be over 2p at maturity.

- For option B, there is a 34% chance of expiring with an intrinsic value of between 0p and 3p and a 16% chance that its intrinsic value will be over 3p at maturity.

- However, the holder will walk away from the option if it expires out of the money, so it is irrelevant to the holder whether the closing share price is 37p or 38p. An option cannot have a negative intrinsic value.

- Hence the greater the volatility, the greater the time value of an option premium prior to maturity.

(iii) Time to maturity of option

The same principles that cover volatility apply to expiry date. The longer the time to expiry, the more time there is for future volatility. The greater the potential future volatility the greater the premium. This always applies to calls, but the 'interest factor' can sometimes counteract the volatility effect for puts. Thus, the only exception to the normal rule, which says that longer the expiry, the greater the premium, can occur with put options at times of high interest rates. (See below for interest rate factor.)

(iv) Short-term interest rate

For an investor who wishes to become a long-term holder of a particular share, there are two possible methods to acquire the share at a known price. One is to buy the share at the outset at today's price. The other is to pay the premium and buy a call option today to give the right but not the obligation to buy the underlying share at the strike price at a future date. Buying the underlying share at the outset ties up more funds at an earlier date than does the call option method. Thus if interest rates rise, the call option method becomes more attractive, and this should result in a rise in the call option premium.

However, an increase in interest rates will generally reduce the premium on a put. If we compare the position of a shareholder who wishes to dispose of his holding at a known price, he has two possible methods. He could sell the shares today for today's spot price, or he could pay the premium on a put option giving the right, but not the obligation, to sell the underlying shares at a future date at a known strike price. The sale of the share at the outset will result in a higher immediate cash inflow for the shareholder than that from buying a put and receiving the sale proceeds at a later date, assuming the option was exercised. Thus when interest rates rise, the cash-flow benefit of selling the shares at once is increased and this makes the put option route less attractive for a shareholder.

(v) Anticipated dividends (cash payouts) prior to maturity if underlying asset is a share (affects intrinsic value)

Let us consider a person who wishes to become a long-term shareholder in a company, but who is uncertain whether to buy the share now or whether to use the call option method. Buying the shares today will mean immediate entitlement to any dividends (assuming the shares are purchased 'cum div'). The greater the amount of dividends between today and the option expiry date, the more attractive the direct purchase route and the less attractive the call option route. The call option premium is usually adjusted downwards by the present value of any relevant dividend.

Similar reasoning for puts shows that it is more attractive to retain the shares and use a put option to set the future sale proceeds. The option premium is usually adjusted upwards by the present value of any relevant dividend on the underlying shares.

9.12 Option pricing models

Option dealers will use computer-based option pricing models to set a base case for the premium. The best known model is the Black Scholes Option Pricing Model. This model incorporates the factors shown above in its calculation of the 'fair value' premium. It also accounts for the fact that share prices are traded throughout the day by applying the principle of continuous compounding. A detailed understanding of the numerical techniques is beyond the scope of this book, but interested readers will find guidance in books such as King, D. *Financial Claims and Derivatives*, Thompson Business Press. In addition there are currently several free option pricing models available by downloading from Internet sources. Because these sources change so frequently, the reader is advised to employ an Internet search engine such as www.google.com and search under 'option pricing models'. Such models can be useful for readers to test out the quoted prices of traded options against the premium the model suggests.

In any event, the option dealer will use the price from the model as a 'base case' for the premium. He will adjust the premium to reflect his own profit margin and any specific market sentiment regarding the underlying share.

9.13   Comparison of stock index futures and stock index options

- There is no premium to pay on a future, but there is always a premium payable to buy an option.

- Both are exchange-traded instruments.

- Futures involve initial and variation margins, but these do not apply to options.

- Positions in the futures markets can result in unpredictable gains or losses unless they hedge a matching position in the underlying share market. Both parties to the futures contract are obliged to fulfil their obligations, but for options only one party (the writer) has this obligation.

- The maximum loss for the holder of an option is the premium, but he retains the right to gain from any favourable price change in the underlying asset.

- The writer of an option has an unlimited potential loss unless this is hedged.

- Options are useful for hedging asymmetric risk. This risk applies where the fund manager believes that the market will rise but where, under the rules of the fund, he has to hedge against any fall. If the manager's forecast is correct, his portfolio will benefit from the rise in the market. His only cost will be the option premium, which can be likened to an insurance premium.

- Futures are useful for hedging symmetric risk, where there is no particular view as to whether the market is likely to rise or fall, but where the fund manager is obliged to stabilize the value of the portfolio.

- With hindsight, the option never gives the best result for a fund manager. If the market moves upwards, he would have been better off not hedging at all, because he has lost the option premium. If the market falls, it would have been cheaper to hedge by taking a position as a seller in the appropriate futures market. However, few of us are gifted with hindsight. Complaining about 'wasting' an option premium with hindsight could be likened to complaining that a fire insurance premium turned out to be a waste of money because the house had not burned down during the insured period.

Conclusion on traded options

The traded option market has expanded very quickly over the last few years (readers should study the *Financial Times* to examine the number of classes and series of traded options available). However, the complexities of this market mean that it must remain the domain of the professional who wishes to speculate or to hedge his position, or alternatively of the speculator who can afford to risk his capital in pursuit of great potential rewards available from the gearing factor. The one saving grace of options as a speculation is that the maximum loss is capped at the premium cost. With futures as a speculation, there is unlimited potential gain or unlimited potential loss. The additional flexibility of an option for the holder, coupled with the additional risk for the writer, is the reason why premiums have to be paid.

9.14   Warrants

What are warrants and why are they issued?

Warrants in a particular company give the holder the right to subscribe for ordinary shares in that company on the terms set out in the articles of association. The price at which the warrant holder can purchase the underlying ordinary shares is called the subscription price, or sometimes the exercise price. Holders of warrants are not entitled to any dividend or voting rights, and if the subscription has not been exercised by the expiry date, the warrant becomes valueless. However, some companies appoint a trustee who will exercise the warrants if the price of the underling shares at maturity is above the subscription price, sell the shares in the market and remit the net sale proceeds minus expenses to the warrant holder. In such a case, on expiry of the warrants, the holder will receive cash, provided the trustee decides that it is worthwhile to exercise the warrants and sell the shares. If he decides it is not worthwhile, the warrants become valueless.

Warrants are dealt with on the Stock Exchange in exactly the same way as any other quoted security. The holder will receive a certificate which usually sets out the number of warrants held, and the terms on which ordinary shares can be purchased. The terms of conversion can also be found in the company's annual published accounts and in the company's Extel card.

Companies have often issued warrants as part of a 'package deal' whereby the warrants and a loan stock were issued together to make the loan stock more attractive. On completion of the issue formalities the warrants and loan stock were then quoted and dealt in as separate entities.

Investment trusts are the main category of company that issues warrants. A quick glance at the Investment Trust sections of the 'London Share Service' page of the *Financial Times* will confirm this fact.

The benefits to the company from the issue of warrants

Reducing the financial burden

No dividends or interest are paid on the warrants themselves. The company has the benefit of the proceeds of the issue of warrants (which are shown as a capital reserve in the balance sheet) at no cost to itself until and unless conversion takes place.

Taking advantage of an overvalued share price

If a company believes its share price to be overvalued, it can sell warrants to outsiders. If the company's share price does indeed fall far enough to make exercising unattractive, then the warrants will not be exercised and the capital reserve will have been acquired at no cost. However, to prevent abuses, the Stock Exchange insists that a new issue of warrants can be offered to outsiders only with the consent of the existing shareholders.

Warrants and investment trusts

By law, new issues of shares in an investment trust must be priced at their asset value. However, prices on the market often fall to a discount. Thus warrants are sometimes an essential 'sweetener' to accompany a new issue of investment trust shares. Once the issue has been made the warrants and shares are dealt with separately.

Enhancing the attraction of other issues in the 'package'

In cases where the warrants are issued as part of a 'package', the accompanying loan stock may be issued at a lower coupon because of the added attraction of the warrant. Once the issue is complete, the loan stockholder can sell the warrants in the market, or choose to hold them with the intention of exercising the warrants at a later date.

An example of a warrant

For example, in April 2001, Omega plc warrants 2002-03 were priced at 102p, and its ordinary shares at 365p. The exercise terms gave warrant holders the right to subscribe for one ordinary share for each warrant held at a subscription price (also called exercise price) of 380p between 2002 and 2003 on any of the 30-day periods each commencing on the dates falling one day after the date of posting of the annual report and accounts and the interim results of Omega plc in those years.

If we ignore dealing costs, we can see that the price of obtaining the shares via the warrants is at a premium of 32.05%. The cost of a warrant is 102p which, when added to the subscription price of 380p, makes a total cost of 482p. This means that the shares cost 117p (482 - 365) more when obtained via the warrants, and there is a premium of:

$$\frac{117 \times 100}{365} = 32.05\%$$

Premiums and discounts

Generally speaking, the premium on a warrant will be higher the longer the unexpired period for subscription, although much must depend on the prospects of the underlying shares. There have been instances, however, where the warrant price has not moved as quickly as the underlying share price, and in these instances a discount can arise.

As the warrant nears the end of its life the premium will tend to disappear as the warrants will either be exercised or will be allowed to lapse.

Time value and intrinsic value

The 'intrinsic value' of a warrant is the amount, if any, by which the current share price exceeds the subscription price. If we look back at the Omega warrant we can see that its intrinsic value is nil (365 - 380). A warrant can never have a negative intrinsic value, since the holder will simply let the warrant lapse if its subscription price on expiry is above the current market price.

The 102p warrant price consists of nil intrinsic value and 102p 'time value', which can be described as the price paid now for the opportunity to acquire the shares at a later date at a predetermined price. Perhaps a clearer name for the concept of 'time value' would be 'speculative potential'.

When the subscription price exceeds the current share price the warrant is said to be 'out of the money', whereas the term 'in the money' applies when the warrant has some intrinsic value.

Gearing

The concept of gearing has already been explained. In short, gearing exaggerates the effect of both the ups and downs of the underlying share price movements.

Let us now consider a warrant with the following features:

- Warrant price   29p
- Share price   160p
- Subscription price   177p (on a one-for-one basis)
- Expiry date   2003

Suppose the underlying share price were to double to 320p by 2003; we could then certainly expect the warrant price to settle at its intrinsic value at least. Thus the warrant could be expected to stand at 143p (320 - 177). (Indeed if the share price were to reach 320p well before 2002, then the warrant price would certainly acquire a time value on top of its intrinsic value of 143p.)

However, if the warrant reaches only 143p its increase in percentage terms is:

$$\frac{143 - 29}{29} \times 100 = 393\%$$

If we look at the converse and assume the share price never rises above 177p, the warrants would be valueless by the expiry date. This would mean that there had been a 100% loss on the warrants whereas the underlying shares could have increased in value by anything up to 10.625%

$$\frac{177 - 160}{160} \times 100 = 10.625\%$$

This hypothetical example shows how gearing on a warrant can magnify the effects of the movement in the underlying share price.

A ratio that is often calculated is the gearing factor. This is given by dividing the share price by the warrant price. For the above warrant, the gearing factor is $160 \div 29 = 5.52$. The higher the gearing factor, the greater the risk, both upwards and downwards.

Capital fulcrum point

We have just seen how gearing exaggerates the effect of the underlying share price. In our example we saw that a rise of 10.625% or less in the share price at the expiry date would result in a 100% loss in warrant value, whereas a 100% rise in the share price would result in a 393% rise in the warrants.

The capital fulcrum point can be defined as the annual percentage equity growth required (between purchase date and expiry date of the subscription rights in the warrant) for an investor to gain equally, in terms of pure capital gain, whether he buys the warrants or the shares. In practice the quickest and easiest method to calculate the capital fulcrum point is by trial and error.

Example of capital fulcrum point for a warrant

The details of a warrant's subscription rights are as follows:

- Time to expiry date   8 years
- Subscription/exercise price 153p
- Today's warrant price   38p
- Today's share price   149p

If the share price grows by 4% per annum compound, after eight years it will rise to 204p. (A simple check is to multiply 149 by 1.04^8 or alternatively multiply by 1.04 then multiply that result by 1.04, repeating the operation eight times in all.) At the expiry date, the warrant price will consist purely of its intrinsic value which will be (204 - 153) = 51p.

If the warrant grows at the same 4% per annum compounded, it will indeed reach 52p after eight years. (Check as before by multiplying 38 by 1.04 or 104% repeating the process eight times in all.)

In the above example the investor will make a marginally better capital gain on the warrants over eight years if the growth rate of the shares exceeds 4% per annum compound. Obviously the lower the capital fulcrum point, the greater the attraction of the warrant as opposed to the equity.

There is, inevitably, a formula for calculating the capital fulcrum point.

$$\left(\frac{E}{S - W} \right)^{1/N}$$

Where:

E = exercise price = 153p

S = spot share price = 149p

W = warrant price = 38p

N = the remaining life of the warrant in years = 8

Applying the formula to the above warrant, we see that the capital fulcrum point is shown as:

$$(153 \div 111)^{1/8} = 1.0409 = 4.09\%$$

Points to bear in mind when evaluating a warrant

If there is a likelihood of a takeover, the warrant holder could suffer very badly if the warrant is 'out of the money'. Under the terms of the issue of almost all warrants there is a clause stating that in the event of a successful takeover of the company, the subscription expiry date will be brought forward to coincide with the bid. The successful bidder must then offer the intrinsic value of the warrants calculated on his offer price to the ordinary shareholders. However, there is no obligation to compensate the warrant holders for lost 'time value'.

Let us revert to our previous example of a warrant, and refresh our memories on the salient points:

- Warrant price   29p
- Share price   160p
- Subscription/exercise price 177p
- Expiry date   2003

The warrant is 'out of the money' because the subscription price exceeds the current share price. Suppose there is a successful takeover at a general offer price of 180p. The warrant expiry date would be brought forward, and the successful bidder would have to offer the intrinsic value of the warrants, i.e. 3p (180 - 177).

The conclusion from all this is that when a warrant's price consists mainly of time value, the warrant holder should sell his warrant on the first news of a takeover bid, unless the offer price is vastly above the current share price. Having no votes, warrant holders cannot exercise any influence on the outcome of the takeover.

Capitalization issues and rights issues

The warrant holder can view such issues with equanimity, because the Stock Exchange requires the company to protect warrant holders from suffering any loss due from a fall in the ex capitalization or ex rights price.

Liquidation

The rights of a warrant holder in liquidation will depend on the terms of the issue. In any event a warrant is classed as capital, and the warrant holder will rank behind all external creditors.

Capital fulcrum point

The lower the capital fulcrum point, the more attractive the warrants.

Expiry date

The longer the expiry date the better, because there is a greater chance of a favourable movement in the price of the underlying shares. The current market price of the warrant could well contain a large 'time value' in recognition of the value of a long timescale.

The company

As with convertibles, the golden rule is not to buy warrants unless the investor expects the company to be successful.

Capital gains tax

Warrants do not constitute a 'wasting share' for CGT purposes, thus an unexercised warrant becomes valueless on expiry of the subscription period, and is classed as a loss for CGT purposes. If the warrant is exercised, the cost of the shares for CGT purposes is the exercise price plus the cost of the warrants.

Conclusion

Because of the gearing factor, warrants are really suitable only for investors who can afford to risk their capital in the hope of a great reward. Remember there is neither dividend nor voting rights unless and until the subscription is made

9.15   Spread betting

Comparison of spread betting to normal share trading

Spread betting is essentially is placing a bet that the price of an index, commodity or share will rise or fall by a certain value per point. For example, if a speculator considered that the price of XYZ stock was likely to fall by a significant amount, he could sell XYZ shares via a spread bet. The spread betting company will make a buy and sell (bid and offer/ask) price on the XYZ shares and the difference between the bid offer price is known as a 'spread'. The spread is effectively the spread betting company's commission, but it incorporates an allowance for tax so any gains from the spread bet are exempt from UK capital gains tax.

Returning to XYZ shares, let us assume a spread betting company is quoting them at 337-340p. The speculator could sell XYZ to the spread betting company an agreed amount per point (a point equates to one penny in the price) at 337. Let us assume the price of XYZ does indeed fall and the amount of the fall is 50p. Assuming the spread remains at 3p, the spread betting company will now quote a spread of 287-290p. Thus the speculator will make a profit of 47 points (337- 290) because he can sell at 337 and buy back at 290. If the amount per point had been set at £100, then 47 points will translate into a monetary gain of £4,700, whereas the gain would have been £47 if the price had been £1 per point.

Obviously, if the price of XYZ had risen, as opposed to having fallen, then the speculator would make a loss. Let us assume the price of XYZ had risen by 50 pence and that the spread remained unchanged at 3 points, then the spread quote would have been 387-390, and there would have been a loss of 53 points.

For the speculator to carry out the same speculative activity in the actual market, he would have to sell 100 shares of XYZ at, say, 338.5p (the bid/offer spread in the actual market would be around 0.5p as opposed to the 3 points spread from the spread-betting quote). He could then buy them back at say 289p. On the face of it, speculation in the real share market is the preferred option, because there is a much narrower bid/offer spread. However, the following need to be considered:

● It may not be possible to 'short sell' shares that the speculator does not actually own, bearing in mind the three-day settlement period for settlement of stock exchange deals in the real market, and bearing in mind that the intention is for settlement to move to a two-day settlement basis.

● There may well be brokers' commission to pay on sales and repurchases of shares.

● There could be capital gains tax liabilities on deals in the real market.

● Spread betting provides a simple and economical technique for speculation below a certain value per point. It is possible to trade for as low as 50p a point, so private investors (speculators) could easily enter such a market. However, the risks are enormous, and spread betting should be undertaken only by investors who fully understand the risks involved.

Comparison of spread betting and futures markets

As with the FTSE 100 Index future, spread betting can be a means of hedging against adverse price movements. If the spread bet shown to sell XYZ shares had been made by someone who actually owned such shares, then, provided the price per point had been set to match the underlying number of shares owned, the bet would have hedged the owner of XYZ shares against a fall in the share price. Any fall in the underlying shares price would have been compensated by a gain on the spread bet, whereas any rise in the share price would have been offset by a loss on the spread bet. This spread bet would have enabled the investor to maintain the value of his wealth without needing to sell the shares and incur brokers' fees and potential capital gains tax.

Thus spread betting is, essentially, very similar to futures trading.

● Gearing applies to both futures and spread betting since both involve trading against a form of margin payment. The winnings or losses will be magnified.

● As on futures markets, spread bets have an expiry date. As the maturity date approaches, the spread bet price will gradually become closer to the underlying share price, in the same way that the FTSE 100 Index futures price will gradually approach the spot index price as the maturity date approaches.

How to start spread betting

In the UK, spread betting companies generally take out stringent credit checks on new clients, so people with a poor credit history are unable to access the facility. With some overseas-based companies, a trading account can be opened literally in a few minutes via the Internet so long as valid credit card details can be produced. Some spread betting companies offer accounts in either investor or player mode. Player mode is for simulated trading and provides the same prices as the real-money investor account. Trying out a player account is a good way of practising your spread-betting skills.

Conclusion on spread betting

The spread-betting business, essentially part of the derivatives industry, has seen explosive growth over the past three years and the UK is leading the way. The spread bet, on say an equity, can be considered as a derivative instrument of that equity, dependant but separate from it, just as a traded option is dependent on but separate from the underlying share. The basic difference between spread betting and derivatives is that spread betting facilities can be accessed with a much smaller initial outlay than is required to access the derivatives markets. Spread bets are suited to short-term speculation of relatively small amounts of money.

9.16   Contracts for difference (CFDs)

Contracts for difference work in a similar way to a future, and they have been described as a type of equity derivative. There is no stamp duty on CFDs, but capital gains tax is payable on profits, although losses on CFDs can be set off against profits for CGT purposes.

The CFDs are over-the-counter (OTC) instruments, so there are no restrictions on the deals that can be arranged between investors/speculators and CFD providers, provided the terms are mutually acceptable.

Minimum initial exposures on CFDs are usually £25,000, and investors usually need to prove that they have liquid assets of up to £100,000 at their disposal. In addition, the Financial Services Authority insists that any investors in CFDs must have experience in equity and margin trading before they can enter into CFDs.

An investor can use a CFD to go long or short on a share. If he thinks the share price will rise, he will go long and he will go short if he thinks a fall is likely. Thus a person who 'goes long' on a CFD will gain on the CFD if the underlying share price rises, whereas a person who 'goes short' will gain if the underlying share price falls. In order to access CFDs the investor will phone or e-mail his CFD provider, advising the provider of the name of the share, how many shares and whether he wishes to go long or short. The CFD provider will quote a price, which will be based on the current share price.

Example of a long CFD contract

The investor wishes to go long on a CFD in 10,000 shares of XYZ plc at 500p, which is equivalent to a total exposure of £50,000.

The investor will be required to pay an up-front margin (similar to the initial margin on a future) but this will usually be 20% of the exposure. The margin here could be £10,000.

Each day a process takes place which is equivalent to the mark-to-market/variation margin process on a future.

If the share price rises to 520p on day one then the long will receive 10,000 x 20p= £2,000 from the CFD provider. If the shares fall to 510p the next day, then the long will pay the CFD provider £1,000, and so on.

Usually there is no pre-set expiry date on the CFD, and the provider will keep the contract in being so long as all margin call obligations have been met.

There is also an interest charge made by the CFD provider. A typical charge would be LIBOR + 2.5% on the balance of a long position not covered by the initial deposit. The interest will be charged over the time the CFD remains in being. There will also be a commission charge of around 0.25% of the total CFD exposure.

The CFD can be closed out at any time by the long and the initial margin will then be returned to him.

On the face of it seems strange that a long has to pay interest to the CFD provider on the balance not covered by the initial margin. However, at the time the CFD is first agreed, the CFD provider may have to invest £40,000 of his own money (£50,000 – £10,000) in XYZ shares to offset his own risks.

If the XYZ shares that are subject to this transaction rise in value, the CFD provider will have protected himself by holding the shares. Any losses (from the CFD provider's perspective) on the long CFD trade will be hedged by the increase in the value of the XYZ shares held by the provider. Conversely, any fall in value of XYZ shares will result in a gain for the provider on the long CFD, but this will be offset by a loss for the provider on the value of the XYZ shares the provider holds.

Short CFDs

These work in the opposite way to long CFDs. Here the short will receive a payment when the price of the underlying XYZ shares falls, and will make a payment when that price rises. Short CFDs are a means whereby speculators can effectively 'sell short' shares they do not own, the price of which they expect to fall. The usual initial margin is payable at about 20% of the exposure.

There will again be a commission charge of about 0.25% of the total exposure on the CFD, but interest on the difference between the full exposure and the initial margin payment will be paid to the short during the life of the CFD. A typical interest rate here would be LIBOR minus 2.5%. Naturally the CFD provider will wish to build in a good profit margin on the interest payments of his CFD positions.

The reason the short receives interest is that the CFD provider could in theory sell the underlying shares today to convert them into cash. From the provider's point of view the hedge would work as follows:

- any fall in the value of the underlying shares will result in a loss to the CFD provider under the CFD

- this loss on the short CFD for the provider will be offset by the fact that the underlying shares have been sold and converted into cash. Thus the wealth of the CFD provider should remain unaffected by his losses on short CFDs.

An overview of derivatives

Derivatives can be used as a risk transfer tool, for example to hedge the value of an underlying portfolio. Alternatively they can be used for speculation by taking advantage of the gearing effect when there is no underlying position in the equity market to hedge. Indeed a derivative can be likened to a fire. It can be used for protection against the cold (as a hedge) or the fire can be a potential source of calamity if it burns you (speculation).

10

INVESTING OVERSEAS

Objectives

After studying this chapter, you should be able to:

● appreciate the motives for overseas investment;

● evaluate the benefits, drawbacks and risks of investing overseas;

● assess the various methods of purchasing overseas shares;

● define and describe the main features of overseas bonds and Eurobonds;

● define and describe bearer securities, marking certificates and depositary receipts;

● assess the impact of the European single currency on overseas investment;

● identify the problems of investing in emerging markets.

10.1   The motives for overseas investment

For most of people their biggest asset is their earning capacity. This ability is sometimes called human capital. A logical conclusion is that, in the long run, returns on human capital will be closely linked to returns on domestic equities. If the UK stock market does well then the earning capacity of UK citizens should also rise, because the returns on both human capital and on domestic equities are linked to the performance of the domestic economy. Thus overseas equities would appear to be an appropriate hedge against the risk of a domestic economic disaster. Let us consider the experience of Japan to illustrate this link and to show how overseas investment can hedge the risk of poor returns on human capital.

Over the last decade the Japanese stock market has fallen by two-thirds at the same time as real wages have stagnated and unemployment has risen. Thus a Japanese investor who has held a diversified portfolio of Japanese equities over this period will have experienced poor returns on human capital as well as on his equities. By investing overseas, this Japanese investor could have hedged his return on human capital, since most non-Japanese stock markets have experienced excellent rises over the period in question.

Returning to the UK now, there are other arguments for international diversification apart from that of hedging human capital. We must remember that the UK accounts for just 6 per cent of the world's gross domestic product, so it is obvious that there must be a vast amount of potential investment opportunities in other economies. Overseas investment exposes the portfolios of UK investors to markets that may be in a different phase of the economic cycle to the UK, and also provides exposure to industries that do not exist at all in the UK, such as diamond and gold mining, or ones where the UK is not a strong competitor. Exposure to overseas investments is therefore considered to provide an additional way of diversifying into investments whose returns may not be strongly correlated to investment returns in the investor's domestic market.

Inevitably, there are arguments against overseas investment. Let us consider the link between the return on human capital and that on domestic equity. For many long-term investors the motive for the investment in equities is the desire to provide an income in retirement. Most of this income could be spent on goods and services that cannot be internationally traded, such eating out, or on nursing care. It could be argued that the return on domestic equities will in the long run be linked to the prices of domestic non-tradeable goods and services. This argument gives a rational basis for investment in domestic equities as opposed to overseas equities.

Another argument against international diversification is that statistics show international stock markets mostly tend to move in a similar way during bear markets. Thus overseas investment will fail to yield the promised protection from diversification just when that protection is needed most. In addition, it can be argued that investment in UK companies gives exposure to overseas economies anyway. Major UK companies such as Shell, British Airways and GlaxoSmithKline are examples of UK companies with a large element of overseas earnings.

Thus, as ever, there is no really clear-cut argument for and against overseas investment. Much will depend on the particular circumstances of the investor.

What is not in doubt is that investing overseas is more complex than investing in the UK stock market and investors are exposed to extra risks, such as currency risk, that need specialist management. This chapter considers the various issues that need to be taken into account when deciding to invest overseas.

10.2   Overseas equity investment

Advantages of overseas investment

The UK stock market is the third largest in the world in terms of total market capitalization, behind the USA, which is the largest, and Japan, the second largest. These three markets are the world's major equity markets. They are commonly known as the 'golden triangle', and due to time differences one of these three is always open.

The European markets are all smaller than the UK with France, Germany, the Netherlands, Spain, Sweden and Switzerland representing the other major European equity markets. As different economies are at different stages of the economic cycle at any one time, there is potential for large gains (and losses) by investing in overseas equity markets. Currency movements between sterling and an overseas currency can generate higher profits when sterling falls against the overseas currency.

In addition to the well-established or developed markets we have discussed, there are also the 'emerging markets' in the old communist countries, and Latin American, Asian and European countries.

10.3   Emerging markets

These markets account for a fairly small proportion of the world's stock markets by market capitalization. There is no definitive definition of an 'emerging market' but economists usually consider that the term applies to a country in the middle-income range in national income per head, which has reasonably well-developed and freely-functioning financial markets.

Many of these countries' listed companies are small in market capitalization compared to international rivals and there may be only a few quoted shares of companies of modest size. Such markets can be very volatile because large buy and sell orders in one stock can move the market dramatically due to a lack of liquidity.

10.4   The risks of overseas investment

Corporate governance

The UK and USA have a very highly-developed system of corporate governance (see Chapter 2). In addition many non-US companies now have a listing on the American stock markets which means that they must comply with the US corporate governance laws. However, for overseas companies that are not in this category, corporate governance can be very rudimentary or even non-existent. In some countries in Europe and elsewhere there are complex cross-holdings of shares, a legacy of the historical influence of banks as shareholders. This can mean that the rights of minority shareholders are not protected by a code of corporate governance, and that there can be scope for conflicts of interest.

Liquidity

In emerging markets, liquidity can be problem. At times when the market is falling it can be difficult to find a buyer. However, this liquidity problem is not necessarily confined to emerging markets. Some partly-privatized European companies can still have a large percentage of their equity in government hands, with only a small percentage available to be traded on the stock market. Companies with complex cross-holdings of shares may be rarely traded on the market. The shares available for trading on a regular basis are known as free float and this free float can sometimes fall below 30% of the shares. Potential investors should always check on the free float if investing in overseas companies that are not major international names listed on the UK or US stock markets.

Foreign currency

Although currency movements can work in favour of the investor, they can also work against him. It is not unknown for a rise in the value of sterling against the currency in which an overseas investment is denominated to wipe out all the profits made in local currency terms. But this works both ways – returns can be enhanced by currency movements. This is called the exchange risk.

Dividends are received in foreign currency, thus the cheque will have to be converted to sterling. There are costs associated with such a transaction and the investor is exposed to the fluctuation of exchange rates.

Political risk

There is a 'political risk' involved in certain countries. Although a country may appear to be politically stable when an investment is made, changes may take place that wreck that stability. This is often thought of as a problem relating to emerging markets, but potentially it can affect any country.

While the UK does not have any exchange-control regulations at present, other countries do have them, or could easily introduce them. If this occurs it may be impossible for an investor to remove his money from that country. This may mean that dividends or sale proceeds cannot be remitted to the UK and no profit on that investment can be realized.

Taxation

Certain countries have made double taxation agreements with the UK. Where these are in place, the UK resident, who is of course liable to UK tax on his overseas investments, will receive a credit to offset against his UK tax liability if the investment has also been subject to tax in the overseas country. For example, if the overseas dividends are subject to a 10% 'withholding tax' levied by the overseas government, the UK tax liability will be reduced by the same amount. The maximum amount of double taxation relief available cannot exceed the UK tax liability of the investor. Thus a withholding tax of 40% is only allowed for up to 10% on dividends for a basic rate taxpayer, the investor 'pays' the extra 30% himself in effect to the overseas government. In the main the investors who suffer most from any withholding tax are non-taxpayers, because in many cases it is not possible to reclaim the withholding tax from the overseas government.

Disclosure and accountancy policies

The standards of accountancy policies, disclosure requirements and internal controls in overseas markets do not always match up to the UK standards. Where this is the case an investor may not be aware of any adverse trends or unhealthy situations until it is too late. However, any non-US companies that are listed on the US stock markets will have to conform to the very strict US accountancy and disclosure rules.

Information

It used to be very difficult to obtain information about overseas companies from the UK press, thus monitoring performance used to be very difficult. However, many of the major overseas companies now have websites which even show analysts' presentations and broker research. In addition, up-to-date price changes can now be followed on various IT-based media. The London Stock Exchange has an International Retail Service (IRS) which gives real-time quotes on 111 overseas companies. In addition, Euronext, The New York Stock Exchange and Nasdaq all have websites with useful data on overseas equities. In addition, the FTSE All-World Index Series enables an investor to follow the general progress of overseas markets in terms of US$. (See Chapter 19 for details of all *Financial Times* Indices.) It is more difficult to find information about companies in the smaller, emerging markets. Any press comment will be in their own national press thus, unless the investor is fluent in a specific language, problems can arise, although English-language business publications are available in many countries. There is now regular emerging markets coverage in publications such as the *Financial Times* and in addition there are specialist emerging market indices such as the IFC Emerging Markets Weekly Investable Indices to help to judge performance. We consider market indices in more detail in Chapter 19.

Settlement periods, board lots and restrictions on non-resident holdings

Different stock exchanges have different settlement periods, and some exchanges deal only in 'board lots', i.e. shares are sold only in multiples of, say, 1,000 shares. For example, in Japan, 90% of quoted stock is available only in lots of 1,000 shares.

Some countries, or sometimes some companies, restrict the proportion of shares that can be held by overseas investors. In such cases, these limited holdings may command a premium price compared to domestic holdings. This higher price may make the shares less attractive to investors, particularly as there is no difference in the amount of dividend paid to national and overseas investors.

Some overseas stock exchanges not only limit the number of shares held by overseas investors, but also place restrictions on the voting rights of overseas investors.

10.5 The various methods of purchasing overseas equities and the risks involved

There are several methods available to investors interested in overseas equity investment. Some are safer than others, and an investor's choice will depend on the amount of risk he is willing to take.

Purchasing shares of an overseas company on an overseas stock exchange

In the past , transaction costs for dealing in overseas equities could be relatively high. However, the London Stock Exchange's International Retail Service (IRS) enables members to purchase any one of 111 major international stocks at the same cost as the purchase of UK domestic stocks. There are plans to include many more international stocks on the IRS. One stock currently available there is Microsoft. For other overseas equities, many UK stockbrokers will be willing to make the necessary arrangements to purchase the shares on the overseas stock exchange. This can be an expensive operation because the UK stockbroker has to deal via a broker in the overseas market, thus incurring heavy dealing costs. This method of overseas investment is suitable only for the institutional investors who have very large amounts to invest, and the necessary expertise available to monitor and manage the risks involved.

A cheaper alternative for the individual investor is web-based trading, with the investor maintaining an account with an overseas broker via the web. But the investor would need to make funds available in the appropriate foreign currency, thereby opening up the exchange risk.

Purchasing shares of an overseas company quoted on the London Stock Exchange

Shares in certain companies are available on their own domestic stock exchange and on the London Stock Exchange (LSE). Some of these shares are quoted fully on the LSE. In the *Financial Times* London Share Service you will find price and yield information for some American, Canadian, Australian and South African shares along with other companies that are included under headings such as 'Oil and Gas, and Mining sectors'. Other overseas companies can be found in other sectors, but these two sectors represent a large number of the overseas companies quoted in London.

The advantages of purchasing overseas shares by this method is that it reduces the problems of exchange risk, because the shares are bought and sold in sterling (although the dividend received may well be in currency). It is also easier to obtain information about these companies from sources such as the financial press because the LSE requires all listed companies to supply certain information as a requirement of obtaining and maintaining a quotation.

Purchasing shares of a UK company with large overseas interests

There are quite a few UK multinational companies whose profits depend quite heavily on their overseas operations. Companies such as GlaxoSmithKline (a pharmaceutical and health care company) export a large percentage of their products to overseas markets and maintain substantial operations in a number of overseas countries. A company such as HSBC provides banking services in a large number of overseas countries, particularly in the Asian and Far East markets as well as in the UK. The success or otherwise of the overseas and exporting activities will be reflected in the profits of these companies.

This method of investment not only reduces the exchange risk but also the problems of accountancy, disclosure and control requirements, because these companies are subject to the UK requirements laid down by the Companies Acts 1985 and 1989 and the Stock Exchange's 'Continuing Obligations'. In addition, this method also removes the problem of finding enough information in the financial press.

Indirect investment in overseas equities

Even though investors may wish to benefit from the opportunities provided by investing overseas, many do not possess the time and expertise necessary to manage direct equity investment, and some investors who would like an element of overseas exposure do not have enough money available for direct equity investment on a large enough scale. To overcome these problems, indirect investment overseas is the answer. This provides professional management and diversification. The three methods that are available are unit trusts, investment trusts and OEICs (Open Ended Investment Companies). (For details of these investment vehicles see Chapters 14 and 15.)

Minimum amounts for direct investment in overseas equities

Direct investment in overseas equities should only be considered for portfolios in excess of £1 million. The minimum amount per share for cost effectiveness is considered by experts to be £5,000 per share.

10.6   Overseas bonds

A bond is an interest-bearing certificate of debt, issued by large companies, governments, banks, supranational organizations (e.g. The World Bank) and by nationalized industries. Most bonds carry a fixed rate of interest, are repayable at or between set future dates and can be traded in the secondary market at any time up to maturity.

The standing of these bonds depends greatly on the standing of the issuer. If the investor is considering overseas bonds as part of his portfolio, he will need to evaluate the risk profile of the issuing country or company as well as taking into account the exchange risk.

Foreign government bonds

As we have seen in previous units, bonds issued by the UK government are called gilt-edged securities. Bonds issued by the government in the US are 'Treasury bonds' or 'T' bonds, in France they are called OATs (*obligation à trésorerie*) and in Japan JGBs (Japanese Government Bonds). With all government securities, their standing depends very much on the government issuing them. Some foreign government securities have virtually 'gilt-edged' status, such as Finnish and Swedish stocks, while others are virtually worthless except as collector's items. An example of one such stock is the pre-revolution Chinese Boxer issue which can be purchased for less than £10 per nominal £100 stock, because the likelihood of a modern Chinese government offering any terms at all for repayment is virtually nil. However, the certificates themselves are collected for their artistic merit and thus have a value in themselves.

Some foreign governments have defaulted on or deferred interest and/or capital payments. In such cases the Council of Foreign Bondholders will exert pressure on the defaulting government to make it pay. The council's main weapon is that eventually defaulting governments will need to raise fresh capital, and when this happens it may have enough power to insist upon agreement being reached with existing creditors before the new loan can be agreed.

A number of foreign government securities have been issued in London in sterling and these have been nicknamed 'bulldog bonds'. Interest is payable in London, in sterling on these bonds, thus there is no problem with exchange risk. However, issues denominated in a foreign currency are affected by the exchange risk, and the fluctuations of the currency must be taken into account when investing.

Eurobonds

A Eurobond is a loan to a government, public body or company underwritten by an international syndicate of banks and sold in countries other than the country of issue. Interest rates can be fixed or floating. A floating-rate note Eurobond (FRN) denominated in US$ has its interest rate linked to the interbank rate for Eurodollars, and this link to market rates should make the bond price stable. The principal currencies of issue are dollars, euros, yen and sterling.

Eurobonds are issued in bearer form, and as with all bearer securities, interest is claimed by submitting a coupon. It is safer to keep the certificate in safe custody, and depositories such as Euroclear provide safe-custody facilities for Eurobonds, in addition to the usual UK banks' facilities. There is no withholding tax on Eurobond interest, although EU pressures on the UK government may change this, but such income must be declared on the investor's tax return. Income tax is payable and any capital gain is subject to CGT.

10.7　Bearer securities

These are stocks and shares issued mainly by overseas companies, public bodies and governments. The issuer does not maintain a register of ownership, whereas with virtually all UK stocks and shares there is a register. Some gilts have part of the issue available in bearer form, one example is 3½% War Loan. A few UK-registered companies also have part of their share capital in bearer form.

Ownership of a bearer security vests in the holder of the certificate and passes by mere delivery, unlike registered stocks and shares where ownership is transferred by the system described in Chapter 5. There is no owner's name shown anywhere on the certificate.

A problem here arises if the share certificate is stolen, and a bona fide transferee for value purchases the certificate from the thief. If this occurred the original owner would lose all his rights to the shares. To safeguard against this occurrence, a bearer certificate should be kept in a safe place such as a bank. Many banks, such as Citibank and Barclays Bank, act as global custodians, whereby they hold bearer securities and claim all dividends due for onward remittance to the owner of the shares.

Keeping a bearer certificate with a bank has other advantages also. Because there is no register of holders, the issuing authority does not know where to send notice of meetings, circulars and dividends. Such items are always preceded by advertisements in the financial press or the Bond Holders' Register. In the case of dividend payments the advertisement will inform holders which coupon to submit in order to claim the dividend and the custodian or bank will claim the dividend for the owner of the bearer security.

Coupons are attached to the certificate and are numbered. Each time a dividend is claimed the relevantly numbered coupon is detached and sent to the issuer or, more usually, a bank acting as a 'paying agent' on its behalf. At some time the coupons will run out and the next set of coupons in numerical order will be claimed by submission of the 'talon' which is the last coupon and is larger than the other coupons. Obviously for the private investor it can be easy to miss the dividend notice, and failure to claim the dividend can lead to forfeiting that dividend. If the certificate is lodged with the bank then there is no likelihood of this happening because the bank is geared up to checking for such items. Another advantage here is that the bank will amalgamate all the coupons belonging to different holders and make one claim. The cheque received is in currency and must be converted into sterling for distribution to the individual holders. The cost of this is divided between all the holders and it is less than the cost to an individual holder with one cheque to convert into sterling. See the Robeco bearer shares for an example of a bearer share, coupons and talon (see Figures 9.1 and 9.2).

Figure 9.1: Robeco Bearer Share Certificate

20 x ƒ 50,—

KC0055164

KC0055164

ROBECO

Rotterdamsch
Beleggingsconsortium N.V.
GEVESTIGD TE ROTTERDAM

Bewijs van
twintig aandelen
AAN TOONDER

ELK GROOT

VIJFTIG GULDEN

ROTTERDAM, 29 APRIL 1979

COMMISSARIS   DIRECTEUR

Dividenden, waarover binnen 5 jaren nadat zij betaalbaar zijn, niet is
beschikt, vervallen ten behoeve van de vennootschap.

KC0055164

KC0055164

Figure 9.2: Robeco Talon and Coupons

In order for a bearer certificate to be sold it must be 'good delivery'. This means that the certificate must be in good condition and all coupons that should be attached must be attached. If there is any doubt as to whether the certificate is 'good delivery' application must be made to the Council of the Stock Exchange, who will rule on the matter.

The final area that can be a problem with bearer securities is the danger of forged documents. Obviously as ownership can pass by mere delivery it is quite feasible that a forged document could escape careful scrutiny resulting in a purchaser holding a worthless piece of paper. Here again the bank would be in a position to verify the genuineness of the certificate purchased.

10.8 Marking certificates (shares registered in a recognized (or good) marking name)

These are shares issued mainly by US and Canadian companies. They are registered shares. The name of the registered holder appears on the front of the certificate and the company maintains a register of holders in exactly the same way as for any registered share.

The difference between marking certificates and ordinary UK-registered shares is that the transfer form on the reverse of the share certificate is blank endorsed. This means that the registered holder signs the form in front of a witness, who also must sign, but then leaves the rest of the form blank. This has the effect of making title pass by mere delivery, i.e. the certificate acquires most of the characteristics of a bearer security. (See Figures 9.3 and 9.4, the BellSouth Corporation certificate.)

Figure 9.3: BellSouth Marking Certificate

Figure 9.4: Reverse Side of BellSouth Marking Certificate

THIS CERTIFICATE ALSO EVIDENCES AND ENTITLES THE HOLDER HEREOF TO CERTAIN RIGHTS AS SET FORTH IN A RIGHTS AGREEMENT BETWEEN BELLSOUTH CORPORATION AND AMERICAN TRANSTECH INC., AS RIGHTS AGENT, DATED NOVEMBER 27, 1989 (THE "RIGHTS AGREEMENT"), THE TERMS OF WHICH ARE INCORPORATED HEREIN BY REFERENCE AND A COPY OF WHICH IS ON FILE AT THE PRINCIPAL EXECUTIVE OFFICE OF BELLSOUTH CORPORATION. UNDER CERTAIN CIRCUMSTANCES, AS SET FORTH IN THE RIGHTS AGREEMENT, SUCH RIGHTS WILL BE EVIDENCED BY SEPARATE CERTIFICATES AND WILL NO LONGER BE EVIDENCED BY THIS CERTIFICATE. BELLSOUTH CORPORATION WILL MAIL TO THE HOLDER OF RECORD OF THIS CERTIFICATE A COPY OF THE RIGHTS AGREEMENT, WITHOUT CHARGE, WITHIN FIVE DAYS AFTER RECEIPT OF A WRITTEN REQUEST THEREFOR. UNDER CERTAIN CIRCUMSTANCES, AS PROVIDED IN THE RIGHTS AGREEMENT, RIGHTS ISSUED TO OR BENEFICIALLY OWNED BY ACQUIRING PERSONS OR THEIR ASSOCIATES OR AFFILIATES (AS DEFINED IN THE RIGHTS AGREEMENT) OR ANY PURPORTED SUBSEQUENT HOLDER OF SUCH RIGHTS WILL BECOME NULL AND VOID.

BELLSOUTH CORPORATION
Relative Rights and Preferences of Classes of Stock of the Company

The Company is authorized to issue one or more series of preferred stock, and the shares represented hereby will be subordinate to each of such series with respect to dividends and amounts payable upon liquidation. The Company will furnish to any shareholder, upon request and without charge, a full statement of the designations, preferences, limitations and relative rights of the common and preferred stocks of the Company and the variations in the relative rights and preferences between the shares of each series of preferred stock insofar as the same have been fixed and determined. The Board of Directors of the Company is authorized to fix and determine the relative rights and preferences of each series of preferred stock at the time of its issuance in the manner provided in Georgia Business Corporation Code Section 14-2-81, as amended, and the Articles of Incorporation. Requests may be addressed to the Transfer Agent named on the face of this Certificate or to the Secretary of the Company in Atlanta, Georgia.

The following abbreviations, when used in the inscription on the face of this certificate, shall be construed as though the words set forth below opposite each abbreviation were written out in full where such abbreviation appears:

TEN COM	-- as tenants in common
TEN ENT	-- as tenants by the entireties
JT ENT	-- as joint tenants with right of survivorship and not as tenants in common

UNIF TRANS MIN ACT — _____ Custodian _____
(Cust) (Minor)
under Uniform Transfers to Minors
Act _____ _____
(State)

Additional abbreviations may also be used though not in the above list.

For Value received, _____ hereby sell, assign and transfer _____ Shares represented by the within Certificate unto

PLEASE PRINT OR TYPE:
SOCIAL SECURITY NUMBER OR TAXPAYER IDENTIFYING NUMBER, NAME AND ADDRESS, INCLUDING ZIP CODE, OF ASSIGNEE

SHARES

PLEASE PRINT OR TYPE:
SOCIAL SECURITY NUMBER OR TAXPAYER IDENTIFYING NUMBER, NAME AND ADDRESS, INCLUDING ZIP CODE, OF ASSIGNEE

SHARES

and do hereby irrevocably constitute and appoint _____

_____ Attorney

to transfer the said shares on the records of the within named Company with full power of substitution in the premises. _____

Dated, _____   _____

IMPORTANT { BEFORE SIGNING, READ AND COMPLY CAREFULLY WITH REQUIREMENTS PRINTED BELOW.

THE SIGNATURE(S) TO THIS ASSIGNMENT MUST CORRESPOND WITH THE NAME(S) AS WRITTEN UPON THE FACE OF THE CERTIFICATE IN EVERY PARTICULAR WITHOUT ALTERATION OR ENLARGEMENT OR ANY CHANGE WHATEVER. THE SIGNATURE(S) SHOULD BE GUARANTEED BY A COMMERCIAL BANK OR TRUST COMPANY, OR BY A MEMBER OF THE EXCHANGE(S) ON WHICH THIS STOCK IS LISTED WHOSE SIGNATURE IS KNOWN TO THE TRANSFER AGENT.

Director.

The registered holder is called the 'marking name' and appears in the issuing company's books as the holder of the certificate. The marking name receives all correspondence, rights and capitalization issue details and dividends. The marking name must then account to the true owner for all of these. It is usual for the marking name to be a member firm of the Stock Exchange, bank or financial institution recognized as being of impeccable standing by the Stock Exchange. Such a marking name is classified as a 'good marking name' or 'recognized marking name', and shares registered in a 'good or recognized marking name' command a higher price than ones in a 'bad marking name', i.e. in the name of someone or a body not recognized by the Stock Exchange for this purpose. The 'good marking name' will give the Stock Exchange an undertaking to pay interest and dividends to the true owner when he claims them. Interest and dividends are paid in the currency of the issuing company's country and the 'good marking name' also undertakes to the Stock Exchange to convert the currency cheques at the approved rate of exchange.

There is no reason why the true owner of a marking certificate should not have the shares registered in his own name. To do so he will complete the form on the back of the certificate, showing himself as assignee. He will then send the certificate and the required fee to the issuing authority who will delete the 'good marking name' from their books as holder and insert the true owner's name. They will then issue a new share certificate showing him as registered owner on the front of the certificate. However, it is inadvisable for the true owner to carry out this operation for four reasons:

- The shares will command a lower price in a 'bad marking name', i.e. in a private individual's name as opposed to being in a 'good marking name'.

- There is a fee to be paid to carry out this operation.

- The shareholder will receive a currency cheque and will have to pay the full cost of converting this into sterling. If his holding is not very large, or the dividend is small, he may find that the charges virtually take the whole of the value of the cheque. The issuing authority itself also deducts a charge for paying a dividend to an individual.

- It takes a long time for ownership to be transferred, one reason being that you are dealing with a company abroad, and postal times can be long.

In conclusion it can be seen that it is better to retain the shares in a good marking name. Because the shares are blank endorsed they are effectively bearer shares, and for safety should be kept in the bank. The bank will claim the dividends due, and in the same way as with true bearer shares, the costs of changing the dividend cheque into sterling is divided between all the holders, thus the true owner will effectively receive a higher dividend than he would if he transferred the shares into his own name.

These certificates have the name 'marking certificates' because in the past each time the dividend was claimed the certificate was marked. However, most banks now do not mark the certificate every time the dividend is claimed.

If a shareholder has a marking certificate registered in his own name, it is recommended that he has the shares registered in the name of a good marking name. The major benefit of having the shares transferred into a good marking name is that all dividend cheques are converted to sterling at a lower fee than charged by most banks and that the price of the certificates will be higher in a good marking name.

10.9 Comparison of bearer securities and marking certificates

There is often confusion as to where bearer securities end and marking certificates begin. Because they are both bearer in nature does not mean they are totally identical. Marking certificates acquire only some of the attributes of bearer shares, and the differences and similarities are best seen by the following table of comparison.

Bearer Securities	Marking Certificates
Stocks and shares of a company which are not recorded in any register of share ownership. Mainly issued by overseas companies.	Shares of companies, usually American, Canadian or Dutch, endorsed on the back by a UK institution such as a bank. They then acquire most of the attributes of a bearer security.
	The marking name is shown on the register of share ownership of the company.
Dividends are claimed by submitting the relevantly number coupon to the issuing company.	Dividends are claimed from the marking name by the beneficial owner.
Bearer bonds cannot be made into registered shares	A marking certificate can be transferred out of the marking name into the name of the beneficial owner by his completing the registration form on the back of the certificate. The certificate will then be sent to the company and they will issue a new certificate showing him as the registered owner.
Bearer bonds must always be 'good delivery, i.e. all coupons and talons that should be attached must be attached and the certificate itself must not be defaced.	Good delivery does not apply.

Common points

All bearer or marking certificates should be kept in a bank or global custodian in safe custody for the following reasons:

- Title passes by delivery and a thief could pass on a good title to a bona fide transferee for value;

- Banks and custodians are geared up to claiming dividends from the company/issuing authority – if a dividend is missed it may be lost forever;

- Because all the claims are amalgamated only one currency cheque is received, thus the costs involved in collecting the cheque are much lower and are divided pro rata among all the beneficial owners of the shares;

- When either security is bought it is dearer than buying a registered security because there are handling fees charged on top of the brokers' commission;

- Secrecy – no one knows that you own these certificates (apart from the bank or custodian who will never disclose the fact).

10.10 Depositary receipts

A depositary receipt is issued by a depositary bank. It represents ownership of shares of a company that is not domiciled in the country where the depositary receipt is issued. One of the benefits to a company whose shares are held as a depositary receipt is that it broadens their potential shareholder base, which can increase the liquidity in the shares. It can also raise the profile of the company in another market. There are two main types of depositary receipt – ADRs (American depositary receipts) and GDRs (global depositary receipts).

American depositary receipts (ADRs)

The first ADR was created in 1927 by J.P. Morgan, to enable Americans to invest in Selfridges – a major UK retail store.

An ADR is a certificate issued by a depositary bank stating that a specific number of a company's shares have been deposited with that bank. ADRs can be traded only on the US exchanges – New York Stock Exchange (NYSE), AMEX or Nasdaq. Some British companies have used the American market to raise funds through primary issues of ADRs, notable names being Barclays Bank and GlaxoSmithKline. ADRs represent a means by which shares of foreign companies listed on foreign stock exchanges can be traded in dollar denominations and in bearer form in the USA. 'Foreign' in relation to ADRs means companies that are not American.

An ADR is created when the shares of a company are purchased on the US stock exchange system and then held in safe custody in a bank. The certificate issued by the bank represents the shares that have been purchased. The holder of the ADR certificate has all dividend rights belonging to the shares, and he has the right to vote at company meetings in the same way as he would if he had purchased the shares direct and held them himself.

From the point of view of the company that can have anything up to 20% of its equity in ADR form, problems arise because it is unable to trace the beneficial owners of its share capital. This is because the ADRs effectively turn registered shares into bearer shares. It can be vital to a company to know who owns its share capital in event of a takeover bid, and it is not impossible that a prospective purchaser of the company could acquire a sizeable holding via ADRs without the knowledge of the directors of the company.

While ADRs are an American creation, some UK institutional investors have purchased shares of UK companies through ADRs in New York rather than on the UK Stock Exchange. ADRs are usually retained in the name of the depositary bank, but, like marking certificates, they can be transferred into an individual's name.

Global depositary receipts (GDRs)

Global depositary receipts are similar to ADRs, but there is no restriction upon which markets they can be traded upon. A GDR can be traded on any major international exchange so long as the issuer satisfies the listing requirements of that exchange. GDRs provide more flexibility to the issuer and holder because they are more widely tradeable.

ADRs, GDRs and emerging-market companies

Many companies that are based in emerging markets use ADRs and GDRs as a way of raising finance in developed markets. There are advantages for issuers and investors. For example, if ADRs are used, funds will be raised in US dollars, which as a 'hard' currency companies will be keen to obtain. Indeed, it may not be possible to raise funds in any other way. A disadvantage from an emerging-market perspective may be a loss of liquidity in the relevant domestic emerging market.

From an investor viewpoint, the emerging market investment is denominated and traded in US dollars, eliminating exchange risk (in the case of US investors) or substituting a dollar-denominated investment (for a non-US investors), which can then be managed in combination with exchange risk arising from other dollar-denominated assets.

10.11 Overseas investment and the euro

The European single currency, the euro, was created in January 1999 as part of the Economic and Monetary Union (EMU) process in the European Union (EU). At the time of writing 12 out of 15 EU member states were participating in the euro and progressing to replacement of their national currencies on 1 January 2002.

The euro has already had an impact on overseas investment opportunities for UK investors. All securities issued in currencies of the participating countries were 'redenominated' into euros on 1 January 1999. This means that government bonds issued by governments of countries such as France, Germany and Italy are now denominated in euros, as are equities issued by companies in those countries. There are clearly significant implications for investment. Exchange risk within the 'Eurozone' has been eliminated, and for investors from outside the zone it has been reduced to the common denominator of exposure to the euro, rather than to individual national currencies such as the Deutschemark, French Franc etc.

There is effectively now a single Eurozone market in government debt, covering the participating countries. This does not mean that all governments can borrow at the same interest rates – that depends on their credibility in the market. But we do have a larger, potentially more liquid market, in which investors will place less emphasis on exchange risk and more emphasis on credit quality of issuers. The same will be true of the corporate debt market.

Equity markets in the Eurozone will also be affected. Investors are already looking less at the nationality of companies, and more at the merits of individual companies and industrial sectors, in evaluating the investment merits of equities within the Eurozone. More cross-border takeovers and mergers are likely to take place. The drive towards a unified stock market in Europe is likely to gather pace.

11

INVESTING IN TANGIBLE ASSETS

Objectives

After studying this chapter, you should be able to:

- analyse the advantages and disadvantages of investing in property, both for residential use and as an investment;

- differentiate between the various methods of financing the purchase of property for home ownership and on commercial basis;

- define chattels and their tax treatment;

- demonstrate an understanding of the types chattels used for investment purposes;

- analyse the advantages and disadvantages of investing in chattels.

11.1　Introduction

Investing directly in the stock market does not appeal to some people – they prefer to purchase a tangible asset such as a property or an antique. However may people decide to purchase their own home, and while they may not consider this an investment at the time of purchase, in later years they understand the value of this asset for their future financial planning. This chapter looks at the benefits and drawback of investing in tangible assets.

11.2　Property

Investment in property is the main aim of the majority of wage earners. Owning your own home is seen as attractive although not every homeowner realizes that he has made an investment. For the majority of people their home is the major valuable asset they own and, apart from money in a bank or building society and perhaps a few shares in privatized or demutualized companies, it will remain their only tangible investment. At the other end of the scale are insurance companies and other institutional investors who own many of the large office blocks and retail shop properties found in our towns and cities. When looking at property as an investment there are two distinct areas to consider: home ownership and investing in property to let.

Home ownership

Property is a very emotive investment. The saying that 'an Englishman's home is his castle' is very true. A house is a tangible asset, one that will not suffer from the problems that can surround paper assets such as stocks and shares, for example liquidation of the company causing loss of the investment.

However, home ownership does have problems that are unique and that must be guarded against, such as fire, subsidence, theft and any resultant damage. All these risks should be covered by insurance. These problems though are far outweighed by the advantages of home ownership.

Advantages of home ownership

Up to the time of retirement, the purchase of a house is usually financed using a mortgage. Housing prices tend to rise at a greater rate than inflation over the long term. For example a house costing £30,000 in March 1982 would, in 2001, be worth around £65,000 if its value simply rose in line with the RPI. However, depending on location, such a house would be worth £100,000 or more today. In London and the South East the value could be considerably higher than this figure.

Mortgage repayments remain fairly static in money terms over the life of the mortgage, while pay increases and inflation reduce them in real terms.

Capital gains on the sale of an owner-occupied house are free of CGT for the main residence and it is usually easy to obtain a mortgage for up to 90% of the value of the property, so the initial sum invested is within the reach of many people. However, care needs to be taken that the mortgage repayments can be comfortably afforded.

If the owner needs at some time in the future to borrow money, a house is a very acceptable form of security. When an investor retires it is possible to use the house to generate an income. There are a variety of schemes set up to provide this facility (see Chapter 16).

Disadvantages of home ownership

The transactions costs involved in buying and selling property are high. It is necessary to use solicitors whose fees also include stamp duty on the purchase of property, which is charged on a sliding scale. If a mortgage is used to finance the purchase the lender will require surveyors' reports which must be paid for. The use of an estate agent also adds to the cost if the investor is selling his property.

Building insurance is compulsory if a mortgage is used to purchase the property, but even if the house is purchased without a mortgage, the property should be fully insured, and this is an expensive annual cost. In addition to this, all repairs and maintenance are the responsibility of the owner.

If the investor has taken out the maximum mortgage he can afford then he may find problems making ends meet if interest rates rise, unless he has a mortgage carrying a fixed interest rate. If he is made redundant he may no longer be able to afford the house and be forced to sell. This may well occur at a bad time, especially if he lives in an area where many people have been similarly affected. This will depress the prices of the houses in the area, and selling becomes difficult. Property valuation is not an exact science. Two estate agents valuing the same house at the same time can give prices that are very different.

Conclusion

Homeowners who have enough cash to repay their mortgages early may wish to remove the 'burden' of a mortgage. Although on a straight comparison of interest earned on cash deposited compared to cost of interest (and repayments of capital on a repayment mortgage) it may seem to be attractive to repay early, care must be taken. Mortgage lenders often levy quite high charges for early repayment. Prior to deciding to repay a mortgage early, the cost of these charges must be considered because it may make early repayment less attractive.

There are advantages and disadvantages to all investments, and home ownership is no exception. However there is far more to be said for owning a property than against. If the decision is made not to buy then accommodation will have to be rented. The rent paid is 'lost' money because you never receive any lasting benefit, and there is the feeling expressed by many people who do live in rented accommodation that 'the house is never your own'.

11.3   Types of mortgage available for home owners

There are various types of mortgage available to investors to meet their requirements. Mortgages can be either floating or variable rate or fixed rate. The interest rate charged on variable-rate mortgages is set by the lender but generally varies in line with the general level of interest rates. Fixed-rate mortgages have a guaranteed rate of interest fixed for a term set at the outset which can be from two to 25 years. Such mortgages are often linked to endowment policies and provide an unchanging amount of monthly interest charges.

Repayment mortgages

Monthly repayments consist of part repayment of capital and part interest. Life cover is often required to protect the lender in case the borrower dies before the mortgage is repaid.

With-profits endowment mortgages

These combine two elements – an interest-only mortgage and an endowment policy (see Chapter 16 for more details on endowment polices). The proceeds of the with-profits endowment policy should not only repay the loan, but also produce a lump sum for the investor. However one form of with-profits endowment policy – the low-cost endowment policy – has run into problems due to the fall in profits which were to be added to the guaranteed sum. These policies were sold on the basis that the mortgage would be paid back in full and a surplus would remain for the investor. The result is that a number of people who purchased this product will not actually receive a sum large enough to repay their mortgage. Thus an investor who currently holds a low-cost endowment policy will need to make further investments to enable him to repay his mortgage.

Flexible-payment mortgages

This type of mortgage is aimed at the more financially aware who know that they may have extra income from time to time that can be used to reduce the amount owing on their mortgage. There are a wide range of these schemes to meet individual needs. These mortgages have the interest calculated daily, and enable customers to increase payments and make lump-sum repayments to reduce the balance of the account. This saves interest, thus shortening the life of the mortgage.

These products can be linked to a fixed-rate loan to give the added certainty of standard monthly payments. These are usually flexible fixed-rate mortgages over a 2- to 5-year period. Some providers link the interest rate charged to bank base rate in a 'flexible base rate tracker mortgage', thus enabling customers who do not want a fixed- or floating-rate loan to have a greater degree of certainty, and to benefit when base rates fall. Another feature of some flexible-payment mortgages is that the customer can take a 'payment holiday', i.e. make no payments for period specified in the mortgage. Such a feature is subject to certain conditions which vary from lender to lender. This feature is useful for some customers, but there is the possibility of getting into further debt if the customer is not self-disciplined.

The most sophisticated of these flexible mortgages are those that link together a current account, savings account, mortgage, other loans and payment holidays in a single account. These accounts usually have a fairly high income requirement and specify that the customers salary is paid into the account. Because this account runs like an ordinary current account there is a danger that expenditure could exceed income into the account, therefore such an account is suitable only for a financially aware, well-disciplined customer.

Pension mortgages

These mortgages are available only to holders of personal pension plans. They operate in a similar way to an endowment mortgage, in that payments of interest only are made during the life of the mortgage and repayment of capital is made at the end of the term. For pension mortgages the capital is repaid by taking a reduced pension entitlement on retirement, using part of the accumulated pension fund to repay the outstanding capital.

For individuals who joined a pension scheme between 14 March 1987 and 14 March 1989 there is an overall maximum 'commutation' of £150,000. For schemes set up after 14 March 1989 the lump sum cannot exceed 11 times the earnings cap, which in the tax year 2001-02 was £95,400, making the maximum 'commutation' £143,100. The earnings cap is linked to inflation and is set each year in the Finance Act.

The pension mortgage is the most tax-efficient form of mortgage, but there is no guaranteed minimum sum available on retirement. In theory the borrower would need to make good the shortfall from his own resources if the pension did not generate sufficient funds to repay the outstanding capital. In practice this is unlikely to happen. The 'extra' tax efficiency of a pension mortgage over an endowment mortgage arises because the pension contributions, which accumulate and are invested, are eligible for tax relief at the investor's marginal rate of income tax.

Occupational and SERPS pensions cannot be used for pension mortgages, only personal pension plans.

PEP and ISA mortgages

These are another form of interest-only mortgage using PEPs and ISAs, and the associated tax reliefs, to accumulate sufficient funds to repay the capital element of a mortgage at the end of the term. PEPs (personal equity plans) and ISAs (individual savings accounts) are discussed in more detail in Chapter 17. Although ISAs have now replaced PEPs, there are PEP mortgages still in existence, and these will be supplemented by ISA investments in order to provide the capital due on repayment. These mortgages are often linked to unit trust or investment trust or OEIC investments via a PEP or an ISA. The maximum annual investment in unit trusts via a PEP was £6,000 and the maximum annual investment in an ISA is £7,000. For high earners this is attractive, especially as the spouse can also take out a plan, effectively doubling the maximum loan, because the tax-free investment that can support capital repayment is doubled. Term life cover is needed in the event of early death.

The tax advantages, especially to high-rate taxpayers, arise because PEP and ISA proceeds are free of all taxes until 6 April 2004. The plan can be encashed at any time without penalty, and the proceeds used to repay the mortgage. This offers greater flexibility than an endowment mortgage, as well as the benefit of tax relief.

11.4   Investing in property to let

Purchasing property to let can take the form of purchasing the freehold of the property or by the purchase of leasehold property. If the property purchased is leasehold then it is usually of a commercial nature, i.e. shops or offices which are then sublet. If the property consists of a flat, this is also usually purchased in leasehold form.

Rack rent

If the property is let to a tenant for its full value, the rent charged is called 'rack rent'. The maximum term of such leases is 50 years. This type of investment can have major problems if the property is let to people to live in. Legislation has been enacted to protect such tenants from unscrupulous landlords who could at one time evict the tenant without notice for no reason at all. For the investor owning such property this legislation has become a nightmare, because it is now an extremely lengthy, and often expensive, business to evict unsatisfactory tenants, even if they have failed to pay the rent due for a long period. The legislation also makes it difficult to increase rents, and in some cases the tenant can have the rent lowered by appealing to a rent tribunal.

This legislation has caused many problems for perfectly fair landlords, and caused a major decline in private rented property as investors found that the problems do not justify the return they received on their capital investment. In order to try to overcome the problem of lack of rented accommodation, the Housing Act 1980 brought in legislation covering a new type of tenancy: protected shorthold tenancies.

Protected shorthold tenancies are for not less than one year and for not more than five years. Such a tenancy applies only to a new tenant and cannot be imposed on an existing tenant. Protected shorthold tenancies provide protection for both the landlord and the tenant as follows:

- The tenant:

    - Provided the rent is paid, and any other terms of the tenancy are complied with, the tenant cannot be evicted;

    - The rent can still be subject to a fair rents tribunal.

- The landlord:

    - At the end of the tenancy the landlord can compel the tenant to vacate the property upon giving three months' written notice;

    - If the tenant fails to comply with the notice at the end of the period, eviction proceedings are quick and easy.

Buy-to-let mortgages

These mortgages have been developed to meet the increased demand for buy-to-let properties. They are available for both residential buy-to-let and commercial buy-to-let.

With the increase in demand for rented housing more people are considering investing in property as an investment. These mortgages enable funds to be borrowed to purchase suitable properties. There are generally limitations on the number of properties that can be purchased – usually a limit of 3 - 5 properties – and a minimum loan of around £40,000 and a maximum loan of around £1,000,000 and a minimum property value around £50,000. Investors entering this market using such a loan need to be aware of the problems that can be caused if there is a recession, house prices fall and there is a lack of tenants. In such a scenario, the value of the property may fall below the amount of the loan. In such a case it may take a number of years to recoup the fall in value, and thus the investor could be in a negative equity situation.

Commercial buy-to-let is more flexible than residential buy-to-let. Most lenders do not specify a maximum number of properties, but a minimum loan of £ 30,000 and a maximum loan of around £1,500,000. The minimum property value is around £40,000.

Advantages of investing in property to let

Property is a good hedge against inflation in the long term, even though commercial property may see major falls in value and fewer tenants able to rent the property during a recession. As a recession ends, there are more tenants available for office properties. Rents may be fixed at a sufficiently high level to gain a good income for certain types of letting where there are no problems with rent tribunals, e.g. assured (not protected) tenancies created by the Housing Act 1980. Upward-only reviews are usually allowed for in the lease.

Property is a tangible asset and there is a certain amount of satisfaction to be gained from holding tangible assets as opposed to paper representing financial assets. One advantage that let property has over financial assets is if the tenant goes into liquidation the owner of the property still has his main asset and it can be re-let. If a company in which the investor holds shares goes into liquidation he will probably lose everything.

Disadvantages of investing in property to let

Capital gains on the property are subject to capital gains tax at the investor's marginal rate of income tax on gains over £7,500. The gain is calculated after allowing for the costs of selling, i.e. estate agents' and solicitors' fees.

Any income is classed as investment income and is subject to income tax. Any costs involved in the collection of the rents, maintenance, repairs or insurance are allowable against the rent in the computation of the amount of taxable income.

All property maintenance falls to the landlord unless the property has been let on a full repairing lease. Commercial properties let in the period from around 1980 onwards are often on full repairing leases. Older leases leave the internal decoration and repairs to the tenant and the external decoration and fabric maintenance to the landlord. The rent charged will reflect which type of lease is used. For private properties the tenant is expected to leave the internal property in the same repair as it was in when he took it over.

With property let to tenants for residential purposes the landlord then runs up against some very special problems created by the Leasehold Reform Act 1967, among other Acts. A tenant has the right to apply to a rent tribunal if he feels his rent is too high. The tribunal will rule in the case and their decision is binding. This can result in the rent being lowered to a figure below the level required by the landlord.

The other major problem caused by the various Acts is that it can be very difficult to evict an unsatisfactory tenant, even if he is in arrears with his rent. Eviction orders are not quickly and easily obtained in many cases, and they always require the aid of solicitors to obtain them. This means a twofold cost – loss of rent and the expense of employing a solicitor. However, the newer protected shorthold tenancies overcome this problem, and virtually all new leases to new tenants are of this type.

The purchase and sale of property plus the costs of drawing up the lease are high. Solicitors' fees, estate agents' fees and other fees such as planning permission are expensive, and while they are allowable against the gain on sale for the computation of the capital gains tax liability, they have to be paid out at purchase and during the letting period. These fees are far in excess of the costs involved in buying stocks and shares.

The length of time involved in buying and selling property renders it a highly illiquid investment. The purchase may take two to three months to complete, and a sale can take a far longer period if a buyer is not readily available.

Unlike stocks and shares which are easily valued, property valuation is very much a matter of opinion. Purchase cost is not a reliable guide to the selling price. Much depends on the market for property at the time, and the condition of the property being sold, which may be better or worse than the original condition.

With commercial property the usage may be limited by local bylaws. Although the investor may have purchased a retail shop in a prime site, if the trade the tenant wishes to carry on in that property is different from the original trade, planning permission may not be forthcoming. This results in the investor holding a property that is empty, thus not generating income, and empty property is a prime target for vandals which will cause even more problems and expense.

A private investor will need a very large sum to purchase just one property. In certain areas of the country this can be in the £25,000-£30,000 range, but in the south and London the figure can be easily £150,000 plus. Even £25,000 - £30,000 will buy only a small terraced-style or small commercial property in the north of England, which will not be in a prime area. To have a good investment in property requires prime-site properties in various centres, and the costs involved here are outside the range of the vast majority of investors. It is really only the institutional investors who have the requisite amount of money for the scale of investment needed to provide a good spread of properties.

In conclusion it must be said that investing in property to let is really outside the range of the majority of private investors. Only the institutions really have the time, expertise and funds to manage property investment successfully. For the private investor who wishes to have a property element in his portfolio then indirect investment is a much more attractive option. There are three main ways in which to invest indirectly in property: property shares, property bonds, and property unit trusts.

11.5   Indirect investment in property

Property shares

Shares in property companies are quoted on the London Stock Exchange and traded in exactly the same way as any other share. The property companies invest in large commercial properties, usually in prime sites in towns and cities in the UK and overseas. The underlying assets of these companies are the properties, and at times this can cause problems.

The property share does not suffer from the illiquidity of direct property investment, and more institutional investors have moved into property shares and out of direct property investment. Although we would expect these investments to have a similar return to the underlying properties, property shares usually trade at a discount to net asset values (see Chapter 12 for an explanation of net asset value (NAV)). The main reason for this is that property companies often have large, dominant shareholdings, and there is a lack of transparency due to the often subjective nature of property valuation.

Property bonds

The other two major alternatives mentioned are somewhat different from property shares. Property bonds are insurance company products (see Chapter 16 for full details of property bonds).

Property unit trusts

Property unit trusts are collective investments. Some property units trusts are authorized by the Financial Services Authority and some are unauthorized unit trusts. The main difference between these is that an unauthorized property trust has more flexibility in dealing with its investments than an authorized trust. (For details of how unit trusts operate see Chapter 14.) These funds will hold a wide range of properties from residential, industrial, retail and office properties both in the UK and abroad.

11.6   Chattels

Otherwise called 'alternative investments' or 'collectibles', chattels are defined for tax purposes as tangible moveable assets. They include antiques, pictures, jewellery, china and wine among others, but do not include motor vehicles (which are classed as 'wasting assets' for CGT purposes), or gold, silver or other precious metals except when made into items such as jewellery. Chattels prices can be very volatile, and valuation can be difficult because there is no standardized market. Prices are set by how much the buyer and seller agree upon, or the highest bid made at auction.

Advantages of investing in chattels

Very large capital gains are possible, especially if you are able to predict the next trend in 'collectibles' and are able to purchase an item at a low price just before the market blossoms. There is a favourable tax treatment for CGT purposes which is explained also below. The bulk of chattels are attractive to own and can bring great pleasure to the owner. As Keats said, 'A thing of beauty is a joy forever'.

Disadvantages of investing in chattels

Although large capital gains can be made, chattel values can fluctuate wildly. To a certain extent the strength or weakness of the dollar is an influence on prices, because Americans are very heavy investors in the UK chattel market. A strong dollar will make UK chattel prices even more attractive, thus pushing up UK prices. When inflation levels in the UK are low, as is now the case, chattels tend on the whole not to rise very quickly in price. It should also be noted that they generate no income whatsoever.

Valuation is difficult. The purchase price of the chattel is not a good guide to its value, especially as some chattels carry 17½% VAT which is not part of the true cost of the item. Dealers' buying and selling prices vary a great deal, and different dealers will quote different prices for an identical item, so it is necessary to 'shop around' to obtain the best price. Many chattel prices are subject to fashion, certain items becoming fashionable to collect, pushing prices up rapidly. If last year's fashion has now gone out of date prices will consequently fall.

Some items such as paintings will require specialist storage to ensure they are kept in good condition. This will either have to be installed, or the painting will have to be kept in a specialist store, each of which adds to the cost of the item.

Chattels are valuable items, thus insurance to protect against damage, fire and theft is essential. For some very valuable items, insurance companies may insist on special alarm systems being installed before they will provide insurance cover. Again this adds to the cost of the item. Many of these items are quite easy to forge, and it takes an expert to detect forgeries. In the art world, forging Old Masters is more difficult, although one artist, Tom Keating, was such an expert forger in this field that several major art galleries and museums paid the going price for the genuine 'Old Master', only to find out later that it was a Tom Keating forgery. The paintings they had paid hundreds of thousands of pounds for were virtually worthless. In fact this particular forger has now become so notorious that his forgeries command a price in their own right, which while well below the price of the genuine article is nonetheless at a high enough level to make his paintings 'collectibles'.

Taxation treatment of chattels

Sale proceeds of chattels are subject to capital gains tax, at the investor's marginal rate of income tax on sale proceeds (not the gain) of over £6,000 per item. The £6,000 applies to each person, thus a chattel jointly owned by husband and wife has a £12,000 exemption. Indexation allowance and taper relief apply as described in Chapter 6.

The £6,000 exemption applies to items that are not part of a set, and while a set is not defined legally, items made as a pair, such as a pair of candlesticks, or an item such as a canteen of cutlery, would be regarded as one item only. If the items form such a set and are sold to the same or associated persons, the £6,000 exemption limit applies to the whole set regardless of the number of items it contains. If an investor owned a set of items but wished to sell only part of the set and retain the rest, he would be able to claim the exemption if he did not subsequently sell the remainder to the same or associated persons. However, he would have to bear in mind that items made as a set command a far higher price than do the individual parts. He may well end up with a larger after-tax gain by selling the set as a whole and paying CGT than by breaking it up to gain the exemption.

How to reduce the risks involved in investing in chattels

Having looked at the many problems surrounding chattel investment an investor may feel that he would still like exposure to the chance of gains to be made in this area, but not wish to have all the problems associated with physical ownership. In this case the main way of gaining this exposure is to purchase the shares of a company that deals in chattels, e.g. Sotheby's. This will give the investor exposure to the rise in value of chattels, but as the companies deal in more than one chattel there is a degree of diversification, especially in the case of Sotheby's who will auction many items apart from chattels, and whose profits depend on the prices paid at auction.

12

Assessment of Company Securities 1: Company Accounts and Ratio Analysis

Objectives

After studying this chapter, you should be able to:

- Assess the information in published accounts from the point of view of a shareholder;
- identify various sources of information on company performance;
- understand the role of management in determining future profitability and growth;
- define 'shareholders' funds', 'net asset value' and 'capital cover';
- calculate a liquidity ratio and understand its significance;
- calculate earnings per share and the price/earnings ratio and understand their significance;
- understand the significance of:
  - dividend yield and dividend cover
  - income cover
  - income priority percentages;
- know the meaning of cash flow and free cash flow and understand its importance;
- interpret information published in the *Financial Times* on company performance;
- define gearing and understand its significance to future company prospects.

12.1 Introduction

In this chapter we consider how a company's financial accounts can be used to assess the immediate past performance of a company. We shall see how the private investor, and the student, can find the relevant information.

12.2 The information to be found in a balance sheet

A balance sheet is a list of the book values of assets and liabilities of a company at a particular date. Obviously assets such as good labour relations or an expanding customer base cannot appear in the balance sheet because they have no direct monetary asset value. Conversely, liabilities, such as product obsolescence, cannot be shown because they do not have a direct monetary claim on the company in the way that a creditor would have.

Shareholders' funds

Here is a simplified balance sheet which shows clearly what constitutes shareholders' funds and what does not.

ABC plc balance sheet as at 31 December 200-			
	£000	£000	£000
Fixed assets			1,020
Goodwill			100
Current assets			
Stock	562		
Debtors	1,094	1,656	
Current liabilities			
Creditors	1,032		
Tax	80		
Dividend	64	1,176	480
			1,600
Represented by			
800,000 £1 ordinary shares			800
Reserves			200
10% Mortgage debentures			200
12% Unsecured loan			160
9.16% Preference shares			240
			1,600

Total shareholders' funds can be calculated in two ways:

> Total assets, less all external liabilities.

or

> All classes of share capital
>
> *plus* reserves
>
> *plus* any credit balance on profit and loss in balance sheet.

Calculations of total shareholders' funds from ABC balance sheet

Note: total shareholders' funds relates to all types of shareholders. Take care when reading a question that you distinguish between total shareholders' funds and ordinary shareholders' funds.

Total assets, less creditors

	£000	£000
Fixed assets		1,020
Goodwill		100
Current assets		1,656
		2,776
Less: current liabilities	1,176	
10% mortgage debenture	200	
12% unsecured loan stock	160	1,536
Total shareholders' funds		1,240

Alternative method

	£000
Ordinary share capital	800
9.16% preference shares	240
Reserves	200
	1,240

12.3 The calculation of net asset value per ordinary share

Note: net asset value is also called 'balance sheet asset value' or, potentially misleadingly, 'break-up value'.

If we take for the moment the balance sheet value of the assets as being synonymous with forced-sale values, and if we assume that ABC went into liquidation as at the balance sheet date, we can calculate the theoretical amount per ordinary share available on liquidation.

All external liabilities must be paid out in full before shareholders can receive anything, and we can assume in the absence of information to the contrary that preference shareholders must then be paid off at nominal value. Any surplus after satisfaction of all these claims will vest in the ordinary shareholders in proportion to their shareholding.

Thus on the basis of our previous calculations, we can see that total funds available to preference and ordinary shareholders are £1,240. From this we deduct the nominal value of the preference shares, and the residue is the amount available to ordinary shareholders.

	£000
Total funds available to all shareholders	1,240
Less: preference shares	240
Ordinary shareholders' funds	1,000

The figure could be calculated in another way:

	£000
Issued ordinary share capital	800
Reserves	200
	1,000

Thus there is anticipated surplus of £1,000,000 to be divided among 800,000 ordinary shares, giving a net asset value per share of 1,000,000 ÷ 800,000 = £1.25 per share. (The number of ordinary shares can generally be found in the balance sheet.)

Note: although the dividend shown in the current liabilities will be paid to the shareholders, do not adjust your calculations. The dividend in practice would be paid out very soon after the balance sheet date.

Why might net asset value calculations be unrealistic?

The £1.25 calculated in the previous balance sheet is the theoretical amount per share payable in a liquidation of the company. However, in practice this amount is unlikely to be realistic because balance-sheet values of assets may well differ from forced-sale values. If fixed assets such as property are shown in the books at original cost, there could well be a surplus on sale. On the other hand, a specialist factory of a failed business may have to be sold below cost, especially in a recession. In addition, there is always a considerable delay while property sales are finalized. Any borrowings that existed at the balance sheet date would continue to be liable for interest until they had been paid off, or until the commencement of any liquidation.

Similar considerations apply to other assets. Goodwill may have no value, but on the other hand, if, for example, the company had a strong brand name, goodwill could be a significant asset, worth more than its balance sheet value. Stock is notoriously difficult to value accurately and debtors may not pay in full. The expenses of liquidation must also be borne in mind.

Furthermore, published balance sheets are not normally available until well after the balance-sheet date. Thus the make-up of assets and liabilities could have changed between balance-sheet date and publication date.

The current assets may now consist of more stock and less debtors if sales have fallen, some capital expenditure may have occurred, or any one of a host of changes may have taken place. Whatever the changes, the published balance sheet will not reflect the profits made, or losses incurred, since its date.

Balance sheets usually record assets at book rather than market values. However, market values may be used for assets that are awaiting sale or are readily marketable and held with the intention of resale, e.g. financial assets.

Financial statements are almost invariably prepared on the basis of the 'going concern' assumption. This means that it is assumed that the business will continue. The assumption is important because when a business is to be wound up many things change – asset values fall and new liabilities appear – for example, redundancy payments to staff, penalties under contracts, environmental clean-up costs.

The relevance of net asset values to investors

Net asset values should be compared with the current share price. As a generalization, a low net asset value compared to the share price means that the company is using the assets effectively, whereas when net asset value is above the current share price assets are being inefficiently used.

This generalization must be examined in more detail because, as with all balance-sheet analysis, the results must be considered in the light of the company concerned.

Companies in the 'people' business such as advertising or public relations companies can be expected to have low net asset values per share compared with the share price. Such companies do not require large factories or vast amounts of plant and machinery; rather they require a highly motivated, professional staff. Thus the main asset of such a business is the 'people' who are employed. Such assets do not appear in the balance sheet.

Significance of goodwill and intangible assets

Intangible assets are of great importance in services industries. Most intangible assets are not explicitly recognized in companies' financial statements. The main exceptions are values of brands and purchased 'goodwill'. Goodwill is the name given to the difference between the price paid when another business is bought and the 'fair' value of tangible assets acquired. It is shown as a separate asset category and is amortized through the profit and loss account (i.e. written off against profits over a period of time). Thus, like depreciation of fixed assets, it is not a cash flow, but an accounting charge allocating the cost of the asset over a number of years. This will be important to bear in mind when we look at cash flow later in the chapter.

We can also view a company's management as an intangible asset, the value of which does not appear in its financial statements, but will be reflected in a company's profitability and share price. So far we have looked at figures as an aid to assessing the past performance and potential performance of a company. We now consider management.

If a company's rate of growth has consistently exceeded those of similar companies, then the reason could well be management. Management changes can therefore be an important factor affecting future performance of a company and its shares.

A good management will be able to spot the potential markets of the future and enable the company to change its operations so as to be able to meet the demands of such markets. A good management will also be able to make the most of current circumstances by generating profits and cash for the benefit of the providers of capital (shareholders and providers of debt). In a takeover, the quality of the management in the two companies can sometimes be a decisive factor in the outcome.

For other companies with large property portfolios, such as a retail consortium, the net asset value mainly depends on when the properties were last valued and on whether the valuation has been incorporated into the balance sheet.

Lastly, manufacturers would be expected to have a fairly high net asset value compared with share price, because of their large investment in factories, plant and machinery, and stocks.

When are net asset values particularly significant?

Net assets per share are important in evaluating the following types of company:

- Investment trusts (for full details see Chapter 15)
- Takeover targets

One of the criteria a potential bidder will consider before fixing the price of his bid is the bidder's assessment of the net asset value of the target's shares.

Part of a successful bidder's strategy may be to recoup some of the cost of the bid by selling off assets or subsidiaries or divisions of the target. The term 'asset stripping' is used to describe this process when subsequent asset disposals are planned to recoup most or all of the cost of the bid.

Generally speaking this net asset value forms a 'back-stop', i.e. the lowest bid that might be successful. Other factors such as potential synergies (e.g. cost savings or cross-selling of products or services to each other's customers) usually mean that the actual offer is above this back-stop net asset value.

Natural resources companies such as oil or mining companies have a net asset value based on proven or probable reserves. Once the reserves have been exploited there will be no earnings, only a 'hole in the ground'. So net asset value is a vital factor for such companies.

Real estate companies By this we mean companies whose main business is dealing in and renting of property, as opposed to companies such as Marks and Spencer which operate from expensive high street sites. Since the main income of the company will be derived from the sale and letting of its properties, the net asset value is very important. Real estate companies such as Land Securities plc invest in all types of real property, such as housing land, industrial estates, retail property and office blocks. Their profits derive from rents received, development profits, and any sales of land made. Real estate company shares often trade at a discount to their net asset value.

Net asset values and profit potential

Apart from the sectors specified in the previous section, a high net asset per share figure compared to a low earnings per share figure can mean:

- The assets appear in the balance sheet at book value, but the true 'forced-sale value' will be less because of the poor profitability generated by the assets.

- The assets figure has recently been increased by capital investment, but the increased profits from this investment have not yet 'come on stream'. Such capital expenditure could be on real, tangible, assets such as manufacturing plant, or intangible assets, such as the purchase of brands or goodwill arising from the purchase of another company at a value in excess of that of the tangible assets acquired.

- Because poor management has resulted in low profits so that the assets are being inefficiently utilized. In such a situation there could be a takeover bid, because the buyer may well acquire the company's assets cheaply.

12.4 Capital cover and capital priority percentages

What is capital cover?

An individual lender is more concerned with the security of his own particular loan than with the indebtedness of the company as a whole. Capital cover is a means of deciding by how much the assets available to a particular lender exceed his debt.

The word 'capital' in this context usually applies to loan stocks, debentures or preference shares, or to medium- /long-term bank loans, i.e. the providers of medium- to long-term capital.

Example of capital cover calculation

To save you turning back to find it, we repeat the balance sheet of ABC plc.

ABC plc balance sheet as at 31 December 200-			
	£000	£000	£000
Fixed assets			1,020
Goodwill			100
Current assets			
Stock	562		
Debtors	1,094	1,656	
Current liabilities			
Creditors	1,032		
Tax	80		
Dividend	64	1,176	480
			(1,600)
Represented by			
800,000 £1 ordinary shares			800
Reserves			200
10% Mortgage debentures			200
12% Unsecured loan			160
9.16% Preference shares			240
			1,600

The conventions for calculating capital cover are as follows.

Assume that all current liabilities will be paid off in full before any repayment of loan capital or preference shares. In practice things may not work out like this, but an assumption must be made to enable calculations to be completed on the same basis.

Calculate the money available to all the providers of loan or share capital. This figure is known as capital employed. It is usual here to exclude goodwill and other intangible assets on the basis that they would have no value in a liquidation, although this may not always be the case.

The figure can be calculated in two ways:

	£000
Fixed assets excluding goodwill and intangibles	1,020
Net current assets	480
Capital employed	**1,500**

or	£000
800,000 £1 ordinary shares	800
Reserves	200
10% mortgage debentures	200
12% unsecured loan stock	160
9.16% preference shares	240
	1,600
Less: goodwill	100
Capital employed	**1,500**

Note: if there had been a deficit in the working capital (current liabilities in excess of current assets) the net deficit would have to be deducted from the fixed-asset totals to calculate the capital employed for our purposes.

The significance of capital cover

In the example just completed, the forced-sale value of the assets could drop to 7.5 times the balance sheet value before the debenture holders were affected in any liquidation:

$$\text{calculated } \frac{\text{Capital Employed}}{\text{10\% mortgage debentures}} = \frac{1,500}{200} = 7.5$$

and 4.2 and 2.5 represent the same falls that could occur before the unsecured loan stockholders or preference shareholders would suffer.

Remember that the presumption is that loan stockholders and preference shareholders will be able to claim the nominal value of their respective securities in the event of a liquidation.

Capital priority percentages

This is simply an alternative way of presenting the same information, and it shows what percentage of the available assets belong to which class of capital.

For ABC plc the capital priority percentage table is as follows:

Capital	Amount £000	Cumulative total	Priority %	
10% mortgage debentures	200	200	$\frac{200 \times 100}{1{,}500}$	$= 0 - 13.3\%$
12% unsecured loan stock	160	360	$\frac{360 \times 100}{1{,}500}$	$= 13.3\% - 24\%$
9.16% preference shares	240	600	$\frac{600 \times 100}{1{,}500}$	$= 24\% - 40\%$
Ordinary shareholders' funds	900	1,500	$\frac{1{,}500 \times 100}{1{,}500}$	$= 40\% - 100\%$
	1,500			

This supplies the same information as for capital cover. Asset values in liquidation could fall by (100 - 13.3) 86.7% before debenture holders suffered any loss. The relative figures for unsecured loan stocks and preference shares are 76% and 60%, respectively.

There is an alternative way of calculating capital cover from this table. Simply divide the priority percentage into 100.

Capital cover for 10% mortgage debenture	= 100/13.3	= 7.5 times
Capital cover for 12% unsecured loan stock	= 100/24	= 4.2 times
Capital cover for preference shares	= 100/40	= 2.5 times.

Liquidity ratio

The purpose of a liquidity ratio is to help to assess whether a company has sufficient cash for its immediate trading needs. If there is a short-term shortage of cash, the classic method of overcoming the problem is the bank overdraft. Although a short-term cash budget would be far more useful than these ratios for the purpose of analysing liquidity, such information is obviously not available to users of financial statements.

There are two types of liquidity ratio:

● Current ratio;

● Quick asset ratio.

Current ratio or working capital ratio

The formula is:

$$\frac{\text{Current assets}}{\text{Current liabilities}}$$

For ABC plc question, the current ratio is:

$$\frac{1,656}{1,176} = 1.41$$

A 'rule of thumb' is that the current ratio should be not less than 1.5, but there are wide variations between different companies, although comparisons between companies in the same sector ought to show similar results. Perhaps of most significance is the change in the ratio over a series of years for the same company.

Do not be misled into thinking that a 'high' ratio is a good sign. Too high a working capital ratio can indicate wasted resources, with too much capital tied up in stock and debtors. Indeed one of the first acts to be taken when a company has a liquidity crisis is to try to 'squeeze' working capital to generate cash.

Obviously too low a working capital ratio can indicate an imminent liquidity crisis. Generally speaking, a manufacturer who has a substantial time lag between receipt of order and receipt of funds will require a higher working capital ratio than a retailer of fast-moving consumer goods.

Quick assets ratio or acid test ratio

This ratio is similar to the current ratio, but it excludes stock, the most illiquid of current assets and the one most difficult to value.

The formula is:

$$\frac{\text{Current assets - stock}}{\text{Current liabilities}}$$

For ABC plc the ratio is:

$$\frac{1,656 - 562}{1,176} = \frac{1,094}{1,176} = 0.93$$

The normally accepted minimum is 1, but, as with working capital, there are many exceptions, for example:

● supermarkets, which can exist on very low acid test ratios because they buy on credit but sell for cash.

● distributors such as motor traders, whose stocks are financed by manufacturers.

● oil and gas companies, whose stocks can be turned into sales very easily.

12.5   Earnings per share

Earnings per share defined

So far in this chapter we have examined the security of capital from the balance sheet. However, liquidations of quoted public companies are rare. Thus capital cover and capital priority percentages are not really as vital as earnings, if we assume that a company will continue as a going concern.

Earnings are found not from the balance sheet but from the annual profit and loss figures, and they represent the net profits of a company available to ordinary shareholders. Earnings can either be paid out to the ordinary shareholders by way of dividend, or they can be retained within the company. The earnings figure remains the same whether or not any dividend is declared. Earnings per share (EPS) is simply total earnings divided by the number of ordinary shares. Total earnings are defined as profit after taxation and any preference dividend, but before any dividend on ordinary shares.

The significance of earnings

Earnings are vital to the share price. If earnings are ploughed back into the company, the reserves or retained profits figure in the balance sheet will rise. Thus the total shareholders' funds will increase, along with a corresponding increase in net asset value per share as the retained earnings are reinvested in increasing the asset base. This should result in a rise in the market price of the shares. Earnings are said to have 'quality' when the company shows steadily increasing earnings, the management is sound, the product range is diversified, and profits are in line with forecasts.

If earnings are paid out by way of dividend, all things being equal the dividend yield will rise, thus making the shares more attractive and causing their price to rise. The decision as to how much of the earnings should be paid by way of dividend is extremely complex. Usually shareholders in companies in mature industries expect that dividends will be constant in real terms or will rise in real terms over time.

However, shareholders in companies in fast-growing areas, such as technology stocks, will be looking for capital growth and low dividends or no dividend will normally be acceptable in such cases. If a company has strong growth prospects, shareholders may be willing to accept no dividend for a long time, if they are persuaded that the company has profitable opportunities to reinvest its earnings. Microsoft, for example, has never paid a dividend, and this is true of several large US technology companies.

Obviously, the other providers of the capital benefit from increased earnings, because higher earnings will mean more cover for the respective interest payments or preference dividend. Growth of EPS year by year is often a stated financial objective of a listed company, and a proportion of senior managers' remuneration may be linked to EPS growth. The prospect of growth of earnings is an important influence on the share price. When earnings grow at a faster rate than inflation there is said to be real growth.

When we wish to compare earnings of two companies from the point of view of an ordinary shareholder we need to relate EPS to the current price of a share. The normal way to relate EPS to price is to calculate a price earnings ratio.

Price earnings ratio (P/E ratio)

This ratio shows the number of times the current share price exceeds earnings per share. The formula is simply:

$$\frac{\text{Current share price}}{\text{EPS}}$$

The P/E ratio is shown for all shares quoted in the 'London Share Service' page of the *Financial Times*. Estimated price earnings ratios in the *Financial Times* are based on the latest annual reports and accounts, and, where possible, are updated on interim figures. As already noted, the EPS is calculated on the net basis, being profit after corporation tax.

The significance of P/E ratios

The main use of a P/E ratio is for comparing one share with another. Shares in sectors with the best growth prospects have relatively high price earnings ratios e.g. companies in the 'Pharmaceuticals' sector compared with those in, say, 'Water'. A high P/E ratio will often indicate that a share is attractive even if it has a relatively low gross dividend yield. Alternatively, a P/E ratio can be relatively high if the last reported earnings have fallen but the share price has not because recovery is anticipated.

Current P/E ratios (along with dividend yields and dividend cover, which we encounter shortly) for different industry sectors can be compared by studying the information in the tables for the FTSE Actuaries Share Indices published in the *Financial Times*.

The P/E ratio of any particular company can be compared with the average for its sector, and appropriate conclusions drawn based on this peer group evaluation. Obviously, if a company has a P/E ratio higher than the sector average this implies that the market believes its prospects to be better than those for the sector as a whole. The opposite would apply if the P/E ratio were to be lower than the sector average.

One method of valuing a company (or of assessing the 'intrinsic value' of its shares) is to try to forecast the earnings for the next accounting period. These earnings can then be multiplied by the average P/E ratio for the sector to calculate an estimated company value (also known as estimated market capitalization). This figure can be divided by the number of ordinary shares to calculate the estimated 'intrinsic value' of a share in that company. Earnings forecasts can also be used to calculate 'prospective' P/E ratios – in other words the same calculation but using prospective or forecast EPS. The reason for doing this is to give a forward-looking rather than historic measure.

Fully diluted earnings

Dilution of earnings applies when a company has issued convertible loan stock, convertible preference shares, warrants or share option schemes. All of these can at some future date at the holder's option be converted into ordinary shares of the company. Until they are converted into ordinary shares these instruments do not qualify for ordinary share dividends. However, as conversion is at the holder's option, it is normal practice for a company that has issued such securities to calculate EPS in two ways. First, the method previously used above, and secondly a calculation reworked on the basis that the relevant securities have been converted into ordinary shares. Obviously this fully diluted method will result in a lower EPS figure, because the calculation will use a larger number of ordinary shares. However, where loan stocks or preference shares have been converted the total earnings figure will be increased by the after-tax amount of interest or preference dividend saved.

Note in the case of warrants, the correct term is to 'exercise' rather than to 'convert'.

Going back to ABC plc, assume that the £200,000 of 10% debenture stock was in fact 10% convertible loan stock. The capital structure would show:

	£000
800,000 ordinary £1 shares fully paid	800
Reserves	200
	1,000
12% unsecured loan	160
10% convertible loan stock	200
9.16% preference shares	240
	1,600
Less: goodwill	100
	1,500

If the loan stock could be converted on the basis of 100 shares per £100 nominal stock and undiluted earnings were, say, 15p per share this would mean that earnings were £120,000 (800,000 shares x 15p).

Fully diluted earnings would be calculated as follows:

After-tax saving on loan stock interest = corporation tax at 30%

$$= (£200,000 \times 10\%) \times (100 - 30)\%$$

$$= £20,000 \times 70\%$$

$$= £14,000$$

Therefore fully diluted earnings

$$= £120,000 + £14,000$$

$$= £134,000$$

Although the company saves the net of tax cost of the loan stock interest, it will have fully diluted earnings of £134,000 attributable to 1,000,000 shares (800,000 + 200,000 converted), reducing the earnings per share from 15p to 13.4p.

12.6 Dividend yield and dividend cover

How dividend yield is calculated

Dividends are the amounts paid out of profits to the shareholders in cash. As we have already learned, the dividend is paid net of a 10% tax credit.

The formula is:

$$\frac{\text{net dividend per share}}{\text{current share price}} \times 100$$

The resultant figure is expressed as a percentage and shows the net dividend as a percentage of current share price.

When comparing dividend yields on shares in two companies in the same sector of the market, do not assume that the one with the higher dividend yield is better value than the one with the lower dividend yield.

The higher dividend yield may have arisen because:

●   Prospects of future dividend rises are considered small.

●   Investors believe that earnings and/or dividends are likely to fall in the future.

In either case, the market will have lowered the share price to reflect future prospects. Hence a past dividend is being compared to a current price which discounts future prospects.

Conversely, low dividend yield and P/E ratios can often go hand in hand, because the current 'high' share price reflects future prospects while the relevant dividends and earnings reflect the past performance.

Dividend cover

The formula is simply:

$$\frac{\text{EPS}}{\text{net dividend per share}}$$

The resultant figure represents the number of times the dividend could be paid out of earnings. The higher the dividend cover the better able would a company be to maintain the dividend rate in the future even if profits were to fall.

12.7   Income cover and income priority percentages

The purpose of the calculations

The principles on which these concepts are based are similar to those for capital cover and capital priority percentages. The purpose of these two calculations is to show the extent to which profits could decline without resulting in the interest or dividend payments being uncovered by profits.

Once again, each provider of capital is concerned with the cover for his own particular interest or dividend payment, so the calculations are worked on a cumulative basis.

How to calculate overall cover and priority percentages for income

- Calculate the net of corporation tax cost of all interest, remembering that the full interest is charged to the profit and loss account before tax is assessed.

- Calculate the total net cost of the preference dividends and ordinary dividends.

- Add back the net of corporation tax cost of the interest payments to the profits after tax and interest. This total represents the profits available to meet interest and dividends.

- Set out the various forms of interest and dividend in order of priority and assess overall cover and priority percentages on the same basis as for capital priority percentages.

Specimen calculations

You are given the following information from the profit and loss accounts of Electra plc. Assume corporation tax to be 30%.

Profit and loss account	£000	£000
Trading profit		4,880
Less: depreciation		1,535
Pre-tax profit		3,345
Less: interest on quoted debt		515
Pre-tax profit after interest		2,830
Corporation tax for year @ 30%		849
Profit after tax and interest		1,981
		£000
Ordinary dividend	720	
Retentions for year	1,261	
		1,981

From the information given above, calculate:

(a) The income priority percentages;

(b) The overall income cover.

(c) What are the investment implications of these calculations?

Answer

£000

$$\text{After-tax cost of interest} = \frac{515 \times (100 - 30)}{100} = \quad 360$$

N.B. the £360 as been rounded up to the nearest £'000.

Net cost of ordinary dividend is £720,000.

	£000
Profit after tax and interest is	1,981
Net of tax cost of interest is	360
Profit available to meet interest and dividends	2,341

Income priority % and overall cover:

Capital	Net cost of interest/ dividend	Cum. total	Income priority %	How calculated	Overall cover
Quoted debt	360	360	0-15.38	$\dfrac{360 \times 100}{2,341}$	6.5
Ord. dividend	720	1,080	15.38-46.13	$\dfrac{1080 \times 100}{2,341}$	2.17
Retained profits	1,261	2,341	46.13-100	$\dfrac{2,341 \times 100}{2,341}$	–
	£2,341				

Note: overall cover is simply the total profits available to meet interest and dividends divided by the cumulative total.

The investment implications are as follows:

Interest. The available profits must fall by 84.62% before they are insufficient to cover the interest (100-15.38). Alternatively, available profits cover interest 6.5 times. Thus interest looks very secure.

The ordinary dividend. Available profits could fall by 53.87% before the dividend was uncovered or, alternatively, the dividend is covered 2.17 times by available profits.

12.8 Cash flow

A company can be profitable, but this may not be reflected in its cash position. It is therefore important to look at cash flow. One measure that analysts pay particular attention to is the retained profit for the year plus depreciation written off in that year. This figure is a monetary amount, not a ratio, nor a percentage.

For Electra plc the figure is:

	£000
Retained profit	1,261
Depreciation	1,535
	2,796

In theory this monetary amount is the cash generated from trading operations. The figure can then be compared with the projected capital expenditure for the following year and any reductions required in current bank and hire purchase facilities over the forthcoming year. If this comparison indicates that the cash flow is insufficient, then some other sources of funds may be needed to service the borrowings, the obvious choices being rights issues or sales of assets. If the funds are to be borrowed as a medium-term loan, then cash flow should be compared to the cost of servicing the loan and any capital repayments required.

Even if the cash flow appears sufficient to service the various facilities over the next year, we still need to bear in mind the following reservations:

● The cash flow is from a past period – a full cash flow projection is of more use;

● The cash flow does not equate with actual cash generated, because some of the retained profit may have gone to finance increased working capital, such as increased stock and debtors, rather than in cash;

● Cash flow is more accurately calculated on the basis of FRS 1 (shown below). However, some investment analysts still use retained profit plus depreciation as a simple but cruder measure.

Cash flow statements in published accounts

Under the first Financial Reporting Standard (FRS 1) of the Accounting Standards Board, all companies with turnover in excess of £2m and net assets in excess of £975,000 will have to produce cash flow statements as part of their published accounts. This will almost inevitably cover all listed companies.

XYZ Limited: A specimen cash flow statement

Cash flow statement for the year ended 31 March

	£000	£000
Net cash inflow from operating activities (note 1)		6,889
Returns on investments and servicing of finance		
Interest received	3,011	
Interest paid	(12)	
Dividends paid	(2,417)	
Net cash inflow from returns on investments and servicing of finance		582
Taxation		
Corporation tax paid		(2,922)
Investing activities		
Payments to acquire intangible fixed assets	(71)	
Payments to acquire fixed assets	(1,496)	
Receipts from sales of tangible fixed assets	42	
Net cash outflow from investment activities		(1,525)
Net cash inflow before financing		3,024
Financing		
Issue of ordinary share capital	211	
Repurchase of debenture loan	(149)	
Expenses paid in connection with share issues	(5)	
Net cash inflow from financing		57
Increase in cash and cash equivalents		£3,081

Notes to the cash flow statement

Reconciliation of operating profit to net cash inflow from operating activities

£000

Operating profit	6,022
Depreciation charges	893
Loss on sale of tangible fixed assets	6
Increase in stock	(194)
Increase in debtors	(72)
Increase in creditors	234
Net cash inflow from operating activities	6,889

The purpose of this format is to provide an accurate statement showing how the company's cash or cash equivalents have altered during the year. Cash equivalents are investments with less than three months to maturity at the time they were acquired.

From the above it can be seen that:

- Cash flow from operating activities adjusts the traditional calculation of operating profit to take account of funds absorbed by extra stocks or debtors or in reduced creditors. This overcomes one major drawback from the traditional simple 'cash flow' calculation, namely that when profits increase, in most businesses cash is absorbed by increased working capital and the actual cash flow is less than the reported cash flow.

- Net cash flow from investing activities shows the new cash flow resulting from capital expenditure less asset disposals.

- Net cash flow from financing shows the amount of money raised from external borrowing or from new issues, and also shows the amounts of loan reductions made over the year.

- Net cash inflow from returns on investments and servicing of finance covers interest and dividends paid or received. Any interest that has been omitted from the reported profit and loss account because it has been capitalized must still be reported here. (An example of such capitalized interest would be where a property developer is charged interest on a loan to develop a property, but that interest is simply added to the capital value of the asset in the balance sheet instead of being charged as an expense to profit and loss.)

- Taxation is the actual amount of tax paid to the Inland Revenue during the year.

- The cash flow statement will provide a useful guide to a company's short-term situation. The 'profit' figure in reported accounts can be very subjective, and very misleading. However, cash flow is not subjective and it has been described as 'the most difficult parameter to adjust in a company's accounts'.

When using cash-flow statements we should be careful to interpret correctly the impact on cash flows of unusual items, for example non-recurring capital expenditure.

12.9 Free cash flow

Another cash flow measure used to evaluate companies is 'free cash flow' The purpose of this measure is to show the amount of cash that is available after meeting all necessary cash payments. 'Necessary' cash payments would include interest and taxation, but not dividends, which are, to some extent discretionary (although shareholders may pressure management to make payments). We should also include part of capital expenditure because some capital expenditure will be necessary for a company to maintain its productive capacity. In the absence of detailed information we would have to make some assumption about what this proportion should be.

Let us return to the example of XYZ Limited. We will assume that £1.2m of the spending on fixed assets is necessary to maintain the company's productive capacity. The company's free cash flow will then be:

net cash flow from operations + interest received - interest paid - taxation paid - capital expenditure (part) = 6,889 + 3,011 -12 - 2,922 - 1,200 = 5,766.

The resulting figure then gives us a measure of the amount of cash generated which can either be accumulated (if the company wants to build cash reserves) or used in various 'discretionary' ways – such as paying dividends to shareholders, increasing capacity, or acquiring other businesses. If the figure is negative, then the implications are clear – the company either needs to generate additional cash from its operations, or raise new finance.

The free cash flow figure for any one year may not be particularly meaningful, but if a picture can be built up over a number of years then a company's cash-generating abilities can be judged.

12.10 EBITDA (earnings before interest, tax, depreciation and amortization)

The significance of EBITDA is that it is a measure of a company's earning power relative to the value given it by the market. The argument for ignoring depreciation and amortization is that these do not reflect cash flows, but simply the allocation of the cost of fixed assets, tangible and intangible. Interest is ignored because it is a cost of financing and in looking at this measure we are not concerned about how the business is financed. Taxation is added back because this is a pre-tax measure. EBITDA is then compared to 'enterprise value':

$$\frac{\text{Enterprise value}}{\text{EBITDA}}$$

The higher this ratio, the more highly valued is the company. Clearly, the measure can be used for comparison to its peer group in the usual way. Enterprise value is calculated by adding market capitalization and the value of debt:-

(share price x number of shares in issue) + value of debt

Where debt is marketable the market value of debt is used; if not, book value.

12.11 Gearing

What is gearing and what effect does it have?

We have already discussed the concept of gearing in connection with options and warrants. In this context we said that gearing magnifies the gains or losses in the underlying securities. With companies a highly-geared share is one where the company has a high ratio of fixed interest capital in relationship to ordinary shareholders' funds. The effect of high gearing, as we shall see, is not only to magnify the effect of profit increases for the ordinary shareholders but also to exaggerate the effect of profit reductions.

Capital gearing

As the name implies, capital gearing is calculated from the balance sheet. There are many different ways of calculating capital gearing, but for the moment we shall use the following:

$$\text{Capital gearing ratio} = \frac{\text{loan capital and preference shares}}{\text{capital employed}}$$

From the following balance sheet, the capital gearing ratio would be calculated thus:

Alpha plc Balance sheet as at 31 December 200-

Assets employed	£000	£000	£000
Fixed assets			
Land, buildings, plant at cost	20,500		
Less: accumulated depreciation	8,000		
			12,500
Current assets			
Stock and work in progress	8,800		
Debtors	6,800		
Cash at bank and in hand	2,900	18,500	
Current liabilities			
Creditors	5,600		
Taxation	1,170		
Dividends proposed	480	7,250	
Net current assets			11,250
			23,750
		£000	£000
Represented by			
Future taxation, deferred liabilities and provisions			2,350
Quoted loan capital			
5.83% debenture stock		3,000	
6.81% unsecured loan stock		5,000	8,000
5% preference capital			2,000
Ordinary shareholders' funds			4,000
Reserves			7,400
			£23,750

$$\frac{\text{Loan capital and preference capital}}{\text{Capital employed}} = \frac{3,000 + 5,000 + 2,000}{12,500 + 11,250 - 2,350*}$$

$$= \frac{10,000}{21,400}$$

Capital gearing ratio $= 0.47$

*Future taxation, deferred liabilities and provisions of £2,350 are not classed as capital because they represent possible depletion of capital in the future.

Notes

● Preference shares are included as fixed interest capital, because no dividend can be paid on the ordinary shares unless the preference dividend has been met.

● As a 'rule of thumb' the ratio should not usually exceed 0.50. However, much depends on the type of business as to whether this 'rule' need be of any concern. Generally speaking, the greater the industry risk and the operating risk the lower the gearing should be. For example, capital goods manufacturers (a risky industry) with high fixed costs (high operating risk) need low gearing.

● Nowadays many bank lending agreements contain clauses, known as covenants, which state that the borrower will be in default if the gearing ratio exceeds a stated figure. In the recession of 1990-92, several companies experienced major problems because their gearing ratio exceeded the limits set out in the covenants. As the recession ended companies made a spate of rights issues to reduce gearing and give room for financial manoeuvre.

● Some analysts calculate the gearing ratio as:

$$\frac{\text{long-term debt}}{\text{shareholders' funds}}$$

It is also usual where a company holds significant cash and/or marketable investments for these items to be deducted from debt in the numerator of the calculation. The rationale for this is that the focus should be on net rather than gross debt.

For some companies, medium- or long-term bank loans perform the function of debentures or loan stocks. It is also usual to see these included in both the numerator and in the denominator of the calculation. When calculating the gearing ratio the inclusion of overdraft and other short-term debt can be justified if these forms of finance are used as long-term finance. Whichever method is used, the principles and conclusions to be drawn are the same.

One of the objectives of financial management is to ensure that a company's gearing is at the optimal level so as to minimize a company's weighted average cost of capital. For most listed companies, for the purpose of assessing the optimal proportions of debt and equity in the capital structure the weightings of debt and equity are based on market values, rather than on book values.

Debt is normally cheaper than equity because lenders will accept a lower return in exchange for the lower risk which debt holders have in comparison with the risks of shareholders. However, as the gearing ratio rises, the overall risks to both shareholders and debt holders also rise. When gearing exceeds a certain level then the weighted average cost of capital will rise. Figure 10.1 illustrates this.

Figure 10.1: Optimal Gearing Level and Cost of Capital

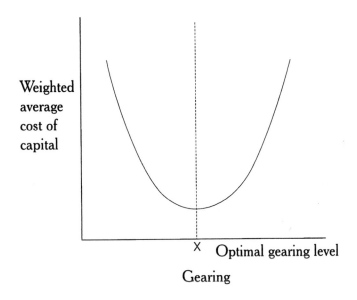

Note: interest is tax deductible, whereas dividends are paid from after-tax profits.

Income gearing

This can be defined as the number of times total available profits exceeds the fixed interest on loan stocks. The generally accepted formula is:

$$\text{Income gearing} = \frac{\text{profit before interest and tax}}{\text{gross interest payments}}$$

Referring back to the profit and loss account of Electra plc (reproduced here again for the reader's convenience) we can see that the income gearing is:

Electra plc		
Profit and loss account	£000	£000
Trading profit		4,880
Less: depreciation		<u>1,535</u>
Pre-tax profit		3,345
Less: interest on quoted debt		<u>515</u>
Pre-tax profit after interest		2,830
Corporation tax for year @ 30%		<u>849</u>
Profit after tax and interest		<u>1,981</u>
		£000
Ordinary dividend	720	
Retentions for year	<u>1,261</u>	
		<u>£1,981</u>

$$\text{Income gearing} = \frac{3,345}{515} = \textbf{6.5 times}$$

The income gearing figure should not generally be less than 2 according to *Money for Business*, published by the Bank of England. However, as with the capital gearing 'rule', the optimal level varies from company to company. Similarly it could be argued that the interest on other forms of debt, if any, should be included in the calculation.

Arguably, the income priority percentages and overall cover are of more relevance than income gearing from an investment point of view, because they take account of the preference dividend. However, income gearing is a useful tool for a lender, as opposed to an investor, because lenders can estimate the potential income gearing ratio when deciding whether or not to grant facilities. Lenders are not concerned with the preference dividend, which is not even an enforceable debt. Ordinary shareholders, on the other hand, must concern themselves with the preference dividend, because the ordinary dividend cannot be paid while the preference dividend is in arrears.

Nowadays lenders often prefer to use a cash-flow based ratio for interest cover. This would compare the forecast cash flows available to service debt over the relevant period against the cash cost of servicing the debt over that period. This is a development of the concept of 'free cash flow' discussed earlier in the chapter.

Why the concept of gearing is important to ordinary shareholders

The easiest way to illustrate the general concept is to study a simplified example. Suppose that the capital employed of LMN plc and CDE plc, and profit records, are as follows:

	LMN plc £000	CDE plc £000
Issued ordinary share capital	500	500
Reserves	500	1,500
10% Loan stock	1,000	Nil
Total capital employed	2,000	2,000

	£000	£000
Net profit before interest – year one	200	200
Net profit before interest – year two	400	400
Net profit before interest – year three	150	150

For simplicity and clarity we shall ignore taxation and also make the simplifying assumption that the capital employed remains unchanged over the three years. In real life such assumptions must not be made, but for the purpose of illustrating the concept of gearing, these assumptions are quite valid.

Let us now look at the distribution of those profits:

	LMN plc Year one £000	CDE plc Year one £000
Net profit before interest	200	200
Less: interest	100	Nil
Available to ordinary shareholders	100	200

	LMN plc Year two £000	CDE plc Year two £000
Net profit before interest	400	400
Less: interest	100	Nil
Available to ordinary shareholders	300	400

	LMN plc Year three £000	CDE plc Year three £000
Net profit before interest	150	150
Less: interest	100	Nil
Available to ordinary shareholders	50	150

From the above we can see: Percentage increase/decrease in profits available to ordinary shareholders between:

	LMN plc	CDE plc
Year one and two	+200%	+100%
Year two and three	-83%	-63%

The above illustrates the point that a shareholder in a highly-geared company relative to one in a company with low gearing will benefit from gearing when profits rise, but he will suffer from gearing when profits fall.

Ratio of market value to sales

There are some measures that can be used in assessing companies without P/E ratios. A company will not have a P/E ratio if it is making losses, such as a high technology company in its early stages of development. In these circumstances two measures are commonly used – the ratio of market value to sales, and 'cash burn'.

$$\text{market value to sales} = \frac{\text{market capitalization}}{\text{sales}}$$

The higher this ratio, the greater the value the market attributes to the company. This ratio could be viewed as a measure of a company's long-term potential, because market capitalization will reflect investors' collective view of the company's prospects. It is also a ratio that tends to be looked at in takeover and merger situations and can be used as a benchmark against companies in the same sector.

Cash Burn

$$\text{cash burn} = \frac{\text{cash and other liquid resources}}{\text{monthly cash outflow}}$$

This measure tells us how many months' expenses a company holds in cash or cash equivalents. The purpose of this ratio is to measure a company's 'comfort margin' in terms of how long it can meet its running expenses until it needs to raise new finance. In practice, new finance would need to be raised well before cash resources are exhausted. This measure is of particular value in assessing companies with little or no sales – a company that it is established and generating revenues and profits should be constantly replenishing its cash resources from its operations. Therefore, companies like Internet or biotechnology start-ups are those most likely to be evaluated using this measure. Monthly cash expenses can be calculated from the cash-flow statement, which is likely to be much simpler than that for an established company – there are unlikely to be any dividends or taxation for a loss-making company. The net cash outflow before financing can be divided by twelve to give a monthly cash outflow. It may be necessary to adjust this figure to take account of any 'lumpy' items such as non-recurring fixed asset purchases or acquisitions of other companies.

12.12 The statistical information in the *Financial Times* London Share Service

Extract of the information (Tuesday to Saturday)

Let us examine the information available for a particular share in the *Financial Times* in a Tuesday to Saturday edition. The edition is 10 May 2001.

Notes	Price	+ or -	52 week High	Low	Volume	Yield	P/E
Sainsbury J. (♣)	398½-	- 1½	438	262¾	1,585	3.6	22.7

Under the column headed 'Notes' various symbols can appear and the reader should refer to the 'Guide to London Share Service' which appears each day at the end of the London Share Service. For Sainsburys the symbol (♣) shows that the company is a member of the 'Free Annual Reports' service by which the latest Sainsbury's published reports can be obtained.

Additional information is available in the Guide to London Share Service, extracts of which are as follows:

● The price is the previous day's closing mid-market price shown in pence unless otherwise stated, and the change since the previous close is shown.

● High and low prices are based on intra-day mid-prices over a rolling 52-week period (i.e. the highs and lows within the last 52 weeks).

● Trading volumes are end-of-day accumulated totals rounded to the nearest 1,000 shares traded. When there is an unusual increase in volumes, then this may well be a sign that the market expects some major change in the company's prospects, such as a takeover bid. Volumes typically rise immediately following company announcements as the market digests news and shareholders adjust their holdings in a company.

● Yields are the net dividend yields based on mid-prices.

● As previously explained P/E is the price earnings ratio based on EPS taken from the latest annual reports and accounts, updated on interim figures.

N.B. There are frequent changes in the information to be found in the *Financial Times* London Share Service. Readers are recommended to purchase a current *Financial Times* and to note any changes.

Examples of information available to managers

The managers of any UK-domiciled company with equity lines of stock listed on the London Stock Exchange are provided with free access to the Stock Exchange Company Report Service. This is a secure website that provides high-quality interactive reports of the company's market performance, covering share price, trading and market value movements over the previous month and in the last 12 months. It allows the managers to select up to five key competitors/peers to benchmark their company's performance against. Obviously, any capable management team will exploit such information as a powerful tool for strategy development.

Other sources of information for use in evaluating companies

Extel on-line and CD-rom systems

Extel has an on-line system that carries information on stocks and shares, company data, financial news, financial systems plus a system that enables accountants to calculate investor's tax liabilities utilizing on-line information.

Datastream

This is a screen-based source of information which carries more information than Extel. In addition to the analysis of the accounts, data relating to the company, its industry and economic prospects are constantly updated. Charts of share price movements plus a wealth of other information, such as a share's beta (β) (discussed in the next chapter), are provided.

Financial Times

We have already discussed some of the details that can be found in this publication. Other information includes:

- Details of interim and final results, and other company announcements, with comments;
- News of rights issues, capitalization issues, takeovers, management changes and industry developments;
- List of active stocks, new share price highs and lows, and major price changes.

Stock Exchange daily official list (SEDOL)

The SEDOL is published by the Stock Exchange on each working day. It lists every stock and share that is quoted on the Stock Exchange. (Not every quoted share appears in the *Financial Times* London Share Service because not all companies are willing to pay the annual fee.)

Details shown in SEDOL include:

- Particulars of the last dividend paid, in pence or %;

- The date the share was last quoted 'ex div';

- The date of the next dividend payments;

- Separate sections for AIM shares, miscellaneous warrants, traded options, suspended securities and takeover disclosures;

- The quotation column on the date of the SEDOL contains the prices of particular stocks or shares, and these prices are used as a basis of the quarter-up method for inheritance tax calculations by the Inland Revenue in connection with lifetime gifts, or with disposals on death;

- Business done, i.e. the range of prices at which deals have been made during the day, including a symbol against intra-firm deals;

- Notice of any selective marketing (placings) of securities;

- The US and Canadian dollar rates at 4.30 p.m., the FTSE 100, FTSE Eurotrack 100 and FTSE Eurotrack 200 indices at close of business;

- The SEDOL code number, which is a six-figure digit. This number appears on contract notes with a prefix number that denotes the type of security, e.g. 0 is for securities quoted in the UK and Eire, while 2 is for securities quoted in North and South America.

- The companies involved in takeovers as notified by the Takeover Panel.

Stock Exchange Year Book

Published annually, it gives details of every quoted company. It provides details of all information recorded at Companies House, but does not include details of the accounts.

Other sources of information

The *Investors Chronicle* and the *Economist* often give in-depth analysis of the prospects of particular companies or industries.

Teletext and Ceefax provide up-to-date information on television relating to share prices, Stock Market movements, company news and other important information relating to operations in the City of London.

There are also a wide range of web sites that provide information. Some of this information is free, but more in depth information is available only by subscription. A list of some of these web sites is shown in the Appendix.

Credit ratings agencies

Another source of information is a company's credit rating. Credit ratings, which rate a borrower's debt, are given by credit ratings agencies, which are commercial organizations that charge fees for their services – often paid for by the company being rated. Potentially this could cause a conflict of interest for the agency, and a small number of large agencies (such as Standard and Poor's, and Moody's) dominate this market. But, in practice, this is not a problem, because they rate large numbers of borrowers, and would soon lose credibility if the ratings they awarded were consistently overgenerous. The agencies also give ratings to countries i.e. they rate 'sovereign' debt.

Thus the classification of a company's debt, which is based on an assessment of a company's financial statements, debt history and prospects, can say much about a company. The most important distinction in credit ratings is between 'investment grade' and 'non-investment grade' debt, which basically states whether a debt issue is a suitable investment for a conservative investor. Non-investment grade debt is also known as 'high yield' or 'junk', because it carries a higher yield to compensate for the perceived greater risk.

Credit ratings are important for investors interested in buying debt securities – much of the analysis has already been done for them by experts. But not every company's debt will be rated and investors will still need to carry out some analysis – for example, in balancing a portfolio if they are investing directly, rather than indirectly, perhaps through a unit trust. Credit ratings also provide clues for equity investors about company prospects.

We must distinguish between credit ratings agencies and credit reference agencies, which perform a very different role, namely providing information about organizations' (or indeed individuals') credit histories, and are likely to be used when sales are made on credit.

13

ASSESSMENT OF COMPANY SECURITIES 2: ANALYSIS TOOLS AND INVESTMENT THEORY

Objectives

After studying this chapter, you should be able to:

● understand the main features of fundamental analysis and technical analysis;

● understand the principles of:

- Dow theory

- Hatch theory

- the random walk hypothesis

- the efficient market hypothesis

- behavioural finance;

● differentiate between systematic and non-systematic risk;

● explain the purpose of beta coefficients;

● appreciate the principles of portfolio theory.

13.1 How professional analysts assess the prospects of a company.

Fundamental analysis

The purpose of fundamental analysis is to suggest whether a share is cheap or expensive compared with its intrinsic (or 'true') value.

In order to assess the 'true value' of a share, the fundamental analyst will make a detailed study of the company's accounts over a number of years so as to study the trends. He will then examine the prospects of the industry and the economy in general, and against this background he will study the company's strategic plan. Naturally, the analyst's opinion of the calibre of the management will have an important bearing on his decision as to whether or not he believes the plan to be viable.

The end result of this detailed study will be a prediction of future profit levels of the company, and perhaps also future dividends. If profits and dividends can be predicted, then a projected price earnings ratio can be calculated, based on the current share price. This projected P/E ratio, adjusted for risk by means of a beta coefficient (which reflects the relative riskiness of a an individual share and which we discuss later), can then be compared with the projected P/E ratio for the sector as a whole.

If the projected P/E ratio of the company appears to be lower than that which would be expected, the share is 'cheap'. The current market price must be below the 'intrinsic price', and thus the share is a 'buy'.

There are other means of calculating whether a share is 'cheap' or 'dear'. One method is to predict the likely amount of the next dividend and future dividend growth rates. This predicted dividend stream can then be discounted at the rate of return thought appropriate for the riskiness of that company. The resultant net present value is said to represent the intrinsic value of the share. The obvious problems are how to predict dividends and their growth. This method is known as the Gordon growth model.

The Gordon growth model

The formula for the Gordon growth model is:

$$P_0 = \frac{D_1}{(r - g)}$$

where: P_0 = intrinsic value of the share

D_1 = next dividend

r = investor's required rate of return

g = dividend growth rate

Example: The next dividend on ABC's shares will be 21p. Future dividend growth is forecast at 5% p.a. and the required rate of return is 12%. The intrinsic value of the share is:

$$\frac{21}{*(0.12 - 0.05)} = \frac{21}{0.07}$$

Intrinsic value of share = 300p

*Note: percentages are expressed as decimals.

Fundamental analysis involves predicting the profits or dividends of a company and comparing these predictions with a prediction of the 'average' profitability of the sector or of the market as a whole. Alternatively, fundamental analysis can involve forecasts of free cash flows, discounted to a present value at an appropriate discount rate.

Fundamental analysis takes a long-term view of investment. In the short term, the 'intrinsic value' of a share may be totally overcome by speculative market forces, and in the long term the fundamentals themselves may change before the share price has reached its 'true value'. Nevertheless, fundamental analysis is considered an important technique judging by the number of such analysts employed in the various City organizations. However, as we shall see in this chapter, there are those who are sceptical about the use of this technique and other techniques which we describe below.

13.2   Technical analysis

Technical analysts, or 'chartists' as they are often called, state that the price of a share is determined by supply and demand, and they totally disagree with the fundamental analyst's view. A chartist predicts future share price movements by plotting charts of share price movements over a period of time. From these charts of price movements he then claims to be able to see trends that forecast where the share price will move next.

There are three different types of chart that the analyst can use. They are:

● Line charts;

● Bar charts;

● Point and figure charts.

Line charts

Figure 13.1: Line chart

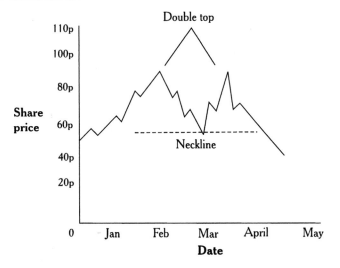

This is the type of chart most commonly understood. It simply plots the closing price of the share each day.

Fig. 13.1 shows a line chart with a trend called a 'double top'. This arises when the share price has risen sharply followed by limited profit taking, which causes the share price to fall. The share then rallies around the previous high figure but again meets resistance. Investors decide that the peak has been reached and they take their profits, causing the price to fall again. The neckline is the support level above or below which the pattern forms. Any breakout through the neckline should be noted. If the price falls below the neckline then the shares should be sold, if it rises above, they should be purchased.

The opposite trend is called 'double bottom', where a share twice hits a price floor, before rising on buying.

Bar charts

This is more sophisticated than the line chart because it shows the high and low trading prices for the day, joined by a vertical line. The closing price is marked by a horizontal line across the bar (see Fig. 13.2).

Figure 13.2: Bar chart

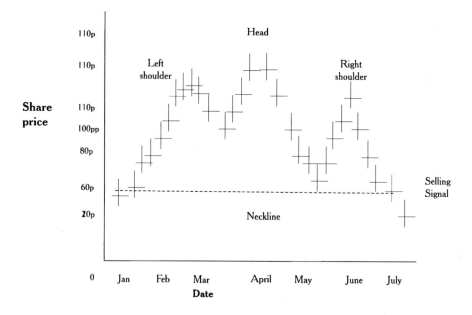

Fig 13.2 also shows the 'head and shoulders' formation. This formation develops when a share price rises quite quickly, falls back due to profit taking (the left shoulder), rises again sharply to a new high because investors think they missed out on the first rise (the head), falls again due to profit taking, rallies again (the right shoulder) then falls due to profit taking. Once the right shoulder has been reached the share price drops quickly, and once it falls below the neckline this is a signal to shareholders to sell.

Point and figure chart

This is a chart with no fixed timescale, although the horizontal axis does represent time. The object of this chart is to show significant price movements. Significant upwards movements are marked by a row of Xs, and downward movements by a row of Os, not both. The rule on starting a new column is that the chartist ignores the highest X in the previous column, but fills all the other squares while the price continues to fall. Once the price rises again a new column of Xs is commenced which starts one square above the lowest O. This can be seen clearly by studying Fig. 13.3.

Figure 13.3: Point and figure chart

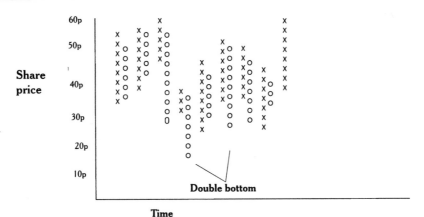

Other patterns

When reading charts certain patterns emerge. One that always seems to occur is after a sharp upward price movement. The following period often has the share price hovering around at a similar level while investors evaluate their next course of action. This period is called 'consolidation' by chartists. If the price then climbs again a 'continuation' pattern forms; if it falls the pattern is called a 'reversal'.

Figure 13.4: The triangle

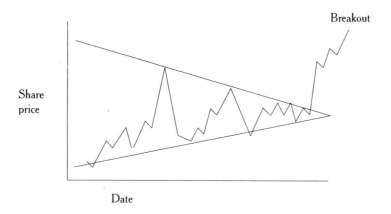

This forms after there has been a strong rise or fall in the share's price. It may produce either a continuation or a reversal pattern when the breakout from the formation occurs. The breakout is always a strong price movement either upwards or downwards.

Figure 13.5: The flag

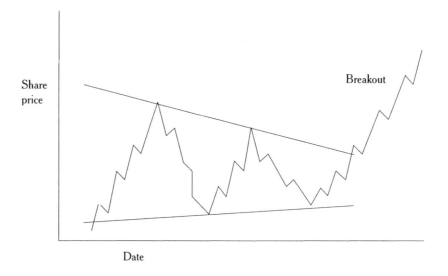

Although this appears similar to a triangle, it has two distinguishing features. First, it always signals the continuation of a trend, and second it forms more quickly than the triangle.

Figure 13.6: The rectangle

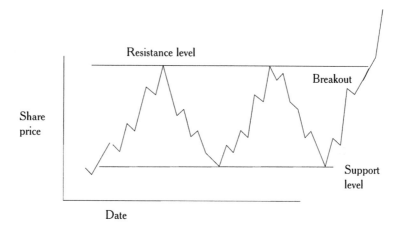

The rectangle-like shape arises when a share's price swings between two points above which it is reluctant to rise, the resistance level, and below which it does not want to fall, the support level.

The resistance level is created when investors feel that they have made enough profit and they decide to take that profit. This will cause the share price to fall. The support level arises because investors feel that the share is now cheap, and buying pushes the price up again. As with the breakout on the other patterns, this can be an upward or downward breakout and signals the end of that particular pattern at that time.

Figure 13.7: Trend lines

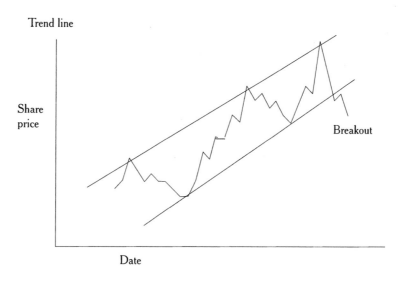

A trend is simply the overall direction taken by the share price. In Figure 13.7 the price is moving up and down between the trend lines, but the overall movement is upwards.

Trends

Chartists watch for three trends developing as an aid to their art:

- The **primary trend** means that the chartist is looking at the share price movements in the long term. In a bull market the primary trend is upwards; in a bear market the trend is downwards. The chartist then looks for any changes in the overall pattern which will indicate a new trend;

- A **secondary trend** is one that lasts for a few weeks, but does not have any effect on the overall primary trend;

- A **tertiary trend** is only a minor movement which lasts for just a few days.

13.3 Comparison of fundamental and technical analysis

Both types of analysis try to predict share price movements as a whole. The fundamental analyst compares the share price with indicators such as the level of interest rates, inflation, the index of employment. He also delves into the company's balance sheet and looks at the industry itself. From this the fundamental analyst claims to be able to say whether to buy or sell a particular share from the point of view of a medium- to long-term investor. The fundamental analyst may also use cash-flow based methods, such as the dividend growth method or discounting of forecast free cash flows, for valuation purposes.

Technical analysts on the other hand disagree with the fundamental analyst's view because they claim that reliance on past performance is a hindrance in judging future prospects. Technical analysts consider that the share price is fixed purely by supply and demand, and past performance as evidenced by the company's accounts is no guide whatsoever. Not surprisingly, the fundamental analysts disagree violently and they compare chartists to astrologers or palmists! Chartists aim to say when to buy, sell or hold a share. Their time scale is short term, whereas that of fundamental analysts is long term.

Neither fundamental nor technical analysts have ever been able to prove that they are 100% right and the other is wrong, and even more confusion reigns because different chartists will sometimes interpret the same chart in different ways.

13.4 The Dow theory

This theory depends on the plotting of daily price indices on charts. It originates in the USA, and in its pure form is related to two US stock market indices – Industrials and Rails. Before any conclusion may be established, the one index must confirm the other. In the UK there is no Rails index, but advocates of the theory claim that it can be successfully applied to other indices.

In essence, it is maintained that there is a primary movement in the market at all times lasting for one or more years. There are also secondary movements usually lasting for a few weeks or months. The daily movements that comprise the secondaries are ignored.

13.5   The Hatch system

This system is based on the argument that if an investor sells at 10% below the top of the market and buys at 10% above the bottom of the market, he is going to do as well as he can reasonably expect. It can be applied to an index, a group of shares or an individual share. There are various ways of operating the system but once the method has been decided upon it must be adhered to, and the signals obeyed.

Example: If an investor purchased a share in March for 250p he would immediately subtract 10%, giving him a sale or 'exit' price of 225p (250p - 25p). If in April the share price had risen to 260p, he would calculate a new selling (exit) price of 234p (260p - 26p). If in May the share price had fallen to 258p, the exit price would remain unchanged because the share price is above the 234p. If in June the share price fell to 230p he would have sold his holding as soon as the price reached 234p. The Hatch operator would then work out a purchase or 'entry' price of 230p + 10%, i.e. 253p, which would be adjusted downwards if the price had fallen on subsequent review days. Whenever the share price rose to the automatic purchase price, he would buy.

A refinement of this system would be to calculate the control selling or buying price using the average price for the previous month, rather than the selling price on a fixed day. The advantage of this system is that it prevents selling too soon in a bull market, or buying too early in a bear market. However, in order to make a profit using this system the market price must rise by at least 20% (in order to cover dealing costs).

Filter rules (that is, systems such as the Hatch System)

These are designed to isolate primary trends from minor price changes caused by random factors. The problem with this method is deciding upon the size of the filter. If it is small, say 3-5%, the investor is constantly buying and selling, thus incurring heavy dealing costs. If it is too large, say 20-25%, much of the price movement will have taken place before the investor acts. (See Fig. 13.8.)

Figure 13.8: Filter method

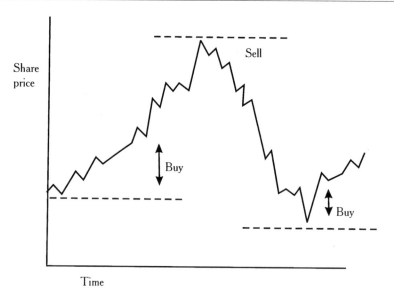

13.6   The random walk hypothesis (RWH)

The RWH views stock markets as highly efficient. At any one time, share prices reflect all the available information about companies and economies, including the best guesses of millions of actual or potential investors about what the future holds. In these conditions prices will change for one reason only: that new information has become available, including any facts or ideas that alter perceptions of the future.

Because new information is unpredictable, future share price movements are unpredictable. Yesterday's share price represented the collective view of yesterday's information. Every day starts out fifty-fifty, so that prices could move up or down depending on the market reaction to new information. Thus the current share price is the best estimate of tomorrow's price, since it reflects all known information and all the estimates and assumptions that investors have made about the future.

13.7   Efficient market hypothesis (EMH)

The EMH developed from the RWH and takes three forms.

Weak form of EMH

The weak form of the EMH seeks to expose the vulnerability of technical analysis by stating that whatever information may be conveyed by charts has already been recognized in the current share price. Thus the current share price already takes account of past price trends and therefore the chart of a share price cannot help in predicting the future share price. One derogatory quotation concerning charts says 'Markets have no memory', referring to the previous comment on the RWH that every day starts out as fifty-fifty.

Semi-strong form of EMH

This theory goes on to say that not only is the chart of the share price (i.e. the price history) reflected in the current price of a share, but that all other publicly available information has been taken into account in the current share price.

The justification for this semi-strong EMH is that all leading companies are under constant examination by a large number of fundamental and technical analysts. Therefore the prices of the shares in these companies reflect the consensus of this expert advice to investors. In addition to investors who deal in a share on the basis of expert advice, there will be non-experts who will buy or sell the shares. However, statistically there is a fifty-fifty chance that a non-expert will be bullish or bearish about a share and therefore the view of the non-experts should cancel out, leaving the expert advisors as the ones whose views move the share price.

As new information becomes available the market will react to it. If the new information changes the market's view of the fundamentals, the share price will immediately adjust to its new intrinsic value.

Strong form of EMH

This strong form states that not only is all publicly available information reflected in the share price of leading shares, but that so too is all privately known 'insider information'. Most 'insider information' in leading companies is quickly available to the analysts because it can be anticipated from other sources. Thus the shares in leading companies are considered to be valued fairly because all information (both public and 'private') is reflected in the present share price.

The strong form of EMH explains and backs up the random walk hypothesis. Leading shares are priced at their current intrinsic values, and their prices will fluctuate in line with changes in information. Changes in fundamentals cannot be predicted and will be instantaneously absorbed into the price, hence share prices will move in a random manner.

13.8 Implications of the EMH for investors

Diversify to reduce risk exposure

Financial commentators have been known to select a portfolio by sticking a pin or dart into the *Financial Times*. The performance of such a randomly chosen portfolio has compared no better and no worse than a carefully selected fund. Thus the investor should simply invest equal amounts in all the leading shares, because every leading share is priced at its intrinsic value. The performance of the portfolio would then represent that of the stock market as a whole, and the investor would be subject to less risk than if he had invested in a single share.

Further research has shown that it is not necessary to invest in every leading share, but that equal amounts invested in 15 different shares from different sectors, chosen at random, will give most of the benefits of diversification, and will prove to be a satisfactory substitute for the 'market portfolio'. This leads us to portfolio theory and index-tracking as an investment management technique, areas we consider later in more detail.

Once the portfolio has been selected, follow a buy-and-hold strategy

There is nothing to be gained by switching once the portfolio of shares has been selected. Switching will involve dealing costs and, possibly, advisory fees. The EMH implies that the shares an investor holds (at whatever price they stand in relation to the original purchase price) are currently valued at their intrinsic value based on currently available information.

Exceptions can arise when changes in market values of the constituent equities mean that particular sectors have become under- or over-represented as a proportion of the total portfolio value. It may then be necessary to switch investments to restore the balance of the portfolio so as to gain maximum benefits of diversification. In addition, it may be beneficial to dispose of certain shares to establish a loss for capital gains tax purposes.

A buy-and-hold strategy may seem to be an inadequate policy when there are market peaks and troughs which signal timely opportunities for active dealing. However, in practice such opportunities become apparent only with the benefit of hindsight. Indeed, very few actively managed portfolios have outperformed the stock market indices consistently over any given period of time, partly because of difficulties in timing major portfolio changes but also because of transaction costs. The rise in popularity of indexed funds, whose portfolios replicate chosen stock market indices, has been heavily influenced by the EMH.

The paradox regarding expert market analysts and advisors

If the current market price represents the intrinsic value of a share, there is little point in individual investors trying to use experts to 'beat the market'. On the other hand, the continuing efficiency of the market may well depend on the efforts of those analysts which will ensure that price movements continually reflect new information. This highlights what is sometimes called the 'free rider' problem – an individual investor may not have the incentive to spend time and incur costs in researching prospects of individual companies, but he does not need to, because these are reflected in its share price.

13.9 The balance of the evidence for and against the EMH

The crash of October 1987

During October 1987, the stock markets of the world experienced a price fall of around one-third. Many writers asked what new information had come to light to cause such a dramatic fall.

In the USA, interest rates had risen, thus driving up the return available from risk-free investments such as Treasury bills. Share prices had to fall so that dividend yields could rise to compensate. In addition, there was a proposed 'merger tax' from the US Congress that would have ended the merger boom. The stocks that fell in price just before the main falls on 'Black Monday' were shares of potential takeover targets.

Some writers claim that the fall was a result of a rational assessment of new information, but others blame mass hysteria, herd instinct, or program trading whereby initial falls in price triggered off automatic computerized sell orders which escalated the price crash.

Monday blues

Some writers quote statistics to show that share prices in general have fallen on Mondays because of sales of shares by private investors. The argument states that private investors make investment decisions over the weekend and then execute these decisions on Monday. Generally speaking, so the argument goes, the private investor is more pessimistic than the institutional investor, and thus the net effect will be to generate sell orders.

Supporters of the EMH would say that if this were true, then other investors would incorporate this information in their investment decision making and would buy on Monday when shares had become temporarily depressed.

The January effect and sell in May and go away

Some writers claim that prices in general have risen in January but have fallen in May. They say that such changes are irrational.

Stabilization techniques for new issues

Issuing houses sometimes make it known that they will buy back a new issue if the price falls in the wake of the launch. Clearly, this means that the price will be artificially supported.

The 'Internet bubble'

Some commentators have argued that the 'irrational exuberance' of the rapid rise and fall in stocks in the TMT (telecoms, media, technology) sector, and in particular those stocks carrying an 'Internet' label, is definitive proof that equity markets are not 'efficient' in the sense of the EMH. How can such dramatic price changes be rationalized on the basis of information flows?

Where does all this leave the EMH?

One point that is important to appreciate is that market volatility does not, of itself, contradict the EMH. If the volatility results from new information constantly being introduced into the market, then it is entirely consistent with the EMH.

However, there is no single 'correct' answer that can prove or disprove the validity of the EMH. The strongest arguments against the EMH are the crash of October 1987 and the inflation and bursting of the 'Internet bubble' in the late 1990s and 2000/1. On the other hand, the failure of professionally-managed funds significantly to outperform the market over long periods of time is quite strong evidence in support of the EMH.

Some would argue that the semi-strong version applies to the shares of major listed companies (i.e. those in the FTSE 100 Index), because of the number of analysts following these shares. The EMH, however, is said to be less in evidence in the shares of smaller listed companies which are followed by fewer analysts. But lower valuations (P/E ratios) for smaller companies is not of itself evidence against the EMH – there can be valid reasons such as weaker market prospects or the dominance of a small number of shareholders in such companies.

Another body of theory known as 'behavioural finance' suggests that investors are influenced by fashions and peer group pressures in their decision-making. This seeks to 'soften' some of the conclusions of the EMH by suggesting that investors may overreact on both the up and down side when market prices are rising and falling respectively. In a rising market, investors overrate their abilities to pick successful stocks and are sucked into the market. Conversely, in a falling market, they lose confidence and rush for the exit. Eventually, 'rationality' reasserts itself and the EMH comes into its own again. However, behavioural finance does suggest that chartism has some validity.

Perhaps the most sensible conclusion about the EMH is that while it generally holds good, particularly in the weak or semi-strong form, there may be quite long periods when it does not, but that the market eventually reverts back and efficiency reasserts itself.

13.10 Directors' share dealings

Directors' dealings in the shares of their companies are often viewed as a useful signal to company prospects. Directors are in a good position to know just how good or bad the companies' prospects are, but in listed companies they are constrained in their share dealings. 'Insider dealing' is a criminal offence and occurs when a person has inside knowledge of happenings, e.g. a prospective takeover bid, and buys or sells shares in order to make a profit from that information. But a director is entitled to buy and sell shares so long as he is not acting on 'price-sensitive' information that is not in the public domain. To prevent any problems the Stock Exchange rules prevent directors from dealing for two months prior to the announcement of interim or final results. Because directors are in a privileged position compared to other shareholders, they are subject to requirements to report their dealings and information is made available about purchases and sales by directors, which can be interpreted to be 'buy' or 'sell' signals for the shares.

'Buy signals'

This is taken as a more significant signal than when a director sells. If he is buying, he is putting his own money 'on the line'. Usually a director will buy because he believes the share price will rise; occasionally he buys as a 'damage limitation exercise' when he feels that the share has been badly depressed and needs bolstering up to aid recovery.

'Sell signals'

These can be misleading, especially if only one director is selling. He may be selling simply to meet personal expenditure such as a large tax bill, or a new house, or a divorce settlement. However, if several of the directors are selling at approximately the same time and in large size transactions, then a 'sell signal' is more likely.

Accuracy of this system

Information about directors' share dealings is now freely available and widely watched. The analysts in this field expect that 75% of the directors' dealings that are interpreted as significant prove to be worthwhile buy or sell signals.

Directors' share dealings are not to be taken in isolation when deciding whether to buy or sell a share, but they are one of the factors professional investors take into account when trying to determine the likely direction of a share price.

13.11 Beta coefficients

The beta coefficient purports to measure the riskiness of a particular share relative to the stock market as a whole. The beta coefficient is an absolute value. If a share has a beta coefficient of one the share is considered to be no more or no less risky than the stock market as a whole. If the beta coefficient exceeds one, the share is considered to be more risky than the market as a whole, and if less than one, less risky.

We are not concerned here how the beta coefficient is calculated, but it is useful to understand a little more about the concept. The total return on a particular share (dividend and capital gain) is compared over a given number of periods with the return on the stock market as a whole for these periods. The beta coefficient represents in a single number the comparative volatility of the return on a share against the volatility of the return on the stock market as a whole.

Generally speaking, a highly-geared share will have a higher beta coefficient than a low-geared share. A 'bullish' investor will look for shares with high beta coefficients, whereas a 'bear' would prefer shares with low beta coefficients. If a share has a high beta coefficient it is said to be 'aggressive', whereas one with a low beta coefficient is said to be 'defensive'.

Other things being equal, shareholders will expect a higher average return from a high-beta stock than from a low-beta stock, since volatility of returns is usually equated with riskiness.

The beta coefficient of each quoted share can be obtained from Datastream. The theoretical basis of beta coefficients is derived from the Capital Asset Pricing Model (CAPM). The CAPM establishes the linkage between returns on an individual security and the market and risk-free rates of return and provides a means by which 'efficient' portfolios can be constructed – we discuss this concept below.

Some writers are not convinced that the beta of a share is an appropriate measure of its risk and hence its expected return relative to other equities. For instance, research has shown that:

- Some low-beta securities earn higher returns that high-beta ones – the opposite of what would be expected.

- Betas change over time. For example, the beta of Marks and Spencer measured from quarterly returns between 1990 and 1999 is 0.68. However, the beta for this company as measured during 1999 based on various 30-day periods of daily returns varied between 0.1 and 1.4.

- Many studies suggest that alphas (returns different from those implied by the beta of a share) can be significantly different from zero. In theory, alphas for individual shares should quickly return to zero as investors buy on excess returns and sell underachievers to bring prices and returns back to those implied by the beta. In practice, this is not always the case.

13.12 Systematic and unsystematic risk

Risks affecting individual shares, and reflected in the betas we have just discussed, are usually classified under two headings.

Systematic risks

Most investments are affected by one of the systematic risks:

Interest-rate risk

This applies to gilts or to any marketable fixed-interest investment. If interest rates in general rise, the price of the stock will fall.

The longer dated the gilt, the more its price will be affected by interest-rate levels. Therefore short-dated stocks can be bought to minimize the risk, because their price will tend to be near to par. Alternatively, bank and building society deposits pay interest linked to market rates and their capital value is not affected.

As a generalization, higher interest rates, or persistent rumours that interest rates are about to rise, usually result in a fall in equity prices, as well as in a fall in fixed-interest stock prices. One reason for this fall in share prices could be that the higher interest rates mean that equity investors will require higher returns from their shares. Thus shareholders will discount forecast dividends or free cash flows at a higher discount rate. Higher discount rates mean lower net present values in any discounted cash flow calculation, and lower NPVs equate to lower share prices.

For example compare the intrinsic value of a share as calculated by the dividend growth method. As we have already seen :

The formula for the Gordon growth model is:

$$Po = \frac{D_1}{(r - g)}$$

where: Po = intrinsic value of the share

D_1 = next dividend

r = investor's required rate of return

g = dividend growth rate

If the next dividend on ABC's shares will be 21p, if future dividend growth is forecast at 5% p.a. and if the required rate of return is 12%, the intrinsic value of the share is:

$$\frac{21}{*(0.12 - 0.05)} = \frac{21}{0.07}$$

Intrinsic value of share = 300p

However, if the required rate for return by equity investors rose from 12% to 14%, the intrinsic value of the share based on the dividend growth model would fall to:

$$\frac{21}{*(0.14 - 0.05)} = \frac{21}{0.09}$$

Intrinsic value of share = 233p

Inflation risk

Rising inflation is usually equated with falling securities prices. The capital value of bank deposits or gilts at maturity will be eroded by inflation, as will the purchasing power of payments under an annuity or fixed-coupon gilt. Inflation equates with uncertainty in the eyes of equity investors, and this can result in share prices being marked down. However, if companies have 'pricing power', and are able to raise the prices they charge in line with, or ahead of, inflation, they may be able to maintain profits in real terms (i.e. after adjustment for inflation). Thus it can be difficult to generalize about the impact of inflation on share prices.

Currently most fixed-interest investments give a 'real' rate of return for basic-rate and non-taxpayers: in other words the monetary return exceeds the rate of inflation. In the long term, equities also have given a 'real' return as shown by the unit trust statistics in Chapter 14. However, the only sure way not to lose from inflation is to buy index-linked NSCs, or index-linked gilts.

The market risk

The performance of the stock market as a whole generally affects the prices of individual shares.

Within the context of direct equity investment, a portfolio of non-durable consumer shares will be less affected by market movements than a portfolio of shares in capital goods producers. This is because the shares of non-durable consumer goods producers generally have low beta coefficients (i.e. are less volatile than the market as a whole), whereas those of capital goods producers have high beta coefficients.

One way to avoid market risk would be to invest in overseas shares but such shares are vulnerable to changes in their own markets and in increasingly globalized financial markets returns in different stock markets are anyway likely to show a high degree of correlation.

In the short run, i.e. up to nine months, investors can buy traded put options on the FTSE 100 or 250 index. If the market as a whole falls, the drop in value of the investor's portfolio will be compensated for by the profit on the traded option.

Unsystematic risks and how to reduce their effect

These are risks that apply to a particular investment, usually thought of in the context of equity investment but also applying to investments such as corporate bonds.

Management risk

Bad decisions can result in poor profits. Try to buy shares in companies with proven management.

Financial risk

Highly-geared companies, or those with heavy liabilities in overseas currency, are at risk here. Study the balance sheets to assess the risk.

Industry risk

Some industries become fashionable investments. The investor needs to be aware of the current 'fashionable' areas, because they often become tomorrow's failures. Similarly, 'out of fashion' sectors can come back into fashion. This is known as 'sector rotation' and we have seen just such a rotation in recent years between 'old' and 'new economy' stocks as the TMT bubble has inflated and then burst.

Reduction of unsystematic risk in a portfolio of shares

Use a mixture of fundamental and technical analysis to select the shares, and spread the risk by buying a minimum of 15 different shares in different sectors. To be cost effective, you need to invest a minimum of £2,000 in each share otherwise the performance of the share will have to be exceptional simply to cover the dealing costs.

Research has shown that most unsystematic risk in an investment portfolio can be diversified away by investing equal amounts at random in 15-20 different shares in different sectors. According to the strong form of EMH, the current share price reflects all information, whether public or private. Thus the current price of any share should equate to its intrinsic value, and new information will affect individual shares in different ways. However, the effects on the performance of the individual shares in a diversified portfolio will tend to cancel each other out, and the portfolio will tend to generate the average return of the market.

Unit trusts, investment trusts and OEICs with professional management and diversification are a means of eliminating most of the unsystematic risk. Buy three or four unit/investment trusts/OEICs under different managers for maximum benefits of diversification.

Note that diversification among equities cannot remove the systematic risk of investing in a particular equity market. Only diversification into other markets and/ or into other forms of investment (such as chattels) can reduce or remove the systematic risk. For this reason, systematic risk is sometimes described as non-diversifiable risk and unsystematic risk as diversifiable risk.

General points on risk reduction

A basic portfolio should include an emergency cash reserve, gilts for guaranteed income, equities with scope for growth of income and capital, and tax-free investments for high taxpayers. In addition, large portfolios benefit from a property element which should be provided by indirect methods such as property bonds. This structure spreads the risk across a range of different types of investment, thus increasing diversification.

13.13   Modern portfolio theory: Background

The view shared by most academics is that the only way persistently to beat the average return generated by the market is to assume more risk than the market average risk. Portfolio theory seeks to explain how portfolio diversification may help the investor to achieve an above market average return without exceeding the average market risk.

The usual way to measure the risk associated with investment in a particular share is via calculation of the *probable variability of future returns*. In other words risk may be measured in terms of the *variance* or *standard deviation* of the expected return. *The higher the variance/standard deviation, the higher the risk.*

For example, let us assume that the average return on a particular share over a period of time, say one year, had been 10%, and that the standard deviation of the returns had been 3.5%. This means, applying standard statistical assumptions, that :

● around 68% of actual measured returns on the share will have been within one standard deviation of the 10% average return;

- around 95% of actual measured returns on the share will have been within two standard deviations of the expected return;

- around 99.73% of actual measured returns on the portfolio will have been within three standard deviations of the expected return.

Therefore, for this particular share:

- measured returns will have been between 13.5% p.a. and 6.5% p.a. (10 +/- 3.5) for around 68% of the time;

- measured returns will have been between 17% p.a. and 3% p.a. (10+/-7) for around 95% of the time; and

- measured returns will have been between 20.5% p.a. and -0.5% p.a. (10+/-10.5) for 99.73% of the time.

Thus, concentrating on the downside risk, if we assume that the future will follow past trends, there is about a 16% chance of return falling below 6.5%, (100- 68) ÷ 2, but only around a 2.5% chance, (100 – 95)÷ 2, of the return falling below 3% p.a., and less than a 1% chance of the return falling to minus 0.5% p.a.

However, an investment in the equity shares of a high-risk company would involve the acceptance of possibly quite variable returns (and in some years negative returns, i.e. losses). As the actual return might vary considerably from the expected average return on a year-by-year basis, the associated variance/standard deviation of the return on the risky equity would tend to be high.

A security generating a stable return with little possibility of that return deviating from the expected level will involve little risk and will have a very small (or even zero) standard deviation. This would apply, for example, to a short-dated gilt-edged stock, or to a three-month Treasury bill.

The relative variability of returns on two securities is known as their *covariance*.

- Where the returns on the two securities have a very close positive correlation (i.e. the returns move up and down together in response to particular events) the covariance of the returns on the securities is high and positive.

- Where the patterns of variability in returns have a fairly random relationship, the covariance of the two securities is small and may be positive or negative in sign.

- Where there is a near perfect negative relationship between the variability of the returns on the securities, the covariance is high and negative.

13.14   Application of modern portfolio theory

We can apply the concept of covariance in constructing portfolios that match investor requirements. For example, if the returns on two securities have a high negative covariance, it is possible to eliminate much of the risk faced in holding each individually by instead holding both securities in a portfolio. Consider the following:

Security	X	Y
Returns in years with hot weather	30%	-10%
Returns in years with cold weather	-10%	30%
Let us assume X is an ice cream manufacturer and Y is a central heating company		

Assuming that the weather is either 'hot' or ' cold' (and hence that all possible outcomes are covered):

● Investing in Security X produces a good return in years when the weather is good, but generates a loss in the years when the weather is bad. If an investor holds just Security X, then a series of years of bad weather could be very damaging financially.

● Investing in Security Y produces a good return in years when the weather is bad, but a poor return when the weather is good.

● By dividing investment funds evenly between Securities X and Y, the investor will receive:

a return of 10% when the weather is good – i.e. (0.5 x 30% return on Security X) + (0.5 x –10% return on Security Y); and

a return of 10% when the weather is bad – i.e. (0.5 x –10% return on Security X) + (0.5 x 30% return on Security Y).

Therefore, irrespective of the weather, by holding the two-security portfolio an investor receives a constant return from year-to-year. Compare this to the outcome of holding just one or other of the securities, when the return will be volatile. In this hypothetical case the risk associated with the return on the two securities has been eliminated entirely and the standard deviation for the returns on this two-share portfolio would be nil.

However, in reality it is most unlikely that the returns on two securities would be so perfectly matched as to eliminate entirely the risk associated with their respective returns. But, so long as the returns on the securities held within a portfolio respond in different ways to developments or economic events (i.e. in technical terms, their returns are less than perfectly correlated), the risk embodied in the portfolio is reduced through diversification.

Thus by adding to a portfolio a security the return on which has a negative covariance with the returns on the securities already held, the risk associated with the portfolio as a whole will be reduced.

Obviously, holding just two different securities does not constitute a diversified portfolio. Fifteen or more different securities is normally thought of as being the minimum number of securities required to achieve significant risk reduction, and generally the greater the number of securities invested in, the smaller will be the impact of fluctuations in one security on the value of an investor's portfolio (remember the old adage – 'don't put all your eggs in one basket').

The key to selecting a diversified portfolio is to be found in selecting securities that are influenced by different sets of economic and financial variables, or are affected differently by particular economic and financial variables. In practice, this means that risks can be reduced by selecting securities from companies in different business sectors. Diversification can take the form of holding shares in different companies (i.e. diversification <u>within</u> a class of assets) and/or by holding different classes of assets (e.g. UK equities, US equities, UK fixed interest securities, real property etc.).

In reality all portfolios of securities, irrespective of the diversity of their content, carry some risk. Selecting low-risk shares, which have returns with negative covariances, may reduce the variability of returns, but it does not eliminate the chance that in any given year losses will be made.

An interesting consequence of portfolio theory is that it may be possible to construct a portfolio with a low level of risk overall, but composed of individually very risky shares, if in combination the risks are low because returns have very low correlation/covariances.

Another important concept here is that of the 'efficient portfolio'. An 'efficient' portfolio is one that delivers a given return for the minimum possible risk (i.e. if there are several different possible portfolios that all have the same mean return, the efficient portfolio is the one with the lowest standard deviation) or the highest return for a given level of risk (i.e. if there are several different possible portfolios that all have the same level of risk – the same standard deviation of returns – the efficient portfolio is the one with the highest mean return). This is sometimes referred to as 'mean-variance optimization' – establishing the best balance of risk versus return.

The calculation of standard deviations and the other statistical methodology associated with betas (β) and Modern Portfolio Theory is beyond the scope of this text. Indeed whole text books have been devoted to these topics. For a very readable yet in-depth study of the EMH, beta, Modern Portfolio Theory and related areas, readers are recommended to study *A Random Walk Down Wall Street*, published by W. W. Norton and Co and written by Burton G. Malkiel.

14

UNIT TRUSTS AND OPEN-ENDED INVESTMENT COMPANIES (OEICs)

Objectives

After studying this chapter, you should be able to:

● define and describe a unit trust;

● differentiate between the roles of managers and trustees;

● explain how unit trusts are regulated;

● describe (briefly) the role of the Association of Unit Trusts and Investment Funds (AUTIF);

● analyse the principles of the pricing of unit trusts;

● differentiate between the different types of unit trusts;

● evaluate the various unit trusts available;

● explain the nature of open-ended investment companies (OEICs).

14.1   Introduction

Direct investments are ones that are selected and reviewed by the investor himself, or by a discretionary manager (see Chapter 2). On the other hand, with indirect investments individuals hand over their money to professional managers who manage the pooled funds on behalf of their investors. In this chapter and in Chapters 15 and 16 we look at the major forms of indirect investment: unit trusts, investment trusts, OEICs, pension funds and insurance products.

14.2   What is a unit trust?

A unit trust is a fund into which investors pool their money. This money is invested by professional managers in a wide range of investments such as cash, shares, gilts, loan stocks, property, warrants, futures and options.

When an investor contributes money to the fund he will receive a number of units of the fund in exchange for his investment. All units of the same fund rank equally, and at any one time the value of a unit reflects the total value of the funds under management divided by the number of units in existence. We shall examine the pricing of units in more detail later on, but for now suffice it to say that the price of a unit is based on the net asset value of that unit.

Unit trusts are 'open ended' so that when new monies are received by the managers new units are created. When investors withdraw their money from the pool the units are cancelled in exchange for their cash value, which is returned to investors.

Obviously when new monies exceed redemptions the managers will have additional cash to invest, but if redemptions exceed new monies then it may be necessary for managers to liquidate some of the fund's underlying investments to meet these redemptions.

The unit trust 'industry' has approximately 17.2 million unit-holder accounts and funds under management valued at approximately £257.286 billion. This makes it a vital part of the UK investment scene. These figures relate to authorized unit trusts as at February 2001.

The role of the managers

The role of the managers is to invest the unit holders' money in accordance with the stated objectives of the trust. They are also responsible for calculating the bid and offer prices of the units, the bid prices being the price at which the managers will buy units and the offer being the price at which they will sell them.

Most individual fund managers are part of a management group which controls a number of different trusts. Generally speaking, there is an overall group philosophy with regard to liquidity levels, the number of securities in which a trust should invest, the size of companies invested in and how actively the fund is to be managed. This philosophy will be influenced by the group's collective view of the UK and overseas economies. The individual fund manager will normally invest in accordance with the parameters laid down by the group as a whole. Fund managers are not necessarily expected to subscribe fully to the group view, but it is unlikely that any radical departures would either arise or be tolerated. This is why performance of an individual trust will tend to reflect the performance of the other trusts under the same management group as well as the benchmark(s) for the sector in which the trust invests.

The role of the trustees

Trustees are substantial financial institutions, and the Financial Services and Markets Act 2000 lays down strict requirements regarding minimum capitalization of trustees. They are also of the highest financial standing and integrity; companies such as Royal Bank of Scotland and Barclays Bank Trust Co act as trustees.

The role of the trustee involves the following:

- Safeguarding the assets of the unit holders. All cash and securities in the fund are held in the trustee's name so that there is no possibility of misappropriation by the managers;

- Issuing certificates to the unit holder or regular statements if the trust is in uncertificated form;

- Ensuring that the relevant unit certificate has been duly cancelled before any proceeds are released to meet the sale of units;

- Collecting the dividend income of the trust and distributing the income by way of distribution to the unit holders (note the correct term is a *distribution*, not a dividend);

- Supervising the register of unit holders;

- Ensuring that the trust is managed within the terms of the trust deed (a formal document that lays down investment guidelines for managers);

- Vetting any advertisement to ensure that it is not misleading and checking that the advertisement states that unit trust prices can fall as well as rise.

Trustee supervision of the investments made by the managers

The trustee must ensure that the investment aims of the trust are complied with, and since all investment is to some extent subjective, there can be different interpretations of how the investment policy should be supervised. Some trustees take this duty to the point of being prepared to veto any investment that they feel conflicts with the unit holders' interests. Other trustees take a more relaxed view and are prepared to veto an investment only where it contravenes the terms of the trust deed.

Payment of trustees

The fee is fixed by negotiation between the trustees and the managers.

14.3   The role of the Financial Services Authority (FSA)

Under the Financial Services Act 1986 only unit trusts that are 'authorized' by the Financial Services Authority are allowed to advertise. All authorized unit trusts are governed by a trust deed which must be approved by the Financial Services Authority (FSA). This deed will cover such matters as maximum management fees, the precise method of calculating the bid and offer prices, and the provisions enabling new investors to join.

As regards the investments made by the managers, an approved trust deed must contain the following minimum requirements:

- Investments must be in securities that are quoted on a recognized stock exchange (although up to 25% of the funds can be invested in shares of companies quoted on the Alternative Investment Market (AIM)), of which 10% may be held in unlisted securities or non-British recognized stock exchanges.

- No single share holding can be acquired which, at the time of its purchase, would represent more than 5% of the value of the whole of the trust's portfolio.

- There can be problems regarding the 5% stipulation if a particular investment increases rapidly in value after acquisition, but as long as its value does not exceed $7\frac{1}{2}$% of the fund the trustees will not be obliged to intervene.

- A unit trust may not hold more than 10% of the share capital of one particular company.

The Financial Services Authority insists on these minimum constraints, although there is nothing to prevent a more restrictive trust deed being drawn up. These constraints ensure that the investments are readily realizable. Thus the managers can buy or sell units at any time and can easily obtain cash if it is required to meet net redemptions of units.

14.4   The Association of Unit Trusts and Investment Funds (AUTIF)

This association is an example of the City of London's desire to keep its own house in order by self-regulation.

The objectives of the association are:

- to make representations to the UK government on legislative, regulatory and taxation matters which affect the business interests of its members;

- to liase with the Financial Services Authority and other organizations in the UK and Europe on regulatory matters and other important issues;

- to increase public awareness and understanding of investment funds;

- to seek to improve the standards of training in the industry;

- to seek to integrate personal finance education into the school curriculum;

- to add value to member companies by providing them with information, guidance and assistance in matters related to their business;

- to offer an information service to external parties interested in the activities of the UK investment funds industry.

AUTIF is a powerful force in the financial services industry, working closely with the regulatory and tax authorities in the UK, the EU and around the world, as well as the other major trade associations and leading financial journalists.

Membership of the association is open to any management company of a unit trust that is authorized by the Financial Services Authority. The work of the association is financed by contributions from members based on the volume of funds managed by each particular group.

One of the most valuable functions of AUTIF is the provision of information. Monthly statistics regarding the number of unit trusts and value of funds under management are published, and any significant developments are chronicled. AUTIF will answer any general enquiries on unit trusts, although it cannot advise on the merits of individual trusts.

14.5   The regulatory authority

The unit trust industry used to be regulated by the PIA (Personal Investment Authority) and IMRO (Investment Management Regulatory Organization). These authorities have now been superseded by the Financial Services Authority which undertakes to ensure that the law governing unit trusts and OEICs as stated in the Financial Services and Market Act 2000 is upheld.

14.6   Pricing of unit trust units

Net asset or creation value as a basis of prices

We have already noted that the value of a unit at any one time will be based on its 'net asset value'. If a fund's assets (i.e. its investments at current valuation together with accrued income and the brokerage costs) totalled £10 million and if there were five million units in existence, then the net asset value per unit would be £2. This net asset value is more correctly called the creation price. If the value of those assets were to increase to £15 million, the creation price of the units would become £3 per unit, provided there had been no new units created and no redemptions. If a unit holder wished to redeem his units when the assets had increased to £15 million, he would receive around £3 per unit. Likewise, a new investor would expect to pay around £3 per unit if he bought units at this time.

Prices are published in the financial press. There are two prices, the higher offer price at which managers will sell to the public, and the lower bid price at which they will buy the units back. The formula for valuing unit trusts is laid down by the FSA. The *Financial Times* does not use the terms 'bid' and 'offer', instead using the clearer names 'selling price' – the price the seller of units receives – is the same as the 'bid price' and 'buying price' or 'offer price' is the price a buyer pays.

The bid and offer prices

In practice some adjustment is necessary to the creation price before the units can be priced by the managers. Administration, dealing costs, trustees' fees, and the manager's own fees have to be paid for. These expenses are allowed for in the spread between the bid and offer prices. The manager's fees consist of the initial charge, which is incorporated in the bid offer price spread of the units, and an annual management fee of, on average, 1-1½%. Most trust deeds specify that the managers can make an initial charge (known as a front-end loading charge) of a percentage of the value of the units purchased, but this charge is incorporated in the spread between bid and offer prices. The average initial charge is about 5%. Under FSA rules, the maximum spread between bid and offer prices would work out at around 10% – but even this is not a statutory maximum figure. However, most managers work to a spread of around 6% between the two prices, since a larger difference may well reduce the attractiveness of the units. Some unit trust managers have reduced the front-end loading charge to around 1% to make the trust more attractive to investors and some intermediaries or brokers offer investers units at discounted prices (by reducing their commission paid out of the initial charge).

In practical terms the significance of the spread to an investor is that the units must rise by the amount of that spread before he can recoup his original investment. In the simplest possible terms, if the offer price of units is 100p and there is a spread of 6%, the investor would buy from the managers at 100p, and if he sold them back the same day he would receive only 94p per unit.

There are no commission charges for lump-sum investments made direct with the managers, but an annual management fee of around ¾-1½% is deducted from either the distribution paid out to unit holders or the value of the fund. Increasingly, the annual fee is levied on the value of the fund,. When the annual fee is deducted from the value of the fund, the published dividend yield will be higher than if the fee is deducted from income. The apparently higher yield, however, is obtained at the expense of capital erosion.

Historic and forward pricing

Unit trusts are valued and repriced daily. In essence, the price of unit trust units is based on creation value with a margin allowed for managers' fees and costs. Pricing can be on one of two methods, historic or forward:

● *Historic pricing.* This is the price calculated on the price set at the most recent valuation. Investors will deal at the price shown in today's newspaper.

● *Forward pricing.* The price for the units is the price to be set at the next valuation. Investors will not know the exact price at which they have dealt until the next day.

Some unit trusts use historic pricing, some forward pricing, some use historic up to a set time then go onto forward pricing, and some switch between the two depending on the mood of the market. The pricing basis is indicated in the financial press for each trust. Investors purchasing or selling units priced on the forward basis are effectively 'dealing blind'. The previous day's price acts as a guide and the movement in the stock market from the previous day should give some indication as to whether the unit price will be higher or lower than the previous day's price. The managers must deal at a forward price on request and may move to forward pricing at any time.

Prices quoted on a bid basis, offer basis and the cancellation price

Note: The *Financial Times* refers to the 'bid price as the 'buying price' and the 'offer price as the 'selling price' . These prices are from the manager's point of view, thus the offer/selling price will be the higher of the two prices quoted.

If the trust is expanding with new monies exceeding redemptions, the managers will usually quote their prices on an offer basis, but conversely when there are net redemptions a bid price basis is often used.

When a price is quoted on an offer basis it means that the managers sell units to investors at the maximum offer price using the FSA formula, with the bid price being set at around 6% below this. If prices are quoted on a bid basis the managers will set the bid price at the lowest possible amount using the FSA formula and will then set the offer price around 6% above this figure. Some management groups are reducing the bid/offer spread from around the 6% mark to around 1% in order to encourage investors into the trust.

Example of offer and bid price calculations

Calculation of the maximum offer price under the FSA formula

Suppose the total value of securities held by a fund, based on the lowest available market dealing offer prices, is £5 million and suppose there are five million units. The value of the securities divided by the number of units is £1.

	Pence
Net asset value per unit of securities (£5m – 5m units)	100.00
Add brokerage (say 0.25%)	0.25
Add accrued interest, dividends and cash (say)	0.75
Creation price	101.00
Add Manager's initial charge (say 5%)	5.05
Maximum offer price	106.05

Calculation of the minimum bid price under the FSA formula

Bid price
Suppose the total value of these securities was £4.9 million when valued at the highest available market dealing bid price. The unit value of a single unit on this basis would be 98p.

	Pence
Unit value (£4.9m ÷ 5m units)	98.000
Deduct brokerage (say 0.25%)	0.245
	97.755
Add accrued income as above	0.750
Minimum bid price/cancellation price	98.505

The maximum spread here is 7.545p - 7.11% of the offer price. However, we have already said that market forces will tend to restrict the spread to around 6%. Thus if the managers were dealing on an offer basis their prices could be:

- offer   106.05p
- bid   99.687p (6% below offer price)

If the pricing were on a bid basis, it would probably be:

- offer   104.7925
- bid   98.505p (6% below offer price)

Notes

1. The cancellation price is the lowest price at which the managers would be allowed to repurchase units from investors. This price in the above example would be 98.505p, which equates to the lowest price under the terms of the FSA formula. When dealings are on a bid basis, the cancellation price and the bid price are the same.

2. The figures have to be adjusted by rounding up or down, because unit prices are usually quoted to two decimal places. The method of rounding up or down is governed by the FSA formula.

3. The manager's initial charge/front-end fee is set out in the trust deed relating to the units. Clearly the higher this charge, the greater the spread. However, the FSA formula imposes limits on the maximum front-end fee.

4. In practice, managers often quote their bid/offer prices somewhere in between the bid or offer basis. In the above example, the bid/offer prices might have been 99p and 105.32p.

Why bid and offer price basis is important to the investor

There is nothing in law to stop the managers changing their basis of pricing overnight, provided the prices are within the figures calculated from the FSA formula. A sudden change in market sentiment could make the managers decide to switch from a bid to offer basis on bullish news and from an offer to bid basis if a bear market seemed imminent. This means that someone who bought units priced on an offer basis could in theory find their 'resale' value had fallen by 10% overnight if the basis of pricing had been changed to bid. In practice the managers would try to smooth the transition over a week or two, but this is not always possible.

Another point for the private investor to bear in mind is that advertisements can be misleading if they quote the unit prices at the start and end of a period on an 'offer-to-offer' basis. If a unit trust unit started the period at 100p and finished it at 115p priced on an offer-to-offer basis, the investor who wished to realize his gain could only sell at the bid price of around 108p. Thus the true gain, ignoring any income distribution, is 8%, not the 15% shown.

The significance of the bid and offer price to the managers

Unit trust managers can buy back their own units, so the concept of 'box management' can be applied when a fund is expanding. However much the net purchases of units by investors, the traffic will be two-way with new purchases exceeding redemptions. The managers can therefore make a tidy profit from buying the units at the bid price and then reselling immediately at the offer price, without the need to disturb the underlying fund as regards these transactions.

The converse applies at times of net redemptions. However, net redemptions usually occur when the market as a whole is in decline so the net asset basis will be falling continually.

Conclusions regarding spreads

Although the spreads are important, market forces have tended to bring most spreads into line. In any event, unit trust units should normally be considered as a long-term investment and in this context it is the investment performance of the units that matters, not their spread.

14.7   Distribution and accumulation units

The differences between these two kinds of unit

The income earned by the trust must be distributed to the unit holders, after deduction of the annual management fee of 1-1½% and other expences such as the trustee's fee and audit fees. Such distributions generally take place twice a year, but some trusts pay out the income more often.

If the trust is a distribution trust, which is the commonest type, the distribution is made in cash. The tax position of the investor is the same as for any other dividend in that a 10% tax deduction is made and basic-rate taxpayer has no further liability. However, non-taxpayers CANNOT reclaim the tax deducted from the gross equivalent, and higher-rate taxpayers pay the difference between 32.5% and 10%, i.e. 22.5% on the gross equivalent. When yields are quoted for unit trusts, they are quoted on a gross basis and are calculated in the same way as the gross dividend yield on a share, i.e. the net distribution is grossed up by 100/90.

Accumulation funds work on the basis that the trust is split into two: one which distributes the income and an accumulation fund which retains income distributions for reinvestment in the fund. Two different prices are quoted for the distribution and accumulation funds.

For example, the Perpetual unit trust managers use this basis for their accumulation units and the price of the two is different as shown from the following figures taken from the *Financial Times* of 4 April 2001.

Perpetual Unit Trust Management Ltd		
	Selling price	**Buying price**
High Income income	182.66	194.32
High Income accumulation	196.31	202.85

On a sale an investor who held funds in the distribution part of the fund would receive 182.66p per unit (bid price), while the holder of accumulation units would receive 196.31p per unit. The holder of accumulation units would have the same number of units at all times (assuming no sales or purchases are made), but his accumulated distribution is reflected in the higher unit price.

At first sight this may seem a wonderful way of avoiding income tax, but in practice this is not the case. The unit trust will issue every unit holder with a tax certificate showing the distribution retained in the fund on his behalf. The sum shown will be the net figure, and the investor will face exactly the same tax consequences as would apply to a cash distribution.

There is one particular advantage of accumulation units. The new units created in lieu of a cash distribution are issued below the published offer price because the administration required is less complex than that needed to create new units for new unit holders.

The significance of 'xd' (ex distribution) on distribution unit trusts

Apart from the final six weeks before income is due to be paid to unit holders, the offer price of a unit trust includes the accrued income since the last distribution. The price quoted in the *Financial Times* is always the 'cum distribution' price unless the letters 'xd' are shown.

The day after its accounting date a trust goes 'ex distribution', and anyone buying units on this date or during the next six weeks will not receive the next distribution. To compensate for this the unit price falls on xd day by the exact amount of the net of 10% tax distribution due.

14.8   Taxation

Income tax position on distributions paid to the investor

All distributions will have tax deducted in exactly the same way as dividends from shares – 10% tax is deducted. This satisfies the 10% and basic-rate taxpayer's liability. Non-taxpayers CANNOT reclaim the tax deducted and 40% taxpayers must pay a further 22.5% (32.5% – 10%) tax on the gross equivalent distribution (gross up 100/90).

Capital gains tax position

The position is:

- As regards the trust itself: unit trusts themselves are entirely exempt from capital gains tax. Thus the managers can buy or sell shares or other securities on their investment merits, without the need to consider CGT.

- As regards unit holders: however, investors are subject to CGT on disposals of the units. CGT is levied on capital gains on disposals of units in exactly the same way as it is levied on disposals of shares or of any other securities.

- From the point of view of the small investor it should be perfectly possible to avoid CGT on unit trusts altogether, simply by using the £7,500 exemption limit and by taking advantage of the indexation allowances.

- Most fund managers do not charge investors extra if they hold their unit trust in the tax-free 'wrapper' of a PEP or an ISA. From an individual investor's perspective therefore, if they hold a unit trust through one of these tax-free vehicles they can escape CGT altogether, as well as enjoying the income tax benefits.

See Chapter 17 for details of PEPs and ISAs.

Corporation tax as regards the trust itself

Unit trusts pay corporation tax at the lower rate of 20% on all income. Distributions carry a tax credit of 10% and interest distributions (from funds investing in fixed-interest bonds) are paid net of 20% tax.

14.9   Dealing in unit trust units

Unit trust units are purchased from the managers at their offer price and sold back at the bid price. There is no secondary market. When a new trust is being created it is usually advertised in newspapers with a fixed price until the closing date of the offer. Funds received prior to the deadline will be allocated units at the set price. Any funds received after that closing date will be allocated units at the offer price ruling on that date. Prices of authorized unit trusts are quoted daily in the *Financial Times*, and the addresses and telephone numbers of the managers are also printed there.

It is quite possible to obtain units through an agent such as a bank, solicitor, stockbroker, accountant or unit trust broker. Generally speaking, the unit trust managers will pay a share of their front-end loading fee as a commission to the intermediary, but the investor himself will still pay only the offer price. The position is quite different when an investor sells unit trusts. Managers will not pay commission on redemptions, and if an intermediary is used to effect the sale he will usually make a separate charge for his services to be borne by the seller. The moral is simple. If you wish to sell your units, deal direct with the managers.

As regards the mechanics of dealing, the process is very simple. On purchase of units an investor receives a contract note specifying the number of units bought, the price per unit and the consideration. Settlement is on 'cash' terms and the certificate will be received in six to eight weeks.

To sell units the investor signs the form of renunciation on the back of the certificate and then sends the certificate to the managers or, in the case of uncertificated trusts, to complete a sale order. The proceeds of the sale should be received within a week.

14.10 Unit trust information in the *Financial Times*

Baring Fund Managers Ltd (1200) H

	Init. Chg%	Notes	Selling price	Buying price	+ or −	Yield Grs
UK Growth	5		160.3	170.90	-2.2	0.2

ACM Investments Ltd. (0830) F

	Init. Chg%	Notes	Selling price	Buying price	+ or −	Yield Grs
Gilt Income	1½		53.53	54.39	+0.06	5.8

Explanation of columns

- Initial charge (Init. Chg.): Manager's 'front-end loading fee' (5% charge or 1½%).

- Selling price: The manager's buying or 'bid' price (i.e. price the seller of units receives − 160.3p or 53.53p).

- Buying price: The manager's selling or 'offer' price (i.e. price the buyer would pay for units purchased − 170.90p or 54.39p).

- + or -: Price movement since the last price calculation (-2.2 or +0.06).

- Gross yield: Equivalent to gross dividend yield on equities, the estimated annual pre-tax yield expressed as a percentage of the quoted offer price (0.2% or 5.8%).

- Time quoted: The time at which the managers' prices are set (8.30 a.m. or 12 noon)

- H or F: The pricing basis H for historic, F for forward.

    In addition there are four symbols that may occur against individual funds: heart, club, diamond or spade. These symbols indicate that the fund is revalued at a different time from the time shown against the manager's name.

Heart   ♥   0001-1100 hours.

Club   ♣   1101-1400 hours.

Diamond ♦   1401-1700 hours.

Spade   ♠   1701-midnight.

The 'Notes' column carries one of two letters:

'C' indicating that all or part of the Manager's periodic charge (management fee) is deducted from capital value of the fund rather than from income, which is more usual.

'E' indicating there is an exit charge on sale of the units. This can apply to funds that do not levy an initial charge, although a few funds do charge both an initial charge and an exit charge. An exit charge is designed to dissuade investors from selling the units and persuading them to become long-term holders.

14.11   Categories of unit trust

The FSA categories of unit trusts

The FSA categorises authorized unit trust schemes into nine types (see below). These categories apply to unit trusts, their managers and trustees and a fund will have to fit into one of these categories for regulatory purposes. However for marketing purposes these nine categories are insufficient to ensure that the target market for the unit trusts is clear about the wide range of funds which are available. AUTIF categorizes funds into 32 categories (see below), all of which will actually fit into the nine FSA-specified broad categories.

	Type of fund	FSA definition of fund
1.	Securities funds	This fund consists of 'transferable securities', but excludes warrants, feeder and fund of funds. 'Transferable securities' is a very broad definition and includes all stocks and shares quoted on a recognized stock exchange.
2.	Money market funds	This type of fund can invest in cash and near cash (a deposit repayable within 6 months), also investments such as bills of exchange and loan stock if repayable within 12 months
3.	Futures and options funds	These consist of derivatives (see Chapter 9). Most or all of the are fully covered by cash, securities or other derivatives. This classification also covers investments in gold.
4.	Geared futures and options funds	Although this has similarities to the futures and options funds, a geared futures and options fund can take on an exposure of up to 20% of its investments at the time of inception of the fund. However, it cannot subsequently borrow.

5. Property funds

The property can be in the UK or abroad. A property fund must obtain £5m during the initial offer period. If it does not achieve this the scheme may be revoked. If the fund is succesful in achieving £5 million it can then be invested within a band of 20% - 80% in 'approved immovables' i.e. any interest in land or in a building subject to certain criteria as laid down in the Financial Services (Regulated Securities) Regulations 1991. The land or buildings can be in the UK, a member state or in certain other countries specified in the Regulations.

6. Warrant funds

Warrants are a form of derivative, and a warrant fund is allowed to invest up to 100% of its money in warrants.

7. Feeder funds

A feeder fund is a relevant pension scheme invested in either a single or regulated collective investment scheme or a single eligible investment trust.

8. Fund of funds

A fund of funds is a scheme that must invest in at least five regulated collective investment schemes (a unit trust is an example of a collective investment). A fund of funds cannot invest in a feeder fund, another fund of funds, or an umbrella fund.

9. Umbrella funds

An umbrella fund can invest in any of the above funds. Thus it has a wider range of funds available than a fund of funds.

The Financial Services (Regulated Securities) Regulations 1991 specifies that most of the above funds have borrowing powers up to 10% of the value of the assets of the fund, subject to stringent conditions laid down in the Regulations. Of the funds listed above only Geared Option and Futures Fund (number 4) CANNOT borrow. Umbrella funds (number 9) are not specifically covered by the borrowing powers because they can invest in funds that can borrow.

The role of AUTIF

AUTIF (Association of Unit Trusts and Investment Funds) has placed the different unit trusts into 32 categories so as to help the investor to narrow down the choice. Since there are currently around 1,600 authorized unit trusts and OEICs this segmentation is of great service to unit holders and potential unit holders.

Perhaps of even more importance is the fact that AUTIF regularly publishes the performance of a 'median' (unidentified) fund in each of the categories. The investor can obtain such information from AUTIF.

Thus investors and potential investors can regularly monitor the performance of their chosen fund against the 'median' for the sector as a whole. Naturally it is of much more benefit to compare a fund with its sector, rather than with trusts as a whole, because there will be times when that sector as a whole compares very well with unit trusts in general, and there will be other times when the reverse is true. At least with this method the investor is able to obtain an impartial benchmark for comparing like with like.

The 32 categories are:

- UK Gilts
- UK Other Bonds
- UK Corporate Bonds
- Global Bonds
- Managed Income
- UK Equity & Bond Income
- UK Equity Income
- Global Equity Income
- Money Market
- Protected/Guaranteed Funds
- UK All Companies
- UK Smaller Companies
- Japan
- Japanese Smaller Companies
- Far East Including Japan
- Far East Excluding Japan
- North America
- North American Smaller Companies
- Europe Including UK
- Europe Excluding UK
- European Smaller Companies
- UK Equity & Bond
- Cautious Managed

- Balanced Managed
- Active Managed
- Global Equity & Bond
- Global Growth
- Global Emerging Markets
- Property
- Specialist
- Index Bear Funds
- Personal Pensions

AUTIF provides a definition of each of their categories on their web site at: www.investmentfunds.org.uk/about_uksector_def/default.htm.

AUTIF also provides graphical examples of the returns from £1,000 invested in various types of unit trust compared to £2,500 minimum invested in an average building society instant access account on a net and gross interest basis and a net and gross income reinvested basis. The examples take returns over periods of 5, 10 15 and 20 years. AUTIF also provides graphical statistics on 'The power of monthly saving'. The graph compares the performance of £50 per month saving in the UK All Companies Fund compared to a building society account for 5, 10 and 15 years (net interest) to the performance of the UK Equity Income sector – net interest reinvested and to the same trust held in a PEP or ISA savings plan. These comparisons are on an offer-to-bid basis with net and gross income reinvested.

The monthly savings show that £50 per month produces the following returns:

	Building Society – net interest	Building Society – gross interest	UK All Companies net income re-invested	UK All Companies gross income re-invested
5 years (£3,000 invested)	3254	3307	3992	4014
10 years (£6,000 invested)	7015	7322	11883	12065
15 years (£9,000 invested)	12355	13719	23698	24667

Figures for the period from 1 September 1990 to 1 September 2000
It is quite clear from these figures that in the long term money invested in a unit trust should produce a considerably higher return than leaving the money in a bank or building society account. Although these figures would imply that investing in a building society (or a bank) would look an unattractive proposition, the investor must understand the risks of investing either directly or indirectly in the Stock Market. One of the main problems that can affect

the return on Stock Market-based investments is the volatility of the market. In the short term it is possible to make very good gains, but equally it is also possible to make very large losses. If the Stock Market falls heavily, as it did early in 2001, when it was declared a bear market, then the performance figures may not look as attractive over the short term.

Of course, there could be a subsequent rise in the market that would compensate for the short-term falls earlier in the year. However, the concept of pound cost averaging will show how these high and lows of the market are evened out by monthly savings.

Pound cost averaging

Because a fixed sum is invested in units every month it follows that the average cost of the units to the investor will be below the average price for any given period. This is because the fixed sum buys more units in a month where prices are low, and fewer in a month when prices are high.

Let us take a simple, exaggerated, example to illustrate the point. Suppose the investor makes a monthly transfer of £20 for three months. Let us calculate the consequences for a given set of prices.

	Offer price	Number of units bought
Month 1	100p	20
Month 2	166p	12
Month 3	200p	10

Average offer price 155p

Average cost £60 ÷ 42 = 143p

The basic effect of what may seem to be a statistical quirk is that your money is never committed at the top of the market, although you can never effect all your purchases at the bottom. Regular savings ensures that all the investors' funds are not committed when the market is at a temporary peak, a danger that can apply to lump-sum investment. Thus, pound cost averaging does bring more stability to the investment.

14.12 Types of unit trust schemes available

Savings plans

The investor arranges monthly transfers, usually for a minimum of £20 per month, to the unit trust managers. The managers allocate units to the investor on the basis of their current offer prices.

Regular savings plans are an ideal savings vehicle. Because there is no contract, the amount invested can be altered at any time or the savings scheme stopped without any tax or other consequences. The units can be sold back to the managers at their current bid price, with little likelihood of capital gains tax because of the current £7,500 exemption. The taxation of distributions, whether distributed or accumulated, is exactly the same as for distributions on lump-sum investments in unit trust units.

Share exchange schemes

Virtually all unit trust managers offer these schemes. Anybody who owns shares direct may be able to take advantage of this type of scheme, whereby the managers would take over ownership of the shares and issue units in exchange. Naturally, the managers reserve the right to refuse any shares which they feel are unsuitable. The benefits of share exchanges schemes for the investor are:

- A reduction, or possibly total elimination of the brokers' commission which would normally arise on a sale of shares.

- The trust could simply acquire the shares directly from the shareholder by taking from him the certificates and signed stock transfer forms.

- The managers may be prepared to credit the shareholder with the offer price value of the shares, and use this as the basis upon which to calculate the number of units to be issued in exchange.

Note: the use of share exchange scheme will still count as a 'disposal' of the original shares for CGT purposes.

Exempt unit trusts

Exempt unit trusts are trusts that are available only to tax-exempt bodies, i.e. registered charities, pension funds and friendly societies. Exempt unit trust holders tend to retain their holdings for much longer than the average unit trust investor, thus this stability means less work for the managers on the buying and selling side of the units. This lower level of administrative work is reflected in lower annual management fees. In addition, the exempt unit trust is exempt from corporation tax, and the investors can reclaim the tax deducted from their distributions.

Ethical unit trusts

The investment objectives of certain unit trusts require them to invest only in companies that do not pursue what are considered to be unethical activities. Some investors prefer not to invest in companies that take part in activities of which these investors disapprove. Examples of such companies are those involved in armaments, drinks, tobacco, and exploitation of workers, animal products, pornography, nuclear industry, pharmaceuticals, depletion of the rain forest, and exploitation of third world countries.

In practice it has proved difficult for ethical unit trusts to find many companies that are 100% ethical. To overcome this problem ethical trusts will invest in either companies that have only 5-10% of their business in unethical areas or in companies that have made a positive effort to reduce the unethical part of their operations. According to Friends Provident, there are 400 quoted UK companies that are believed to satisfy ethical criteria.

Indexed (or tracker) funds

Many fund managers (unit trusts included) have failed to produce returns that match the average as measured by whichever index is deemed most suitable, e.g. FTSE 100 or FTSE Actuaries All Share Indices. As a result there has been a growth in indexed funds. These funds are aimed at both professional and private investors, and some unit trust managers have introduced index-tracking funds.

A computer will design and run a portfolio to match a particular index (e.g. FTSE 100). Most indexed funds only partly replicate (reproduce) the chosen index. They use various techniques to provide an overall portfolio with a beta factor of one, i.e. no riskier than the index chosen. The more common name for funds that partially replicate a chosen index is tracker funds.

Many tracker funds are available to private investors as well as to institutional investors. Some funds track overseas indices, or a chosen part of the FT World Index Series, e.g. Japan, or the index in that chosen country, e.g. Japan's Nikkei index.

The benefits of indexed funds are:

● They are cheaper to run than a 'managed' fund – the *Economist* quotes the cost as being one-third;

● Performance will match that of the index.

The only 'decision' to make is which index to match. The performance will, by the very nature of the funds, be only 'average'. However, as many fund managers have failed to obtain even an 'average' performance, this method may well produce better results. Care needs to be taken in choosing a tracker fund, because statistics show that they have virtually all underperformed their chosen index. The major factor for underperformance is the level of the front-end fee but other factors contributing to underperformance are the dealing costs involved in switching the shares to keep the correct weightings and the annual management charge and other expenses.

Emerging markets

Investing overseas in countries that are only relatively new to an efficient stock market is very risky. Unit trusts investing in the emerging markets provide a diversified portfolio and professional management that is fully conversant with the problems and risks of these markets. This enables an investor to benefit from rises in the market without the extra problems that emerging market investment carries. However, as with any type of investment, there is always a risk, and even with professional management the risk profile of emerging market investment is still high. See Chapter 10 for more details of emerging markets.

14.13 Guidelines for unit trust selection

There are around 1,600 authorized unit trusts in the UK and this number tends to increase every month. Despite the fact that unit trusts are one form of collective investment that provides investors with a simple doorway to the stock market and professional investment management, the choice of trusts must be bewildering to the average unsophisticated investor. However, he can make a rational choice by using the following considerations.

Deciding whether he should invest in unit trusts at all

The investor must have an emergency cash reserve invested in a bank or building society before he can even contemplate investing in unit trusts. The rate of growth in unit trusts is not steady and the investor should be able to choose the moment when he sells, rather than being forced to do so when the market is temporarily depressed. An emergency cash reserve will, it is hoped, prevent the investor from becoming a forced seller.

Linked with this point is the timescale of the investment. Although high short-term gains can be seen, unit trusts should be regarded from the outset as a long-term investment.

Deciding on the investment objective (assuming unit trusts are appropriate)

The investor must choose a trust that mirrors his own objectives. The simplest way is to ascertain which of the AUTIF categories would be most suitable. His objectives may be for high income, capital growth or a mix of both. He may prefer to stay mainly in trusts investing in UK equities, or may be willing to take a higher degree of risk by choosing some of the new emerging markets such as Latin America.

Selecting a trust from those within the appropriate category

Factors to consider are:

● Past performance;

● Consistency of management;

● New trusts;

● Size;

● Redemptions/new monies position.

Past performance and management

It is possible to obtain details of the performances of other trusts in the required category so that their progress can be compared with the median fund. Information on the various trusts' performances is available in the *Unit Trust Year Book*, the financial press, *Money Management*, or from the managers themselves. The fund's performance can also be checked against that of a median fund from statistics provided by AUTIF.

It is possible that management companies showing a good performance record for all their trusts over a one-year period will also exhibit a better performance record in the long term. This can be attributed partly to the probability that trust managers with a good past performance record can point to proof of their expertise and are therefore keen to try to maintain these results. However, recent work by the FSA has cast doubts on whether past performance can be taken as any indicator of likely future performance.

Consistency of management

Maintaining a good performance is partly dependent on continuity. Frequent changes in investment management can bedevil overall group performance because of changes in investment policy.

New trusts

A new trust has a virgin pool of cash that can be invested in accordance with current market conditions which will have been carefully researched. Existing trusts, however, are to some extent committed to their past investment decisions. It is not easy in practice to liquidate a large holding of shares that has already fallen in value because this would convert a 'paper loss', which could possibly be recovered, into a 'cash loss', which would be irrecoverable.

In addition, new trusts often waive or reduce the front-end loading charges to encourage new investors by the attraction of a lower initial offer price. They sometimes offer a discount if investors respond by a set date.

Investing in a new trust at a time when the market appears bullish can be an excellent means of achieving a good result, provided the bullish expectations of the market are fulfilled. Naturally, the investor will wish to check the past performance of the management group.

Size

In theory, a small fund should be able to respond more quickly than a large one to changing market conditions. In practice there is little statistical evidence to support this theory. What evidence there is suggests that very large funds very rarely appear at the top or at the bottom and tend to perform around the average for trusts of that type. One of the reasons for this may be that large funds behave like 'closet index trackers' – managers are under pressure to match benchmarks and the very size of funds forces them to invest in the largest companies and hold fairly well-diversified portfolios.

An investor who did not wish to take an above average risk should invest in a large fund as opposed to a small fund.

Redemptions/new monies position

Because unit trusts are open ended, the managers will eventually have to sell some of the underlying investments if there are net redemptions for a long period. Forced sellers of equities frequently find that market conditions are not ideal for the sale of the equity concerned, and so the sales could be at a temporarily depressed price.

In addition, the mere prospect of forced sales of the underlying assets may influence the managers to switch from an offer price base to a bid price base. Someone buying such units just before the change of pricing could see a fall of 10% from the offer price at which he purchased to the current bid price.

Invest in more than one unit trust

Bearing in mind that the minimum lump-sum investment is around £200-500, it would be better to split a larger lump sum available into three or four equal amounts, with each part being invested in a suitable trust under a different manager. Even a good manager can have a bad year, and this diversification cushions the investor against such an occurrence. This will provide the maximum diversification.

14.14 Benefits of unit trust investment

Diversification

The Efficient Market Hypothesis and other research indicates that an investor should spread his investments among 15 different shares in different sectors of the market to avoid the unsystematic risk. The minimum economic investment in a single share is around £2,000 (because of the minimum broker's commission) hence £30,000 would be the absolute minimum to invest in a directly-held, diversified, equity portfolio.

With unit trusts the minimum lump-sum investment can be as low as £200, and this gives the investor an indirect interest in a diversified portfolio. Most unit trusts invest in between 50 and 100 different shares.

Professional management

Most private individuals lack the time or expertise to manage a portfolio. Decisions on which shares to buy, which to sell and whether to take up a rights issue are taken by professional managers who have access to detailed research by their own analysts or stockbrokers.

Elimination of paperwork

The investor merely records the purchase or sale of the units on his tax return, together with the distributions. All other matters, company reports, bonus issues, rights issues, and takeovers, are dealt with by the managers.

Overseas investment

Dealing costs with direct investment in shares quoted on an overseas stock market are very high. Unit trust investment is one of the most economic ways of obtaining a diversified portfolio of overseas investments. The professional managers can keep in touch with overseas market developments and can monitor the exchange risk. Some trusts may have investment powers allowing them to use derivatives or other methods of hedging exchange rate risks.

14.15 Commodity unit trusts

As the name suggests, these funds invest in commodities. Commodities are very wide ranging and include items such as metals, sugar, soya beans, coffee, wheat, barley and pigs. Under FSA rules such trusts cannot be authorized, because the underlying investment is not liquid enough to meet a sudden spate of net redemptions.

It is as well to remember that an authorized unit trust, while being unable to invest directly in commodities, can invest in the shares of companies dealing in commodities.

14.16 Offshore unit trusts

From the point of view of a UK investor, an offshore unit trust based in the Channel Islands, the Isle of Man or Bermuda should be as secure as an authorized one, provided the managers are UK clearing banks or their subsidiaries or some other reputable City institution. These three countries are classed as 'designated territories', i.e. the UK regulatory authorities consider that their investor protection laws are equivalent to those of the UK. Funds in these countries can apply under the Financial Services Act to market their funds in the UK as 'authorized offshore funds'.

Other offshore unit trusts should be regarded with caution, unless the managers are well known and undoubted. Offshore funds can invest in almost anything, but currency deposits or even high-interest sterling accounts are common.

Suitable offshore funds appeal to expatriates and other non-residents because there are potential tax benefits. However, such benefits do not apply to UK-resident investors.

The problems of unauthorized unit trusts

When the managers of the unauthorized trust are asked for information, their response is not restricted by AUTIF or the FSA. Yields on some unauthorized gilt-edged unit trusts have been quoted at higher figures than those for an authorized gilt trust, purely because the basis of the calculation formula was more favourable to the trust than the strict rules laid down for adverts for authorized unit trusts. The moral is plain: make sure the managers are reputable.

14.17 Open-ended investment company (OEIC)

The OEIC is in many ways a cross between a unit trust and an investment trust. They are pooled investments which are legally a company but have the ability to create or cancel shares i.e. it can expand and contract as supply and demand for its shares determines. Thus as a unit trust is open-ended it can create and cancel units, an investment trust is legally a company thus cannot expand or contract the number of shares. Under the specially written company law covering OEICs, they can expand or contract the number of shares issued.

Both OEICs and investment trusts issue shares, whereas unit trusts issue units. However the pricing of OEICs is different to both unit and investment trusts. Unit trusts have dual pricing, i.e. a bid and an offer price, investment trust shares also have dual pricing – the market maker's bid and offer price. OEICs have a single price, i.e. buyers and sellers pay/receive the same price. This does not mean that there are no dealing costs or manager's fees, just that these are shown separately.

OEICs prices are based on net asset value, as is the case with unit trusts, thus there will be no discount/premium to net asset value (NAV) as is seen with investment trusts. (See Chapter 15 for a comparative table of unit trusts, investment trusts and OEICs.)

A number of unit trust management companies have converted their unit trusts into OEICs because they offer them greater flexibility.

14.18 The unit trust fund managers' perspective

Fund management companies generate income from the initial charge on new units, the dealing spread on units traded 'out of the manager's box' (see section 14.6 above), and annual management charges levied on the funds they manage. Their main expenses are the costs of fund management (mainly the managers themselves and administrative support) and the costs of advertising and promotion, including commissions paid to financial advisers.

If fund management companies are to increase their income, they need to increase the value of funds under management – this boosts the annual charges (because these are a percentage of fund value). Outperformance of competitor funds and benchmarks will tend to attract new investors. Poorly performing funds will probably not attract new investors but may not lose old investors due to investor inertia – investors' lack of scrutiny or slowness to respond to poor performance.

Successful fund management companies will market themselves effectively, both to investors and the advisers through whom many sales are made. Performance is an issue in attracting investors but so is spotting market trends. New funds tend to be launched in 'hot' investment areas – in recent years these have included sectors such as technology and pharmaceuticals – in order to attract investors. 'Style' funds have come into vogue in recent years. Such funds tend not to concentrate on geographical markets but on investment styles across a range of markets – say, 'global income' or 'aggressive (i.e. high-risk) growth' and invest in securities that match the set criteria.

Fund management companies may also launch new funds to cover gaps in their ranges. From a strategic perspective, fund managers have to decide whether to offer a full range of funds covering all market sectors or whether to concentrate on niches – say, fixed-interest funds or

UK equity funds. Another important decision is whether to offer index tracking funds. Although now widely available, fund managers were reluctant to offer these type of funds because management charges on these funds tend to be much lower than on actively-managed funds. But the 'passive' management of index tracking funds means that they are significantly cheaper to run than actively managed funds because they do not need expensive fund managers – they rely on computer systems to determine how they allocate their investments.

Good managers may move between fund management companies and gravitate to larger funds where they will be better remunerated and have more funds under their control.

The use of unit trusts, OEICs and investment trusts by institutional investors

Institutional investors themselves use unit trusts, investment trusts and OEICs as a means of gaining exposure to various markets instead of investing directly in them. These reasons are very similar to those why individual investors use these funds – convenience in investing in markets where management would otherwise be difficult, or where they could not achieve the level of diversification they believe necessary, or where direct investment would not be cost-effective due to the small volume of funds available to commit to a particular market. For example a fund such as Fleming Japan (an investment trust) holds not only direct investments in Japanese shares, but also holds investments in their own Japanese Smaller Companies fund which can provide a greater level of diversification than could the Fleming Japan fund which has a wider investment remit. By holding an indirect investment as well as direct investment, Fleming have a wider exposure to the Japanese market.

The role of financial advisors

Financial advisers play a major role in selling unit trusts. Many advisers analyse fund performance and managers (or buy in such research), and make recommendations and rate individual funds and managers. As we have noted, such advisers receive commissions from fund managers, which are paid for out of charges levied on the unit trusts and OEICs (but not investment trusts, which are not able to pay commissions to advisers – an important difference). These commissions are paid out of initial and annual charges, although some advisers may reduce their commissions to attract business from investors (effectively giving back to investors some of their own money – but if investors receive a service from an adviser, they should expect to have to pay something for it).

15

INVESTMENT TRUSTS, EXCHANGE TRADED FUNDS, ENTERPRISE INVESTMENT SCHEMES AND VENTURE CAPITAL TRUSTS

Objectives

After studying this chapter, the reader should be able to:

● differentiate between an investment trust, a unit trust and OEICs;

● assess the relevance of discounts and gearing;

● explain methods of removing discounts;

● define and describe limited-life and split-level trusts;

● analyse the benefits and drawbacks of warrants;

● evaluate the benefits investment trust savings schemes;

● explain (briefly) the role of the Association of Investment Trust Companies;

● interpret information on investment trusts published in the financial press;

● analyse the nature of exchange traded funds;

● assess the benefits and drawbacks of venture capital trusts.

15.1   The legal structure of an investment trust

An investment trust is a limited company with a fixed share capital whose shares are listed on the Stock Exchange. The capital of the investment trust is invested in quoted shares, unquoted shares and overseas shares. Thus an investment trust offers its shareholders an indirect interest in a professionally-managed portfolio of securities.

Investors deal in the stocks and shares of an investment trust via a broker in the usual way that any securities are dealt with. The exception is the savings scheme run by some trusts.

As with any limited company, an investment trust is allowed to have loan capital or other forms of capital, and we have already seen in Chapter 10 how the warrant market is dominated by investment trusts. Thus the underlying assets of an investment trust are similar to those of a unit trust but the legal position of the shareholders is quite different from that of unit holders.

15.2   Taxation and investment trusts

The position of an investment trust shareholder

The investment trust shareholder will be treated for tax purposes in the same way as a shareholder of any other limited company. Dividends will be paid net of 10% tax, however non-taxpayers CANNOT reclaim the tax and 40% taxpayers are liable to extra tax at 22.5% (32.5% - 22.5%). Capital gains on disposal of investment trust shares are liable for CGT in exactly the same way as are gains on any other share.

The tax position of the investment trust itself

Capital gains tax

As with unit trusts, all capital gains made by the trust itself are totally tax free of CGT (Finance Act 1980). In order to qualify for this exemption, the investment trust must be 'approved' within the terms of s.359, Income and Corporation Taxes Act 1970 as amended by s.93, Finance Act 1972.

For approval to be granted, the investment trust must:

● Be resident in the UK;

● Be listed on the UK Stock Exchange;

● Derive its income wholly or mainly from shares or securities;

● Not invest more than 15% of its assets in any one company (except in another investment trust);

● Not retain more than 15% of its income from stocks and shares;

● Not distribute any capital profits from the sale of its investments as a dividend to shareholders.

15.3 The importance of an investment trust being closed-ended as opposed to open-ended

An investment trust is a closed-ended fund, unlike a unit trust which is an open-ended fund. Purchases and sales of the investment trust's shares on the secondary market do not result in cash coming into or out of the investment trust itself. These secondary market transactions simply affect the price of the investment trust's shares on the secondary market. Thus, because their capital is fixed, investment trusts have the benefit of continuity, and investment trust companies can plan their investment strategy on a long-term basis. Investment trusts therefore can take a very long-term view of the underlying investments without needing to worry about short-term performance. Thus this investment medium benefits from a relatively stable structure and lower stock turnover.

15.4 The significance of discounts on investment trust shares

What is meant by 'discount' in connection with investment trust shares?

In Chapter 12 we explained the concept of net asset value of a share which, briefly summarized, can be defined as total shareholders' funds divided by the number of shares. We have also explained that share prices are set by market forces, and that for most successful companies the current share price should be above net asset value. However, for investment trusts, the share price is generally below (i.e. at a discount to) net asset value.

Why are most investment trusts priced at a discount?

A number of factors cause this apparently strange position to arise.

- If the investment trust were to liquidate itself, it might not be possible to realize the full net asset value. Unlisted shares may not fetch their expected value, and there will be the usual brokers' and other selling costs to bear. In addition, there may be a penalty to pay for early redemption of any fixed-term loans taken out by the trust.

- The Stock Market still generally expects to see investment trust shares priced at a discount to net asset value. If the discount narrows or is eliminated, investors begin to feel that the share price is too high. The resultant fall in demand for the investment trust's shares will make their price fall, without any effect at all on their underlying net asset value.

- The annual management expenses and corporation tax on unfranked income reduce the flow of income from the underlying investments to the investment trust's shareholders. In other words, the shareholders would receive a slightly higher income if they could invest directly in the underlying assets, rather than investing indirectly via the trust.

What is the effect of the discount?

There are three major points an investment trust shareholder should bear in mind.

Increased income

Suppose an investor buys 1,000 shares in an investment trust when the share price is 200p and their net asset value is 266p.

The cost to the investor would be:

	£
Consideration 1,000 x 200p =	2,000.00
Commission at 1.65% (say)	33.00
Stamp duty	10.00
	2,043.00

In the above example, £2,043.00 acquires assets of 1,000 x 266p = £2,660. These assets are earning income for the investor.

This can be contrasted with a unit trust where the investor would expect to obtain £1,941 of assets for an investment of £2,043 (£2,043 less a 5% spread). Other things being equal, which they rarely are, the same amount of money should generate more income from investment in an investment trust than would be received from a unit trust investment.

Additional capital gain in a rising market and additional losses in a falling one

Discounts on investment trust shares tend to narrow in a rising market, and to widen on a falling market. Hence in a rising market the net asset value will rise, but the share price will rise even more as the discount narrows. Conversely, as the market as a whole falls, the discount will widen, hence the share price will fall at a greater rate than net asset value falls. Thus the discount can be said to contribute a gearing factor.

Acquisition of the underlying shares at a discount or premium

When an investment trust is standing at a discount the effect is that the value of the underlying assets are being purchased at a lower price than an investor would pay if he purchased those shares directly. The share price would be standing at a discount to net asset value (NAV). When the situation is reversed, the share price is above the value of the underlying assets, then the investment trust shares will stand at a premium to net asset value.

What causes the discount to change?

As was previously stated, discounts tend to narrow on a rising stock market, and they will also narrow when a particular trust is expected to perform better.

Instances of this would occur when:

- The trust is invested in a particularly popular sector of the market, e.g. the emerging markets, then supply and demand will drive up the share price. This does not affect the net asset value because the underlying assets are totally separate from the investment trust shares.

- There is a change in management or of investment policy which is likely to improve performance.

- There is a fall in interest rates which makes the returns on equities look more attractive. The classic illustration of this would be a narrowing of the reverse yield gap.

- There is a possibility of a takeover which would make the shareholders anticipate that they were likely to receive the net asset value of the shares in the near future.

- Investment trust savings schemes have had the effect of narrowing the discount. While the amounts saved are small in relation to the value of the investment trust sector, there has been a stabilizing influence from this growth of small investors. Small investors prefer to retain their share holding, so this has the effect of stabilizing the share price. Institutions, however, tend to trade actively, which can have a destabilizing effect on the share price.

Discounts will widen when performance is expected to worsen. Examples are:

- If there is a sale of a large number of the shares by a institutional investor, this will depress the share price and widen the discount.

- If there are only a few shareholders, there tends to be a narrow market in the shares, and this usually results in a wider discount.

Gearing and discounts

We have already said that an element of gearing is introduced by the discounts on investment trusts. Investment trusts can 'gear up' by way of preference shares, debentures, loan stocks, bank loans, or foreign currency loans. However, the major factor that determines how highly geared the shares are is the amount of fixed-interest capital compared to shareholders' funds. Investment trusts can borrow money, subject to the usual restrictions imposed by the memorandum and articles of association, in just the same way as can any other limited company. As with any share, on a rising market, gearing should beneficially exaggerate the share performance of the underlying assets in its effect on the share price and dividends of the investment trust share. However, the usual downside still applies in that gearing will also exaggerate the fall in share price and dividends in a bear market.

One way of removing the discount would be to liquidate the trust. This would entail the trust winding itself up with the shareholders' approval. The assets would be realized at around net asset value, which will be close to the full market value less dealing costs. Problems arise with this option for private investors because they will be repaid and thus have a disposal of shares for CGT purposes and a potential CGT liability.

15.5   Types of investment trusts

Limited-life trusts

These trusts consider it desirable that the shareholders have the opportunity to decide whether the company should continue or be liquidated. The articles of association accordingly specify that at periodic intervals (usually five years) the shareholders must vote on whether or not to liquidate.

Split-capital trusts

Split-capital investment trusts have a capital structure that can provide for the specific needs of the investor. There are a number of types of shares issued – zero-dividend preference shares, stepped preference shares, income shares and capital shares. There is a set date, or predetermined period, when the split-capital trust must be wound up.

Zero-dividend preference shares

These shares, known as 'zeros', are issued at a price below their par value. On the redemption date the trust will redeem the zeros at the predetermined redemption value, provided there are sufficient assets available. Redemption of the zeros will take priority over redemption of the other classes of shares, but they rank after repayment of any loans the company may have taken out or loan stock they may have issued. 'Zeros' provide a fixed capital return in the form of a redemption value. They do not provide any income. Zeros are normally the first class of share to be repaid upon winding up of the trust.

In the same company, zeros are the least risky category of shares because of their priority on winding up. The price of zeros is affected by changes to bond yields, rather than dividend yields. This is because they pay a fixed rate of dividend. The other factor that influences the price of a zero is how well the present and future assets of the trust are covered. (See Chapter 12 for capital cover calculations.)

Stepped preference shares

These shares offer dividends that rise at a preset rate plus a guaranteed redemption value on winding up.

Income shares

During the life of the investment trust all or most of the income accruing to the trust is paid out by way of dividend on the income shares. At the winding up date the income shares are redeemed at a predetermined capital value, which may be the nominal value but need not be. The income will rise over the life of the trust, but the capital value will fall up to redemption. These shares are suitable for investors requiring a high and growing income who are willing to accept a capital loss on winding up. Once the shares have been purchased the capital loss on redemption can be identified. The investor can calculate an approximate gross redemption yield based on assumptions of dividend growth, using the Gordon growth model. (See Chapter 13.)

Capital shares

The capital shareholder receives little or no income during the life of the trust. On winding up he receives all the remaining money after all prior loans and classes of shares have been repaid.

An analysis of M & G Equity split-capital investment trust

	Winding up date	Repayment terms	Price	Gross div yield %	NAV (p)	Discount (+ve)/ Premium (-ve)
Income Shares	31 March 2011	At par	34½	12.9	0.56	-
Capital Shares		All surplus assets	23½	-	67.65	65.6
Zero-Dividend Preference Shares	8 March 2011	46.09p	53½	6.5	46.0	-11

The price of the zero preference share tends to move in line with the net asset value as can be seen above where the price is 46.09p and the net asset value 46p.

Since the redemption date is ten years away (taking the date now as 2001) the price of the income shares is heavily influenced by the amount of dividend they will generate. However, as 2011 approaches the price of the income shares will tend to approach par, with an allowance for accrued dividends. The same principles apply as apply to short-dated gilts just prior to redemption, provided the value of the trust's portfolio is sufficient to cover the redemption commitment.

Turning to the capital shares, their price was at a discount of 65.6% to their net asset value. At this stage of the trust's life these shares are speculative. No income is generated so the price is dependent purely on the market's view of the net asset value in 2011. There are few analysts who would even attempt to predict so far ahead, so a large discount applies to take account of the uncertainty.

As redemption date approaches, the discount on the capital shares will narrow; the price will then stabilize at a small discount unless there are major price movements expected in the market as a whole.

Conclusion

For an investor who requires a high and growing income for a long period, and who can accept a capital loss in the long term, income shares of a split-level capital trust are an ideal vehicle provided the redemption date is well ahead.

Conversely, a high taxpayer, who prefers capital gains to income, would prefer a capital share. If he wished to speculate, he would buy a long-dated capital share, but if he required a safer investment, a capital share with a shorter redemption period or a zero-dividend preference share with a relatively low hurdle rate would be preferable.

Warrants

Investment trusts may issue all types of capital, including warrants. The warrant market is dominated by investment trusts. Warrants issued by conventional investment trusts can be exercised for ordinary shares in the trust. Warrants issued by split-level capital trusts will specify the class of capital into which they are exercised, e.g. a capital share or zero-dividend preference share.

Warrants may be issued free when a new investment trust is launched. The warrants can be sold on the market or held and executed in the future. Warrants are a risky investment and likened to long-term share options. More detail about warrants and warrant arithmetic can be found in Chapter 10 (Derivatives).

Suitability of the different types of share capital for different investors

Consider the following table.

Share capital	Type of investor
1. Zero-dividend preference shares.	Investors who need a fixed capital sum at a set future date. The investor would tend to be a little risk averse, but willing to invest in these shares in preference to gilts which are safer but offer a lower guaranteed return. Also may be a 40% taxpayer who prefers capital gains to income.
2. Stepped preference shares.	An investor who wants a growing income that is to grow at a preset rate, along with a guaranteed capital sum on winding up.
3. Income shares.	Investors who need a high level of income, but are willing to take a loss on capital on winding up. Also 40% taxpayers who wish to put these shares into an ISA and withdraw the income tax free.

Share capital	Type of investor
4. Capital shares.	Investors who do not want or require income but are willing to take a higher risk, in that all prior claims and classes of capital must be repaid before they can receive any money. The investor is likely to be a 40% taxpayer who prefers capital gain to income.

Investment trust savings schemes

These work in a similar way to unit trust savings schemes and have the same advantage of 'pound cost averaging'. There has been a rapid growth of investment trust savings schemes since their introduction. The schemes start with monthly contributions as low as £20, and dividends can also be reinvested with the same effect and tax consequences as unit trust accumulation units. Some schemes also accept lump-sum investments from as little as £250. The money is pooled and the investment trust purchases its own shares in the market and allocates them to the new shareholders. This is a cheap way of purchasing shares for the private investor because dealing costs are shared among all the investors pro rata rather than each saver having to pay brokers' commission at top rates on his own dealings. The cost works out at about 0.2% of the amount invested against broker's commission of around 1.5-1.65%. Most schemes also offer the facility to sell shares purchased through this scheme at similar, low rates of commission. For the investment trust it has the added advantage of reducing the discount to net asset value. This reduces vulnerability to takeover because the trust is increasing its number of shareholders while retaining its original share capital.

Share exchange schemes

Some investment trusts have introduced share exchange schemes whereby an investor can give any shares he owns to the investment trust, and in return he will receive investment trust shares. The system operates in much the same way as share exchange schemes with unit trusts (see Chapter 12).

15.6 The role of the Association of Investment Trust Companies (AITC)

This body performs a similar function for investment trusts to that performed by AUTIF for unit trusts. Information and statistics are available on all aspects of investment trusts. Although the AITC cannot advise on the selection of an individual trust, it is prepared to send, free of charge, a list of firms of brokers who are prepared to offer advice and handle investment trust shares for private investors.

AITC Investment trusts categories:

- Global Growth
- Global Growth And Income
- Global Smaller Companies
- Global Emerging Markets
- Global High Income
- Overseas Growth
- UK Growth
- UK Income and Growth
- UK Smaller Companies
- UK High Income
- North America
- North American Smaller Companies
- Far East – Including Japan
- Far East – Excluding Japan
- Japan
- Japanese Smaller Companies
- Far East – Excluding Japan (Single)
- Europe
- European Smaller Companies
- European Emerging Markets
- Latin America
- Venture Capital Trusts
- Country Specialists: Europe
- Country Specialists: Far East
- Country Specialists: Other
- Sector Specialists: Biotechnology/Life Sciences
- Sector Specialists: Endowment Policies
- Sector Specialists: Financials
- Sector Specialists: Global Mining

- Sector Specialists: Property

- Sector Specialists: Restaurants and Pubs

- Sector Specialists: Smaller Companies, Media Communication and IT

- Sector Specialists: Tea Plantations

- Sector Specialists: Technology Media Telecommunication

- Sector Specialists: Utilities

- Sector Specialists: Zero Preference Shares

15.7 Investment trust information in the *Financial Times*

The *Financial Times* classifies Investments Trusts under 'Investment Companies'.

Extract details in Tuesday to Saturday Editions of the FT

Stock	Price	+ or -	52 week High	Low	Yield net	NAV	Dis or PM(-)
Candover	1057½	-5	1160	975	2.8	1020.7	-3.6
British Smaller Companies	67½	-	93½	65	4.1	85	20.6

Explanation

- Stock: Name of the stock.

- Price: The closing mid-market price on the previous trading day.

- + or -: Change in price from the previous trading day.

- High/low: The highest and lowest price the share has reached over a rolling 52-week period.

- Yield: Net dividend yield. This is based on the mid price.

- NAV: Net Asset Value. This is in pence per share. It assumes prior charges at par value, convertibles converted, and warrants exercised (if applicable). This should be compared to the share price to establish the premium or discounts.

- Dis or Pm (-): Discount or premium in relation to the closing share prices.

- The price is at a discount when the NAV exceeds the current share price, and at a premium when the share price exceeds the NAV, thus Candover is standing at a premium of 3.6 and British Smaller Companies standing at a discount of 20.6. An explanation of the premium calculation for Candover is as follows: 1020.7 x 1.036 = 1057.5 (the share price).

Note: Investment trusts never have a price/earnings ratio because it would be meaningless due to the nature of their business.

15.8   Investment trusts versus unit trusts and OEICs

As far as private investors are concerned it is difficult to choose between an investment trust, a unit trust and an OEIC. For investments of under £1,000 a unit trust may be more suitable, since the 'spread' between bid and offer price is usually less than the dealing costs for purchase and sale of £1,000 worth of investment trust shares, although this may not be the case if a discount stockbroker is used. For the large investor, investment trusts tend to provide better returns, taking into account their gearing and discounts. However, this is by no means certain because the performance at the end of the day is influenced by the success or otherwise of the manager's investment policy. For small investors, the investment trust savings schemes offer both monthly savings and lump-sum options. These provide excellent value for the small saver.

The FTSE All Share Indices contain an Investment Companies index which measures the performances of this sector as a whole. *Money Management* also provides performance statistics grouped according to the aims of the trust.

15.9   Summary of main differences between investment trusts, unit trusts and OEICs

Investment Trusts	Unit Trusts	OEICs
1. Control is exercised by directors, subject to the normal approvals required from shareholders at meetings and subject to the memorandum and articles of association.	A unit trust is a trust where each unit holder is entitled to share in the assets of that trust in proportion to the number of units owned. Control is exercised by managers, subject to approval by trustees within the terms of the trust deed.	As for unit trusts.

Investment Trusts	Unit Trusts	OEICs
2. An investment trust is closed-ended. The shares of the investment trust are dealt with on the secondary market. Hence the purchases or sales of the trust's shares do not result in cash payments to or from the trust managers. No new shares are created, nor are any liquidated, because of dealings on the secondary market.	A unit trust is open-ended. Sales or purchases by unit holders result in cash payments to or from the managers. Hence net redemptions of units will mean that the managers have to sell some of the trust's underlying investments to meet such redemptions. Some units will then be liquidated. Conversely net new monies cause new units to be created and increase the underlying investments.	Open ended (as for unit trusts), but **shares** not units are issued and dealings are via the managers.
3. The shares are bought or sold on the Stock Exchange in the same way as any other shares. Hence, dealing costs are based on the usual brokers' commission, stamp duty, and PTM levy.	Unit holders buy and sell units from the managers. There are normally no commission charges as such, the 'cost' to the investor is the difference between the bid and offer prices.	As for unit trusts.
4. The price of investment trust shares is not laid down by any formula, but in the same way as for other share prices, the level depends on market forces.	The price of units is based on the net asset value, with a maximum spread between bid and offer prices as set by the FSA formula.	The price is based around the net asset value, but there is only a single price.
5. Dual pricing.	Dual pricing.	Single pricing.
6. Generally the price of an investment trust share is at a discount to net asset value.	See 4 above.	The share price closely reflects the underlying value of the assets.

Investment Trusts	Unit Trusts	OEICs
7. Investment trusts can have different types of capital. If investment trusts have loan capital, then the concept of gearing applies.	Unit trusts can only have one class of unit for each trust. Every unit is treated equally. The concept of gearing cannot apply. (The only time that there can be two classes of unit is where there are accumulation units as well as distribution units. Both types ranks equally)	As for unit trusts.
8. Investment trusts cannot invite the public to buy their shares through advertising. (There is an exception to this in the case of a new issue of investment trust shares.)	Authorized unit trusts are permitted to advertise to invite the public to purchase units.	As for unit trusts.
9. Annual management fees tend to vary between ½% and 1% of the value of the assets under management.	Annual management fees are usually 0.75% - 1.5% of the value of the funds under management.	As for unit trusts.

15.10 Exchange-traded funds

An exchange-traded fund is a form of investment company where the investment objective is to achieve the same return as a particular index. It is similar to an index fund in that it will primarily invest in the securities of companies that are included in a selected market index. An exchange-traded fund will invest in either all of the securities (full replication) or a representative sample (tracker) of the securities included in the index.

Exchange-traded funds combine the features of unit trusts, investment trusts, electronically traded shares (via SETS) and an index fund. They are actually open-ended investment companies (OEICs).

Although exchange-traded funds are legally classified as open-ended investment companies they differ from traditional OEICs in the following ways:

● Exchange-traded funds do not sell individual shares directly to investors and only issue their shares in large blocks that are known as creation units.

- The main purchasers of creation units are the institutional investors. They buy creation units with a basket of securities that generally mirrors the exchange-traded fund's portfolio. Private investors do not usually purchase creation units.

- After purchasing a creation unit, the institutional investor can split up and sell the individual shares on a secondary market. This permits other investors to purchase individual shares (instead of creation units).

- Investors who want to sell their exchange-traded fund shares have two options:

    (a) they can sell individual shares to other investors on the secondary market, or

    (b) they can sell the creation units back to the exchange-traded fund. In this case the investor would usually be an institution. Exchange-traded funds generally redeem creation units by giving investors the securities that comprise the portfolio instead of cash.

- A share in an exchange-traded fund is a stake in an open ended investment company (OEIC). The value of an exchange-traded fund share moves with the value of the fund owned by the investment company which in turn, closely follows an index.

For example, an exchange-traded fund invested in the shares contained in the FTSE 100 would give a redeeming shareholder the actual shares that constitute the FTSE 100 Index.

Exchange-traded funds were created in the USA in 1993. The first US exchange-traded fund was the SPDR (Standard and Poor's Depositary Receipt), more commonly called Spider. Spiders track the S&P 500 Index in the USA. These funds have developed successfully in the USA, and the best known after the Spider is the 'cube', or QQQ which tracks the Nasdaq 100.

iShares (sic) are exchange-traded funds – a new investment product that captures the benefits of both shares and funds and can provide a core building block for an investment portfolio.

Exchange-traded funds were launched in the UK in April 2000 and the first exchange-traded fund tracked the FTSE 100 Index. iShares are exchange traded funds which allow investors to buy into an index by way of a share. The first index was the iFTSE100 and the index is fully replicated. The iShares are traded on extraMARK.

The iShares structure allows large investors to create and redeem shares in the fund at NAV on a daily basis. This is done in large blocks of shares, typically worth more than £1 million, which represent a creation or redemption basket. New shares that are created can then be traded in the secondary market. iShares should trade at a price close to their net asset value, because if a discount were to exist, a large investor could arbitrage this opportunity for a risk-free profit. In the USA this has proved to be an extremely efficient mechanism for ensuring that the price trades in line with the underlying NAV.

Exchange-traded funds are not currently subject to stamp duty in the hands of an individual investor. This is because they are trading already created shares. The spread on iFTSE100s should be less than the spread on the underlying shares in the FTSE100. The management fees are quite low because there is no selection involved of the underlying shares, the exchange-traded fund merely tracks the chosen index.

Dividends are paid and the management fees of around 0.35 - 0.5% are deducted from the dividend yield earned by the exchange-traded fund. The price of an exchange-traded fund is close to its net asset value. Exchange-traded funds are not allowed to borrow, thus gearing does not apply, and because the price is always very close to the net asset value premiums and discounts do not occur.

Exchange-traded funds have the advantage of diversification because they are collective investments that fully or partially replicate a specific index.

Arbitrage

As an exchange-traded fund grows it provides units in itself to new investors. Most open-ended funds do this by accepting cash for units, but this does not happen with an exchange-traded fund. The critical feature of an exchange-traded fund is that securities dealers enable the subscription process with a transfer of physical shares. To meet subscriber demand new units are created when the shares are transferred into the fund, so enlarging the assets of the exchange-traded fund. The process is completely transparent since the constituents of the fund are known, and the price of the fund is known as are the constituents. The mechanism of arbitrage available to the professionals in creating new units and redeeming old units should continually correct the price to accurately reflect the underlying assets.

Institutional investor expertise available for all investors

The arbitrage activity and basket trading that exchange-traded funds require remains the preserve of institutional traders. Similarly the low cost of management charges levied against the exchange-traded fund is usually only available to very wealthy investors who can create economies of scale for their managers.

However due to the exchange-traded fund being available on an exchange and equally available to investors large and small, anyone can now participate in the benefits of such institutional expertise.

The market price of an exchange-traded share

The price of a share in an exchange-traded fund on extraMARK will reflect the net asset value of the fund managed by the company. Therefore, if an exchange-traded fund iShare opens at £15 and the index is at 5894 and the index closes at 5962 the exchange-traded fund should be trading around £15.17 (a rise of approximately 1.15% reflecting the percentage rise in the index) at the close, ignoring dividends payments.

15.11 Enterprise Investment Scheme (EIS)

The Enterprise Investment Scheme (EIS) was created to help certain types of small higher-risk unquoted trading companies to raise capital. It does so by providing a range of tax reliefs for investors in qualifying shares in these companies.

These are high-risk investments, thus suitable for investors who have a well-balanced portfolio of shares and are interested in more speculative investment over the medium to long term. Alternatively the EIS will be attractive to investors who wish to be involved with running the business as a paid director. In this case the individual must not have been connected with the issuing company or carrying on in the trade in any capacity during the two years before and five years after the issue of the shares in the EIS. The maximum shareholding in a single company is 30%.

Rules governing EIS shares

Subscriptions must be for new ordinary shares only. The shares must be held for a period of 3 years – the 'lock in' period to gain income tax and CGT exemptions. Throughout the period of five years from the date of issue, the shares must not carry any preferential rights to dividends or to the company's assets on its winding up, neither must the shares carry any right to be redeemed during the five year period.

Qualifying companies

Companies must meet certain conditions for any of the reliefs to be available for the investor:

- the company must be unquoted (which includes AIM shares);
- the company must be carrying on business wholly or mainly in the UK whose trading activities are not excluded;
- all the shares in the issue must raise money for the purpose of a qualifying business activity;
- the money raised by the share issue must be invested within a specified period by the company;
- the total gross assets of the company must not exceed £15m before the share issue and £16m immediately after the issue.

Main exclusions from the definition of qualifying trades

- finance, legal and accountancy firms,
- leasing (except certain ship chartering),
- property development,
- hotels,

- nursing or residential homes,

- farming and market gardening,

- forestry and timber production,

- a trade of receiving royalties or licence fees is excluded EXCEPT where the income arises from films or from research and development or from an intangible asset, the greater part of which has been created by the company.

Income tax relief

Investors may be given income tax relief at 20% on their investments of up to £150,000 per tax year. Thus the maximum amount of tax relief is £30,000. Income tax relief on up to one-half of the amount invested between 6 April and 5 October can be carried back to the previous tax year, subject to a maximum of £25,000. This will generate a tax rebate from the previous year.

CGT exemption

Gains on the disposal of EIS shares are exempt from CGT unless the income tax relief is withdrawn.

CGT deferral

Gains made on the shares can be deferred by re-investing the gains in EIS qualifying shares. There is no limit to the amount of gain which can be deferred.

15.12 Venture capital trusts (VCTs)

Venture capital trusts were created in the Finance Act 1995 as a method of enabling new and unquoted companies to raise money from investors. They are very similar in legal structure to investment trusts. The aim of venture capital trusts is to provide capital finance for small expanding companies while making capital gains for investors. They must hold at least 70% of their investments in qualifying unquoted companies, including AIM-listed shares.

Venture capital trusts are a tax-efficient way to invest larger sums of money and are aimed at medium to large net worth private investors. The maximum investment per tax year is £100,000. They qualify for income tax relief in the form of a 20% income tax refund of the amount invested subject to the £100,000 calculated as £100,000 x 20% = £20,000 maximum. The tax relief is not at the investor's marginal rate of tax.

Dividends from ordinary shares in VCTs are exempt from income tax (except for the 10% tax levied at source on all dividends) subject to the rule about the maximum investment in a VCT being £100,000.

VCTs also qualify for a special form of CGT deferral provided that the investment qualifies for VCT income tax relief. There is no CGT payable at the time on any gain in VCT shares provided that the gain on the shares is re-invested. The re-investment period starts 1 year before, but ending 1 year after the date on which the gain arose. This means that it is possible to straddle three tax years, thus meaning that a total of £300,000 can be sheltered. However, CGT is only deferred until encashment of the VCT, when CGT will be chargeable at the investor's marginal rate of tax.

Investors must be willing to accept a higher level of risk than investing in established companies listed on the Stock Exchange. A higher level of risk surrounds the smaller quoted and unquoted companies. It is advisable that an investor does not consider venture capital trusts unless they can accept this level of risk and already have a well-balanced portfolio of stocks and shares and can afford to invest up to £100,000 in a venture capital trusts. The investment should be looked on as a long-term investment vehicle.

Most venture capital trusts aim to invest the majority of assets in qualifying unquoted companies trading wholly or mainly in the UK. Of these companies, 80% of are established companies or management buyouts. As venture capital trusts become more sophisticated they are investing in funds such as smaller company funds or funds of hedge funds, to maximize returns. (See Chapter 9 Derivatives for details of hedge funds.)

Rules governing venture capital trusts

- At least 30% of the holdings must be in ordinary shares.
- No single holding can be more than 15% of the total investment.
- Loans or securities that are guaranteed are excluded.
- At least 10% of the total investment in any company must be in ordinary shares.
- Companies quoted on AIM qualify for inclusion in a venture capital trust providing they are carrying out a qualifying trade.
- The maximum permitted investment is £100,000 per tax year.
- The venture capital trust must not retain more than 15% of it income from shares and securities.
- The money raised by the venture capital trust must be at least 70% invested after 3 years and the maximum amount that can be invested in one company in one tax year is £1m.
- The venture capital trust does not have to invest its funds immediately; the money received can be invested in high-interest accounts, government stocks (gilts) and fixed-interest securities until the funds are invested.
- In addition the total gross assets of the company must not exceed £15m immediately before the venture capital trust purchased the holding, nor £16m immediately afterwards.
- Venture capital trust shares can be sold or bought at any time, but initial income tax

relief is available only on the new issue of shares with a minimum holding period of three years to retain the relief.

Venture capital trusts shares are traded on the Stock Market as with any other quoted company.

Eligibility to invest in venture capital trusts

Any UK tax payer over the age of 18 can invest in a venture capital trust. The initial tax relief granted is limited to the amount of tax the individual pays.

Tax benefits of investing in venture capital trusts

To encourage investment, the Finance Act 1995 has given special tax breaks to investors. These are:

- Investors receive tax relief at 20% on their initial investment up to £100,000 per annum. (This relief is claimed from the Inland Revenue.)

- If the shares are sold within 5 years (other than to the holder's spouse or on the holder's death) tax relief will be withdrawn.

- Dividends are free of the higher rate of income tax, but the 10% tax credit on dividends cannot be reclaimed.

- There is no liability to CGT.

- Capital gains rollover relief is given to investors re-investing up to £100,000.

Main exclusions from the definition of qualifying trades:

- Companies dealing in land

- Finance, legal and accountancy services

- Property development

- Farming and market gardening

- Forestry and timber production

- Hotels and nursing or residential care homes.

Venture capital trusts are a high-risk investment, only suitable for a high-rate tax payer who already has a large, well-diversified portfolio and who is willing to take a higher risk than average. Management fees tend to be higher than those charged on investment trusts due to the added complexity of the operation of venture capital trusts. It has been suggested that an investor should have no more than 5% of his portfolio in a venture capital trust. Valuation of a venture capital trust is difficult because most of the shares are not freely traded. Many shares on AIM have a very thin market, thus the bid-offer spread will be very large. There is little secondary market trading in venture capital trusts because most investors are holding them for the 5-year period to gain maximum tax benefits.

There are currently three main types of venture capital trusts:

- AIM trusts
- Technology-based trusts – mainly invested in unquoted technology companies
- General trusts which spread investments between AIM-listed companies and unlisted companies. They often have a policy of investing in companies that are already or very nearly profitable.

16

INSURANCE, PENSIONS AND FRIENDLY SOCIETIES

Objectives

After studying this chapter, the reader should be able to:

● evaluate the functions of life insurance companies as providers of policies that offer protection and/or investment;

● analyse the features and benefits of the range of products available from life insurance companies;

● understand the features of mortgage annuities/home income plans;

● understand the principles of pensions;

● differentiate between SERPS, occupational pensions, self-invested personal pensions (SIPPs), stakeholder pensions and personal pensions;

● analyse the tax treatment of these investments.

16.1   Introduction

One thing that insurance companies, pensions funds and friendly societies all have in common as an investment is that they are all able to provide the investor with a vehicle whereby money invested now provides a future return, usually at a known date. With insurance products this varies according to the specific product; with pension plans a pension is paid upon retirement; with friendly societies a sum is payable on maturity or earlier death. Each type of institution is different and the insurance industry has a very wide range of products. This chapter covers the various types of products that are offered by insurance companies, pension funds and friendly societies.

16.2   Insurance products

Insurance products cover a wide range from life insurance, both qualifying and non-qualifying policies, to annuities.

The taxation treatment of life insurance companies and life insurance policies

The life insurance company

All life insurance companies pay tax. The insurance company pays a special corporation tax rate of 22% on income. It also pays a special CGT rate of 22% on all capital gains realized.

When a life insurance policy matures the insurance company will make a deduction from the gross proceeds in respect of its own CGT liability. This deduction cannot be reclaimed by investors who are not subject to CGT.

The life insurance policy

The proceeds of all qualifying life insurance policies are totally free of all income and capital gains tax in the hands of the investor because the insurance company itself has paid tax on its profits and capital gains.

Rules for qualifying life policies

For a policy to be classed as a 'qualifying policy' it must adhere to certain rules:

- Premiums must be payable for a minimum of 10 years, except in the case of term life policies.

- Premiums must be paid annually or more frequently, and those paid in one year must not exceed twice those paid in another year, nor must they exceed one-eighth of the total over the first 10 years.

- The sum assured under an endowment policy must be no less than 75% of the total premiums payable during the term of the policy, although these rules are relaxed when the life assured is over 55 years of age.

- The sum assured under a whole life policy, which carries a surrender value, must be no less than 75% of the total sum payable if death occurred at the age of 75.

- The life insurance company must have an office in the UK and be trading there also.

Tax relief on life insurance premiums

The 1984 Finance Act changed the position regarding tax relief on qualifying life insurance premiums. Prior to 13 March 1984 life insurance premiums were eligible for tax relief of 15% of the premium provided the premiums were paid annually or more frequently for a minimum period of 10 years. The tax relief also had a ceiling of one-sixth of taxable income or £1,500 per annum whichever was the higher for the taxpayer. Policies taken out after 13 March 1984 do not attract any tax relief on premiums for the investor. This has made life insurance a less attractive savings vehicle.

If an investor is paying premiums on a qualifying policy taken out before 13 March 1984 he should make every effort to continue paying the premiums because he will retain tax relief at a rate of 12½% – Finance Act 1988. (The rate of LAPR (Life Assurance Premium Relief) was lowered from 15% to 12½% by the Finance Act 1988.) The tax relief is deducted from the gross premium payable to the insurance company, which means that the investor pays only £87.50 for every £100 of cover purchased. The insurance company reclaims the 12½% from the Inland Revenue.

Non-qualifying life policies

If a life policy does not qualify for tax relief under the rules it is classed as a non-qualifying life policy. Most of these non-qualifying policies come under the umbrella heading of 'single premium bonds'.

The difference between protection and investment

With the investment management syllabus the products that are of interest lie on the life assurance (or insurance) arm of the insurance industry's products, rather than on the house insurance and car insurance products.

There are a variety of life insurance policies available to suit an investor's needs. Some simply provide a sum of money if the life assured dies before a set date but nothing if he survives, and they are pure protection policies also known as term life policies. Others are mainly a savings vehicle, but provide protection in the event of premature death. Endowment policies are examples of the latter.

With life insurance there are three parties to the policy: the proposer, the life assured and the beneficiary. The proposer is the person who pays the premiums to the insurance company. The life assured is the person on whose life the policy is based, and it is that person's age and health that determines the level of premiums to be paid by the proposer. If the life assured dies prior to maturity of the policy then the proposer pays no more premiums, and the insurance company will pay out the sum due to the named beneficiary. It is quite common for all three parties to the policy to be one or two persons only. In these cases the proposer and life assured will be the same and the beneficiary will be either the same person or a third party. This is most commonly seen when a husband takes out life cover on his own life, payable on his death to his wife, or vice versa.

From the point of view of giving investment advice when a customer asks for it, one of the questions must be whether he or she has adequate life cover. What may seem adequate to a customer is not necessarily adequate from the viewpoint of the professional adviser. The minimum amount of life cover a customer should have is enough to pay off his mortgage and any other debts if he should die before the final payment is due. If the customer is married, then on top of this an extra provision should be made for his or her family in the event of his or her early demise.

Husband and wife should both have their lives insured, first so that they can at least afford to cover funeral expenses, which are quite high, and even more importantly if there are children, to be able to provide help in the home to look after them in the event of the early demise of a parent. This type of advice may seem morbid, but without adequate life cover an investor's family would be in great trouble if he or she died young.

For a young couple with children the sum assured (i.e. the amount that is guaranteed to be paid out on death) should be at least 10 times the annual salary of the life assured, so for someone earning £30,000 p.a. the sum assured should be £300,000. This may seem to be a large amount, but company and state benefits and pensions are not very high for younger couples with children, and it is advisable to provide enough money so that the same standard of living can be maintained.

If the children are young, say pre-school age, it must be remembered that they will be at school until they are at least 16 years of age, and expenses are very high during this period. In addition the advent of student tuition fees has meant that children could now be financially dependent on parents until the age of 21 or 22. It is equally important for the wife and the husband to carry adequate life insurance, for if he or she dies leaving a young family, the spouse will either have to stop working with the resultant lowering of the standard of living, or employ people to run the house and care for the children. With adequate life cover the second option would be available.

From the savings side the investor is looking to provide himself or herself with a lump sum at a set future date. In the event of death before this date a guaranteed sum will be paid out, but the real purpose is to provide a lump sum in the future to coincide quite often with a known event, say a child's eighteenth or twenty-first birthday, or retirement. In this case the investor would choose the life insurance vehicle that provided a guaranteed minimum sum plus profits at the required date. This is called a 'with-profits endowment policy' and is described fully below. In this case the investor is relying on the expertise of the insurance company in investing his money in a good spread of underlying assets that will generate good profits. Some insurance companies are more successful than others, and the investor would be well advised to look at the league tables of results published in the financial press from time to time. There is a vast difference between the amount he would receive from the top and bottom performers.

Types of life insurance policies available

There are three distinct types of life assurance:

- Protection;
- Investment/protection;
- Investment.

As regards protection, life insurance is unique, but life insurance should be compared with unit trusts and investment trusts as regards its investment merits.

- Protection only is provided by products such as term life, critical illness and permanent health policies.

- Investment/protection is provided by the various forms of endowment policy and whole life policies available.

- Investment is provided by single premium bonds, where the protection aspect is very small compared to the investment potential of the policy.

Term life insurance

This is the cheapest form of all life cover available. The policy pays out only if the life assured dies before a set date. If he or she survives this period then nothing is paid out. Premiums are paid for the term of the policy and, if the life assured dies during this term, the beneficiary will receive a preset guaranteed sum. Donors who make potentially exempt transfers under inheritance tax should take out a seven-year term assurance written in trust to cover the potential inheritance tax liability.

These term life policies are purely protection policies, and are often found marketed under different names, the most common being mortgage protection policies, family income protection policies, critical illness policies and permanent health policies.

Mortgage protection policies are usually needed when an investor takes out a repayment mortgage with a bank or building society. The lender will insist on such cover being held to pay off the mortgage if the borrower dies before the end of the term of the mortgage. This type of policy is a term life policy

Family income protection policies are marketed to provide the surviving spouse with enough capital to carry on living at the same standard, and provide any necessary extras should the other spouse die before a predetermined date.

Critical illness insurance pays out a lump sum on either the diagnosis of a specified range of illnesses, or the progression of such an illness so that becomes impossible to carry on working. In such a situation many people may not receive a full salary for the duration of the illness. Thus can result in financial hardship both in repaying loans and meeting daily living expenses. State benefits are often insufficient to enable a normal lifestyle to be maintained.

Permanent health insurance is designed to produce an income for people unable to work due to ill health from any cause. An income, which can be inflation protected, until retirement is paid. The individual can decide the amount of his gross income that he wishes to insure. This is usually up to 50-65% of the gross income. The policy will normally pay out after a preset date, usually 3, 6 or 12 months after the illness has meant that they cannot carry on working. The shorter this period, the greater the premium. As with most insurance policies, the premium will depend on age, occupation and sum insured, and will normally exclude pre-existing conditions.

Whole of life insurance

This type of policy pays out a guaranteed sum upon the death of the life assured. There is no payout during the time the life assured is alive, and thus it is not a savings policy which benefits the life assured. However it is a way of providing for the family after the death of the life assured. The cost of this form of life cover is more than for term cover, because the insurance company will have to pay out at some time, but the premiums are lower than those for endowment policies.

A whole of life insurance policy can be with or without profits.

Endowment policy

There are four forms of endowment policy, with or without profits, unit-linked and unitized with-profit endowment. In the case of a with/without profits policy a guaranteed minimum sum is paid out after a set period, or on death of the life assured, whichever occurs first. The money is paid out to the named beneficiary of the policy. Approximately 10% of the premium paid is used by the insurance company to cover its costs and provision of the death benefit in the event of the life assured dying before the policy is due to mature. The remaining amount is invested by the insurance company to provide the sum paid out on maturity.

Without-profit endowment policies

These are the cheaper of the two types of straight endowment policy because they pay out only a set sum upon maturity or earlier death. The premiums are higher than for a whole life policy, because the guaranteed sum has a known payout date (assuming no prior death).

With-profits endowment policies

These policies pay out a guaranteed sum plus profits on maturity. At the end of the term the guaranteed sum is paid out plus profits. In the event of death prior to the preset maturity, payment will be made on the death of the life assured.

The profits are added to these policies in the form of two types of bonus: reversionary and terminal. With both bonuses, their size depends on the level of profits made by the insurance company. (Profits refers to the profit the insurance company has made on the underlying investment fund. A with-profits endowment policy shares in these profits.)

The reversionary bonus is added to the policy each year and is based on the sum assured. Once the reversionary bonus has been declared (i.e. added to the policy) it cannot be withdrawn. The level of the reversionary bonus does not always reflect the level of the insurance company's profits for that year. If the profits were high, the company could retain some profits to enable it to at least maintain the level of bonus in a year when profits were poor. The level of the reversionary bonus usually increases steadily each year.

The terminal bonus is paid out on maturity of the policy and it is a reflection of the success of the insurance company's investment management over the life of the policy. Terminal bonuses have on occasion been cut when the insurance company has had a poor profit performance. The last time this happened on a large scale was in 1974 when the property market collapsed. Because insurance companies are one of the largest owners of commercial property the collapse seriously affected their profits. For similar reasons, but to a much lesser extent, some life companies cut terminal bonuses in 1990. Terminal bonuses are not guaranteed.

One very important factor an investor must take into consideration when investing in a life policy is whether or not he will be able to afford the premiums throughout the period of the policy. If a premium is not paid then the life cover is invalidated. If by unhappy circumstances an investor does find that he can no longer afford the premiums he has one of three options available to him if the policy is a whole of life or endowment policy. He can either surrender the policy, which means that the insurance company will pay him a cash sum in return for the policy; he can sell the policy; or he can have the policy made into a paid-up policy. With the first option there is no guarantee that the investor will receive back the amount he has invested.

During the early years of a policy the surrender value is very low, and is always less than the premiums paid (typically for the first 18-24 months). This is because the insurance company has heavy costs to cover in setting up the policy, and in organizing a surrender, and these costs must be covered from the premiums paid before paying out anything on surrender. However, if the investor is desperate for cash this may be one option available. An alternative is to take out a loan against the surrender value of the policy, and this can be obtained from the insurance company itself. Provided the premiums can still be met this is the better option. Up to 90% of the surrender value can be borrowed and the capital is repaid from the proceeds of the policy on maturity.

If the investor does need cash from his life policy, a better way of increasing the amount received is to sell the policy at auction via one of the firms that specializes in this area. However, if it is impossible to meet the premiums but a cash sum is not required, then the policy can be converted into a paid-up policy. No more premiums will be due, and the policy will mature on its due date. Even this option is not usually attractive because the conversion terms do not favour the investor. However, it does still supply the element of life cover that may be necessary.

Before an investor starts to pay premiums on a life insurance policy, and more specifically on a with-profits endowment policy, he must choose the life insurance company carefully. Not all companies are the same. Some have far superior profit records, thus the amount paid out on a with-profits policy is much higher if a top-performing company is chosen.

One area that affects the payout on the policy is whether or not the insurance company pays fees to intermediaries for introducing customers. Some top-performing companies refuse to pay commission to intermediaries, whereas others pay a relatively low rate of commission. The low intermediary commission has been a major factor in these companies' success, especially when you consider that other companies pay up to 100% of the first year's premiums as commission.

However, the investor can simply approach the company direct to obtain life cover, thus avoiding intermediary commissions. If for any reason he needs to obtain life cover from a company paying commission to intermediaries, the investor should still approach the company direct and enquire whether he would receive a better deal as no intermediary is involved. In some cases the insurance companies which pay intermediary commission will give better value if approached directly.

Unit-linked and unitized with-profit endowment policies

Unit-linked endowment

Strictly, unit-linked policies are not endowments as such. They have similar purposes, however, and are often grouped in the same portfolio as with-profits policies. Both with-profits policies and endowment policies are commonly used to repay the capital on a mortgage.

The sum payable on maturity of a unit-linked endowment policy depends on the performance of the underlying fund which is run like a unit trust. There are no bonuses added to unit-linked endowment policies. Approximately 10% of the premium paid is used to purchase term life cover, the remainder is invested in the underlying fund. On death there is usually a guaranteed minimum sum paid out (which comes from the percentage of the premium used to purchase term life cover). If the value of the units in the underlying fund exceeds this sum, then that extra value is also paid out on top of the guaranteed sum.

For an investor who survives the term of the policy, the sum paid out will depend on the value of the units. If the investor purchases a policy with a fixed maturity date then it is possible that he could receive back less than he has invested. This would occur if the stock market had fallen badly on the maturity date, because the value of the policy is calculated on the value of the underlying fund. The investor can guard against this occurrence by taking out a policy with a flexible maturity date, thus if the market is low he can retain his policy until a more favourable time.

The main advantage of these policies ceased with the abolition of LAPR in the 1984 Finance Act. Prior to 13 March 1984 all unit-linked endowment policies were eligible for tax relief on premiums. This of course improved their performance because the tax relief increased the sum available for investment, but with the abolition of LAPR these policies are not as attractive as they once were. Policies that were issued before 13 March 1984 still qualify for LAPR at 12½%. If an investor wishes to invest in a savings scheme, and does not require life cover, then he should consider a unit or investment trust savings scheme or an ISA. These schemes offer more flexibility because payments can be stopped at any time without the problems associated with lapsing insurance policy premiums.

Unitized with-profits endowment

The other type of unit-linked policy is called a unitized with-profits endowment policy. This policy operates in much the same way as the unit-linked endowment but there are bonuses added to the policy. These are safer than unit-linked policies, but do not have the potential for such large gains (or losses).

Comparison of unit-linked endowment policies and direct unit trust savings plans

Unit-linked policies	Unit Trust savings plans
1. The insurance company makes a deduction from the proceeds in respect of its own CGT liability.	1. Unit trusts managers are not liable to CGT.
2. Policies taken out prior to 13 March 1984 attracted 12½% tax relief on premiums.	2. There has never been any tax relief on the amount invested.
3. The proceeds of a qualifying policy are free of income and capital gains tax in the hands of the investor.	3. The proceeds of a unit trust savings plan are subject to income tax on the dividends and capital gains tax on the gains in the hands of the investor.
4. Missing a premium invalidates the life policy.	4. Missing a premium merely means that no units are purchased that month
5. The policy can only be surrendered, sold or made fully paid.	5. Units can be sold at any time while continuing with the plan.
6. A guaranteed minimum sum paid out on the death of the life assured prior to maturity of policy. Policies automatically pay out on death of the life assured.	6. Only the value of the units is paid out on death. Alternatively, the units can be left to a beneficiary. Death does not mean that the units are automatically sold.
7. If the life assured survives the term of the policy, the proceeds are paid out, with the payment value being based on the value of the underlying units. It may not be possible to defer payment if the stock market is low, thus the return may not be very good in such a situation. Hence investors should purchase only those unit-linked policies that have a flexible maturity date.	7. The value of the units depends on the price quoted by the managers. However, the unit holder is free to sell the units when he so desires.

Comparison of unit trusts, investment trusts and life assurance as a savings vehicle

Life assurance

The 1984 Finance Act abolished the tax relief on premiums of all new insurance policies. Any policies in existence prior to the 1984 Finance Act are a good investment because they attract the 12½% tax relief, which is a valuable bonus on the sum invested.

However, for an investor considering life assurance as a vehicle for new savings the position is different. Life cover is vital for all investors who have dependents, and term, whole life or without-profit endowment should be used according to the investor's needs. League tables of the best-performing companies are published and investors should choose the best company for all forms of life cover. As a savings vehicle, life insurance must be compared to a regular monthly unit trust savings plan and investment trust savings plans. With-profit endowment policies are the savings vehicle.

Life Assurance – With-Profit Endowment	Unit Trust Savings Plan	Investment Trust Savings Plan
1. Guaranteed minimum sum payable on death or maturity. Sum paid out on death/maturity will be at least equal to amount paid in, plus any bonuses accrued. (Provided not a unit-linked policy where the problems are similar to unit and investment trust savings schemes.)	1. Sum paid on encashment depends on the price of the underlying securities. Thus less than the money invested could be paid out.	1. When the shares are sold, the price is set by supply and demand on the stock market. The investor could get back less than he paid.
2. The insurance company makes a deduction in respect of its own tax liability, but the proceeds of the policy are free of all taxes in the hands of the investor.	2. The unit trust is not itself liable to CGT, but the proceeds of the sale of the units are subject to CGT in the investor's hands, and interest is subject to income tax.	2. As with unit trust savings plan.
3. Professional management and diversification of underlying investments.	3. Same.	3. Same.

Life Assurance – With-Profit Endowment	Unit Trust Savings Plan	Investment Trust Savings Plan
4. Missing a premium invalidates the life cover.	4. Missing a payment merely means no units are purchased that month.	4. As with unit trust savings plan.
5. Payments should be kept up for 10 years to get a good return. If payments cease in the early years the sum repaid may be less than the sum invested due to deduction of insurance company costs.	5. Payments can cease at any time. Obviously sales should only be made when the market is high to avoid a loss.	5. As with unit trust savings plan.
6. Some insurance companies pay commission to insurance brokers who introduce business. If a new client comes direct, these insurance companies keep the commission for themselves.	6. Many unit trust companies pay commission to intermediaries which reduces the sum available. Plans should be taken out directly with the managers.	6. Some investment trusts pay commission to intermediaries. If this is the case, the sum available for investment is reduced.
7. No costs (apart from 6) involved in investing in life insurance.	7. Front-end loading charges and annual management fees are deducted from investments.	7. Broker's commission and PTM levy are charges on purchase of shares – but all bulk purchases are made once or twice a month, thus the broker's commission is very low. These charges are divided between all investors. No front-end loading charges, but annual management fees are charged.

16.3 Single-premium bonds – non-qualifying life policies

These are non-qualifying life policies where the investor pays a lump sum to the insurance company. A small percentage (around 10%) is used to purchase life cover, and the remainder is invested in units in the underlying fund. The units reflect the value of the assets held in the fund, plus the accumulated income of the fund. When the bond is encashed the proceeds depend on the value of the underlying fund.

The life cover element provides only a basis on which to calculate the amount payable on death, it is not used to calculate the value of the bond on encashment. Some life companies purchase term life cover which gives a guaranteed minimum payment on early death of the bondholder, while others use the life cover element on death to ensure that the bondholder's estate receives at least the same amount as was originally invested in the bond. In the second case the formula used to calculate the sum due on death uses the life cover element as its basis, but the exact formula varies from company to company.

The minimum investment in single-premium bonds varies from company to company, but is around £500. There is no income paid during the life of the bond, but the investor can withdraw 5% cumulative per annum of the capital sum invested for up to a maximum of 20 years. This facility is free of income tax at the time of withdrawal and capital gains tax on the partial withdrawals, but the total encashed is added to the value of the bond to calculate the investor's tax liability.

There are several types of single-premium bond available:

● Property

● Managed – of which there are the following types:

 – Balanced Managed

 – Stockmarket Managed

 – Cautious Managed

 – Defensive Managed

● UK All Companies

● UK Equity Income

● UK Smaller Companies

● UK Gilts

● UK Fixed Interest

● Money Market

● Guaranteed Funds

● Distribution Funds

- Global Equities
- Global Fixed Interest
- UK Index-Linked Bonds
- Money Market
- Europe Excluding UK
- North America
- Australasia
- Far Eastern Including Japan
- Far Eastern Excluding Japan
- Japan
- Emerging Markets
- Currency
- Commodity and Natural Resources
- Friendly Societies – Tax Exempt.

While an investor may make his initial investment in, say, the money market fund, he can at any time move his investment into one of the other bonds within the same company without encashing the bond. The switching between funds is done on a bid price-to-bid price basis.

The insurance company deducts an initial sum of around 5% of the amount invested (depending on the company) which is the 'front-end loading charge'; it also charges an annual management fee of around ¾% which is not fixed but can be raised at the company's discretion.

The investor should look very carefully at the funds mentioned above and compare them with the performance of unit trusts in the same field. Investment in the index-linked gilt fund should be compared to direct investment into index-linked gilts. For a money market fund, comparison should be made with direct investment into a bank or building society money market account. In the case of many of the funds listed above the investor will almost certainly be better to use the alternative vehicles, one major reason being that the insurance company will make a deduction from the value of the bond on encashment in respect of its own CGT liability, whereas the investor will have his annual exemption to offset gains made on the alternative forms of investment that produce taxable capital gains. In addition direct investment into money market or fixed interest stocks are free of CGT, whereas the insurance company has to deduct money for its own CGT liability.

Taxation treatment of single-premium bonds

The tax treatment of single-premium bonds in the hands of the investor is different from the treatment of qualifying life policies.

The Inland Revenue treats the proceeds of single-premium bonds as income, not capital gains. The bond is deemed to have suffered basic-rate income tax because the insurance company has paid tax itself on its income at 22%. The proceeds are free of capital gains tax because the insurance company has paid liability on the gains it has made.

Partial encashment

An investor can withdraw 5% cumulative per annum of the initial investment in the bond for a maximum of 20 years free of tax. If in year one no withdrawals are made, then in year two, 10% can be withdrawn. If in years one and two no withdrawals have been made then in year three, 15% can be withdrawn, and so on.

On final encashment

Ascertain the total profit (encashment proceeds plus any partial withdrawals, less the original cost of the bond).

If the bondholder's marginal tax rate is 40% in the year of encashment, he will be liable to income tax at 18% on the whole of the gain (the rate is the marginal tax less basic rate of 22% (40 - 22 = 18%)).

If the bondholder's marginal tax rate is less than 40% calculate the total gain above and divide it by the number of years the bond has been held. This average gain is then added to the investor's taxable income to see if it takes him into the next tax bracket. The amount unused of the 22% tax threshold is used up, and the remaining amount times number of years held, in excess of the 22% tax threshold, is taxed at 18% (i.e. 40% - 22%). There is no point in averaging the gain if the bondholder's marginal tax rate is 40%, since this is currently the highest rate of income tax.

If the investor's marginal tax rate is 22% after adding the 'averaged gain' to his taxable income, he will not pay any tax at all on the gain.

Non-taxpayers and lower-rate (10%) taxpayers cannot reclaim the tax deducted from the proceeds of the bond.

Example of top-slicing calculation

An investor purchases a single premium bond for £10,000. He holds it for five years then surrenders it, receiving £25,000. He has withdrawn 5% of the purchase value of the bond each year. Calculate whether he has any further tax liability on encashment of the bond in the following circumstances:

(a) He has a total taxable income of £10,000.

(b) He has a total taxable income of £45,000.

(c) He has a total taxable income of £27,000.

First the total profit is calculated:

	£
Sale proceeds	25,000
Plus 5%, withdrawals (£500 x 5)	<u>2,500</u>
	27,500
Less original cost	<u>10,000</u>
Total profit	<u>17,500</u>

(a) As he has a total taxable income of £10,000 he is a basic-rate taxpayer. The profit must be annualized, and added to his taxable income to see if he becomes a 40% taxpayer.

Annualized profit = $\dfrac{17,500}{5}$ = £3,500

Total taxable income = £10,000 + £3,500

= <u>£13,500</u>

Thus, he remains a basic-rate taxpayer and has no further tax liability.

(b) With a total taxable income of £45,000 he is a 40% taxpayer. Thus the whole of the profit is subject to top slicing i.e. 40% - 22%.

Income tax payable on profit = $\dfrac{£17,500 \times 18}{100}$ = £3,150

(c) The annualized profit of £3,500 is added to his total taxable income of £27,000.

= 27,000 + 3,500

= £30,500

Thus the profit takes him into the 40% tax band. The tax payable is calculated thus:

Unused part of basic rate tax band	= £29,400 - £27,000
	= <u>£2,400</u>
Annual profit = £3,500 - £2,400	= £1,100
Tax at 18% (40% - 22%) on	£1,100 x 5 years

$$= \frac{(1,100 \times 5) \times 18}{100}$$

$$= \frac{5,500 \times 18}{100}$$

Income tax payable   = <u>£990</u>

16.4 Property bonds

A property bond is a single-premium insurance bond where the underlying assets consists of a range of commercial and industrial property. These bonds provide the investor with an indirect interest in a professionally managed portfolio of properties that are situated on prime sites and are let to first-class tenants.

The minimum sum that can be invested in property bonds is £500 and for the investor who wishes to have property in his portfolio, these bonds are one very good way of providing it. For a high-rate taxpayer property bonds are an attractive addition to a balanced portfolio.

Disadvantages of property bonds

There are, however, certain disadvantages with property bonds that must be considered before investing.

- The value of the bond depends entirely on the value of the underlying property. If the property market collapsed as it did in 1974 and 1990 the underlying assets could be so reduced in value that the investor would make a loss.

- Valuation of property is subjective. Different experts will give widely different values on the same property at the same time. This makes accurate valuation of the underlying fund difficult, although the property bond holder can easily obtain a valuation of his bond because the bid and offer prices are published in the *Financial Times*.

- The percentage of the initial sum used to purchase pure life cover will not give as high a sum assured as would using the same amount to purchase a term life policy directly from the insurance company. However, there is no way that the bondholder can avoid the deduction for life cover from his initial premium.

- If too many bondholders encashed their bonds simultaneously the insurance company could be forced to sell some of the property to repay the bondholders. This could depress the property market and start a downward spiral of property values.

16.5 Managed bonds

These are also single-premium bonds and have all the characteristics of such bonds. The underlying fund is invested four ways: fixed-interest stocks, equities, commercial property and cash. The investment principle behind managed bonds is that the insurance company can switch from a fund that is performing badly to one that is doing well. However, this advantage is more theoretical than practical. The time to leave an investment is when it is doing well and the investor has made a good gain. Likewise he should invest in new areas when the investment is just starting to look attractive. This is called 'good timing'. The theory behind the managed bond completely reverses this policy and is one that should not be pursued. Another problem arises if it is the property fund that is doing badly. Property takes a long time to sell, and the value of the insurance company's property holding would fall dramatically if it sold a large part because the sales at such a level would reduce property values.

One advantage that a managed bond has over a property bond is that the managed bond has one of its funds invested in cash, thus a large number of bondholders simultaneously encashing their bonds will not depress the value of the bond as much. At certain times it can be advantageous to have a high level of cash, particularly when interest rates are high and the stock market is depressed. The cash part of the bond is as actively managed as the other three elements of the managed bond.

The diversified portfolio of holding in four different areas reduces the risk to the investor of sudden adverse movements in the value of the bond. However, it also reduces the benefits of upside movements.

16.6 Suitability of the various insurance products for various investors

Figure 16.1 is a brief summary in connection with term life cover, endowment policies, single-premium bonds and unit-linked life policies.

Figure 16.1: Insurance products compared

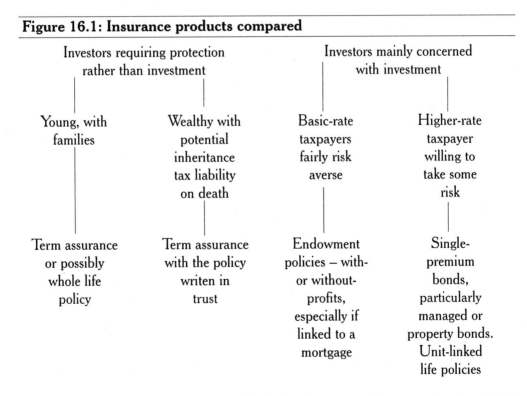

Note: a basic-rate taxpayer would normally find endowment policies attractive when linked to a mortgage. However, if he is looking for investment rather than a mortgage repayment vehicle, he would be better advised to consider a unit or investment trust savings scheme because of the flexibility of these schemes compared with life policies. (See Chapters 15 and 16.)

16.7 Guaranteed growth, guaranteed income bonds and guaranteed capital bonds

A lump sum is invested in an insurance company at a fixed interest for terms of one to 10 years. The rate of return is guaranteed at the outset, and in the case of income bonds the income is paid out net of basic-rate tax and with growth bonds it is rolled up in the bond. At the end of the term the investor receives back the capital sum invested, and with the growth bond the accumulated interest. Whether the interest is accumulated or paid out is irrelevant for tax purposes, it is treated as being paid net of basic rate tax. Non- and lower-rate taxpayers cannot reclaim the tax. The bonds are treated as single-premium bonds for tax purposes, thus are subject to the top-slicing rules.

The returns can be attractive for basic-rate taxpayers, provided they can afford to lock up their money for a fixed period. In most cases the investor is unable to withdraw the sum invested early, and the bonds that do allow early encashment carry heavy penalties for such an operation. The average minimum investment is £5,000.

An example of the average interest rates paid compared to gilts is given below, all rates being quoted in April 2001 (income paid annually).

Guaranteed	1 year term	4.1% net basic tax
income bonds	2 year term	4.15% net basic tax
	3 year term	4.2% net basic tax
	4 year term	4.15% net basic tax
High coupon	1 year to maturity	4.9%
gilt gross redemption	2 years to maturity	4.9%
yield	3 years to maturity	4.85%
	4 years to maturity	4.88%

From this table it is obvious that the income bonds can give the better return to a basic-rate taxpayer (gross up income bonds 100/80). The two advantages of gilts are that they are marketable, thus can be quickly sold if the capital is needed, and secondly that a non-taxpayer can have the interest paid gross. It may not be advisable, however, for a basic-rate taxpayer to take out a bond for over four years because the interest rate remains fixed. Thus the general level of interest rates and inflation may rise over a longer period, eroding the purchasing power of both interest and capital. A higher-rate taxpayer has to pay tax calculated under the 'top-slicing rules' on the income.

The principle behind these bonds is quite simple. The insurance company purchases a large amount of fixed-interest stock and sells off slices as income or growth bonds. The maturity date of the bond and the stock is the same, hence the guaranteed return.

16.8   Annuities

An annuity is a lump-sum payment to an insurance company which in return guarantees to pay out a set sum for a guaranteed period or until death, whichever is later. The sum paid to the insurance company is never returned unless the annuity is a capital-protected annuity.

The guaranteed sum is paid at regular intervals yearly, half-yearly, quarterly or monthly, and the more frequent the payments the lower they are. The amount paid out depends on the age at the commencement of the annuity and sex of the annuitant and whether there are any special provisions involved. Men have a lower life expectancy than women, thus men receive a better return. The other deciding factor in determining the amount paid out is the general level of interest rates at the time the annuity is taken out. The higher the general level of interest rates, the higher the annuity. This type of annuity is called a 'level-term annuity'.

Special provisions available

On a sole life paying a fixed sum per annum until the death of the annuitant. This method gives the highest level of income.

The variations available are:

● The income will be paid for a guaranteed minimum period, usually five or 10 years. If the annuitant dies during this period the income continues to be paid into his or her estate or to a named beneficiary until the period ends.

● Escalator annuities. These start with a lower initial income and the income rises each year by a set percentage or by the rate of inflation.

● Joint and last survivor annuities are taken out on the joint lives of husband and wife. They continue paying until the last survivor dies. The income paid out is lower than for a basic annuity because the insurance company is committing itself to what may possibly turn out to be a larger payment over the term of the annuity.

Taxation treatment of annuities

The tax treatment of annuities is favourable. Part of the payment is treated as return of capital and is tax free, the remainder is classed as interest and is subject to tax at the 20% or 40% rate depending on whether the taxpayer is a 10%, basic or 40% taxpayer. The capital element of the payment is at levels laid down by the Inland Revenue, and the greater the age of the annuitant on commencement of the annuity, the greater the capital element for tax purposes.

Example of returns available on annuities

An indication of the amounts received under annuities purchased for £10,000 is given below.

	Male aged 70	Female aged 70
Level-term annuity	£991	£870
Escalator annuity, scalating at 5% p.a.	£657	£545
Joint and last survivor (male 75/female 70)	£800 (no reduction on first death)	
	£880 (reducing by 2 on male death)	

From the above rates it may seem that the return for age 70 is reasonable compared to gilts, however the returns are fixed, the capital cannot be repaid and as the individual could easily live for 20 or more years, the fixed return will be severely depleted in real terms by inflation. However, the older the investor, the higher the return because the insurance company will be paying out over a shorter period of time.

Disadvantages of investing in an annuity

Unless special provisions are made that will reduce the amount paid under the annuity, the initial sum invested is lost completely to the heirs on the annuitant's death. The annuitant can never reclaim the sum paid to the insurance company.

Unless the annuity allows for the annual income to keep pace with inflation, the purchasing power of the annuity is eroded by inflation. If the annuitant lives to a very old age inflation can effectively wipe out the purchasing power of the annuity.

To get a good return the investor needs to be at least 70 years old at the time an annuity is taken out. To receive back the amount invested, the annuitant needs to live for around ten years from the date of purchase. From the investor's point of view he or she should be in good health to enjoy the annuity for many years. However, it is possible to get better rates for 'impaired life' e.g. for a smoker or someone with a chronic life-shortening illness.

Conclusion

For an investor aged at least 70, in good health and with a family history of longevity, the investment can be attractive because he or she should be able to live long enough to reap its benefits. However, with the current low inflation and low interest rate climate, returns on annuities are low. A potential investor needs to consider the impact on the purchasing power of an annuity if inflation rises, contrary to the current consensus of forecasts. If inflation rises then the purchasing power of the annuity will fall. For this reasons it is not advisable to commit all available funds to an annuity because later on a capital sum may be needed for unexpected expenses. For an investor over 70 who has no need to utilize the capital spent, it is worthwhile to consider committing part of his or her capital to an annuity and invest the remainder in a balanced portfolio. Portfolio planning is covered in Chapter 18.

16.9 Mortgage annuities or home income plans

For many investors their only asset of real value is their home, yet they need to be able to boost their income. A mortgage annuity (also called a home income plan) allows them to do this provided they are over 70, and own an owner-occupied house free of mortgage. The usual amount that can be borrowed is 15% to 75% of the value of the house depending on the age of the individual. For a joint and survivor mortgage annuity the joint ages must be at least 150. These limits are laid down by the companies operating these schemes.

The lender takes an fixed-rate interest-only mortgage over the house and the investor uses the sum raised to purchase an annuity. The investor pays only the interest to the lender. The annuity payment is treated as part repayment of capital, which is tax free, and the remainder as income which is subject to tax at the investor's marginal rate. The annuitant is allowed to retain up to 10% of the sum lent in cash and the remaining 90% must be invested in an annuity.

The loan is repaid only on the death of the annuitant by the sale of the house. Any excess of sale proceeds over the loan amount is paid into the deceased's estate. This does pose one problem for many elderly people, in that they will not be able to leave the whole value of their house to their heirs, but for those whose heirs have no need of the house, or for pensioners who are childless, the mortgage annuity scheme enables them to unlock capital tied up in their home. One advantage a mortgage annuity/home income plan has over a straight annuity is that as the value of the property increases it is possible to take out further top-up annuities, thus enabling the annuitant to increase his income.

Note: it is only advisable to take out a fixed-rate mortgage. A floating-rate mortgage may be cheaper in times of low interest rates but if interest rates become high, the interest on the mortgage may exceed the amount of the annuity payment, thus causing severe financial difficulties.

For individuals who receive housing benefit care must be taken because the extra income from this investment could reduce the entitlement to benefit.

16.10 Home reversion schemes

All or part of the house is sold to a company specializing in this area, and the house becomes the property of the company. In return a cash sum is paid which can be invested as the individual wishes. There is no loan involved and thus no interest to pay, and the company sells the house on the death of the occupier (or if the occupier moves permanently into a nursing home). Although this may seem a better scheme than a mortgage annuity, there are some important disadvantages:

- The house is no longer owned by the person/couple, thus cannot be left to their heirs. The person/couple only retains the right to live in the house until their death.

- The amount paid for the house is substantially below its market value, 35-60% below market value is not uncommon. Any rise in value belongs to the company.

16.11 Pensions

A pension is a method whereby an individual pays into a pension scheme a proportion of his earnings during his working life. These contributions provide an income (pension) on retirement which is treated as earned income and is taxed at the investor's marginal rate of income tax. The contributions to the pension are deducted from the investor's income before arriving at taxable income, thus gaining tax relief at the investor's marginal rate of tax.

Example A single investor whose gross earnings are £34,000 contributes 5% of his earnings to a pension scheme. His marginal rate of tax is 22% calculated:

	£
Gross income	34,000
Less: Pension contributions	
(5% of £34,000)	1,700
	32,300
Less: basic personal allowance	4,535
	27,765

This is within the 22% tax band of up to £29,400. Without the pension contributions his marginal rate of tax would be 40%. So it is a very tax efficient saving for retirement.

A variety of schemes are available, detailed in this section.

Occupational pension schemes

These are schemes run by employers and they come in two basic types: 'contracted-in' and 'contracted-out'. The maximum annual contributions are generally limited to 15% of earnings. Upon retirement a tax-free lump sum of up to 1½ times final salary up to a maximum of £150,000 salary can be taken in cash, and a reduced pension received if the scheme was joined before 14 March 1989. After that date the figure is £143,100 (1½ times the earnings cap of £95,400).

Contracted-in schemes

A 'contracted-in' scheme is contracted in to SERPS (State Earnings-Related Pension Scheme), and does not have to give any minimum guarantees. These schemes can be based either on 'final salary' or on 'money purchase'. A 'final salary' scheme means that the pension will be an amount based on a proportion of your salary, the proportion depending on the number of years worked in the company. A 'money purchase' scheme is not related to employee earnings but to the success of the pension fund managers. All contributions to pension schemes receive full tax relief.

Contracted-out schemes

A 'contracted-out' scheme is so named because it has contracted out of SERPS. This has a guaranteed minimum pension equal to at least what would have been received via SERPS. A contracted-out money purchase scheme is also known as COMPS. A contracted out scheme means that the employee receives a company pension and basic state pension only.

Should an employee stay in or opt out of a company scheme?

An employee has the right to opt out of his company scheme into a personal pension plan (PPP). Before he changes he should consider the following points:

- Is the company scheme a money purchase or final salary scheme? All PPPs are run on a money purchase basis, but if the company scheme is a final salary scheme it may be best to stay in (bearing in mind the next two considerations).

- Is the employee likely to move jobs? If so, a PPP may be more suitable than a frozen pension from a series of past employers.

- Does the employee want a flexible retirement age? PPPs allow for retirement at any time between the ages of 50 and 75, whereas company schemes tend to be much less flexible.

- If the employee transfers to a PPP how much, if anything, will the employer contribute, bearing in mind the employer has no obligation to pay into a PPP? If employers will not contribute to a PPP it will probably be better for the employee to stay in the occupational scheme.

- Is the scheme a COMPS one? Employees under 45 (male) or 40 (female) will probably be better off staying in the COMPS scheme. For those over these ages it will probably be better to stay in a SERPS scheme.

Personal pension plans (PPPs)

These are not available to anyone who is already in an occupational scheme unless there are earnings from other sources.

All contributions to a PPP are tax deductible, and therefore attract tax relief at the investor's marginal rate of income tax. The maximum contribution that can be made is on a sliding scale according to age and varies between 17½% and 40% of 'net relevant earnings'. 'Net relevant earnings' are defined basically as pre-tax salary for the employed, and taxable profit for the self-employed. The contribution limits are subject to a maximum of £95,400 gross for 2001-02 and are:

Age at 6 Apr	% of net relevant earnings	Effective maximum contribution i.e. of £95,400
35 or less	17.5%	£16,695
36-45	20%	£19,080
46-50	25%	£23,850
51-55	30%	£28,620
56-60	35%	£33,390
61 and above	40%	£38,160

This increasing scale means that older employees can boost the size of their pension fund, which is tax advantageous, so that they can enjoy a greater pension and tax-free lump sum on retirement if they wish.

The pension fund itself pays no tax except for the 10% tax credit on dividends, thus the potential investment return is higher when compared to alternative investments.

Finally, on retirement a lump sum is available. Up to 25% of the available sum can be commuted, i.e. taken as a tax-free lump sum, but the maximum amount of the tax-free lump sum is limited. The remainder is used to provide a guaranteed income for life.

The scheme is set up by the investor directly with a pension fund. The employer is not bound to make any contribution into a PPP as he is with the SERPS or occupational schemes. So why should an employee opt for a PPP? If he/she is likely to stay with the same employer all their life then the company scheme will be more likely to be beneficial, especially if it is a final salary scheme. However, many people nowadays change jobs regularly and with a company scheme the pension can be frozen, which means in real terms that it may be worth very little on retirement. A PPP operates on a money purchase basis, so the employee needs to have a long period before retirement to build a good fund.

The employee can arrange a 'buy-out' plan whereby his company scheme is transferred to a PPP. This does not mean that the employee will have the same value transferred in relation to the number of years service with the company, but a reduced number.

PPPs are more flexible in relation to retirement age. The benefits can be drawn from the age of 50 onwards, unlike company schemes where the age will be 60 or 65. For anyone planning early retirement a PPP is more flexible. They are also the scheme to use if the individual concerned is self-employed.

SERPS (State Earnings-Related Pension Scheme)

The amount received is paid for out of higher National Insurance contributions and the benefits are directly linked to earnings. For older employees (men over 45 and women over

40), if they are already paying into the SERPS scheme, then they will be better to stay in. The employer is bound by law to contribute to an employee's SERPS scheme. Younger employees are better off out of this scheme which is being reduced in value after the year 2000.

If the individual opts out of SERPS into a PPP, the plan must be an appropriate personal pension plan as certified by the Occupational Pensions Board.

Appropriate PPPs relate only to schemes that result from transferring from SERPS. All other PPPs are classed as 'approved' PPPs.

Position of self-employed, of those employed in pensionable employment, and those relying only on SERPS

Self-employed people have always been allowed to contribute to pension plans, subject to the age-related 17½%-40% of net relevant earnings rule.

Those employed in company pensions will have the right to transfer any pension rights accumulated in a company scheme into a PPP. Alternatively, the employee could let his company pension scheme continue, but make additional voluntary contribution into the company scheme or into an FSAVC.

Rights of those in SERPS

Individuals have the right to contract out of SERPS. They will then qualify for a rebate of the National Insurance contributions which would normally have gone into SERPS. This rebate will be paid directly into the nominated PPP. Alternatively, an individual should be able to continue in the SERPS scheme, but make regular payments to a PPP.

Topping-up pension schemes

Most employees pay around 5-6% of their gross earnings into a pension scheme, but the maximum actually allowed is 15% of gross earnings for occupational schemes and a sliding scale with a minimum of 17½% for PPPs. If an individual wishes to increase the value of his pension fund he has three options – AVCs, FSAVCs or a PPP.

AVCs (additional voluntary contributions)

These are extra payments made into the company scheme by the employee. Depending on the scheme, the employee may be able to increase his monthly contributions, purchase full years or put in lump sums as and when convenient. The terms vary between the schemes. The total contribution to the occupation pension plus AVC must not exceed 15% of net relevant earnings.

FSAVCs (free-standing AVCs)

These are individually set up schemes not paid to the company scheme but purchased directly from a pension fund. The employee continues to pay the usual pension contributions to the employer's schemes, but pays FSAVCs elsewhere. This route would be chosen if the individual did not find the company AVC scheme suitable. FSAVCs are money purchase schemes.

PPPs (personal pension plan)

These schemes can also be useful if an employee has non-pensionable earnings from other sources, e.g. royalties or fees.

The pension funds are run by a variety of institutions including pension funds, insurance companies, building societies, banks and unit trusts. In all cases the tax position is identical. The fund itself is free of tax except for the 10% tax credit on dividends and the contributions receive tax relief at the investor's marginal rate of income tax. On receipt of the pension it is treated as earned income and taxed at the investor's marginal rate of income tax.

Using PPPs to fund mortgages (pension mortgages)

'Pension mortgages' work along the following lines.

● The lender (say, a bank) agrees to lend a sum of money for house purchase. The house is mortgaged as security for the loan.

● The borrower takes out a PPP with agreed contributions. The projections should show that the tax-free commutable sum at retirement will at least equal the loan. In addition, term life cover is taken out, and the premiums for this will qualify for tax relief if they and the pension contributions do not exceed the age-related percentage rule.

● The borrower pays interest only on the bank loan, and pays the pension contributions. Normal PPP benefits apply, so the contributions are tax deductible and the PPP itself is free of all taxes.

● On retirement the commutable lump sum pays off the mortgage, and there is money left over to purchase an income for life.

Comparison of 'pension mortgages' with 'endowment mortgages'

An endowment mortgage is an interest-only loan with the capital to be repaid from the maturity proceeds of a life policy. The performance of the underlying investments will presumably be similar if the PPP is managed by an insurance company. There is no tax relief on the life policy premiums, however, and the insurance company will be subject to a special corporation tax rate of 22%. Thus the same total contributions will be much more beneficial if a PPP rather than an endowment policy is used.

SIPPS (Self-Invested Personal Pension Plans)

This type of personal pension plan is aimed at wealthier, more experienced investors, who have at least £100,000 in their pension fund or who can afford large annual pension contributions. The pension holder can decide on the investments to be held in a SIPP rather than pay a fund manager to do so. The maximum amount that can be invested is calculated in the same way as for other personal pension plans. The pension provider usually charges an up-front fee of between £500 - £700 and an annual fee of around £400.

The main eligible investments are:

- Stocks and shares listed on the UK Stock Exchange (main market and AIM)
- Stocks and shares listed in a recognized overseas stock exchange
- Debenture and other loan stocks, including gilts
- Convertible stocks
- Permanent interest-bearing shares
- Through any futures and options exchange in the world:
  - Currency, Equity and Bond futures – either long or short positions
  - Currency, Equity and Bond options – either put or call
- Warrants (equity)
- Unit and investment trusts and OEICs – authorized or unauthorized, subject to regulation by the Financial Services Authority or any other UK statutory regulatory organization for the purposes of the Financial Services Act
- Traded endowment policies
- Land in the UK or overseas including development land, farm land and forestry
- Insurance company managed funds
- Deposit accounts
- Commercial property in the UK or overseas purchased by a party not connected to the holder of the SIPPS

SIPPS allow the investor flexibility in planning for retirement. At a younger age the investor may look for higher-risk investments, but 5 to 10 years prior to retirement he may decide to change his strategy to a more conservative one in order to lock in the gains (as far as is possible).

The inclusion of commercial property is particularly attractive to the businessman who trades from his own property. He can place the property in his SIPP.

16.12 Stakeholder pensions

Stakeholder pensions commenced in April 2001. This is a very flexible pension scheme that enables anyone, whether in employment (subject to certain constraints shown below) or not, to save for a pension. There is no lower age limit to start a stakeholder pension, and parents or grandparents can start saving for their child/grandchild's pension via a stakeholder pension. Stakeholder pensions are available from banks, building societies, investment companies, insurance companies and pension companies.

The minimum amount that can be invested in a stakeholder pension is £20. There is no commitment to making regular payments into the fund. The maximum amount that can be invested each year is £3,600, subject to the earnings cap of £95,400 (2001-02). Contributions to a stakeholder pension are subject to tax relief at the investor's marginal rate of tax, with basic rate tax relief being given at source. Thus the maximum contribution of £3,600 would cost a basic-rate tax payer only £2,808 (£3,600 minus 22%).

Employees can use a stakeholder to top-up their pension in the same way as they can currently use AVCs. However stakeholder pensions are not available for employees who are already member of an occupational scheme and earn over £30,000 p.a. or to controlling directors, or people over 75.

Employers can offer stakeholder pension instead of a company scheme. If they employ five or more employees they are bound to offer a stakeholder pension if they do not offer an occupational pension scheme. Stakeholder pensions must meet certain standards laid down by the government covering charges, flexibility and information.

Charges

The maximum charge for managing a stakeholder pension is 1% of the value of the fund per annum. The charge is deducted from the fund.

Flexibility

Contributions can be made on a regular basis or occasionally. If the stakeholder pension is being provided by an employer, then contributions can be deducted from the weekly or monthly salary at source.

Stakeholder pensions are also portable. If the holder changes jobs the pension can be transferred without any charges being levied. This is advantageous compared to current occupational schemes where someone leaving the company cannot usually take the whole value of the occupational scheme to the new employer or has to opt to leave a frozen pension with the old employer. This will mean that at retirement the pension would be lower than that gained from a stakeholder pension which received the same amount of contributions over the period.

Information

The pension provider must give regular information about the fund, including annual statements of amount paid in and the value of the fund.

On retirement the investor can withdraw a lump sum from the stakeholder pension of up to

25% of the fund. This is tax free. The remainder of the fund will be used to purchase a pension annuity.

16.13 Friendly society bonds

A friendly society is a tax-exempt body except for the 10% tax credit on dividends, which gives it a major advantage over life insurance companies. All returns on a friendly society bond are tax free, thus the combination of the tax-free status of the society and the returns in the hands of the investor make these bonds very attractive to any investor who can afford to tie up his money for 10 years. The policy must run for at least 10 years with the premiums paid for a minimum of 10 years. If the premiums cease during the first 10 years the most that will be returned is the amount paid in.

Policies taken out prior to 13 March 1984 receive the 12½% tax relief on premiums, as do life insurance policies taken out prior to that date. Policies taken out after 13 March 1984 do not qualify for tax relief on premiums. The maximum sum assured is £2,050 and maximum monthly premium is £25. If the premiums are paid annually the maximum is £270 p.a. Husband and wife can each have friendly society bonds. It is possible to make a lump-sum payment into a friendly society bond, and this amount is around 20% lower than the cost of 10 years premium, i.e. the sum is £2,160. The interest earned by the friendly society on the sum deposited makes up the shortfall, although the interest itself is subject to income tax at the investor's marginal rate.

With all friendly society bonds the investor has four options open to him at the end of the 10-year period:

- He can encash the bond free of all tax;
- He can partially encash the bond as and when desired leaving the remaining sum to grow;
- He can leave the entire sum in the bond to continue growing tax free;
- He can continue to make payments.

While the amounts invested are small, these bonds can be attractive to high-rate taxpayers. For a basic-rate taxpayer who is certain that he can afford to tie up his money for 10 years the returns are also very attractive. It is possible for an annual premium of £270 over 10 years to realise in excess of £6,000, which is a growth rate of approximately 9% per annum.

Many friendly societies have now brought out plans aimed at parents, grandparents or other adults who wish to save money for a child. The advantage of these plans is the same for the beneficiary (whether child or adult) in that they are totally tax free. Friendly society bond funds invest in a wide range of investments – building society accounts, UK and overseas government stocks and shares.

17

Cash and Tax-free Investments

Objectives

After studying this chapter, the reader should be able to:

- identify the interest rates available on bank and building society accounts;

- differentiate between and evaluate the benefits and drawbacks of NSB accounts, National Savings Certificates; National Savings Income Bonds; Pensioners Guaranteed Income Bond; National Savings Capital Bonds and Premium Savings Bonds;

- Also Savings Children's Bonus Bonds; ESOPs; PEPs; TESSAs and ISAs;

- identify and assess the benefits of the investments that are totally exempt from income and capital gains tax in the hands of the investor;

- differentiate between investments that provide instant to one-month's access to capital; investments that have a withdrawal period of one month to one year; the investments that mature between one and 10 years; longer-term (five years plus) investments;

- evaluate the benefits of investments that provide a monthly savings scheme.

17.1   Introduction

Cash investments

These are funds placed with:

- National Savings, representing loans to the government;

- Banks and building societies.

These funds are generally repayable on demand or at very short notice. They are also capital guaranteed – the customer cannot make a capital loss unless the institution with which he invests becomes insolvent. They usually incur few if any charges. Those charges which are made are published in a tariff by the institution in keeping with the Code of Banking Practice, to which most institutions subscribe.

Note: all interest rates quoted in this and subsequent chapters are as at 1 May 2001.

Tax-free investments

These are investments that are exempt from income tax and capital gains tax under government regulations. They include many National Savings products, individual savings accounts (ISAs), personal equity plans (PEPs) and employee share option schemes (ESOPs).

17.2 Bank and building society accounts

Most banks and building societies offer savings products that are broadly similar in nature. There is one particular difference in that savers with a building society are members of that society. If a society demutualizes and becomes a bank, members may receive shares in the 'building society' which are tradeable on the Stock Market.

Current accounts

Retail banks are the main providers of current accounts. Generally, current accounts providers pay very low rates of interest (or no interest at all) on balances held, because money is available on demand. Interest-bearing current accounts pay interest on a net basis, i.e. with 20% tax deducted at source (which satisfies a basic-rate taxpayer's liability).

High-interest cheque accounts

Most large banks have 'premium' rate cheque accounts, aimed principally at high net worth customers. These products usually have a minimum opening balance, with interest paid reducing to a very low rate if the balance falls below a certain level. As long as a reasonably substantial balance is held, interest rates are quite competitive. Better rates can be obtained, however, on savings and investment accounts on which cheque book facilities are not available.

Savings accounts

All banks and building societies offer a range of savings and term accounts. Most offer instant access. The longer the term and the higher the balance, the better the interest rate paid.

Money-market deposits

All banks and building societies offer these deposits, usually for amounts in excess of £25,000. The period of investment is agreed at the outset and the return is fixed for that period. Interest on balances in excess of £50,000 is paid gross and the investor is liable for tax on this. Balances below that threshold receive interest with tax deducted at source. Money-market accounts are especially useful for the investor who needs time to construct an investment portfolio, because the rates paid are about the best available.

Calculation of after-tax returns from bank and building society accounts

Investors will need to know how much interest they receive on these accounts, after taking into account their marginal rate of tax. The following calculations shows how they calculate the rate of interest they receive after tax is deducted.

17.3 Taxation treatment of bank and building society interest

Non-taxpayers can reclaim the tax deducted from interest, or they can receive the interest gross upon signing a declaration that they are non-taxpayers. The interest must still be entered on a non-taxpayer's tax return so that the Inland Revenue can establish the correct marginal rate of tax. When the interest has been entered on the investor's tax return, the Inland Revenue will gross it up and add the grossed-up figure to the investor's other income. If the gross interest alters the investor's marginal rate of tax, there will only be further tax to pay if the investor becomes a 40% taxpayer. In this case a further 20% tax on the gross interest will be paid. A 10% and basic-rate taxpayer have no further tax liability because the 20% tax deducted at source satisfies their liability to tax.

17.4 National Savings Bank

National Savings Bank Ordinary Account

The NSB accounts are opened at the Post Office. The ordinary account has a minimum investment of £10 and a maximum of £10,000. Cash withdrawals of up to £250 per day (or £500 per day if the account is classed as a 'Regular Customer Account') can be made, and standing orders can be raised to meet regular payments.

The interest paid is on two levels.

- Balances of under £500 – interest of 1.25% gross p.a.
- Balances of £500 or more that were in the account by 31 December and remain above £500 for the whole of the following year until 1 January of the next year – interest of 1.35% gross p.a.

Thus the £500 balance must be in the account on 31 December 2000 and remain above £500 until 1 January 2002 to attract the higher rate. If the account is opened during the year only 1.25% per annum is paid that year. This also applies if the balance falls below £500 during the year.

The first £70 of interest is free of income tax and a husband and wife are each entitled to £70 interest tax free, thus they can receive £140 interest tax free. The interest, while tax free, must be recorded on the investor's tax return.

Interest is paid only on each whole pound on deposit for complete calendar months. Money does not earn interest in the month it is deposited or withdrawn. This makes the timing of deposits and withdrawals very important.

- Incorrect timing: A deposit made on 1 April and withdrawn on 31 July will earn interest only on the two complete months of May and June. This has the effect of reducing the rate of interest paid.

- Correct timing: A deposit made on 31 March and withdrawn on 1 August earns interest for four complete months – April, May, June and July.

Thus, making deposits on the last day of the month and withdrawals on the first day of the month gives an extra two months' interest, yet the money has been deposited for only two days longer.

For a 40% taxpayer who has deposited £500 or more for a full calendar year, and only makes deposits or withdrawals in accordance with the 'Correct Timing' section above, the interest rate of 1.35% is equivalent to an after-tax return of 2.25% from a bank or building society.

$$\frac{(1.35 \times 100)}{60} = 2.25\%$$

In order to keep with the £70 per annum interest that is tax free, the maximum deposit is £5,185. For this sum, the highest bank and building society rates are paying around 4% gross, which is equivalent to 2.4% for a 40% taxpayer. Given the complexity on the Ordinary Account and the poor returns quoted above, it is not worth a 40% taxpayer investing in this account. For a basic- or lower-rate taxpayer the Ordinary Account is very uncompetitive.

For a non-taxpayer this account should be avoided despite the interest being paid gross because the return of either 1.25% or 1.35% can be bettered by other savings accounts. If immediate access to money is needed, the instant access account in a bank or building society gives a better return because interest can be paid gross to non-taxpayers.

National Savings Bank Investment Account

This account is also available via the Post Office and offers a far more attractive return than the Ordinary Account. The minimum deposit is £20, the maximum holding £100,000 plus any accumulated interest. Interest on this account is paid gross on a banded rate from 4% on balances under £500 to 5.2% on balances of £50,000 and over.

The NSB pays all interest gross, unlike banks and building societies who can pay gross only to non-taxpayers. Interest is calculated on a daily basis on each whole pound deposited and is subject to tax at the investor's marginal rate. Interest on this account is paid only once a year, on 31 December. All withdrawals are subject to one month's notice, which runs from the day the application is received at the National Savings Bank in Glasgow, not at the local Post Office. Money can be withdrawn without notice, provided the amount has been in the account for at least 30 days. Thirty days' interest will be lost on the amount withdrawn.

The account is not attractive to non-taxpayers because the interest rate is between 4% and 5.2%. They may find a bank or building society instant access account paying higher rates. The 5.2% gross is only worth 4.16% to a 22% taxpayer, and 3.12% to a 40% taxpayer. Remember that interest is subject to tax at 20% for a 22% taxpayer, and at 40% for a 40% taxpayer.

17.5   Other National Savings investments

57th Issue Fixed Interest National Savings Certificates

National Savings Certificates can be purchased through most post offices and banks. The 57th issue carries a guaranteed return equivalent to 3.55% compounded over five years, and the return is free of income tax and capital gains tax. The minimum investment is £100, the maximum £10,000, purchased in units of £25. Any returns from these certificates do not have to be recorded on an income tax form. The repayment value increases at the end of the first year and at the end of each subsequent three months. If the certificates are encashed during the first year, only the purchase price is repaid. If the certificates are encashed early, they receive a lower rate of interest depending on the time held.

These certificates are attractive to 40% taxpayers because they give a gross equivalent return of 5.92% tax free.

$$\frac{(3.55 \times 100)}{60}$$

National Savings Certificates that are not redeemed at the end of the five years continue to receive interest at the general extension rate of 2.61%.

19th Issue Index-linked NSCs

These NSCs guarantee a return that is a real return over the rate of inflation. Interest equivalent to 1.65% compounded p.a. over five years is added and this is on top of the inflation proofing. The minimum investment is £100, the maximum £10,000. At each anniversary of purchase the whole certificate is revalued in line with the retail prices index plus the guaranteed return. If the certificates are held to maturity they receive the guaranteed return plus index linking. The formula used to calculate the index linking is:

$$\frac{\text{Purchase price} \times \text{RPI in month of encashment}}{\text{RPI in month of purchase}}$$

If the RPI on the date of purchase was 144.7, and 172.3 on encashment, £1,000 invested in Index-Linked NSCs would be worth:

$$\frac{1,000 \times 172.3}{144.7} = £1,190.74$$

For the higher-rate (40%) taxpayer these certificates offer an attractive return. The 1.65% is equal to 2.75% gross PLUS the index linking. These certificates are attractive to basic-rate taxpayers only in times of high inflation.

Note: On top of the £10,000 for the 57th issue and 19th issue index-linked NSCs, investors can invest the proceeds of any previous issues of NSCs with no maximum limit. NSCs purchased in this manner are called reinvestment certificates.

General extension rate and reinvestment certificates

At the end of the five-year period all NSCs from the 7th issue onwards (apart from the index-linked issues) receive the same rate of interest: the 'general extension rate' of 2.4% (correct at time of writing). It is inadvisable for investors to retain issues of NSCs after their 5-year guaranteed interest period, because the general extension rate is always below the rate paid on the current fixed-rate NSCs.

Other short-dated, fixed-rate National Savings issues

In addition to the 5-years issues of NSCs, there are also 2-year NSCs, both index-linked and fixed-rate.

There are also a range of short-dated fixed-rate bonds, with durations of six months and two years. For full details of these see www.nationalsavings.co.uk.

National Savings Income Bonds

These bonds, like all National Savings and National Savings Bank investments, pay interest gross. The interest rate is 5.15% gross on balances under £25,000 and 5.4% on amounts over £25,000. The minimum holding is £500, the maximum £1 million. All interest received is subject to tax at the investor's marginal rate. The bonds pay interest on a monthly basis. This can be very useful for an investor who requires a regular income. However, the rate of interest is variable at six weeks' notice, hence it is not possible to predict the exact income received over a year or more. If interest rates look set to rise then this account is attractive for non-taxpayers who require monthly income. However, if interest rates are falling the non-taxpayer should consider purchasing a high-coupon dated gilt which will ensure a fixed level of income until redemption.

For a basic-rate taxpayer the 5.15% gross return is worth 4.12% after 20% savings rate tax. If he requires a monthly income he should compare this to a building society 90-day account which provides this facility. Three months' notice of withdrawal for NS Income Bonds is required. Withdrawals must be in multiples of £500 and at least £500 must remain invested, but the interest received depends on how long the income bond has been held:

● Repayment in first year: Interest at half rate from date of purchase to date of repayment on amount paid;

● Repayment after first year: Interest paid in full.

A bank or building society account is more flexible than the NS Income Bond as only 90 days' notice need be given to withdraw without loss of interest, or instant access with loss of 90 days' interest is also possible. If repayment is made during the first year, and the amount paid out as monthly interest exceeds the amount due under the 'half rate' rule, then the overpayment of the interest is deducted from the capital repaid. Interest is calculated from the date of purchase on a daily basis and is paid on the fifth of each month. The first interest payment on the bond will be made on the first interest date after the bond has been held for six weeks, and includes all interest due from the date of purchase. Each bond has a guaranteed initial life of 10 years from the first interest date after the date of purchase. The bond will be redeemed at par either at the end of the guaranteed initial period, or on any interest date thereafter on the Treasury giving of six months' notice.

Pensioners' Guaranteed Income Bonds

As with the National Savings Income Bonds, Pensioners' Guaranteed Income Bonds also provide a monthly income. The rate of interest on these bonds is guaranteed if held for five years from the time of purchase. Early withdrawals are subject to 60 days' notice and 60 days' loss of interest. Withdrawals without notice are subject to 90 days' loss of interest on the amount to be withdrawn. The minimum investment is £500, the maximum £1 million and these bonds are available only to people aged 65 or over.

The rate of interest is 4.75% gross but is subject to tax at 20% for a basic-rate taxpayer and 40% for a 40% taxpayer.

National Savings Capital Bonds

Capital Bonds are designed for investors with a lump sum to invest who do not wish to receive any income. The interest paid is rolled up into the bond and on repayment the investor receives his capital back plus the accrued interest.

Interest is paid gross on the bonds at the fixed rate of 4.8% gross, and is added to the capital once a year but it is subject to tax as described above in the year the interest is added to the capital. This makes these bonds unattractive to any taxpayer because there is no facility available to defer tax until final encashment, as there is with a single-premium bond. The minimum holding is £100, the maximum holding is £250,000. Purchases must be made in multiples of £100. The minimum withdrawal is £100. The rules regarding withdrawals and the rate of interest paid apply as those detailed for National Savings Income Bonds.

Premium Savings Bonds

These do not give any guaranteed return at all and, indeed, are not a true investment because they guarantee only capital back. However, premium bonds pay out prizes that are totally free of income tax and capital gains tax.

Prizes range from £50 to £1,000,000. The minimum purchase is £100. However, the minimum holding is £1. The maximum holding is £20,000. Each £1 unit gives the holder one chance per week or month to win a prize. The odds against winning any prize at all are in the region of 20,000 to 1. Thus, an investor with £20,000 worth of Premium Savings Bonds should, on average, receive a prize 12 times a year, but this is only a mathematical model and in practice does not hold true because the prizes are picked electronically at random. These bonds cannot be recommended as an investment. However, if an investor wishes to have a 'flutter' and holds a balanced portfolio then it is one alternative to consider among other riskier investments, the risk being loss of income and erosion of capital value.

National Savings Children's Bonus Bonds

This is a lump-sum investment of between £25 and £1,000. The rate of interest is fixed for the first five years at 4.45% per annum compounded. At the end of five years a new rate of interest is fixed. The bond can be encashed at any time, but should be encashed on the child's 21st birthday. No interest is earned after the 21st birthday. Children's Bonus Bonds do not pay out interest – it is rolled-up in the bond. The interest is totally free of income tax and capital gains tax even when the bond has been purchased by a parent. These bonds are useful if the parent is giving money to the child and the total interest from such gifts would exceed £100. With other investments when the income exceeds £100 p.a. gross the whole of the income is treated as the parent's for tax purposes and taxed at the donor parent's marginal rate of income tax.

Calculation of gross equivalent from income tax and capital gains tax exempt investments

Investors must also be able to compare returns on investments that are totally free of income tax and capital gains tax with those that are taxable. To do this, the gross equivalent return is calculated for the tax-exempt investment and compared to the gross return on taxable investments. This will indicate the most attractive investments.

The following investments detailed in this chapter are totally free of income and capital gains tax.

- All National Savings Certificates
- Premium Savings Bonds
- National Savings Children's Bonus Bonds
- PEPs
- ESOPs
- TESSAs
- TOISAs
- ISAs

Some of these investments do not give a guaranteed return; these are Premium Savings Bonds, ESOPs, PEPs, TESSAs, TOISAs and ISAs. The return on these depends on other factors such as interest rates (TESSAs), performance of the stock market (ESOPs and PEPs), ISAs (performance of the underlying investment see section 10) and 'luck of the draw' (Premium Bonds).

17.6   Personal equity plans (PEPs)

PEPs are no longer available for new investment. However, investments held in a PEP can be retained and have the benefit of tax-free income and capital gains. The investments that can be held in a PEP are the same as those which can be held in an ISA. The investments must be listed on a recognized Stock Exchange, and can consist of gilts, company loan stocks, unit trusts, investment trusts and OEICs. Overseas investments are allowed if they comply with these rules.

Suitability of PEPs for investors

For high taxpayers who also have capital gains each year in excess of the £7,500 figure these plans are attractive. An investor who already holds PEPs needs to consider whether to retain or transfer all or part of the PEP into an ISA (see section 7). The drawback is that on the year of transfer the investment will count as being part of the annual amount invested into an ISA. Thus no further investment in an ISA will be possible for that year. In addition there may be costs incurred for withdrawing funds from the PEP. The investor who holds shares in his plan will retain all the rights of an ordinary shareholder. He will receive notice of meetings, annual reports and shareholders' concessions (if any). As PEP fees tend to be higher than unit trust fees this can make the PEP plan rather expensive in the early years. Fees tend to be around 5% of the initial investment and subsequent annual management fees are between 1.25% and 1.5%. Some managers levy a flat annual fee varying from £20 to £120.

Single-company PEP fees are somewhat lower. Some managers do not charge an initial fee, and many fees are in the 0.75-1% range. Annual management fees vary from 0.5%-1.5%

17.7   ISAs (individual savings accounts)

ISAs are tax-free savings accounts which have replaced PEPs and TESSAs. They have been available since 6 April 1999. The maximum amount that can be invested in an ISA per annum has been set at £7,000 up to April 2006. The investments held in an ISA are cash, stocks and shares, unit and investment trusts, life insurance and national savings. Basically ISAs are divided into three investment categories: cash, insurance and stock market.

ISAs are free of income tax and CGT. Where shares are held in an ISA, the tax credit will be paid back into the ISA account for the 5-year period ending 5 April 2004. This 'repayment' of the tax credit applies only to shares held in an ISA.

Investments held in an ISA must be listed on a recognized Stock Exchange, and the investments can consist of gilts, company loan stocks, unit trusts, investment trusts and OEICs. Overseas investments are allowed if they comply with these rules. Shares from profit-sharing schemes or employee share option schemes can be transferred into an ISA within 90 days of issue, provided the total amount held in the ISA does not exceed the annual limit of £7,000 (2001/02). Shares purchased via a new issue or a demutualization CANNOT be transferred into an ISA.

CAT marks have been introduced by the government for ISAs. This is NOT a guarantee of performance, but indicates that the ISA complies with stipulated conditions in relation to charges, access and terms. Even with CAT-marked ISAs, the tax savings may not be sufficient to cover the charges for non- and basic-rate taxpayers.

The CAT (Charges, Access and Terms)

	Charges	Access	Terms
Cash ISA	No charges of any kind.	Minimum deposit/withdrawal no greater than £10, withdrawals within 7 working days or less.	Interest rate no lower than 2% below base rate, must follow base rate increase within one month.
Insurance ISA	Annual charge no more than 3%, no other charges.	Minimum premium no greater than £250 a year or £25 per month.	Surrender value must reflect the value of the underlying assets and be at least equal to premiums paid after 3 years
Stock market ISA	Annual charge no more than 1% of net asset value, no other charges.	Minimum saving no more than £500 a year, or £50 per month.	Can invest in shares, authorized unit trusts, OEICs or certain investment trusts (not split capital), units and shares must be single priced at mid-market price.

The CAT (Charges, Access and Terms) (cont.)

	Charges	Access	Terms
Any ISA Provider	Decent straight-forward treatment of customers, use of plain English, no requirement to buy other linked product, no limitation of ISA investments to existing customers, undertaking to keep to the CAT standards after the investment is started.		

A basic-rate taxpayer must look at the situation regarding tax benefits and charges and compare these to the performance of the fund in order to decide whether an ISA is an appropriate investment vehicle.

ISAs come in two forms – mini and maxi.

MINI ISA – limits

	2001/02
Cash ISA	£3,000
Insurance ISA	£1,000
Stock market ISA	£3,000

A mini ISA allows the investor to choose the best fund manager, bank or building society or insurance company for each element of the fund. The only restriction is that of the monetary limits per type of ISA are observed.

MAXI ISA – limits

	2001/02
Cash ISA	£3,000
Insurance ISA	£1,000
Stock market ISA	£7,000

A maxi ISA has all the investments purchased from the same management company. All classes of investments are available via a maxi ISA. There is some restriction on how the money is invested in a maxi ISA e.g. all the £7,000 can go into a stock market ISA.

It is important to note that an investor CANNOT have both a mini and a maxi ISA in the same tax year; the choice of ISA will depend on the investor's needs. For example, if stock market investment is the sole choice, then a maxi ISA should be used because the limit is higher. Although the proceeds of existing PEPs can be transferred into ISAs there is little obvious benefit for so doing as switching costs would be incurred which would reduce the value of the investment. PEPs do not have a set life span. The investor cannot put any more money into the PEP, but can still change the investments within the PEP according to the PEP rules.

17.8. Employee share option schemes (ESOPs)

This is a scheme whereby employees can save a fixed sum up to a maximum of £250 per month over five years, making a total of 60 payments in all. At the end of the five-year period a bonus equivalent to 15 monthly payments is added; if the money is left a further two years the bonus paid equals 30 monthly payments. The bonus is free of all taxes, and the minimum and maximum payments are £10 and £250 per month, respectively. When the employee joins the scheme he is given the option of buying a fixed number of shares at a preset price at the end of the five- or seven-year period. The price of the shares is effectively fixed at the outset, as is the number of shares that can be purchased. The maximum discount at which the shares can be offered on the day the ESOP option is granted must not be 'manifestly less' than 20% of the market value. The investor can either take his return as cash or use it to buy the number of shares specified. If the shares have risen in value the investor can immediately resell the shares at the current market price. If the investor chooses to do this the profit is free of income tax but subject to capital gains tax. If the shares are held then there may be a liability to capital gains tax when they are eventually sold. If the investor chooses to take the cash option then it is free of income tax and capital gains tax. The scheme is a method of either benefiting from a long-term rise in the shares of the employing company or simply achieving a good tax-free return if the shares are not worth buying. The scheme can be set up only if the employer agrees, and it must then be approved by the Inland Revenue. Minimum conditions of eligibility state that the employees must have been employed by the company for over five years and work full time. However, companies can alter these rules to include part-time workers and those who have just joined the company.

17.9 Tax-exempt special savings accounts (TESSAs)

TESSAs were savings schemes whereby a maximum of £9,000 could be invested over a period of five years, the interest being paid free of tax provided it is not withdrawn from the account. The interest does not have to be shown on a tax return provided, again, it is retained in full in the TESSA for five years.

Rate of return

The interest rate paid on a TESSA is not fixed (although providers can offer a fixed rate), but subject to market fluctuations. The rate is set by the bank, building society or other institution authorized under the Financial Services and Markets Act 2000 running the TESSA, so rates vary according to the provider. A TESSA is suitable for retention by high-rate taxpayers who can afford to tie up the money for five years. However, interest rates vary between providers, so the investor should shop around for the best terms.

TOISAs - Tessa-Only ISAs

TESSA proceeds can be transferred into a TOISA which is a special account where the monetary limit of the transfer is £9,000. As a TESSA has a life span of 5 years, this method enables the tax-free element of the savings to be maintained.

17.10 Summary of savings and investments

This section covers all the details of the various investments that are available, as detailed throughout the book, including this chapter. In Chapters 18 and 19 we cover the construction and management of portfolios.

Investments that are totally free of income tax and capital gains tax in the hands of the investor

These are:

- All issues of NSCs
- PEPs
- TESSAs
- TOISAs
- ISAs
- National Savings Children's Bonus Bonds
- Premium Bonds
- ESOPs
- Proceeds of qualifying life policies
- Friendly society bonds

Note: The NS Ordinary Account does not come under this heading because the interest must be declared to the Inland Revenue, even though the first £70 of interest is tax free.

Investments that provide instant access or access with up to one month's notice

These are:

- Bank and building society current accounts
- Bank and building society high-interest cheque accounts
- Bank and building society money-market deposits at call
- Premium Bonds
- National Savings Certificates
- National Savings Children's Bonus Bonds
- TESSAs, provided only net interest is withdrawn
- ISAs

Investments where repayment is made in one month to one year without penalty

These are:

- Bank and building society notice accounts
- Bank and building society money-market deposits for a fixed term up to one year maximum
- National Savings Bank Investment Account
- Short-dated gilts with one year or less to maturity provided they are held to maturity
- 6-months Fixed-Rate National Savings products

Investments that mature between one and 10 years

These are:

- Bank and building society term deposits (at the end of the term)
- Employee share option scheme (five to seven years)
- Guaranteed income bond (two to 10 years)
- Guaranteed growth bond (two to 10 years)
- Local authority fixed-term loan (at the end of the term)
- Yearlings (one to two years)
- National Savings Income Bonds (one year for full interest to be paid, can be left in for 10 years)
- National Savings Capital Bonds (one year for full interest to be paid, can be left in for 10 years)

- National Savings Certificates
- Personal Equity Plans
- Short- and medium dated gilts (one to 10 years to maturity)
- Dated company loan stocks with one to 10 years to maturity, provided they are held to maturity
- TESSAs

Long-term investments (over five years)
Return guaranteed at the outset
These are:

- Medium- or long-dated gilts held to maturity
- Dated company loan stock held to maturity
- Annuities and mortgage annuities
- Employee share option schemes (five to seven years life)
- National Savings Children's Bonus Bonds
- PEPs
- ISAs

Return variable depending on performance of stock market and/or managers
These are:

- With-profits endowment life assurance policies
- Unit-linked life policies
- Friendly society bonds
- Pension plans
- Single-premium bonds
- Unit trusts
- Investment trusts
- Equities
- PEPs
- ISAs invested in equities

High-risk investments

These are:

- Direct investment in overseas equities
- 'Penny' shares
- Chattels
- 'Stagging' new issues
- AIM shares
- Warrants
- Options
- Traded options
- Stock Index Futures
- Spread betting
- Contracts for difference
- Enterprise Investment Schemes (EISs)
- Venture Capital Trusts (VCTs)

Monthly savings schemes

These are:

- Life assurance policies
- Pension plans
- Friendly society bonds
- Unit trust savings schemes
- Investment trust savings schemes
- Employee share option schemes (ESOPs)
- Personal equity plans
- ISAs

Monthly income schemes

These are:

- Building society term accounts (including 90-day accounts)
- Annuities

Investment Management

- Mortgage annuities
- National Savings Income Bond
- Unit trust withdrawal plan
- Unit trust monthly income schemes
- Pensioners' Guaranteed Income Bond

18

PORTFOLIO PLANNING, ASSET ALLOCATION AND RISK

Objectives

After studying this chapter, the reader should be able to:

- understand the importance of a clear asset allocation strategy and the role that risk plays in creating a portfolio strategy;

- appreciate the significance of timing;

- list the information required from an investor in order be able to give advice on portfolio planning and apply such information to practical situations;

- analyse the principles that influence how a portfolio should be constructed;

- evaluate the factors that could influence the basis on which investments are selected.

18.1 Asset allocation

Investors need to be aware of the problems and risks of failing to provide a well-diversified portfolio of investments. The risk is not just related to the performance of the stock market, but to the whole spread of investments held by an investor. Because investors are individuals, a good asset allocation strategy for one person might be totally wrong for another.

Asset allocation strategy is about trying to achieve the most effective blend of risk and return for each investor depending on the investment aims and the time horizon of the investment strategy. The asset allocation decision will depend on a combination of:

- the expected level of returns available from each asset class

- the expected level of risk associated with each asset class

- the investor's time horizon

- the investor's attitude towards risk.

The major asset classes

There are three main asset classes – cash, fixed interest and equity or equity-based. None of these classes is risk free. Inflation and interest-rate movements affect returns on fixed-rate cash and fixed-interest investment. Equity and equity-based investment is better able to cope with the effects of inflation in the long term. The Barclays Equity-Gilt Study 2001 shows the value of £100 invested in 1945 with income re-invested:

Table 18.1 Extracted from the Barclays Equity-Gilt Study 2001		
Asset class	**Value**	**Real return (taking inflation into account)**
Cash	£4,165	£177
Gilts	£3,296	£140
Equities	£97,023	£4,132

A portfolio does need balance, and although the return shown on cash is very low, there must be a cash element in a portfolio to ensure that living expenses and other costs, such as a new car or a holiday, can be paid for without having to disrupt the carefully created portfolio.

Likewise the overall return on gilts looks unattractive, but the purpose of gilts in a portfolio is to provide stability via a guaranteed income and a known repayment date which can be tied in to future needs.

From the figures in Table 18.1 it is clear that equities have an important role to play in a portfolio. Equity or equity-based investment (unit/investment trusts and OEICs) provide long-term growth of income and capital. The aim with equity-based investment is not to use these investments to provide needs at set dates or to meet emergencies, but to provide growth of income and capital over the long term. Having to sell equities to meet a specific need is ill advised. The stock market may have fallen (as seen in early 2001), or a previously good, strong company may have hit a bad patch in its business that has driven its share price down (for example, Marks and Spencer).

Within these three asset categories, there are varying levels of risk and return. With cash the risk of loss on capital is virtually nil provided that the money is deposited with a bank or building society, or other body covered by the compensation scheme set up under the auspices of the Financial Services and Markets Act 2000.

Gilts are free of the risk of default, but are subject to interest-rate and inflation risks. The impact of inflation can be seen in Table 18.1. Company and other loan stocks (bonds) have varying risk profiles, and should be considered taking into account the judgement of a Credit Rating Agencies such as Moody's and Standard and Poors (see Chapter 17).

Understanding the investor's risk profile

Risk can apply to the cash and fixed-interest elements of the portfolio. When interest rates fall, the cash element will yield a lower income if the rate of interest is linked to base rate or LIBOR. For conventional fixed-rate gilts, the danger lies when interest rates rise, because gilt prices will then fall. Inflation erodes the purchasing power of capital and interest when the capital is invested in cash or fixed-interest stocks. However, inflation is currently at relatively low levels.

To minimize the interest-rate and inflation risks, investment in shares is utilized. However, there is risk involved in investing in shares. The company may cut its dividend, or go into liquidation.

Each investor must identify his own risk profile. For example an investor who is due to retire in 5 years time should bear in mind the risks of being heavily exposed to the stock market, which may have fallen at the time of retirement. In such a case the investor may not have the desired level of income and capital at hand on retirement, which will have an adverse effect upon his quality of life. It has been suggested that the percentage of savings invested in the stock market should be 100 less the investor's age. Thus for an individual aged 60, this would suggest that the maximum amount invested in equity or equity-based investment should be 40% of his funds, whereas for someone aged 30, this would be 70% of his funds. However this technique must not be applied blindly to an investor's portfolio, because the investor may prefer a different split between equity and other investments.

Another widely used asset allocation is 10% cash, 30 - 45% fixed-interest and 45 - 60% equity or equity-based investment.

Risk is either systematic (the risk of a portfolio after all unsystematic risk has been diversified away) or unsystematic (applies to a specific investment). The greater the diversification the lower the unsystematic risk. Provided the investor has sufficient funds to invest directly in a minimum of 15 shares in different sectors, with a minimum of £2,000 each for cost effectiveness, then he can manage away (as far as is possible) the unsystematic risk. If the investor does not have this amount of cash, then he can invest indirectly, through unit/investment trusts and OEICs. These investments provide a well-diversified portfolio of holdings that are professionally managed. However, just because they are well diversified does not mean that the risk level of each fund is similar.

The Association of Investment Trusts recognizes the differing levels of risk across the whole range of trusts, with UK income growth being classed as low risk, and emerging markets classed as high risk. One of the major risks of investing overseas is that the level of corporate governance (see Chapters 2 and 10) in many companies falls woefully short of the UK and US standards, thus increasing the risk due to possible conflicts of interest or lack of disclosure of information.

Unit/investment trusts and OEICs are particularly suitable for giving investors exposure to specialist market sectors where an individual investor would face practical difficulties or be unable to achieve a reasonable level of diversification. This is likely to be particularly true of investment in overseas markets or in illiquid assets such as property.

18.2　The importance of timing

Timing is a vital point to bear in mind when investing, because success or failure with timing will have drastic consequences. If an investor is forced to sell some of his holdings to meet unexpected bills, then the timing of the sale is totally wrong. Sales should be made when the investment is showing a good profit. Obviously it is not always possible to buy just as the market is taking off and to sell just before the market begins to fall, but it should be possible to avoid buying when the market is very high and to avoid selling when the market is very low. Timing of the sum to be invested in a portfolio is vital. The whole sum should not be invested in one fell swoop just because it is available. The investor should wait for the right opportunities to present themselves. While he is waiting the money should be placed where it will gain the most interest yet remain easily accessible. A money-market deposit or bank or building society high-interest account should be used. The choice is a simple one: the money is invested in whichever gives the best return after tax to the investor.

Tax reasons may have some influence on timing. For example, if an investor is to use his annual CGT allowance, thereby reducing or eliminating his CGT liability, he may need to sell investments at particular times. But the tax 'tail' should not wag the investment 'dog' – making investment decisions solely for tax reasons can be damaging to wealth and returns.

It is also important to note that transactions cost affect long-term investment returns, and that regular transactions can run up significant costs in commissions, stamp duty etc. An investor who is tempted to believe that he can 'sell at the top' and 'buy at the bottom' of the market is unlikely to be right (professional investors find it difficult enough to call the top and bottom of markets and individual asset prices), but will probably incur transactions costs which erode long-term returns.

18.3　Information required from an investor

Before it is possible to advise a customer as to suitable investments, the adviser must elicit information that will aid the correct choice of investments. The portfolio of investments recommended to a customer will be based upon accurate usage of all the information provided by the customer.

In an examination question certain information will be given. Before repeating a whole list of questions, read the information given and then specify only the questions that are pertinent to the customer and consider what is relevant to the situation.

The questions to be asked

An investor is an individual and thus has specific ideas about what he does or does not want or require. Having said that, there are general guidelines by which a portfolio is constructed.

Before starting to invest money certain information must be elicited from the investor to aid portfolio planning. All advice must take into account the stage the investor is in in his lifecycle (see Chapter 1, section 1.2).

- What is the customer's marginal rate of tax?

- Marital status. Is he willing to transfer freely any assets into his wife's name for her beneficial use, if this would be advantageous for tax purposes?

- Age of the customer (this will give an indication of the customer's time horizon – obviously a 90-year-old has a somewhat shorter time horizon than a 30-year-old). Usually young married people require income from their investments, as do retired people. Middle-aged investors whose children are no longer dependent on them often require capital growth to build up capital prior to retirement.

- Is the customer employed? If so, is his job secure?

- Does he have an adequate pension scheme? If not, could he make AVCs or is he eligible to take out his company's scheme or freestanding AVCs, or is he eligible to take out a personal pension plan or a stakeholder pension?

- Does he have adequate life and health insurance such as permanent health and critical illness insurance, and if married or living with his partner, is his wife's or partner's life also insured?

- Age of any dependent children. Any other dependants, e.g. aged parents, that he supports? The age of children may identify specific dates, e.g. eighteenth birthday, when a capital sum may be required.

- Does he have any other income apart from his salary?

- Does he have any other investments?

- Does he own his own home? If so, is there a mortgage? What is the amount outstanding, the type of mortgage, and is there life cover on the mortgage to repay it in case of early death?

- Does he have any other outstanding debts that it may be better to repay first? This is especially important if he has loans at a high rate of interest.

- Does he wish to make any provision for his dependants?

- Are there any major purchases he wishes to make, e.g. a car or a world cruise? (This is important as the sum available will have to be adjusted when constructing a portfolio.)

- Is he a non-resident? (If so, he is not liable to any UK taxes.)

- What is his level of risk aversion? The higher his aversion to risk, the more difficult it becomes to construct the best possible portfolio since some otherwise suitable investments will have to be omitted to minimize his perceived risk profile.

- Are there any areas of investment he wishes to avoid, e.g. is he an ethical investor who may wish to avoid companies involved in chemical manufacture, or tobacco companies? Are there any shares he wishes to buy purely because of the concessions that are attached to them?

- Does he require income, capital growth or a mixture of these from his investment?

- Does he have any specific known future commitment to provide for, e.g. a child going to university, a wedding or his retirement? If so, suitable investments can be chosen to mature at this time.

18.4 Portfolio construction

A general guide to the construction of a portfolio is easily learned, but it is important that the customer's own views are always taken into account. With very large sums there will be a larger number of investments available that will fit into the customer's requirements. The tax position of the customer will also indicate various investments that are suitable, e.g. a high taxpayer will find the return on National Savings certificates attractive, while a non-taxpayer could obtain far better returns elsewhere. It is also important to realize that anyone who has inherited or otherwise received a large sum of money may well end up paying income tax at a higher marginal rate than previously. Thus it is vital that the gross income generated by the portfolio be calculated and added to the investor's other income to ascertain his tax position. For example, if a single person earns £18,000 per annum gross he will be a basic-rate tax payer. If he then inherited a sum £500,000 which when invested gave a gross yield of 4% he would have a total gross income of £18,000 + £20,000 = £38,000. When the basic personal allowance is deducted from this it leaves a gross income for tax purposes of £33,465. This will make his marginal rate of tax 40% (over £29,400). Obviously this will affect the type of investment that can be chosen to give the most benefit to the customer. If £20,000 were invested in a high-coupon gilt it could yield £1,340 per annum at 6.7% gross interest yield. After tax this would be worth only £804. If instead an index-linked gilt were used the income could be around £500 per annum gross at a rate of 2.5%, £300 after tax. There would also be the benefit of inflation-proofed guaranteed income and capital sum in addition to the capital gains on gilts being free of capital gains tax. This could make the index-linked stock more attractive for this taxpayer. However, the investor should compare the net redemption yield of the gilts to find the best return, which may not always be given by a low-coupon gilt even for a 40% taxpayer.

A portfolio for an investor with less than £50,000-£60,000 should be constructed along these lines:

- 10% liquid funds;

- 30-45% fixed-interest stocks;

- 45-60% equity-based.

If the portfolio is large, say £100,000 plus, the breakdown between fixed interest and equity will not be up to an equal split as for a smaller portfolio. It is quite likely that someone with a considerable amount to invest is, or may become, a 40%, taxpayer. In such a case tax-exempt investments should be considered. These would include NSCs and ISAs. The NSCs would take part of the fixed-interest funds, with a maximum invested in gilts of £30,000-

£45,000, then direct equity investment would be suitable if the portfolio is large enough, and professional management provided via discretionary management (see Chapter 20) or by the investor if he has the expertise and time to manage the portfolio himself. An ISA should be used for three of the equities for tax efficiency. If the customer is a high-rate taxpayer then the most suitable tax-free investments should also be included. While these investments do not give an income, the returns are very attractive to the high-rate taxpayers. In addition, to extend the degree of diversification the high taxpayer with a large portfolio should consider property and overseas elements for the portfolio. We shall shortly examine how this is achieved.

The liquid reserve

A liquid reserve of up to 10% of the value of the portfolio should be provided. It should be easily accessible and carry the best after-tax rate of interest from the available investments. It is essential to have liquid funds to enable unexpected bills to be paid, 'spur of the moment' purchases to be made, and any new investment opportunities that may arise to be taken advantage of, e.g. a rights issue. If there were no liquid reserve then the investor would have to sell some of his holdings to meet any unexpected needs, The timing of a sale may coincide with a fall in the Stock Market or in a specific sector of the market, thus crystallizing a paper loss.

Taxpayers, irrespective of whether their marginal rates are nil, 10%, 22% or 40%, should use the bank or building society high-interest access account for their liquid funds. The rate of around 4.5% net of basic tax is the rate obtainable on readily available deposits.

18.5   The fixed-interest element

There are several investments which fit the bill as fixed-interest investments. Depending on whether the taxpayer wishes to receive a high income, capital growth or a mixture of both, a suitable stock can be found.

Gilts

These are 100% secure in money terms; the only risk run is that of inflation eroding the purchasing power of the interest and capital. Even this can be avoided by investing in index-linked gilts, whose only drawback is that the low coupon makes such stocks suitable only for high taxpayers.

Local authority stocks

If purchased under par local authority stocks will provide a capital gain that is free of capital gains tax. Technically, they are not as secure as gilts but the main problem is that they are not very marketable (i.e. they are infrequently traded thus there is a wide bid-offer spread).

Debentures and loan stocks

These are issued by companies and their security depends on the class of stock and the standing of the company. A debenture has a fixed charge over certain of the company's assets and thus will be paid off from the sale of these assets in the event of liquidation. Loan stocks are usually unsecured and rank with the other creditors regarding repayment in the event of liquidation. While company debentures and loan stocks are saleable, there is a wide spread between the bid and offer prices indicating the far lower level of marketability when compared to gilts which have a very narrow bid/offer spread.

For the private investor, gilts are the best option. There is a range of coupons, interest and maturity dates and the investor's needs can be satisfied by an appropriate gilt. Because the highest marginal rate of income tax is now 40%, low-coupon gilts are not necessarily the most attractive option for a 40% taxpayer. To find the best stock he should compare the net redemption yield of various stocks to find the best return.

To emphasize this point let us look at four stocks quoted in 2001 as follows:

Calculate the net redemption yields for a 40% taxpayer on the following stocks. Recap to Chapter 7 if necessary.

			Price	Gross yields Int	Redemption
3½%	Funding	1999-04	95.91	3.65	4.9
12%	Treasury	2003-05	112.99	10.62	4.98
7¼%	Treasury	2007	112.21	6.46	5.04
12%	Exchequer	2013-17	164.65	7.29	5.01

The net redemption yields for a 40% taxpayer are:

3½%	Funding	1999-04	-	3.44%
12%	Treasury	2003-05	-	0.73%
7¼%	Treasury	2007	-	2.46%
12%	Exchequer	2013-17	-	2.09%

From these calculations it can clearly be seen that a high-coupon gilt will not automatically be the most suitable for a higher-rate taxpayer. In fact in this case a low-coupon gilt provided the best return and a medium-coupon gilt the second-best return.

However, index-linked gilts could also be considered for long-term investment for high-rate taxpayers, so a large portfolio would probably contain a mixture of gilts, including index-linked ones.

18.6   Equity content

A portfolio should include some equities to provide growth of income and capital. A portfolio needs careful management and this applies especially to the equity content. To have a well-diversified direct equity holding there should be at least 15 shares, each in a different sector of the market. This will ensure adequate diversification of the unsystematic risk, although monitoring would be essential. It is not cost effective to invest less than £2,000 in one share because the dealing costs will take too long to recoup. Before a share can show a real profit the price rise has to cover the costs of both purchasing and selling, thus the larger the percentage of the dealing costs, the larger the rise in price of the share must be to cover them.

The other problem facing the private investor is whether or not he has the time and expertise necessary to manage his portfolio. In the vast majority of cases this very essential area will be outside the expertise of the investor. However, a portfolio does need an equity content but one that is professionally managed. The alternatives to direct equity investment are unit trusts, investment trusts, OIECs and single-premium bonds.

Unit trusts/OEICs

There is a whole range of unit trusts/OEICs available which will provide exactly what the investor requires. Higher-rate taxpayers will generally prefer capital growth-oriented unit/investment trusts/OEICs. The income is low, but is taxed at the investor's marginal rate of tax. The capital gains are subject to CGT at his marginal rate of income tax on gains over £7,500 p.a. The majority of investors are unlikely to realize enough gains, when the indexation allowance or taper relief is applied, to have to pay any CGT.

For a taxpayer who wishes to strike a middle way between income and capital growth, a fund that tracks an index such as the FTSE 100 is more appropriate. This will provide growth of both capital and income in the long term. For an investor who requires emphasis on income, income unit trusts are suitable. They will not only give a good level of income, but also, over the long term, the level of income should grow to provide a hedge against inflation. If the investor is a non-taxpayer, it must be borne in mind that the tax deducted from the dividends at source cannot be reclaimed from the Inland Revenue.

Investment trusts

These are quoted companies that have an underlying portfolio of stocks and shares. As with unit trusts/OEICs, there is a range of investment trusts available to meet the investor's needs, although there are far fewer to choose from than with unit trusts. Dealing costs on investment trusts are competitive with unit trust dealing costs as incorporated in the bid offer spread, and the performance of investment trusts has been very good. Thus a mix of unit/investment trusts/OEICs is advised for indirect equity investment. Having said that, investment trust shares are very attractive for certain types of investor. A high-rate taxpayer requiring capital growth would be well advised to consider including in his portfolio a capital share in a split-level investment trust. These shares do not normally provide any income at all during their life. When the trust is dissolved at the predetermined date the income shareholders are paid back at the preset rate and the remaining gains are divided between the capital shareholders. The gains are subject to capital gains tax in the hands of the shareholders, but

because it is a closed-end investment

the indexation allowance and/or taper relief will reduce the taxable gain. Where CGT is payable the rate is at his marginal rate of income tax on taxable gains over £7,500 p.a.

The income shares of these trusts can be attractive to investors who require a high and growing level of income, because all, or nearly all, of the income generated by the trust is paid to the income shareholders. The disadvantage, however, is that on redemption the amount income shareholders receive will probably be less than the price they paid for the shares. The share price of the income shares is relatively high in the early years, but as maturity approaches the price will tend to gravitate down towards the preset redemption figure. This loss should be allocated on an annual basis and deducted from the expected gross dividend yield. If the resultant figure is much higher compared with the yields on an income-oriented unit trust it is worthwhile considering including in the portfolio an income share of a split-level investment trust.

Even though unit/investment trusts/OEICs hold a wide portfolio of stocks and shares, a particular trust may not perform well one year, thus affecting the return for the investor. In the same way as the investor should not hold only one share, he should not invest in only one unit or investment trust. To provide adequate diversification the investor should use three or four unit/investment trusts/OEICs under different managers. Each trust should, of course, match the aims of the investor. There are tables of unit and investment trust median fund performances which can be compared with the records of the managers of any trust being considered. (Full guidance on the choice of unit trusts and OEICs was given in Chapter 14 and on investment trusts in Chapter 15.)

Single-premium bonds

These bonds come in various forms, but the most appropriate two for inclusion in a portfolio are managed bonds and property bonds. Both will provide a property element to the portfolio. However, single-premium bonds are really more attractive to a higher-rate taxpayer who wishes to defer his income tax liability until a time when his marginal rate of tax has fallen, e.g. on retirement. The 5% p.a. cumulative withdrawal facility gives quite a reasonable return to 40% taxpayers because the withdrawal is tax free at the time it is made.

Overseas content

It is advantageous to have an overseas content in a portfolio. It gives exposure to different markets, each of which may well be at a different stage of growth. It also gives exposure to industries that simply do not exist in the UK, e.g. the diamond mining industry. In addition, overseas investment can hedge the returns on human capital. (See Chapter 10, section 10.1.) The many problems inherent in investing directly overseas would often preclude direct investment. However, indirect investment by way of a unit or investment trust which specializes in overseas stocks will ensure that these problems are taken care of by experts. The unit or investment trusts investing overseas can be chosen for income, capital growth or general emphasis and for investment in a particular geographical area. So when including unit or investment trusts in a portfolio aimed at growth, one of the three or four trusts chosen should have an overseas content.

If a portfolio is large enough to include 15 directly-held shares it will still benefit from overseas exposure which should be obtained by including a unit or investment trust investing overseas. Even experienced, professional portfolio managers who operate portfolio management services for their clients advise unit or investment trusts for the overseas content of the portfolio.

Tax-exempt investments

These are investments whose proceeds do not have to be declared on an income tax return. They are particularly attractive to higher-rate taxpayers who will find that the returns may exceed anything they could find on other fixed-interest investments. The tax-exempt investments have been covered in full in Chapter 17.

18.7   Higher-risk investments suitable for large portfolios

If there is a large sum available for investment, it is worthwhile considering some slightly higher-risk investments, as the returns can be very good. In this area the investor will generally be a higher-rate taxpayer, thus these investments are aimed more at capital growth or deferral of income tax liability until the investor's marginal rate of tax should fall. It would be advisable not to commit more than 5 - 10% (depending on the size of the portfolio) to any one higher-risk investment area, and this sum should be split between two or three types of investment in that area to give a further degree of diversification.

Two of the higher-risk investments – split-level investment trust capital shares and single-premium bonds – are suitable only for the larger portfolio because they generate no income. Few small investors can afford to forego income entirely.

The higher-risk investments to consider are:

● Capital shares in a split-level investment trust;

● Single-premium bonds, particularly managed or property bonds;

● Unit/investment trusts or OEICs investing in the emerging markets covering a number of countries;

● Shares listed on AIM

18.8   Very high-risk investments

Some investors express a wish to use some of their capital for 'fun money', i.e. they want to invest in areas that may show phenomenal growth but that could also flop. Any investor who wishes to do this must realize that he could well lose all his money. Some investors, both individuals and institutions, follow what is described as a 'core/satellite' approach to investment. This means that the majority of their funds are held in mainstream, well-diversified investments (e.g. index-tracking funds), with a small proportion allocated to riskier, more exotic, investments. The advantage of this approach is that they can boost returns through the riskier 'satellite' investments, while remaining confident that the 'core' of their portfolio is safely invested. Provided he is aware of this and already has a balanced portfolio, the areas that are open to him are:

- Chattels (unless for personal pleasure);
- Emerging market unit/investment trusts/OEICs investing in one country only;
- Warrants;
- 'Stagging' new issues;
- 'Shell' situations;
- Penny shares; takeover situations;
- Options;
- Traded options;
- Futures;
- Spread betting;
- Contracts for difference;
- Enterprise Investment Scheme (EIS);
- Venture capital fund (VCT).

The investor should be advised not to invest all his 'risk money' into one specific area. Diversification can help offset losses, and he would be well advised to choose two or three of the above options to achieve the aim of minimization of losses.

18.9   The selection of investments

This is best covered by using specimen questions with full answers.

For continuity, the following income returns are assumed in all questions dealing with portfolio planning.

Bank/building society high-interest
instant access account   3.6% net basic tax

Gilts   high-coupon, say   6.7% gross
             low-coupon, say   4% gross
             index-linked, say   2.5% gross

Equity or equity-based investment

income, say	2.6% gross
capital growth, say	2% gross
overseas, say	1% gross

Note: the rates ruling at the time of the examination must be used, not the above rates.

Specimen question 1

You are consulted by three customers (briefly described below) about their investment situations. In each case detail the types of investment that would be appropriate and construct a suitable investment scheme based on a selection of the types of investment discussed. Explain your reasons for the selection made.

All three customers have suitable houses with outstanding mortgages and none of them intends to alter these arrangements.

(a) Customer A is a married man aged 45, with four children aged 5, 8, 10 and 14. His salary is £18,000 per annum and he has £40,000 to invest. He pays 5% of his salary into a SERPS pension. He requires maximum income to supplement his earnings. His wife does not work but has income from inherited investments of £5,000 p.a. gross.

(b) Customer B is a married man aged 45. His salary is £25,000 per annum. His wife earns £3,500 a year. They have no children. He has £40,000 to invest and requires a capital appreciation over a 20-year period. He is paying 6% of his salary into his contracted-out pension scheme.

(c) Customer C is a single man aged 45. His salary is £30,000 per annum. He has a non-contributory pension scheme, which is contracted out of SERPS. He plans to save £150 per month for 20 years in order to build up a capital sum for his retirement. He does not have any dependants.

Suggested answers

Mr A

Customer A has a gross salary of £18,000, thus he will be a basic-rate taxpayer. Even with gross interest from the portfolio of, say, 4.5%, he will still be a basic rate taxpayer. Mrs A will be a 20% taxpayer after the basic personal allowance is deducted from her investment income.

Investment Management

Mr A tax	£	£
Gross income		18,000
Less: basic personal allowance	4,535	
pension contributions (5%)	900	5,435
Taxable income		12,565

Tax payable:	£
£1,880 at 10%	188.00
£10,685 at 22%	2,350.70
Tax payable	2,538.70

Thus he pays £2,538.70 income tax.

Mrs A	£
Gross income	5,000.00
Less: basic personal allowance	4,535.00
Taxable income	£465.00
Tax payable = £465 @ 10% =	£46.50

She is a 10% taxpayer.

First, Mr A must have a liquid reserve to meet any unexpected bills. This must be easily accessible and give the best possible return on the sum invested. 10% of the portfolio, £4,000, should be invested in a bank or building society high-interest account paying 3.6% net of basic tax. The remaining sums should be split between fixed-interest and equities. The fixed-interest stock should be gilts, and he should purchase gilts to give the best net redemption yield. The gilts should have different maturity dates to coincide with his children's eighteenth birthdays, when a capital sum could be advantageous to meet any expenses incurred then. He will be liable to tax at 20% on the interest. All gains on gilts are free of CGT. We shall assume that medium- and high-coupon gilts yielding around 6.7% gross will give the highest net redemption yield.

The equity content should provide a growing income and capital value over the long term. To gain the benefits of diversification he needs a minimum of 15 shares in different sectors, plus the time and expertise to manage them. With only £18,000 (45% of £40,000) available for equity-based investment it is certainly not cost effective to invest directly. Instead he should use three or four unit/investment trusts/OEICs under different managers aimed at income. Even with unit/investment trusts/OEICs it is unwise to invest in only one trust. If the managers have a poor year the investor's returns will suffer, thus a spread of trusts under different managers should iron out any poor performances.

Investment	Amount(£)	% Gross rate	Gross income
Bank/building society	4,000	4.5	180
Medium/high-coupon gilts	18,000	6.7	1,206
Unit/investment trusts/OEICs	18,000	2.6	468
	£40,000		£1,854

$$\text{Gross yield on portfolio} = \frac{1,854 \times 100}{40,000}$$

$$= 4.63\%$$

Mr A will have an approximate gross income of £1,854 from the portfolio. As Mr A requires maximum income to supplement his earnings, the fixed-interest and equity elements each account for 45% of the value of the portfolio. By setting the portfolio out as above, all your recommendations are put together in a clear manner, and the investor can see the level of gross income he can expect to receive from his portfolio. Note: bank/building society interest rate assumed is 3.6% net of 20% savings rate of tax, which is 4.5% gross

$$\frac{(3.6 \times 100)}{(80)}$$

Mr. B

Mr B, with his salary of £25,000 gross, will be a basic-rate taxpayer. Mrs B, with an income of £3,500 gross will be a non-taxpayer.

Mr B tax payable

	£	£
Gross income		25,000.00
Less: basic personal allowance	4,535	
Pension contribution (6%)	1,500	6,035.00
Taxable income		£18,965.00
Tax payable:		
£1,880 at 20%		188.00
£17,085 at 22%		3,758.70
Tax payable		3,946.70

He pays £3,946.70 income tax.

Investment Management

Mrs B tax payable	£
Gross income	3,500
Less basic personal allowance	4,535
Taxable income	Nil

She has no liability to income tax, because her gross income is below the income tax threshold.

Again, as in (a), the income generated from the £40,000 will not take Mr B into the next tax band.

Mr B will require a liquid reserve invested as in (a) of £4,000. For the capital appreciation he should consider gilts, giving the best net redemption yield and maturing in 20 years' time. He should also consider index-linked gilts if he expects inflation in the future to rise. (The portfolio assumes that medium/high-coupon gilts are more attractive.) For capital growth purposes, 30% of the portfolio should be in fixed-interest.

For the equity content three or four unit/investment trusts/OEICs aimed at capital growth, with one investing overseas, is a more suitable option than direct equity investment. Indirect investment gives professional management and a wide diversification of holdings in the unit/ investment trusts/OEICs. For growth purposes 60% of the portfolio should be in equity investment. The tax-free investments of NSCs do not offer an overly attractive return to a basic-rate taxpayer.

For a slightly riskier way of achieving capital growth Mr B could consider a capital share in a split-level investment trust. He will receive no income during the term of the trust, but will share in the gains made after the income shareholders have been repaid at the predetermined rate. Another alternative is a managed bond, which is an insurance company product with the underlying assets invested in property, fixed interest, equities and cash. This provides a property element to the portfolio. The gains on the bond are paid net of basic-rate tax when the bond is surrendered, in accordance with top-slicing rules. As capital growth is the main objective, an investment of £2,000 in a managed bond and a split-level investment capital share would be appropriate.

Investment	Amount (£)	% Gross rate	Gross return (£)
Bank/building society	4,000	4.5	180
Medium/high-coupon gilt	12,000	6.7	804
Unit/investment trusts/OEICs			
Growth	16,000	2	320
Overseas	4,000	1	40
Capital share investment trust	2,000	Nil	Nil
Managed bond	2,000	Nil	Nil
	40,000		1,344

Gross yield on portfolio = $\dfrac{1,344 \times 100}{40,000}$

$$= 3.36\%$$

As Mrs B is a non-taxpayer, with an income of £3,500 gross, there is an unused part of her basic personal allowance of £4,535 amounting to £1,035. It would be tax efficient for the couple for Mr B to transfer around £20,000 to his wife for her beneficial use, and for her to invest that in a gilt giving the best gross net redemption yield (she is a non-taxpayer) and income-oriented unit/investment trusts/OEICs.

Mrs B's portfolio:

	Amount (£)	% Gross rate	Gross return
Gilts	10,000	6.7	670
Unit/investment trusts	10,000	2.6	260
	£20,000		£930

Gross yield $\dfrac{930 \times 100}{20,000}$ = 4.65%

Note: she could opt for accumulation units or reinvestment of dividends on the unit/investment trusts/OEICs. This would boost the value, but have no extra tax consequences.

(c) Mr C will be a basic-rate taxpayer.

Mr C tax payable

	£
Gross income	30,000
Less: basic personal allowance	4,535
	£25,465

Note: the pension is non-contributory, so no payments are shown as deductions against income.

Tax payable:

	£
£1,880 at 20%	188.00
£23,585 at 22%	5,188.70
Tax payable	£5,376.70

He pays £5,376.70 income tax

There is no mention of any liquid reserve, thus this must be provided. A reserve of around £2,000 would seem reasonable in view of his salary and stated saving aim of £150 per month. This should be accumulated with a bank or building society. He should build this up in an instant access account paying around 3.6% net basic tax. Once this has been achieved Mr C should look to provide himself with adequate pension cover. He should enquire whether he can pay any more into his company pension scheme. The extra payments are called 'additional voluntary contributions' (AVCs). If the company scheme is not attractive, or he is intending to change jobs, free-standing AVCs or a stakeholder pension would be more suitable.

A friendly society bond is another attractive investment. The maximum sum payable is £25 per month, but as both the friendly society and the proceeds of the policy are not liable for tax the returns are attractive even for a basic-rate taxpayer.

The final recommendation would be a unit/investment trust/OEIC savings plan. This will carry the advantage of 'pound cost averaging' and the plan can be linked to a capital growth oriented trust. The money should be invested in two or three trusts under different managers. He should opt for accumulation units in the unit trusts and reinvestment of dividends in the investment trust to boost his capital further. These savings plans will provide long-term growth of capital and income.

Suggested answer

Build up £2,000 liquid reserve. Once completed, the following breakdown of savings is recommended:

	£ per month
Unit/investment trust/OEIC savings scheme	100
Pension plan/ AVCs/FSAVCs/stakeholder pension	50
	£150

Specimen question 2

Mr and Mrs Jones

You have been consulted by Mr and Mrs Jones (briefly described below) about their investment problems. You are required to set out an investment strategy for each customer. Mr and Mrs Jones are both aged 60. Mrs Jones receives a retirement pension of £1,751. Mr Jones has just retired and will receive a pension of £8,000 per annum, together with a lump sum of £14,000. In addition he has bank and building society accounts amounting to £11,000. The house is paid for and the children are independent. He estimates that he and his wife will need a net income of approximately £190 per week.

Suggested answer

Mr Jones' tax position

	£	£
Pension		8,000
Less: basic personal allowance		4,535
Taxable income		£3,465
Tax payable £1,880 at 10%		188.00
£1,585 @ 22%		348.70
Tax payable		£536.70

After-tax income is £8,000 less £536.70 = £7,463.30

As Mr Jones is aged 60 he does NOT receive the higher basic personal or married couple's allowance even though he is retired.

Mrs Jones

As her pension is less than her basic personal allowance of £4,535 she will be a non-taxpayer.

Total net income for couple	=	£7,463.30 + £1,751
	=	£9,214.30
Net annual income required	=	£190 x 52
	=	£9,880
Shortfall (after tax)	=	£9,880 - £9,214.30
	=	£665.70

To make up the income shortfall the investment of £25,000 will need to yield 2.66% net. Thus the portfolio should be aimed to provide a balance between long-term growth of income and capital, which will enable Mr and Mrs Jones to maintain their standard of living. The total sum available is £14,000 plus bank and building society funds of £11,000 = £25,000.

Ten per cent of the sum should be kept as a liquid reserve. A bank or building society high-interest account provides a return of 3.6% net of basic tax which is the best available return on easy-access money. Thus, they have too much invested here and this should be reduced to £2,500. The remainder should be split between gilts and unit/investment trusts/OEICs to provide both guaranteed income from the gilts, and growth of both income and capital from the unit/investment trusts/OEICs. Three or four unit/investment trusts/OEICs under different managers will give good diversification. The gilts should provide the best net redemption yield to provide the required level of income in the long term. If the income generated is in excess of their needs it should be reinvested in a unit or investment trust savings plan which complements the existing investments. The unit/investment trusts/OEICs should be aimed at income. This will still give a growing income, with long-term growth of capital. If they do not require all of this income at present they can opt for accumulation units. There is not sufficient available to invest directly in equities on a cost-effective basis because a minimum of 15 shares in different sectors are required for a well-diversified portfolio, plus the time and expertise to manage them.

Investment	Amount (£)	% Gross rate	Gross return £
Bank/building society	2,500	4.5	112
High-coupon gilts	10,500	6.7	703
Unit/investment trusts /OEICs	12,000	2.6	312
	£25,000		£1,127

$$\text{Gross yield on portfolio} = \frac{1,127 \times 100}{25,000} = 4.51\%$$

Income after tax from portfolio:

	£
(£112 + £703) £815 @ (100-20%)	652.00
£312 @ (100 -10%)	280.80
Income after tax	£932.80

	£
Net income for the couple:	9,214.30
Net income from portfolio	932.80
	£10,147.10

This is meets their stated need of an income after tax of £9,880. It would be advisable to transfer sufficient of the capital to Mrs Jones for her beneficial use to utilize the unused part of her basic personal allowance.

Note: when answering a question that specifies either an amount per week/annum or a percentage return on the investment, it is vital to show the calculations. When a set sum is required first calculate the after-tax income that is already received, then look at the shortfall to decide on investment policy.

Specimen question 3
Mr C
Your customer Mr C is a married man aged 60. His earned income is £40,000 per annum.

He owns his house and he holds the maximum entitlement of the 55th issue (£10,000) of National Savings Certificates. He has £30,000 available for investment and is looking for capital growth over the next five years. When he retires in five years' time he will need income from his investments to supplement his pension. Mrs C has no income of her own. Mr C is not willing to transfer assets into his wife's name.

(a) Detail the types of investment which would satisfy Mr C's requirement of capital growth over a five-year period.

(b) Discuss how a change of policy could be implemented after five years to increase income, and mention any difficulties you might expect from such a policy switch.

Suggested answer

Tax position

	£
Gross income	40,000
Investment income at, say, 2%	800
	40,800
Less: basic personal allowance	4,535
Taxable income	£36,265

This makes him a 40% taxpayer. Thus it would be tax advantageous to transfer the £30,000 into his wife's name because she is a non-taxpayer. However, he has stated that he is unwilling to do this.

Equities are totally unsuitable for a five-year period. Equity investment should be made only on a long-term basis with a view to selling when the price shows a profit. Equity-based investments, including by definition unit/investment trusts and OEICs are unsuitable for a short-term investment which may have to be realized at an unfavourable time.

(a) Investments which give guaranteed growth over five years

(i) 19th Issue Index-Linked National Savings Certificates. On top of the index linking, interest equal to 1.65% p.a. plus index linking over the five-year period. The maximum holding is £10,000 per person. All returns are tax free.

(ii) 57th Issue NSCs can be encashed after five years to give a return of 3.55% p.a. over the five-year period. The maximum holding is £10,000 per person. All returns are tax free.

(iii) Index-linked gilts due to mature in five years' time will give capital growth which is free of CGT. The capital is index-linked on redemption using the RPI eight months prior to redemption and eight months prior to issue. The coupon is also index-linked.

iv) Conventional short-dated gilts, due for redemption in 5 years. They will provide a guaranteed income over the period and a known value on redemption. Mr. C will need to choose the gilt giving the best net redemption yield for a 40% taxpayer. Although any capital gains are free of CGT, there is no inflation proofing on these gilts.

Suggested portfolio

Investment	Amount	% Gross rate	Gross return
55th Issue NSCs (retained)	10,000	Nil	Nil
57th Issue NSCs	10,000	Nil	Nil
19th Issue Index-Linked NSCs	10,000	Nil	Nil
Index-linked or conventional gilts	10,000	3	300
	£40,000		£300

He will have to pay tax only on the income from the gilts – £300 at 40%, the rest of the investments being tax free. The 55th issue NSCs will reach their 5-year term before he retires, and unless he re-invests them or encashes them at this time, they will receive only the general extension rate of 2.4% (correct at time of writing), which is less than the current rate paid on NSCs. None of the above investments will carry any charges on repayment or redemption.

(b) The main problem with a switch of emphasis from capital growth now to income in five years' time is that interest and inflation rates in the future are unknown. If they have fallen over the period then Mr C will obtain a lower rate of income than he could have received otherwise. A policy of avoiding income in the short term is rather short-sighted, and it would be preferable to construct a balanced portfolio now which will meet Mr C's long-term requirements.

The portfolio should have 10% invested as a liquid reserve to meet any unexpected bills. The best return is from a bank or building society high-interest account paying 4.5% net of lower rate tax.

The returns on the 55th and 57th Issue NSCs and 19th Issue Index-Linked NSCs are attractive to a 40% taxpayer. However, as he already has one older issue of NSCs, the full holding of all three NSCs would leave the portfolio overweight in this section. He would be advised to retain his existing certificates until maturity and consider then whether reinvestment in either or both of the current issues of NSCs was still attractive, or whether to invest the money elsewhere.

The gilt part of the portfolio should be aimed at income, thus gilts with the best net redemption yield should be purchased to give a guaranteed return over the long term.

The equity content should be in the form of equity-based investment rather than direct equity investment, which requires a minimum of 15 shares in different sectors plus the time and expertise to manage them. As he is a high taxpayer at the moment, £5,000 invested in a managed bond would be suitable. If in five years' time the bond shows a profit he can encash it, and provided the annualized profit does not make his gross taxable income exceed 22% it will be tax free. He can also withdraw 5% p.a. cumulative tax free at the time of withdrawal if he wishes.

The remainder of the equity-based content should be invested in three or four unit/ investment trusts/OEICs under different managers aimed at capital growth. When he retires he may be able to switch to income units in the same management group without incurring too much cost. Most unit trusts allow switching between funds on a bid price to bid price basis. There may be a potential capital gains tax liability for the investor but as the annual exemption limit is £7,500 now, and as the taxable gain is reduced by the indexation allowance/taper relief, it is highly unlikely that he will actually have to pay any CGT.

Investment	Amount	% Gross rate	Gross return
Bank/building society	3,000	4.5	135
55th issue NSCs (retained)	10,000	Nil	Nil
Gilts long-dated with best net redemption yield	5,000	6.7	335
Managed bond	5,000	Nil	Nil
Unit/investment trusts/OEICs	17,000	2	340
	£40,000		£810

$$\text{Gross yield on portfolio} = \frac{810 \times 100}{40,000} = 2.03\%$$

Note: the NSCs and managed bond do not pay out any income, so nothing is shown in the % gross rate and gross return columns. The gross return on the gilts of 6.7% assumes that this also gives the highest net redemption yield.

Example – Monthly savings

A single man aged 20 has recently been promoted, with a pay rise that will enable him to start saving for his future. Currently he lives at home with his parents and pays them rent of £200 per month. He owns a car, but has no other valuable assets. He has little knowledge of the various types of investment available and has consulted you for advice on an overall strategy for his savings. After completing a fact find, he has decided that he can afford to save £250 per month towards buying his own home in the future. He is in an occupational pension scheme. Detail the advice you would give him, and recommend with reasons the investments that he should consider as his priorities.

Suggested answer

The priorities for a small saver are:

1. To build up a <u>cash reserve of around 3 months outgoings</u> so that any unexpected bills can be paid without disrupting his savings plans.

2. To save towards buying your own home because:

   (a) The value of the house will rise over the long term

   (b) Rental money is 'dead money' in that there he will be forgoing the long-term benefit from home ownership.

3. To build up sufficient cash for a deposit for a house, a tax-efficient way of achieving this is by using a mini-cash ISA, where up to £3,000 per annum can be invested in a high-interest bank account, and the interest is paid gross with no liability to income tax. He could also consider a mini-share ISA. (Maximum amount £3,000 for long-term capital and income growth free of CGT and income tax.) If he chooses to have a mini-share ISA it would be advisable, due to the small amount to be invested, to choose an unit/investment trust/OEICs that has a monthly savings scheme. This would provide him with the benefits of pound cost averaging as well as professional management and diversification. However, he does need to appreciate that indirect investment in the Stock Market can mean that the value of the investments can fall in the short term, although in the long term performance has been upwards. If he wants to have a set date by which he will have his deposit, it would be wiser to limit himself to a mini-cash ISA.

4. Although he currently has no dependents, it would still be wise to ensure that he has adequate life cover, because the premiums will be far lower at his age, and he may need to have life cover in order to take out a mortgage.

5. He would be well advised to look at the types of mortgage that are available in order to identify the most suitable type for him in the near future. This will also help him to focus on the best type of life insurance for the form of mortgage he will take out.

6. Mortgage payments can be fixed or floating rate, although there are some flexible payment mortgages available. However, these are less likely to be available for a first-time buyer, but should be considered when he is established in his career and looking to buy a larger property.

Suggested aims

1. Build up a cash reserve to meet any unexpected bills, building up a sum of around three months' outgoings.

2. He should take out adequate life assurance which can be used to provide protection for his mortgage.

3. Once this has been achieved start a mini-cash ISA with the provider offering the best rates of interest. This is more likely to be a non-traditional provider rather than a bank or building society. It will be more likely that a supermarket bank or Internet bank will provide a higher return.

4. If he wishes to have exposure to the stock market, having taken into account the risks involved, it would be advisable to split the £250 (less the amount payable for insurance premiums) into two equal parts, with one in a mini-cash ISA and the other in a mini-share ISA.

Consider this

(a) It often happens that people come into possession of lump sums of capital on retirement either from pension commutations, maturing endowment policies, or from the sale of a business. What are the advantages and disadvantages of this aspect of financial planning from the point of view of the individual concerned?

(b) What key factors should be taken into account when formulating an investment strategy for retired people?

Suggested answer

(a) Advantages

(i) At retirement many people feel they would like to splash out on a good holiday, refurbish their home, or even move to a more convenient home. A lump sum enables them to do this to their satisfaction.

(ii) It is tax advantageous to build up a lump sum through pension or life policies because the proceeds are tax free in the hands of the investor.

(iii) A lump sum in the hands of the investor provides flexibility. It can be invested to meet the needs of that individual. For example, if the income from the pension is sufficient at the present, then the lump sum can be invested to provide capital growth; if extra income is the priority then this can be achieved through a balanced portfolio.

Disadvantages

(i) For many people this will be the first time they have had such a large sum in their possession, and they may not invest it properly if they do not obtain expert advice. The temptation for many is just to put the money in a bank or building society account where inflation will erode its purchasing power.

(ii) It can be difficult to persuade an investor who requires income that his interests would best be met by splitting the money between gilts and equities. Yields of 6.7%, gross on gilts look far more attractive than 2.6% on equities, yet the effects of inflation must be explained and the fact that the equities should provide a rising income and long-term capital growth which will help combat inflation.

(iii) At certain times it is difficult to know whether to invest for the long or short term. If interest rates are low it can be difficult if not impossible to meet the target income figure. A decision would have to be made as to whether to stay fairly liquid and hope that the interest rates will rise in the near future so that a suitable portfolio can be constructed then.

(b)   Retired people have certain needs that do not always apply to other investors.

(i)   Security. The investments made must be secure. Retired people have little chance of rebuilding any lost savings because they no longer have an earning capacity.

(ii) Income. This is generally more important than capital growth as they will be living on a reduced level of income, and while they no longer have all the expenses that someone in employment has, they still need a good level of income in order to live comfortably.

(iii) Protection against inflation. Although the state pension is inflation proofed to a large extent, an occupational pension may not be. Also the income generated by the investment must allow for it to rise thus equity-based investment is important.

(iv) Liquidity. There should be an adequate emergency reserve to smooth out any irregularities in income. For example, if the investments pay dividends only twice a year there needs to be a cash reserve to allow withdrawals between the receipts of the dividends.

(v)   Simplicity. While by no means does retirement mean that the investor's mental capacity has been diminished, it is advisable to keep the portfolio straightforward so that the investor is not burdened either by having to run it himself or by paying high fees for someone else to run it. Many retired people have never had any dealings with investments, thus they require an easily understandable portfolio.

Nowadays many people are retiring at age 50 onwards. Those between 50 and 60 (women) and 65 (men) will not receive a state pension until they reach 60/65. They may, however, be able to supplement their income from employment on a part-time basis – an option that is not readily available to those in receipt of the state pension.

18.10 Summary of portfolio planning for individuals

Each time an investor requires advice it is necessary to cover the various suitable alternatives, quoting the interest rates paid, tax situation of the investment and approximate gross income generated.

Once the options have been explained a suggested portfolio should be drafted that shows not only the average rates of interest available on gilts and equities but also the gross income generated by the portfolio, and the gross yield of the portfolio. The portfolio also shows how much is invested in each area, which is just as important a guide for the investor. After all, no investor wishes to receive a list of all the options open to him and then have to decide how much to invest in what area! He is coming to the investment advisor for guidance, and in the examination you are the investment advisor.

Why not just leave the money in a bank or building society?

You may have noticed that the gross returns on some of the portfolios drafted in this unit are below the gross return available from a bank or building society. An investor may well ask why he should bother with stocks and shares when he can get a higher return from a bank or building society.

The problems with bank and building society investments are:

● The interest rate moves in line with the general level of interest rates and if the rate falls then the investor loses out on income;

● The capital value remains static, thus inflation erodes the purchasing power of the capital.

Table 18.1 shows how the real value of cash investments has fallen well below the real value of equity investments.

To overcome these problems a portfolio has three elements: liquidity, fixed-interest and equity. The fixed-interest element provides a guaranteed income until maturity, irrespective of changes in interest rates. Equity or equity-based income provides a lower initial income, but over the years the income and capital value will grow. Statistics have shown that equity investment has outstripped bank and building society interest and rises in the RPI in the long term.

18.11 Portfolio planning and institutional investors

Institutional investors share many of the same objectives as individual investors. For example, they often need some liquidity, they have views about the level of risk they are comfortable with, and they are looking for diversification in their investment portfolios. Some institutional investors are also in 'life cycle' positions – for example, pension funds have age profiles of members. A pension fund whose members are predominantly in retirement and receiving pensions will need to invest in a different way from one whose members have predominately not yet reached retirement age. The need to generate income will differ between funds with these different membership profiles. (See Chapter 21, section 21.8 for more details.)

Another similarity between institutional and individual investors is that institutions may also have the choice between managing funds for themselves (using in-house fund managers) or appointing external fund managers. Where this happens, external fund managers compete to be appointed in 'beauty parades', where they display their virtues (e.g. strong historical performance, expertise in managing comparable funds, expertise in particular investment markets etc.).

Where institutional investors differ from individual investors is that they usually have much greater levels of investment funds. This has several consequences. They can diversify their portfolios more easily, so they may hold a wider range of investments and may choose to hold some relatively illiquid investments which can generate good long-term returns (e.g. commercial property). They are more likely to invest directly in markets (such as overseas equity markets) where individual investors would not invest directly due to lack of knowledge, practical difficulties in trading, or high transactions costs. They are able to demand much lower rates of commission from brokers etc. due to their greater 'buying power'. They are also able to get easier access to individuals such as company directors and stock market analysts. They may have sufficient voting power to affect company behaviour. Because of their closeness to the markets they may be able to make investment decisions more quickly than individual private investors, but large market positions may be difficult to buy or sell – a 'nimble' private investor may be in a better position to make major changes to his portfolio than an institution which will hold large blocks of shares and other investments.

19

PORTFOLIO MANAGEMENT AND REVIEW

Objectives

After studying this chapter, you should be able to:

- describe the range of stock exchange indices and the methods by which they are calculated;

- assess the significance of the information provided by indices;

- understand the problems of comparing performance of unquoted and overseas securities;

- understand some techniques by which portfolio performance can be measured;

- review a portfolio.

Introduction

This chapter introduces you to a number of techniques that are used to aid portfolio management. The range of indices that can be used to measure the performance of a share, sector, country or geographical region are discussed. Then the difficulties in assessing the performance of unquoted and overseas shares are discussed and finally the portfolio management considerations that private investors need to consider to enable them to manage their portfolios effectively are covered.

19.1   Stock exchange indices

All stock markets have indices, the aim of which is to try to capture movements in market prices in a representative way. Usually, the larger and more sophisticated the market, the wider the range of indices available. Individual exchanges tend to provide an index or indices for their own exchange. There are a number of major providers of indices at an international level, the most important of whom are FTSE International (the *Financial Times* and the London Stock Exchange), MSCI (Morgan Stanley Capital International, owned by the investment bank Morgan Stanley), Dow Jones and Frank Russell. In discussing indices, we concentrate on those provided by FTSE International.

The performance of fully-quoted shares on the UK Stock Market can be measured by reference to the indices grouped into the FTSE UK Series. The performance of international shares can be measured by reference to indices grouped into the FTSE All-World Index Series or the FTSE European Series.

The FTSE UK Series

The following are calculated on a real-time basis:

- FTSE 100 Index
- FTSE 250 Index
- FTSE 250 Index excluding Investment Companies
- FTSE 350 Index;
- FTSE 350 Index excluding Investment Companies
- FTSE Actuaries All Share Indices
- FTSE Actuaries All Share Indices excluding Investment Companies
- FTSE Actuaries All Share Indices excluding Multinationals
- FTSE Actuaries All Share SmallCap.

The following are calculated on an end-of-day basis

- FTSE All-Share Sectors
- FTSE 350 Higher Yield
- FTSE 350 Lower Yield
- FTSE Fledgling
- FTSE All-Small
- FTSE All-Small excluding Investment Companies
- FTSE All-Small sectors
- FTSE AIM
- FTSE techMARK 100.

In addition there is the FT 30 Share Index, which, while not part of the FTSE UK Series, does provide some relevance to portfolio management (see below for details of this index).

FTSE All-World Index Series, the FTSE European Series

These two categories of indices enable investors to assess the performance of shares listed on overseas markets.

FTSE All-World Index Series

- FTSE World Index

- FTSE World Europe
- All World Developed
- All World Emerging
- All World Advance Emerging
- All World Emerging
- All World excluding US
- All World excluding UK
- All World excluding Japan
- All World Developed excluding US
- All World Developed excluding Eurobloc
- All World Nordic
- All World EuroPacific
- FTSE World Index Multinational Indexes
- Global Islamic Index.

FTSE European Series
- FTSE Eurotop 100 Index
- FTSE Eurobloc 100 Index
- FTSE Eurotop 300 Index
- FTSE EuroMid Index
- FTSE European Series.

A further category is:

FTSE eTX Index Series
- FTSE eTX All Share
- FTSE 50 and FTSE eTX Euro 50 Indices
- FTSE eTX sub-sectors Indices.

Overall comparison of world stock markets can be made from data on 'World Stock Markets' published in the *Financial Times* and *Investor's Chronicle*.

FT 30 Share Index
The index commenced on 1 July 1935 with a base value of 100 and was originally wholly

based on industrial companies. Hence its original full title was the FT Industrial Ordinary Share Index. As some industrial companies have declined and other sectors have risen, the constituents have now changed and now include retailing, and oil and gas companies. The 'Industrial' part of the title was dropped in 1984. There was a time when the industrial bias made this index unrepresentative of the market as a whole and, while this has now changed, the Ordinary Index still has a heavy industrial bias. Because of this bias the index is unsuitable as a method of measuring long-term portfolio performance comparison. Indeed, it was never intended to perform this function.

The index is an unweighted, geometric mean index of the price relatives of the top 30 leading shares, and is calculated by multiplying the price relatives of the 30 shares and taking the thirtieth root. The price relative of a share is the current share price divided by the share's price at a base date. In practice the current prices of the 30 shares are multiplied together divided by a constant, and then the thirtieth root is taken. The 30 shares comprising the index represent approximately 25% of the total market capitalization of all UK-quoted shares.

The index is calculated hourly. The 'close' position is based on the position at the end of the day's trading at 5.15 p.m., which is taken from the final prices obtained from the market makers' offices at that time.

The FT 30 Share Index, as published in the *Financial Times*, has the ordinary dividend yield and price earnings ratio. The index also has the hourly changes and the high and low figures for the year.

The purpose of the FT 30 Share Index is to give a guide to short-term market sentiment. It can be very volatile. One reason for such volatility is due to the method of calculation. The unweighted geometric method means that a change in the price of one share has the same effect as the same change in any other share, irrespective of the original market capitalization of the two companies. In an extreme case if one share price fell to zero, the whole index would fall to zero. However, this would never occur in practice because the constituents of the index are changed to take into account any decline in one constituent. When this occurs a replacement share is brought in. On the other hand, however, the geometric mean method means that the index will not rise as far, if one share rises, whereas if the arithmetical mean had been used the volatility of the index would have been greater.

Although the 30 companies represented are diverse in nature, they are all blue-chip shares (shares in major, well known companies). Such shares are generally first to respond to changes in market sentiment, hence the use of this index to measure short-term market mood.

FTSE 100 Index

This is a broader-based index than the 30 Share Index. It was introduced on 3 January 1984 with the value at that date given the index number 1,000. It is a weighted arithmetical mean index based on the share prices of 100 of the largest companies. This gives a far more balanced spread of companies over the different sectors and thus it is a more useful guide to portfolio performance than the FT 30 Share Index. The constituents of the index are reviewed each quarter.

Since this index is recalculated every minute (real time) it is very sensitive to the mood of the market. The FTSE 100 is nevertheless not as volatile as the FT 30 Share Index due partly to its broader base of constituents, and partly to the method of calculation.

This index was introduced for several reasons. First, the LSE is in competition with overseas stock exchanges for international business. Many large sophisticated overseas investors are used to having information on a minute-by-minute basis, especially in the US markets. The FTSE 100 provides an equivalent service to that given in the US stock markets thus adding to the attraction of our market to overseas investors, especially to those from the USA. At the time it was introduced, the FTSE 100 was the only index able to give a minute-by-minute recalculation of the relevant figure. In the UK investors had for a long time been able to hedge against price movements in individual shares by the use of options and traded options, but they had never been able to hedge against movements in the market itself. There is now a traded option series available based on the FTSE 100 and also the FTSE 100 Index Future, which enables institutional investors to hedge against price movements in the market itself. In September 2000 LIFFE introduced the Mini-FTSE100 Index Future, which is more appropriate for private investors who can access this derivative more easily because of the lower initial cost of entry. (See Chapter 9 for details of these derivatives.)

Although it may appear that only 100 shares out of a total of over 2,000 quoted shares is not representative of the market as a whole, in fact the 100 shares represent approximately 75% of the total market capitalization of all UK equities. As a demonstration of how representative the FTSE 100 Share Index would have been if it had existed in the period 1978-83, research showed that the 'Top 100' companies over that time period underperformed the FTSE All Share Index by approximately 0.5% per year. As the All Share Index consists of approximately 760 shares, this difference is small.

Worked example to compare geometric mean and arithmetical mean when the price of a single constituent share rises

Let us take a hypothetical index that consists of four shares, each of which has a current price of 50. Using the geometric mean method, the index would be calculated thus:

$$\sqrt[4]{50 \times 50 \times 50 \times 50} = 50$$

Under the arithmetical mean method, the index would also equal 50:

$$\frac{50 + 50 + 50 + 50}{4} = 50$$

Suppose one share's price rises to 60p, while the others are unchanged.

Under the geometric mean method, the index would be calculated as:

$$\sqrt[4]{50 \times 50 \times 50 \times 60} = \sqrt[4]{7,500,000} = 52.33p$$

Under the arithmetical mean method the result would be:

$$\frac{50 + 50 + 50 + 60}{4} = 52.5p$$

Hence it can be seen that the geometric mean method will understate the effect of rises in individual shares when compared with the arithmetic mean method.

Note that the geometric mean method will always result in a lower index figure than the arithmetic mean method. This applies equally if share prices are falling, except when all the figures are the same.

The FTSE 250 Index

This covers the next 250 companies by market capitalization after the FTSE 100 companies. At the time of writing these companies had a market capitalization of between £280 million and £1.8 billion. It is calculated on two formats, one which includes investment companies and one which excludes investment companies. The base date of the index is 31 December 1985, and the base value is 1412.60.

The FTSE Actuaries 350 Index

This combines the FTSE 100 and 250 indices. This index is a real-time index and is the basis for the real-time figures on sector performance intended to mirror the all-share sector figures. The FTSE 350 is calculated in four formats – with and without investment companies, the higher yield and the lower yield. The 'higher yield' comprises stocks with an annual dividend yield above the average yield on the FTSE Actuaries 350 Index, and the 'lower yield' with a below average annual dividend yield on the 350 Index. The FTSE 350 higher and lower yield indices are calculated once a day at close of business. The base date at the index is 31 December 1985 and the base value 682.94.

The FTSE SmallCap Index

This index measures the share price performance of around 550 smaller companies. At the time of writing these companies were capitalized at between £40 million and £280 million, and include the smaller 450 companies in the FTSE Actuaries All Share indices. This index, like the 250, is also calculated in two formats, including or excluding investment companies. The index is calculated daily at close of business.

FTSE Fledgling Index

This index includes approximately 800 companies too small to be included in the FTSE Actuaries Share Indices. It is calculated daily including and excluding investment companies. The index accounts for less than 2% of the UK equity market by value, but contains nearly the same number of companies as the FTSE Actuaries All Share Indices.

FTSE techMARK 100

Launched on 4 November 1999, this index consists of technology companies with market capitalization of under £4bn. It is designed to enable investors to track the performance of small and medium-size technology companies. Thus the large technology companies such as Vodafone and BT are excluded from this index.

FTSE Actuaries All Share Indices

This is a weighted arithmetical mean index consisting of the prices of around 760 shares which represent about 98% of the total market capitalization of all UK equities. The index started on 10 April 1962 with a base value of 100. This is a 'real time' index. The constituent shares are segmented into equity groups and subsections, the breakdown in May 2001 being:

Indices	Number of shares
Resources	15
Basic industrials	51
General Industrials	52
Cyclical Consumer Goods	7
Non-Cyclical Consumer Goods	70
Cyclical Services	218
Non-Cyclical Services	23
Utilities	16
Information technology	90
Non-financials	542
Financials	218
FTSE All Share Indices	760

The main use of this index is as a measure of portfolio performance. Each of the above groups has subsections that have their own index figures. For example, the non-cyclical consumer goods section has its constituent groups as:

● Beverages,

● Food Producers and Processors,

● Health,

● Packaging,

● Personal Care and Household Products,

- Pharmaceuticals,
- Tobacco.

Each sector has its own index. The following data are available for each:

- Index value in £ sterling terms,
- Day's change in % terms,
- Index value in euro terms,
- Index value in £ sterling terms at previous day's close,
- Index value in £ sterling terms 1 year ago,
- Actual yield %,
- Dividend cover,
- P/e ratio,
- Ex-dividend adjustment for the year to date,
- Total return,
- High and low index value in £ sterling terms for the year to date and since compilation began.

This information can aid investors in comparing the performance of individual shares against sector indices and the All Shares indices as a whole.

FTSE All-World Index Series

This series was introduced in March 1987 with the base value of 100 at the base date of 31 December 1986. It is a weighted arithmetic mean index, as are all the other indices except the FT Ordinary Share Index. The index was introduced to provide a benchmark for measuring the performance of the growing number of overseas funds. It represents at least 70% of the total market capitalization of the world's main stock markets even though there are only 2,284 shares (at 10 May 2001) in the index. It consists of national and regional markets with the number of stocks represented in each market shown.

The three largest markets, USA (509), Japan (337) and the UK (145) provide about half the stocks. (Share numbers are approximate because the constituent companies change regularly.) The reported information on the index also includes a US dollar version of index, % change in the index on the day, % change on the month, % change on the year to date, and yield %. The index is calculated nightly.

There are a number of other indices published in the *Financial Times* which can be used to check the performance of shares that may not be in the main indices described above.

Overseas stock exchanges

In addition to market index data, the *Financial Times* also publishes information relating to major companies listed on other countries' stock exchanges. The information published for each company is: the closing share price shown in the local currency (except for Eurozone countries where the price shown is in euros); change in the share price from the previous day's close; the high/low price on a rolling 52-week basis; gross dividend yield; P/E ratio; and volume of shares traded.

The countries for which this detail is published in the *Financial Times* are:

North America
United States
Canada
South/Central America (the only two countries included being Brazil and Mexico)
Europe (EMU)
Austria
Belgium/Luxembourg
Finland
France
Germany
Greece
Ireland
Italy
Netherlands
Portugal
Spain
Europe – non-EMU
Denmark
Norway
Sweden
Switzerland
Africa
South Africa
Pacific
Japan
Australia
Hong Kong
Malaysia
Singapore

Information is given separately on the main US markets – NYSE (New York Stock Exchange), NASDAQ and AMEX.

The major markets in the world are London, New York (USA) and Tokyo (Japan); these are called the 'golden triangle', and due to time differences one of these markets is always trading.

FTSE European Series

There are a number of indices representing Europe's stock markets. The three main ones, which track the European large capitalization stocks, are: FTSE Eurotop 100, FTSE Eurotop 300 and FTSE Eurobloc 100.

FTSE Eurotop 100

This is a basket of the 100 most-traded European stocks. It is a 'fixed basket' construction which makes it useful for derivatives trading.

FTSE Eurotop 300

This measures the performance of the largest companies in terms of market capitalization. It has separate sector and regional sub-indices.

FTSE Eurobloc 100

This index includes stocks from those countries participating in European Monetary Union (EMU). The top 60 stocks are selected by market capitalization and the remaining 40 added on a basis of sector weighting. It was designed with derivative trading in mind.

FTSE EuroMid

The FTSE EuroMid consists of those stocks that make up the European section of the FTSE World Index but that are too small to qualify for the FTSE Eurotop 300. This index enables investors to judge the performance of this group of stocks on a standalone basis.

The FTSE eTX Index Series

This is the first European technology index representing all the relevant stocks from large to small cap. The constituents of the FTSE eTX indices are technology stocks trading on Europe's main markets, as well as on NASDAQ Europe and the Euro.NM markets.

19.2 Weighting methodology and free float

The purpose of weighting in indices such as the FTSE 100 is to ensure that a change in the price of one of the largest constituent companies has a bigger effect on the index than a similar change in the price of one of the smaller constituents.

Traditionally, the basis of weighting was market capitalization, which is the number of shares in issue multiplied by the share price. However, there is a major problem with this basis, namely that for some companies not all the shares are available for Stock Exchange transactions. For instance, in the UK there are limited companies such as J. Sainsbury and BSkyB where a significant proportion of the shares are in the hands of the founding family and these shares would not normally be traded. In continental Europe and in some emerging markets there are many listed shares that have large government holdings or complex cross-holdings which are hardly ever traded on the stock market.

The problems here are twofold:

● It is considered inequitable that companies with large holdings of rarely traded shares should be given an overstated weighting which makes the index unrepresentative.

● There can be a shortage of stock as index tracker funds try to obtain sufficient holdings of these shares to reflect what is an artificially high weighting. Thus prices of these stocks are supported by such demand.

The response to this problem has been to adjust weightings to represent the market capitalization of the number of shares actually available for trading, and this principle is known as 'free float'. The FTSE 100 adopted the free float measure on 18 June 2001 and Morgan Stanley Capital International will have adjusted its indices by May 2002. It has been estimated that the UK's weighting in the MSCI world indices will rise by 5% while Europe's will fall by 3.3% due to the adoption of the free-float policy. US shares will also have greater weightings in the MSCI indices. The aim of free float is to make the indices more representative of the overall performance of the shares of companies represented.

19.3 Problems of comparing the performance of unquoted companies and overseas companies

Unquoted companies

While there are indices available to measure the performance of shares with a full or AIM quotation, there are no comparable indices available to measure the performance of shares in unquoted companies. An investor may at least be able to compare the current share price (where one is available) with the price he paid. But for a completely unquoted share there will not be a price available for comparison, because a buyer must first be found before a share price can be obtained. This is one reason why the ordinary investor should steer clear of investing in unquoted companies.

There are various methods that can be used to value unquoted shares. Examples are net asset value, future dividends, net present value based on projections of future net cash flows discounted at a rate adjusted for risk, or price earnings-based methods. However, such methods can at best only be indicative.

OFEX Facility

OFEX is an unregulated trading facility for share dealing in unquoted companies. It is operated by J. P. Jenkins Ltd. in association with Newstrack Ltd. Prices for shares traded through OFEX are published in the *Financial Times*. The information published for each company is the company name, mid-price of the shares, day's charge, market capitalization (£m) and the year's high and low prices.

Overseas shares

Although the closing prices of the major shares on the major stock markets are published daily in the *Financial Times* along with index figures for the main indices in the major centres, the volume of published information readily available for overseas shares is less than that for UK companies. In addition to the relative lack of readily available information, currency fluctuations can seriously affect the size of profit or loss made on the sale of an overseas share. A good capital gain on a share can be wiped out if the value of the currency in which it is denominated has fallen against sterling, and, vice versa, a rise in the value of the currency against sterling can increase the gain. The FTSE World Series does provide some guide for measuring portfolio performance on a currency-adjusted basis. If the shares are in Europe then the FTSE Eurotop 100 and 300 indices are useful measurement tools.

19.4 Portfolio management methods for the private investor

Some investors take an active interest in the stock market and prefer to manage their portfolios themselves. To do this they must be able to use the available information to their best advantage. One thing they need to do is read the quality financial press on a regular basis. The *Financial Times* and *Investor's Chronicle* are invaluable sources of information. For investors in unit trusts, OEICs, investment trusts, single premium bonds and some offshore funds, *Money Management* provides a monthly source of performance statistics. In addition information is available from various websites some of which are shown in the Appendix. The Internet is a potentially powerful research tool for the individual investor. Many listed companies maintain websites on which they post information for investors such as financial statements, results announcements, press releases, and the detail of presentations given to institutional investors. Individual investors are thus able to access this information more quickly than previously

Sites such as www.hemscott.net allow access to vast amounts of information about listed companies that may be useful in making investment decisions. Brokers' research on companies may be available on the web, as may credit ratings (see, for example, www.moodys.com). Fund management companies maintain websites giving information about their own funds (e.g. portfolio composition and performance data) and performance data for the population of funds available can also be obtained.

We now set out some general principles for the review of an investment portfolio by an investor. The value of the portfolio should be calculated and the gross yield for each investment found or calculated. The investor should check his marginal rate of income tax and identify any realized capital gains that will count against his CGT allowance. The individual components of the portfolio should be examined.

The liquid reserve
The investor should check:

- The available interest rates to ensure that the investor is getting the best return net of tax.

- The size of the liquid reserve against the value of the portfolio. If it exceeds 10% then unless this is for a specific purpose the excess should be invested elsewhere in line with the investor's overall strategy.

The fixed-interest content
The investor should:

- Check the value and the redemption dates of the stocks noted to see if any will shortly be redeemed.

- Calculate the net redemption yield of each stock to ensure it still matches his income tax situation.

- Check the current and anticipated levels of inflation and interest rates to see if any stocks need to be switched in view of the likely trends. Switching should ideally be done just before the changes take place in order to benefit the investor.

- Ensure that the value of any individual holding does not unbalance the structure of the portfolio.

However, bear in mind that all gilts are equally secure in that they are all government backed. A mixture of stocks is still required to ensure that there is a good spread of redemption dates. If the investor has included company loan stocks (corporate bonds) the information he will need to judge the suitability of the bond will include all the information relating to gilts, and in addition the current credit rating of the company, which is given by agencies such as Standard and Poor's and Moody's. These credit ratings are based on an in-depth analysis of the company and its future prospects and performance. The rating agency then gives each bond a rating ranging from AAA (also called Triple A) to D in the case of Standard and Poor's and C in the case of Moody's (see Chapter 12 for a discussion of credit ratings.)

The tax-exempt content
The investor should:

- First ensure that these investments are still suitable in view of his tax position.

- If any of the investments are nearing maturity, check whether they are automatically repaid on maturity or whether they will continue to receive interest after maturity. If they are due to be repaid the investor should look at any new schemes available that are suitable for reinvestment. If, as in the case of NSCs, they continue to receive either index-linking or interest at the general extension rates then these rates should be compared with those available on similar investments before a decision is taken about retaining them or not.

● If tax-exempt investments are still suitable, then, provided the investor does not find a more attractive alternative for this element, check to ensure that the portfolio is still properly balanced in relation to this element. In general tax-exempt investments are unsuitable for non- and basic-rate taxpayers.

The equity content

Direct equity investment
The factors that should be considered are:

● The investor should ensure that he has at least 15 shares in different sectors to provide adequate diversification to eliminate most of the unsystematic risk.

● Each holding should be valued and performance should be compared to the average of its Actuaries Indices sector where applicable, or some other appropriate benchmark.

● For each holding the yield should be compared to the yields given for the FT Actuaries Indices for that share's sector.

● The overall yield on the equity part of the portfolio should be compared to the yield on the Actuaries All Share Indices.

● Any holdings that have got too large should be scaled down. The value of holdings should be about equal, and any shares that show a good gain will unbalance the portfolio. In this case some of these shares should be sold to bring the value into line, but care should be taken that disposals are within the exemption limit for CGT purposes.

● Any underweight holdings should be carefully examined. If the performance has been poor and prospects for a quick recovery are slim it would be better to cut the losses and use the proceeds along with any others realized to invest in a complementary holding.

● Apart from comparing an individual share's performance with past performance, the investor should also look at future prospects for both the company and the industry. If there is a major crisis looming that will affect the company then it would be better to sell the share before the price is affected and move into a more promising sector. The key is, of course, to anticipate such events correctly which, as we have seen in our discussion of the Efficient Markets Hypothesis (see Chapter 13), may not be easy.

Indirect equity investment

The factors that should be considered are:

- Each holding of unit trusts, investment trusts, OIECs and single-premium bonds should be valued and its performance compared to the appropriate benchmark for that type of holding.

- The holdings should maintain the balance of the portfolio.

- In the case of single-premium bonds, consideration should be given to whether or not total encashment would result in a taxation payment under top-slicing rules. If this were the case the whole profit would be taxed at the investor's marginal rate less basic rate.

Other considerations to bear in mind

Other factors that the investor should consider are:

- Look at any new investment opportunities available and evaluate them to see if they will suit his needs and fit comfortably into the balance of his portfolio.

- If any investments are due to be redeemed, the trends of interest rates, inflation and the market must be considered. It may turn out that for a short period it would be advantageous to retain these funds in liquid form. If, for example, a new investment was being launched in the near future, or a particularly attractive company was being floated on the stock market, then it might be better to remain liquid for the period to enable the opportunity to be taken up.

- Before making any buy, sell or hold decisions the investor could employ the techniques of either fundamental or technical analysis to guide his decision making. The fundamental approach attempts to say whether a particular share should be bought, sold, or held, while technical analysis attempts to say whether the timing is right for carrying out the transaction.

- The investor should ensure that any major changes in taxation policy introduced in the Finance Act are taken into account when carrying out the review.

19.5   Portfolio review

When a customer brings in a portfolio of investments for review there is certain information that must be obtained from him, and then the portfolio review procedure can be undertaken.

Information required

You need to ask the following questions.

- What is the investor's age? If he is young or retired then income is the more likely requirement. If he is middle-aged with no dependent children then the aim will more likely be towards building up a 'nest egg' for retirement.

- What commitments does he have? Are his children in private education? Are they in higher education? If so, money will be needed to meet their school fees and expenses. Are there any other relatives to support?

- Has he adequate life and pension cover?

- Does he own his own home? If so, what is its value and what is the mortgage outstanding on it?

- What is his salary and other income and his marginal rate of tax? How does the income from the portfolio affect his tax position?

- What other investments does he have, if any? If so, do they fit into the existing portfolio, do they complement it?

- What is his attitude to risk? How does this affect the selection of the most suitable investments?

- Are there any ethical considerations such as areas he wishes to avoid, e.g. breweries or tobacco companies? Or are there any shares he wishes to purchase for the concessions?

- Is he a UK resident or a non-resident? If he is a non-resident he is exempt from UK capital gains tax on stocks and share deals. He is also eligible to receive income from gilts free of income-tax liability.

- What are his requirements from the portfolio?

Assessment of the existing portfolio

This should be carried out in the following order to ascertain the suitability of each holding.

- List the investments held to show their price, current value, and gross and net yields.

- Compare the performance of the portfolio as a whole with the FT Actuaries All Share Indices.

- Compare the performance of each equity with the performance of the individual sector index in the FTSE Actuaries All Share Indices. If there are any overseas holdings, either directly-held shares or unit or investment trusts investing overseas, compare the performance with the FTSE World Indices or FTSE Eurotop as applicable.

- Have there been any sales during the year? If so, is there a potential capital gains tax liability?

- Is there an adequate liquid reserve invested in the most efficient manner with regard to the investor's marginal rate of tax?

- Are the fixed-income and equity content balanced?

- Is the fixed-income element of the portfolio suitable to the investor's needs? Are any stocks due to be redeemed shortly?

- Are the coupons and yields of the fixed-interest stocks suitable for the investor's tax position? Do the maturity dates of the stocks meet his needs?

- Where there is direct equity investment, are there at least 15 shares in different sectors to provide most of the benefits of diversification of the unsystematic risk?

- Are the values of any of the share holdings very small or large? If small should the holding be increased or sold? Small holdings of individual shares are usually not cost effective to manage. If large then the holding should be scaled down and the funds realized reinvested in a complementary holding.

- If the investor is a higher rate taxpayer does he have the maximum holdings of the current tax-free investments, i.e. NSCs and ISAs?

- Would the equity content benefit by inclusion of unit trusts investing overseas, single-premium bonds or split-level investment trusts?

- Are there any new investments available that would fit the investor's needs?

Reviewing the portfolio: an example

A customer aged 59 asks your advice on his investments, a list of which is given below. He is married, his wife is aged 61, they have children but they are no longer financially dependent on him. He is a company executive and pays income tax at the top rate. He is not averse to reasonable risk. He owns his house and has sufficient cash available to pay off the outstanding mortgage of about £5,000 but no other resources. His wife is a basic-rate taxpayer.

	Price	Value	Interest yield %	Redemption yield %
£20,000 3½% Funding 1999/04	95.91	19,182	3.65	4.9
£40,000 7¾% Treasury 2012/15	121.23	48,492	6.39	5.15
£25,000 5½% Treasury 2008/12	102.97	25,743	5.34	5.01
£7,500 2½% Treasury 1975 or after	48.83	3,662	5.12	–
		97,079		

Indicate the general investment policy you would recommend to your customer and state, with reasons, what changes, if any, you would suggest in his present portfolio.

General Investment Policy

(a) He has accumulated enough cash to pay off his £5,000 mortgage. If it is a repayment mortgage it will almost certainly be near the end of its term because he is 59. In this case it may be wise to repay because most of the payments now will consist of repayment of capital. If it is an endowment or pension mortgage he should retain it. We shall assume it is an endowment mortgage, thus the £5,000 is available for investment.

(b)   Check he has adequate pension and life cover.

(c)   The existing portfolio consists entirely of gilts. These do not provide for any growth of income over the long term or protection from inflation. Two of the gilts are priced over par, which will result in a capital loss if held to redemption. One is undated and will not produce any guaranteed capital gain. All capital gains on gilts are free of CGT but no relief is given for capital losses.

(d)   With a portfolio valued at around £102,079 (including the accumulated cash), overseas and property elements could be included.

The overseas element should be provided via unit or investment trusts investing overseas to provide growth in the long term from other expanding economies, and to spread risk.

The property element should be provided via a property bond. This is a single-premium bond that does not pay any income. On encashment the profit is subject to top-slicing rules, so that if encashment is deferred until he retires and he then becomes a basic-rate taxpayer, there will be no further tax liability.

However, with both of these investments, the emphasis is on long-term capital growth, thus it may be better to avoid these investments as he is due to retire in 6 years time.

(e)   He has not taken advantage of the various tax-free investments such as NSCs or ISAs. Any NSCs purchased now would mature in 5 years time when he is due to retire (presuming retirement at 65). The returns are tax free and guaranteed on the NSCs. ISAs do not have a maturity date and are free of all taxes, but the return depends on the success of the ISA managers.

(f)   Does the customer's wife use up her full basic rate tax allowance? If not, is he willing to transfer capital into her name to fully utilize this allowance?

Suggested changes to the portfolio

(a)   The 3½% Funding matures in 2004 and its market price is under par. No change: retain. It will provide funds to further develop the portfolio for his retirement.

(b)   The other three gilts should be sold. The 7¾% Treasury and 5½% Treasury are both giving a reasonable return. He needs to ensure that any gilts he holds or purchases give the best net redemption yield for a 40% taxpayer. With all his investments in gilts this area of his portfolio is overweight. The 2½% Treasury is undated and is unlikely ever to be redeemed. Undated gilts give a return that is entirely of interest. For high taxpayers this is not suitable.

(c)   He should retain his cash as a liquid reserve to meet any unexpected bills. He already has £5,000 cash, which could be increased to £10,000 (10% of the value of the portfolio) if he felt that he may have some larger expenses or wish to take advantage of any new investments in the future. A bank or building society high-interest account would give the best rate of return for liquid cash.

(d) Although he could consider investing in NSCs for tax efficiency and to mature in 5 years time, it would be excessive to have both the fixed-interest and index-linked issues, especially as inflation is low and projected to remain low over the next few years. Thus it would be advisable to invest in the 57th issue NSCs to provide a tax-free return of 3.55%, equivalent to 5.92% for a 40% taxpayer over 5 years.

(e) The inclusion of an ISA provides tax-free income and capital gains. He should put the maximum of £7,000 in a maxi-ISA investing either in two shares or indirectly in unit/investment trusts/OEICs depending on whether the equity content is invested directly or indirectly.

(f) He could invest directly in equities with the sum available provided it is professionally managed. He has sufficient funds for holdings in 15 different companies in different sectors. Alternatively he could use unit and investment trusts to provide professional management and diversification. Three or four trusts under different managers aimed at growth would provide protection against poor performance by one manager.

Note: These suggestions assume there is no advantage in transferring any capital to his wife.

Suggested portfolio

	Amount £	Gross Rate/ Yield %	Available Gross Income
Bank/building society high-interest account	5,000	4.5	225
£20,000 3½% Funding 99/04	19,182	3.65	700
1 Long-dated gilt with best net redemption yield	15,000	6.7	1005
57th Issue NSCs	10,000	Nil	–
ISA	7,000	Nil	–
15/20 holdings in shares professionally managed – growth companies	45,897	2	918
	102,079		2,848

Gross Yield on portfolio = $\dfrac{2,848 \times 100}{102,079}$ = 2.79%

Upon retirement the NSCs and the Funding stock will have matured. The proceeds can then be re-invested to provide income if required.

The ISA using the full £7,000 allowance complements his existing holdings. All income and capital gains are free of tax.

The new portfolio provides the basis for his retirement, while maintaining tax efficiency. There will also be an extra amount of cash, which he may want to utilize, for example, by taking a holiday upon retirement, and this will mean that the new portfolio will not be disrupted to provide for this expenditure.

Example

The following portfolio of investments is held by a new client

Fixed Interest

Holding	Stock	Price	Value	Int. Yield	Red. Yield
£9,426	Treasury 6½% 2003	103.71	9,776	6.27%	4.95%
£5,780	Treasury 9% 2008	£124.23	7,180	7.24%	5.05%
£4,498	Treasury 5¾% 2009	£105.19	£4,731	5.47%	5.0%
			£21,687		

Equity

No. of shares	Company	Price	Value	Div. Yield
1,000	Lincat	308p	3,080	5.3
300	Railtrack	487p	1,461	5.6
400	Wyndeham Press	181p	724	4.5
2,500	Thistle Hotels	126p	3,150	4.0
500	Rolls Royce	221p	1,105	3.6
750	Allied Domecq	416p	3,120	2.8
2,000	Express Dairies	38p	760	8.9
			£13,400	

Total portfolio value (Gilts + Equities)   £35,087

Note

All the shares currently have yields higher than the average of the FTSE Actuaries All Share dividend yield of 2.26% and the current holdings are all in different sectors.

Required

You are asked to examine the portfolio and discuss its suitability for the client described. What changes, if any, would you make?

The client is a 70-year-old widow whose other sources of income do not provide the standard of living which she enjoyed when her husband was alive. She is a basic-rate taxpayer. She owns a detached house, with no mortgage outstanding and has two married sons who are well established in their professional careers. The pension she receives from her husband's former employment is inflation-linked. She is in good health and, for the time being, she wishes to be independent of her children. She was widowed 3 years ago.

Portfolio review
She needs to maximize her income from this portfolio. The fixed-interest and equity elements should be split equally to give her a high level of initial income with long-term capital growth.

Although all the gilt holdings have good interest yields, she is overweight in the section. It is suggested that she retains the 9% Treasury Stock and purchases another, longer-dated, gilt giving the best net redemption yield. This will provide a further long-term guaranteed high income element to the portfolio.

The equity content consists of only 7 shares, whereas a minimum number of 15 are needed to give the maximum benefits of diversification, with a minimum value of £2,000 each for cost effectiveness. However the emphasis on income is too great at the expense of long-term capital growth, thus some restructuring of the equity portfolio is needed, with the sale of shares and their replacement with shares or indirect investment into unit/investment trusts/ OIECs giving an average yield of nearer 3%. Unless the lady has the time and expertise necessary to manage the equities, it would be better to sell them and use professional management.

Unit trusts could be purchased via a share exchange scheme to minimize dealing costs. The trusts should be aimed at income and a selection from different managers chosen to give protection against poor performance. Such holdings will provide growth of income and capital in the long term. Investment trusts and OIECs could also be used alongside the unit trusts.

She does not appear to have a liquid reserve to fall back on in case any unexpected bills arrive and this will be provided from the sale of the 5¾% and 6½% Treasury Stock. £3,500 invested in a bank or building society high-interest access account paying, say, 3.6% net of basic tax, should be sufficient for her needs.

New Portfolio

	Value £	Gross Interest Rate/Yield	Gross Income
Bank/building society instant access a/c	3,500	4.5	158
*£5,780 Treasury 9% 2008	7,180	7.24	520
High-coupon long-dated gilt	8,800	6.7	590
3/4 unit trusts/ OIECs aimed at income, say	15,607	2.6	406
	35,087		1,674

Gross yield on portfolio $\dfrac{1,674 \times 100}{35,087} = 4.77\%$

* When the nominal value is given the gross income from coupon x nominal can be calculated to give the exact monetary amount received.

Example

James Winter is a 43-year-old senior executive in an IT company based in London. His wife aged 40 is the head of a large school and, with their combined income they are able to have a satisfactory standard of living and are able to meet the education fees for their 13-year-old son. Their elder son of fifteen has a free scholarship to an independent day school and it is expected that both boys will to go on to university. Both parents are in good health, their lives are adequately insured and they both have good pension schemes. They are both 40% taxpayers. Their mortgage is fully covered by an endowment policy and they also have ample life and critical illness insurance.

James has little knowledge of the stock market and has not previously made any provision for his portfolio to be reviewed. He chose all the holdings himself. The gilts were chosen to coincide with the children's 18th birthdays and the shares were chosen by James based on share tips in the financial press and purchased randomly over a period of 5 years. James says that he is interested in the stock market, but neither he nor his wife have sufficient time to manage a share portfolio. He has a high-interest bank account with a balance of £10,000 which he feels is sufficient for his needs.

He has asked you to review the portfolio and to develop a new portfolio that will met the needs of the children's university fees and expenses at the age of 18, and to give long-term capital growth for their future retirement at the age of 65. James is not willing to transfer any of the investments to his wife.

Current portfolio

Cash   £10,000

	Fixed Interest	Price	Value	Int. Yield %	Red. Yield %
£10,000	Treasury 6¾% 2004	105.73	10,573	6.38	4.97
£ 5,990	Treasury 8½% 2007	118.07	7,072	7.2	5.06
£4,700	Exchequer 8¾% 2017	141.95	6,672	6.16	4.96
			£24,317		

	Equity	Price	Value £	Div. Yield %
3,200	Royal & Sun Alliance	507	16,224	5.1
2,300	Rio Tinto	1372	31,556	2.8
980	Lloyds TSB	738	7,232	4.1
2,500	Cranswick	411	10,275	3.8
2,500	Invensys	135	3,375	5.7
1,800	Marconi	378	6,804	1.4
2,000	Tesco	247	4,940	2.0
			80,406	

The total value of the portfolio is £114,723 (including the cash element).

The existing portfolio is split, cash 9%, fixed interest 21% and equities 70%. This is weighted a little too much towards the equity content. For a portfolio for a client such as Mr Winter would be better with a maximum of 60% in equity or equity-based investment. He holds sufficient cash to meet his needs, but the portfolio lacks tax efficiency. He should consider investing in the 57th issue NSCs, which give a return of 3.55% over 5 years, equal to 5.19% for a 40% tax payer. The younger son will be going to university in 5 years' time, so the timing of this investment would be suitable for the expenses incurred at this time.

The two Treasury stocks are dated to meet each son's entry to university and should be retained. The Exchequer stock is long dated and should be retained provided it gives the best net redemption yield.

The seven equities are worth £80,406, but the values are quite unbalanced – from £3,375 to £31,556. At the very least the equity part of the portfolio needs tidying up. If shares are sold or scaled down care should be taken about any potential CGT liability. The size of the portfolio would indicate that direct equity investment was suitable. Around 15 - 20 shares in different sectors are needed to minimize unsystematic risk. Given James' interest in the stock market, direct equity investment is suitable, however James does need professional management due to his lack of time to manage the portfolio. He could consider an advisory service so that he would have a major influence over the shares chosen, while benefiting from the high quality of advice such a service can offer. Alternatively he could opt for discretionary management if he felt that he would not have sufficient time to manage the portfolio, but still wanted to track the performance of the shares himself.

Tax efficiency should be included by means of an ISA, whereby £7,000 per tax year can be invested in a maxi-ISA investing in directly or indirectly in shares. There is no liability to income tax or capital gains tax within an ISA. If possible he should try to invest the maximum into an ISA each tax year to increase the tax efficiency of his portfolio.

The new portfolio should be geared to long-term growth of capital because James and his wife have more than 20 years to go until retirement. The inclusion of an overseas investment base will provide exposure to different economic cycles and would complement the new portfolio. Overseas investment should be carried out via professional management using unit/investment trusts and OEICs. The complexities of overseas investment are such that private investors are well advised to use professional management.

Suggested Portfolio

	Value	% return	Gross income
Bank/Building Society	10,000	4.5	450
57th issue NSCs	10,000	-	–
£10,000 Treasury 6¾% 2004	10,573	6.38	675
£ 5,990 Treasury 8½% 2007	7,072	7.2	509
£4,700 Exchequer 8¾% 2017	6,672	6.16	411
ISA	10,000	-	-
15/20 shares – growth	43,406	2	868
Indirect investment overseas	10,000	1	100
	£104,723		£3,013

Gross yield on portfolio $\dfrac{3,013 \times 100}{104,723} = 2.87\,\%$

The new portfolio is aimed at long-term capital growth and tax efficiency. The life events of university are taken into account as well as the long-term nature of the portfolio with retirement not taking place for over 20 years.

20

INVESTMENT MANAGEMENT SERVICES, INVESTOR PROTECTION AND TAKEOVERS

Objectives

After studying this chapter, the reader should be able to:

- differentiate between the investment management services offered by banks, stockbrokers, independent advisers and accountants;

- assess the extent of protection offered by the various regulators to investors in banks, building societies, insurance companies and financial services;

- assess the significance of the main provisions of the Financial Services and Markets Act 2000 as regards investor protection;

- analyse the principles behind takeovers and mergers.

20.1 Investment management services

Investment management services are offered by a large number of different organizations: clearing banks, stockbrokers, merchant banks, independent advisors and accountants. The services range from simple 'dealing only', to 'advisory' and 'discretionary' management. This chapter looks at each of these organizations and the types of service they provide.

Polarization

All financial institutions have been affected by the Financial Services and Markets Act 2000 in the area of giving investment advice. They cannot sell both their own in-house investment products and other companies' investment products. They have had to decide whether to be independent intermediaries, selling only other companies' investment products, or to be tied agents selling only their own products. However, in the Finance Bill 2001, a major change was announced which means that a financial services organization can now be either tied to a single provider, be 'multi-tied' advisers, able to sell the products of a range of companies, or be independent intermediaries. The vast majority of banks and building societies are tied, which limits them to selling the products of one provider. However the new multi-tied status broadens the range of products that can be sold, while not providing the same breadth of products that are available to an independent intermediary.

20.2   Discretionary management and advisory services

Discretionary management

Private clients who want advice tend to be steered towards discretionary management if their portfolio is below £50,000. From the manager's point of view it is much quicker and cheaper to deal with a portfolio if he can take decisions unilaterally. Discretionary management clients receive valuations yearly or half-yearly, and year-end tax summaries are issued.

Clients need to be aware of the danger of 'churning' a portfolio under discretionary management. 'Churning' is a term used to describe switching for switching's sake so that the managing broker can obtain commission income. 'Churning' is forbidden under the Financial Services and Markets Act 2000. If churning is suspected, the onus is on the firm to prove that the deals carried out were justified.

Advisory services

The manager, along with the client, sets up an initial portfolio, which is then monitored by the manager. Before any deals can be done, the manager must obtain the agreement of the client. This service will be of interest to investors who understand the stock market and wish to be involved with the management of their portfolio, but who lack the time to monitor performance on a regular basis.

20.3   Retail banks and building societies

The general nature of the retail banks' and building societies facilities

All retail banks and building societies offer investment management services, and generally the minimum investment accepted is £20,000 to £25,000. Investors with smaller sums will normally be directed towards their own investment vehicles. A full discretionary service is preferred, but advisory services may be available for larger portfolios. The fees are usually ¾% per annum and these compare favourably with the annual fee charged by unit trust managers.

The major selling point for a clearing bank's discretionary management service is that it amounts to a 'total financial package' which covers capital gains tax, inheritance tax, insurance, pensions, wills and income tax as well as investment management.

In particular, banks and building societies will usually recommend investments such as National Savings Certificates which may be particularly suitable for high taxpayers. Discretionary management services are particularly appropriate for busy people who have no time to look after their financial affairs. The equity content, whether in equities or unit/investment trusts and OEICs, will be managed on a conservative basis, and the 'total financial package' concept means that the investor's money is managed efficiently.

20.4 Services of stockbrokers

The growing importance to stockbrokers of the private investor

Because commission rates are (technically) negotiable, it now depends on the standing of the investor as to how high or low dealing costs will be. For institutional investors rates will be low because of the size of their deals, thus many brokers are now looking to private clients to make up for some of the lost earnings.

Fees for advice and for dealing are likely to be separated, and brokers are aiming to segment their services into:

- A 'no frills' dealing-only service. This is simply a dealing-only service which does not offer advice. Investors who wish to deal in small sums should check the minimum commission which the broker will charge. No advice is available from the broker with this type of service.

- Dealing-only services are becoming popular with small investors, especially as many of these services are highly competitive on price, and a number of specialist firms have set up business purely for this purpose. A number of these services are available via telephone and Internet brokers.

- Advisory services involve the broker, in consultation with the client, setting up an initial portfolio, and thereafter managing it on behalf of the investor. Before any changes are made, the broker must consult the client. Since such consultation is costly many brokers now set a minimum amount for an advisory service.

Deposit facilities

Many brokers also arrange for clients to keep money on deposit with them, and this is a particularly useful facility when the client is 'between investments'. The brokers can pool their clients' cash so as to obtain near money market rates from a clearing or merchant bank for deposits that are made up of relatively small individual deposits.

Services for small investors

The broker constructs a basic portfolio of gilts and unit/investment trusts and OEICs for investors with anything between £2,500 and £25,000 and the advice is usually given free of charge, because he will be remunerated by his commission from the fund managers. Obviously dealing costs on the gilts and investment trust shares will be charged to the investor.

The scheme generally operates as follows: the investor discusses with the broker his income and capital needs, and then the broker recommends a mixture of gilts and unit/investment trusts and OEICs. Annual or half-yearly valuations are then issued to the client.

20.5 Merchant banks

Merchant banks tend to specialize in the selection of an equity portfolio geared to growth. Usually the minimum investment a merchant bank is prepared to manage is £100,000. Fees are usually in the region of 0.5% to 1.25% per annum, based on the value of funds managed. Discretionary management is always insisted upon, because when investments of this size are switched, speed is essential to take advantage of any useful bargains.

20.6 Independent financial advisers

There are many independent firms that act as financial advisers. They can advise on virtually all financial matters, including for example:

● The best building society rates currently available;

● ISAs;

● Unit trust and OEIC outlook;

● Gilts;

● Tax planning;

● Insurance and pension products.

Some of these independent advisers charge the investor a fee for the advice, and will remit any commission received on, for example, unit trust deals, against the fee. This type of financial adviser may provide a better service than commission-based advisers because there is no pressure to sell services for commission purposes. Other independent advisers will provide the best advice on a range of products from different companies and earn their remuneration from the commissions received. They do not charge the investor a fee.

20.7 Services of accountants and solicitors

The larger accountancy and solicitor's firms have always offered a 'total financial package' to the higher net worth investor. Most larger firms cater for the executives of the companies that they audit. They will not recommend specific shares for a client's portfolio, but will suggest the basic outline with the proportions of gilts and equities and possibly risk capital. Other items recommended will include pension plans, life assurance, tax planning and executor services. The client will then be referred to a stockbroker for advice on a specific equity selection. These services are fee-based, not commission-based.

20.8   Investor protection

Banks and building societies

Banks and building societies are regulated by the Financial Services and Markets Act 2000. They are known as authorized institutions. Investors should beware of making deposits in any organization that claims to be a bank but is not recognized as one authorized by the Bank of England under the Financial Services and Markets Act 2000.

20.9   Financial Services and Markets Act 2000

Background to the Act

In 1984 Professor Gower produced a report on investor protection, and this report formed the basis of a White Paper which was published on 29 January 1985. The theme of the White Paper was self-regulation within a statutory framework so as to provide investor protection while allowing the UK financial services industry to operate efficiently and competitively. This White Paper formed the basis of the Financial Services Act 1986. The Financial Services Act 1986 was becoming rather dated because the industry has evolved greatly since it was first drawn up. In response to these changes the Financial Services Act 1986 is due to be repealed and replaced by November 2001 by The Financial Services and Markets Act 2000.

The changing regulatory framework

The regulation of financial services has, historically, been the responsibility of a range of different bodies such as the Securities and Investment Board, the self-regulating organizations ('SROs'), the Investment Management Regulatory Organization (IMRO) and the Securities and Futures Authority (SFA). In addition there were other non-regulatory bodies overseeing the industry, such as the Building Societies Commission, the Friendly Societies Commission and the Registry of Friendly Societies.

The Financial Services and Markets Act 2000 Act provides the framework within which a single regulator for the financial services industry – the Financial Services Authority – will operate. All the old self-regulating organizations have ceased to exist. The Act also establishes the framework for single ombudsman and compensation schemes to provide further protection for consumers.

Businesses authorized and regulated under the Act include:

● Banks

● Building societies

● Insurance companies

● Friendly societies

- Credit unions

- Lloyd's

- Investment and pensions advisers

- Stockbrokers

- Professional firms offering certain types of investment services

- Fund managers

- Derivatives traders

The main provisions of the Act are:

- the definition of the scope of regulated activities;

- the powers of the Financial Services Authority to authorize, regulate, investigate and discipline authorized persons;

- the recognition of investment exchanges and clearing houses;

- the provision of financial services by members of the professions (e.g. solicitors and accountants);

- regulation and marketing of collective investment schemes (e.g. unit trusts, investment trusts and OEICs).

The Financial Services and Markets Act 2000 will broadly continue the regime for recognized investment exchanges and clearing houses under the Financial Services Act 1986 although the Financial Services Authority's powers under the Financial Services and Markets Act 2000 will be widened as compared with those under the predecessor legislation. The Financial Services Authority will have powers to regulate the Lloyd's insurance market. The recognized professional bodies regime under the Financial Services Act 1986 will be abolished by the Financial Services and Markets Act 2000. Professional firms (such as solicitors, accountants and actuaries) carrying on mainstream regulated activities will be authorized and regulated directly by the Financial Services Authority.

The Act is intended to coordinate and modernize financial regulatory arrangements which are currently established under a number of different statutes such as:

- the Insurance Companies Act 1982

- the Financial Services Act 1986

- the Building Societies Act 1986

- the Banking Act 1987

- the Friendly Societies Act 1992

- the Policyholders Protection Acts 1975-97

- the Insurance Brokers (Registration) Act 1977.

20.10 The Financial Services Compensation Scheme

The new single compensation scheme is a key element of the FSA's framework for protecting consumers and promoting market confidence. The new scheme will provide a single point of access to consumers. The Financial Services Compensation Scheme is an important part of the safety net for consumers providing compensation to those who would otherwise lose out if a firm collapsed owing them money. The aim of the scheme is to protect investors who are least able to sustain a loss and provide compensation arrangements that are easily understood by, and accessible to, the people who need them.

The scheme provides compensation as follows:

- 100% cover for the first £2,000 of claims relating to deposits and non-compulsory general and life insurance;

- the maximum amount payable on claims relating to deposits is £31,700;

- deposit protection is to be extended to deposits in all currencies.

The Financial Services Authority is seeking to provide a reasonable level of compensation to investors that have lost money through the collapse of a bank, building society, insurer or investment firm.

The Financial Services Compensation Scheme will bring together the Deposit Protection Scheme, the Building Society Investor Protection Scheme, the Policyholders Protection Scheme, the Friendly Societies Protection Scheme, the Investors Compensation Scheme and the Section 43 Scheme (which covers business transacted with listed money-market institutions).

20.11 Conflicts of interest in the large financial conglomerate

Over the past few years demarcation lines in the financial services industry have crumbled, and the new financial services conglomerates now carry out all the services that were once offered separately by different organizations. After the 'Big Bang' in 1986 the last of the legal 'demarcation lines' have ceased to exist. Many investment banking groups offer:

- Fund management;
- Securities dealing both as principal and as agent;
- Corporate finance;
- Conventional banking.

Possible conflicts could arise, for example:

- The banking section will probably be the first to learn of a corporate customer's financial difficulties. This department may pass on the information to the securities dealing section.

● The broking section could then advise its private clients to buy shares in the corporate customer which the 'market maker' section wished to dispose of because of the 'tip' from the banking section.

The problem is approached by the physical separation of the different functions. This separation can take the form of separate incorporation, or of separate physical location in different buildings or on different floors of the same building. This separation has been called 'Chinese walls' and has been regarded by some critics as 'a fortification of doubtful value'.

In order to strengthen these 'Chinese walls', there are compliance departments, which have the responsibility of ensuring that in all situations where conflict could arise appropriate procedures for the protection of clients should be observed.

Most major broking or jobbing firms already stipulate that staff cannot deal for the account, nor can they stag an in-house new issue.

20.12 Takeovers

Why takeovers occur

Takeovers are intended to boost the profits of the bidder in the long term.

The reasons for takeovers are:

● To enable the bidder to diversify its interests;

● To obtain for the bidder an increased market share of an industry;

● To help the bidder ensure supplies by taking over a supplier;

● To enable the bidder to impose improved management on the target and thus the bidder will obtain added value by more efficient operation of the target;

● To acquire retail outlets to help to distribute the bidder's products;

● To enable the bidder to take advantage of synergies which will result from combining the activities of the bidder and the target. Synergies can arise for many reasons, the most common of which is cost reduction due to rationalization of operations.

Takeovers can be classed as fulfilling the corporate objectives of the bidder in the following ways.

Horizontal integration

The takeover is made by the bidder taking over another company that is in the same industry and at the same stage of production, e.g. a direct competitor. This will increase market share and sales, thus (hopefully) increasing profits. A problem that may arise here is when the size of the two companies exceeds 25% of the market share in that industry. The 25% figure is deemed to be a monopoly, and the bid may be referred to the Monopolies and Mergers Commission. The MMC have the power to refuse to allow the bid to continue.

Vertical integration

The takeover is made by the bidder taking over a company that is either a supplier or outlet. The benefits of a vertical takeover are that the bidder can control either the supply or sale of the products cutting out the middleman and (hopefully) increasing profits. It is possible that a vertical integration bid may exceed the 25% rule, and the bid will then be referred to the MMC.

Diversification

Some companies have grown by taking over totally unrelated businesses that the bidder feels are not being run efficiently. Such a bidder may well sell off part of the company after takeover to recoup some of the costs of acquisition, and then put its own management team in to turn the company around.

Disposal synergies

As mentioned above, it is not uncommon for disposal of part of a business to occur. In the mid-1990s it is significant that several companies have moved towards the creation of separate strategic business units, set up by de-mergers.

Some takeover bids are extremely hostile, with the target company trying to fight off the bid by all legitimate routes. There is considerable controversy in the UK concerning takeovers. Some would argue that the threat of a hostile bid will ensure that managements continuously work to maximize shareholder value. Others would say that takeovers inspire short-termism on the part of the managements of potential targets and that takeovers mean that the management of bidders are free, at shareholders' expense, to act out their empire fantasies.

The procedures for carrying out a takeover

To acquire control of a target company the bidder requires over 50% of its voting shares. Such a holding will give the bidder a majority of votes and therefore he will become the controlling shareholder. However, a company needs 75% of voting shares to be sure of passing special and extraordinary resolutions. The significant stages are shown below.

3% or more of the target company's voting shares acquired

The process of acquiring shares of the target company can be commenced by the bidder buying the shares in the open market. Under S.198 of the Companies Act 1989 any person who acquires (or disposes of) more than 3% of the voting shares of a public limited company must notify the company in writing within two working days. The 3% figure is calculated by totalling the holdings of the bidder, his family and friends, and any others acting on his behalf in a 'concert party'. This prevents a number of associates from each acquiring 2.9% of the shares and not having to notify the target company. If the target company thinks the 3% limit has been breached it can require the suspect to confirm or deny the fact. When the holding is in the name of a nominee company, the target company can insist that the nominee discloses the name of the beneficial owner if he has acquired 3% or more of the shares. Failure to supply the target with the required notification can eventually result in an application to the court to deprive the bidder of his voting rights, dividends and the right to sell, a rule which makes it very difficult for a bidder to acquire a substantial interest unbeknown to the target company.

10% of the target's voting shares acquired

If the bidder has acquired more than 10% of the voting shares in the 12 months before it makes a full takeover bid, the bid must be for cash or contain a cash alternative at the highest price paid during the previous 12 months.

A bidder is not allowed to acquire 10% or more of the voting rights of the target in any seven-day period if together with shares already held they comprise between 15% and 30% of the company's voting rights except by purchasing the shares from a single shareholder or through a tender offer to all shareholders. The 10% figure is laid down by the City Code on Takeovers and Mergers and includes any shares acquired by associates acting as a concert party.

30% or more of the target's voting shares acquired

It is considered that a 30% holding is sufficient to give a bidder effective control of most public companies. If the bidder, together with any associates acting as a concert party, acquires more than 30% (laid down by the City Code on Takeovers and Mergers) of the target company's shares, he is required to make a general offer to all the other shareholders at the highest price paid in the previous 12 months. The 'bid price' will have to be set above the current market price, or at least above the market price that prevailed before the news of the bid. The consideration offered can be for cash, for shares or other securities such as convertible loans in the bidding company, or for a mixture of the three. Often the target company's shareholders will be offered a choice of cash or securities. Usually the shareholder will learn about the bid from his newspaper. Shortly afterwards he will receive a formal offer document from the bidder.

50% or more of the target's voting shares acquired

At this stage the bidder has gained control of the company.

90% or more of the target's voting shares acquired

Under ss.428-430 of the 1985 Companies Act, the successful bidder is allowed to acquire the shares of minority shareholders under certain circumstances.

If within four months of the offer 90% in value of the shares has been acquired by the bidder, then the bidder may, within the next two months, serve notice on dissenting shareholders requiring them to transfer their shares on the same terms as the other shareholders. The transfer must be put into effect unless the shareholders petition the court within one month, in which case the court will decide whether there is a good reason for the transfer to be blocked. (The '90%' figure is calculated as 90% of the shares not owned by the bidder when his offer was made.) Likewise, after expiry of a successful offer that acquired 90% of the shares for the bidder, the minority shareholders may, within three months, require the bidder to acquire their shares on the same terms and conditions as the other shares were obtained.

The position of a shareholder of a target company

Agreed bids

An agreed bid occurs when the directors of the target company recommend acceptance. In such circumstances the shareholder will receive a letter from his directors recommending that the bid be accepted, as well as the formal offer document. In these circumstances it is fairly certain that the bid will prove successful and the investor has two choices: sell his shares in the market or accept the bid by returning his share certificate and completed acceptance form to the bidder. The market price of the shares will usually be a few pence below the bidder's price, so it will usually be better to accept the bidder's terms, although the shareholder should leave acceptance until the final date indicated in the formal document, just in case a larger, rival, bid is received in the meantime.

If the bidder offers his own shares as consideration, it could pay the shareholder to sell out in the market if he expects the bidder's shares to fall in value.

The bidder must state a level of acceptances that will make his bid 'unconditional' and once the offer has become unconditional, the shareholder may as well accept. The required level of acceptances is usually reached when the bidder has acquired 50% of the share capital, so there is no possibility of another bid after this stage has been reached. While the offer is still open the level of acceptances will be announced by the press, so the investor can watch the progress.

Contested bids or 'hostile' bids

When the board of the target company objects to the bid, the bid is said to be contested or hostile. In such circumstances the shareholder will be bombarded with literature from both parties, and he must decide:

- Whether the bid is likely to succeed at the initial offer price;
- Whether the bid is likely to be referred to the Monopolies and Mergers Commission:
- Whether the bidder will offer a higher price;
- Whether another bid may come from a rival bidder;

- Whether the target will find a 'white knight'. A 'white knight' is a company by which the target is willing to be taken over.

Normally, the market price of the target's shares will be below the offer price, and if the bid is likely to fail, it may be worthwhile accepting the terms while they are available. A reference to the Monopolies and Mergers Commission probably means that the bid will lapse, because the bidder will have reserved the right to drop the bid if such a reference is made. It is possible for a bidder to avoid a reference to the Monopolies and Mergers Commission if it agrees in advance to sell parts of the combined business so as to overcome any danger of preventing competition in a particular market. When the target company's shares stay above the bidder's terms it means that the market expects the opening bid to be merely a 'sighting shot', with an improved offer likely. Normally the first offer period lasts for a minimum of 21 and a maximum of 60 days from the date the offer documents are posted. During this time the bidder can revise (upwards) his terms as many times as he likes. However, since shareholders must be allowed 14 days in which to consider any new proposals, terms cannot be improved after the forty-sixth day of a 60-day offer.

The 60-day timetable can be extended subject to the agreement of the Takeover Panel if:

- A new bidder emerges;
- The target company announces potentially significant 'trading information' after day 39.

Any shareholder who has accepted earlier terms is entitled to receive the benefit of any revisions. Indeed, a shareholder who has accepted the bidder's terms can revoke the acceptance altogether, if he wishes, from 21 days after the first closing date of the initial offer. However, this right of revocation is lost if the offer has become unconditional. Conversely, if the bidder fails to obtain 50% of the shares of the target by the sixtieth day all acceptances are null and void and the bid fails.

Summary of the takeover timetable

The takeover timetable runs for 60 days. The timetable starts when the bidder sends out its first formal offer documents after making its bid intentions clear.

The deadline can be extended when a rival bidder becomes involved. The timetable is put on hold if the bid is referred to the Monopolies Commission and recommences if the Monopolies Commission does not block the bid.

Day 0   Formal documents posted.

Day 14   Target can issue a defence document up to this date.

Day 21   The minimum period under the City Code for a first offer. This is the earliest possible first closing date of offer.

Day 22   The first close. A second offer can be made.

Day 39   The defence can issue no more material of significance.

Day 46   Final terms and offer documents are posted. Closing date (day 60) specified.

Day 60   Offer closes.

The City Code for takeovers and mergers

The City Code works on the following basic principles:

- All shareholders of the same class should be treated equally. This principle is illustrated by the Code's rule that the bidder must make a general offer to all shareholders once a 30% stake has been acquired.

- Such rules prevent the old practice of making a high bid to certain large shareholders, and later acquiring the other shares at a lower price.

- Shareholders should be given adequate information to form a proper judgement. All documents issued to shareholders must be prepared to the same standards as are required for listing particulars. Profit forecasts should be prepared with great care.

- The bid must be put to the board of the target company in the first instance, and this board must seek competent independent advice in the interests of its shareholders.

- The bidding company should only make an offer that it has every reason to believe can be fulfilled.

- The creation of false markets in the shares should be avoided.

- Most forms of 'knocking copy' advertising are banned.

- When assessing whether the bidder has acquired a 50% plus controlling interest, only shares backed with immediate delivery of a share certificate can be counted.

The nature and purpose of the City Code for takeovers and mergers

The Code was last revised in April 1985 and its official title is 'The City Code for Takeovers and Mergers and the Rules Governing Substantial Acquisitions'. In 2001, the Code is going through a consultative process overseen by the FSA with the aim of bringing it up to date. The nature and purpose of the Code can be summarized from the following extracts from Section A.

The Code represents the collective opinion of those professionally involved in the field of takeovers on a range of business standards. It is not concerned with the financial or commercial advantages or disadvantages of a takeover which are matters for the company and its shareholders, or with those wider questions which are the responsibility of the government, advised by the Monopolies and Mergers Commission. The Code has not, and does not seek to have, the force of law, but those who wish to take advantage of the facilities of the securities markets in the United Kingdom should conduct themselves in matters relating to takeovers according to the Code.

On 24 May 2001, the FSA published draft rules on the endorsement of the takeover code. The position currently is that if an authorized firm fails to comply with the code or with a ruling of the Takeover Panel, the Panel can request the FSA to take action against the firm. Thus the power of the Code and Takeover Panel has been strengthened by the Financial Services and Markets Act 2000 as follows:

- The Takeover Panel has the formal power to ban any investment company, including merchant banks, from taking part in takeover activity if the company has breached the Code.

- The Financial Services Authority (FSA) is able to 'require' merchant banks and others to cooperate in Panel investigations.

- The Panel has access to 'sensitive' data which until now has only been available to the Department of Trade or the Bank of England.

'Shells' and reverse takeovers

'Shells' are quoted companies whose main asset is their quotation. Such companies are usually capitalized at under £2 million. Sometimes a person with substantial private business interests may wish to obtain a 'back door' quotation for his business. Such an investor will take over the 'shell' and then inject his own private business into it. This is known as a reverse takeover. A more common operator is the stock market entrepreneur who wishes to raise some capital in the City to start a new business.

Rather than using the conventional new issue methods for his business, it can be quicker and easier to take over a 'shell' and raise capital for that 'shell'. Generally speaking, the entrepreneur will have arranged a placing to raise the necessary extra capital, or he may choose to use a rights issue for the 'shell' immediately prior to taking it over. The Stock Exchange will not automatically allow the 'shell' to retain its listing if it is unhappy about the company taking over the 'shell'.

These reverse takeovers are usually made at a price above the 'shell's' current value, and speculators are very keen to try to anticipate potential 'shells'.

Vendor placings and vendor rights issues

With vendor placings, the purchase price of a takeover is paid for in new shares of the bidding company. However, these new shares are immediately placed with clients of the bidder's merchant bank so that the target company's shareholders are effectively paid in cash. A vendor rights issue is a term used to describe the making of a rights issue by the bidder to finance a bid.

Capital gains tax and takeovers

If the shareholder accepts a cash offer, then this counts as a disposal for CGT, but if the shareholder accepts shares or other securities in the bidder, the transaction is not considered to be a disposal for CGT purposes. When the new securities are eventually sold, the taxable capital gain will be the net sale proceeds of the new securities, less the original cost of the target company's shares, with appropriate indexation allowances.

Other considerations for a shareholder in a target company to bear in mind

The shareholder should examine the formal offer document. The information in this document will enable him to compare the records of both companies, the profit forecasts and asset valuations. It should also provide information on the reasons for the bid, whether the target's board recommends acceptance, how many shares have been already committed to the bidder, whether any cash offer is underwritten, and whether the City Code has been complied with.

If shares are offered, the shareholder should decide whether the bidder's shares are likely to complement his existing portfolio. He can calculate the value of this bid by using the current market price of the bidder's shares. For example, if the bidding company 'B's' shares are quoted at 100p and 'B' offers one of its shares for every two in the target company, the bid is worth 50p a share. If the target company's shares stand at 40p in the market, then there is a premium of 10p. If the bid seems likely to fail, the target's shares will remain around 40p in the market, but if a higher offer or counter offer seems likely the market price could rise.

Once the offer has become unconditional, the shareholder has the choice of accepting, selling in the market, or becoming a minority shareholder. His choice will depend on his perception of the way the price of the bidder's shares is likely to move, but it is unlikely to be worthwhile becoming a minority shareholder. As was previously mentioned, accepting a cash offer could involve capital gains tax liabilities, but accepting an offer of shares does not involve any immediate CGT liability.

In most cases the success or otherwise of a takeover will be decided by the institutional shareholders.

Insider dealing

Since 1980 'insider dealing' has been a criminal offence that could result in imprisonment. This rule was confirmed by the Companies Act 1985, and extended by the Criminal Justice Act 1993. One of the problems in proving that the offence of insider dealing has occurred is the definition of what constitutes 'price sensitive information'. If an individual who has price sensitive information trades on that information, or encourages another person to trade (whether or not that person knows the information is price sensitive) he could be found guilty of insider dealing.

21

TRUSTEE INVESTMENT

Objectives

After studying this chapter, the reader should be able to:

● assess the significance of the role of a trustee;

● understand and describe the main provisions of the Trustee Act 2000 and the Charities Act 1993 relevant to investment;

● apply the provisions of the above acts to the portfolios of investments of registered charities, family trusts and will settlements;

● understand probate valuations;

● assess the significance of the provisions of trust legislation relevant to pension funds.

21.1   The duties of trustees

The word 'trustee' in this connection refers to trustees acting under a will or settlement, or in other capacities appointed by legislative deed. Until the present century, trustees were generally private individuals; nowadays there is also the Public Trustee Office (a government office) as well as the trustee departments of the banks , other financial services institutions solicitors and accountants.

The primary duty of a trustee is to carry out the terms of the trust. These will usually be laid down in the trust instrument by the person or body creating the trust, but may be provided by statutory provisions. It is essential that the trustee ensures the security of the trust property and, in so far as the trust fund does not consist of authorized investments, to invest it appropriately.

An 'investment' in the context of a trust is strictly interpreted as the purchase of an income-producing asset (re *Power's Will Trusts* (1947)) and authorization may come from the trust instrument or by statute. The general power of investment allows a trustee to place funds in any kind of investment, including land, as though he or she was the absolute owner of those funds. This often gives trustees a much greater range of possible investments to create the portfolio.

Section 4(1) of the Trustee Act 2000 lays down the standard investment criteria that trustees must adhere to. These are:

- To have regard to the suitability to the charity of the investment proposed to be made or being reviewed; and

- To have regard to the need for diversification of the charity's investments, in so far as is appropriate to the circumstances of the charity, not only when exercising the power of investment, but also when reviewing investments.

Trustees must undertake their duties in accordance with their general duty of care. However there are specific requirements to which trustees must adhere when exercising investment powers and discharging their duty to review existing investments. These are to:

- take proper advice (unless the trustees reasonably conclude it is unnecessary or inappropriate do so); and

- have regard to the 'standard investment criteria', in accordance with Section 4(1) of the Trustee Act 2000.

These duties apply to investments made by trustees generally, whether or not under the powers conferred by the Trustee Act 2000.

'Suitability' relates both to an investment that is considered for inclusion in either a new portfolio or when considering adding investments to the existing portfolio. In addition the suitability of existing investments need to be reviewed on a regular basis. Areas that must be considered for suitability include:

- the size and risk of the investment;

- in the case of endowed charities, the need to be even-handed between the interests of present and future beneficiaries of the charity;

- any ethical considerations as to the kind of investments that are appropriate for the trust to make.

The Trustee Act 2000 enables charities to invest in almost any share which is deemed suitable by the trustees. For example a share may be deemed unsuitable by the trustees if the Trust Deed specifies that the charity is an ethical investor which does not invest in alcohol. Thus the shares of companies that are involved in the brewing and selling of alcohol would be avoided.

It is possible for the trust instrument to authorize the purchase of non-income producing assets such as works of art. However, these will not qualify as investments and thus the wording in the trust deed as to what exactly may be purchased must be precise.

Balancing the interests of two or more beneficiaries

Regardless of the extent of the trustees investment powers, or how they arise, where there is more than one beneficiary the trustee is subject to an overriding requirement to act impartially between beneficiaries. The effect of this in an investment context is best illustrated where the trust has a life tenant, A, entitled to the income of the fund to the date of his death, and a remainderman, B, entitled to the capital on that date. Clearly, investment in assets providing a high income but no capital growth, or vice versa, would benefit one beneficiary to the detriment of the other. In such cases impartiality is best achieved by the purchase of a variety of investments of different types. The Trustee Act 2000 reinforces this by requiring trustees to give due regard to the diversification of the trust investments.

21.2 Trustee legislation

The principal legislation concerning trustees was the Trustee Act 1925; however, the investment powers of this Act tended to reflect the attitudes of the 19th century when the purchasing power of money remained constant over long periods. At that time investment in equities was considered highly risky and thus inappropriate for a trustee. Because the purchasing power of money started to fall due to the impact of inflation it became necessary to revisit the restrictive powers of investment granted by the Trustee Act 1925. As a result, the Trustee Investments Act 1961 repealed most of the investment provisions of the 1925 Act, and it was the Trustee Investments Act 1961 that provided the statutory provisions for trustee investments until the new Trustee Act 2000 came into being. It should, however, be noted that most modern wills and settlements usually provided for extensive powers of investment and that the investment powers of the modern trustee are only likely to be based on the Trustee Investments Act 1961 when the trust instrument is an old one (i.e. pre-dates the Trustee Act 2000).

Relevant provisions of the Trustee Act 1925

Although the statutory investment powers of the 1925 Act were repealed with the passing of the Trustee Investments Act 1961, some of its provisions remained relevant to investment matters. The most important are as follows:

- Section 4 provides that trustees shall not be liable for a breach of trust by reason only that they continue to hold an investment which has ceased to be an authorized investment. This, therefore, provides for the retention of such investments, provided of course the trustees continue to consider it suitable, but it should be classed as special-range property.

- Section 10(3) permits trustees to concur in reconstructions and mergers and accept any resulting securities, as well as to subscribe to rights issues in respect of shares held.

The Trustee Investments Act 1961

The Trustee Investments Act 1961 applied to family trusts, will trusts, pension funds and charities. This Act did not require a trustee to follow its provisions if he did not wish to do so, provided the trust deed granted the trustee the widest investment powers. The trustee was bound by the provisions of the Act only if he wished to invest in equities when the trust instrument did not grant this power. A person creating a trust since the 1961 Act was passed could exclude its powers and create trustees' investment powers to a far greater extent than is allowed by the Act.

If the provisions of the Trustee Investments Act 1961 applied, the initial division of the fund was into two equal parts, the narrower range and the wider range. In certain circumstances a third range, special range, could also be held.

Rules governing investment

Overriding conditions

There were certain overriding conditions that qualified a trustee's investing powers, and any potential investment had to comply with all of them. They were as follows:

Suitability and diversification

This required the trustee to have regard to the:

- Need for diversification of trust investments;

- Suitability of the proposed investment.

In all cases, such conditions had to be exercised in the context of the trust's particular circumstances.

Advice

A trustee usually had to obtain advice on each proposed investment before the investment was made. He had to obtain periodic advice on the securities held, and the frequency of this is determined by bearing in mind the nature of the particular investment. Such advice could only be given by a person authorized by the Financial Services Authority.

Place of issue

The UK had to be the place of issue and registration of any investment and all payments made or received had to be in sterling. Thus direct investment overseas was not allowed.

Quotation

The securities had to be quoted on the London Stock Exchange.

Division of the fund

The 1961 Act stated that trust funds be divided into two parts, 50% narrower range and 50% wider range. The definition of narrower and wider range was somewhat arcane and meant that a number of investments could not be made by a trust governed by the Trustee Investments Act 1961. The Act divided investments into four categories:

- Narrower range without advice investments – broadly speaking, National Savings investments and building society deposit accounts.

- Narrower range investments with advice – broadly speaking, all types of fixed-interest securities, including gilts and company loan stocks.

- Wider range investments – broadly speaking, all classes of UK issued share capital, unit trust units and building society accounts except building society deposit accounts, which come under the heading of narrower range with advice.

- Special range investments – which are any investments that are not in the narrower or wider range areas.

For an investment to have 'trustee status', it must have been listed for five years and paid dividends in each of those years.

Criticisms of the Trustee Investments Act 1961

The Act became law 40 years ago, and as a result it does not take into account the changing face of investment nowadays. The main criticisms of the Act are:

- There were no powers to invest in companies that have been privatized, until they have been quoted and paid dividends for the statutory five years. This rule effectively debarred investment in any of the privatization issues made from 1970 onwards – despite the fact that many of these were sound investments, such as the gas, electricity and water industry.

- There was a requirement for a company to have £1 million paid-up capital to be eligible for trustees. This amount was very outdated, it would now represent a very small quoted company. Such companies are higher risk than the majority of larger quoted companies.

- The different treatment of building society deposit account (narrower range with advice) and all other building society accounts (wider range) was very dated. Banks and building societies are effectively as secure as each other and hence both should have been treated equally.

Charities Act 1993

This Act, which related only to registered charities, was intended redefine trustee investments as mentioned above. Under previous statutes charities were restricted on the percentage of their funds they could invest in equities and gilts. These restrictions were abolished by the Charities Act 1993. The change was well overdue, because the restrictive regime that governed equity-based investment has meant that over the years charities have been unable to benefit fully from the rise in capital values and income from shares.

21.3   The Trustee Act 2000

The Trustee Act 2000 applies to family trusts, will trusts, pension funds and charities. The statutory powers and duties of trustees relating to investment have previously been defined mainly by the, now repealed, Trustee Act 1925, the Trustee Investments Act 1961 and the Trusts of Land and Appointment of Trustees Act 1996. Over a period of time, these Acts have become out of date due to the changing nature of the types of investment available and to the impact of the changes in the economy – particularly the period of low inflation and low interest rates. The old Acts did not give trustees the powers needed to provide the most appropriate types of investments for the current scenario, thus making it difficult to administer the trusts effectively.

The main changes to Trustee Investment in the Trustee Act 2000 are:

● new, wider powers of investment;

● new powers to acquire land and to insure property;

● appropriate safeguards including a duty to take proper advice in relation to investments and a statutory duty of care.

These changes enable trustees to invest in a far wider range of investments so as to better meet the aims of the trust while still maintaining a high level of statutory controls to safeguard the trust itself and beneficiaries of a trust.

The statutory duty of care of a trustee

The Trustee Act 2000 states that a trustee, when exercising any of his or her powers under the trust deed or carrying out any other duties, must exercise such care and skill as is reasonable in the circumstances having particular regard to:

● any special knowledge or experience that they have or hold out that they have; and

● where they act as a trustee in the course of a business or profession, to any special knowledge or experience that it is reasonable to expect of a person acting in the course of that kind of business or profession.

This is known as 'the duty of care'. It applies to the way in which the trustees exercise their powers of investment and their obligation to review the investments of the charity. The only time that there can be any exception to the statutory duty of care is when the trust deed states otherwise.

21.4 Common investment funds

Charity fund managers have two methods by which they can invest their funds, firstly by using a professional manager who will create and manage a fund for the charity (the segregated route), and secondly by using common investment funds (CIFs).

Common investment funds

Common investment and common deposit funds enable charities to pool financial resources for investment purposes. They are particularly suitable for small charities which would not be able to create such a well-diversified portfolio.

Under the Charities Act 1993 there are three types of fund:

- the Capital Fund;
- the High Yield Fund; and
- the Gross Income Fund,

which can be used for the purpose of the investment of money in common investment funds. The investment manager is responsible for administering the funds in accordance with the following objectives:

- the Capital Fund – with a view to securing high long-term capital growth with some growth in annual income but with less emphasis on the level of annual income; and
- the High Yield and Gross Income Funds – with a view to securing a high annual income with some long-term capital growth.

The investment manager is responsible for the management of the investment strategy that has been designed to achieve these objectives. Dividends payable on the Gross Income Fund are paid without deduction of income tax.

CIFs provide a balanced portfolio of holdings, covering cash, equity and fixed-interest (not just gilts, but also company loan stocks). CIFs are particularly suitable for small charities with less than £100,000 to invest, where segregated funds would be more expensive to manage and the performance may not be as good due to the smaller value of the holdings and limit on the number of holdings due to the relatively small amounts invested. The management fees are lower on CIFs than segregated funds because they are pooled funds. CIFs managers can reclaim the tax deducted from dividends up until 5 April 2004. After that date charities will be subject to tax on the dividends they received at the prevailing rate levied on dividends.

21.5   Registered charities (charitable trusts)

The rules governing charitable status were laid down by Lord MacNaughton in 1891. There are four different types of charitable trust:

- For the advancement of education;
- For the advancement of religion;
- For the relief of poverty;
- For any other purpose beneficial to the community.

The last of these categories has further additional guidelines which mean any body with any hint of political association will be refused charitable status.

If the Inland Revenue and Charity Commissioners grant a charitable trust registered status, it will not be liable to any UK capital and income taxes.

Charities often require a high level of income to fund their works, thus investment in high-yielding, fixed-interest securities is used for this purpose. To provide growth of income and capital, equity or equity-based investment is used. This can be undertaken through segregated funds, or CIFs if the charity either does not have enough cash available to invest directly in shares, or the investment manager does not have the time to manage direct equity investments.

The considerations relating to charity investments is best shown by considering the following example

A charitable trust has been set up with £100,000 cash. The trustees have wide powers of investment. They intend to invest on a long-term basis and are looking for a reasonable level of income, together with growth of capital value and income. Advise the trustees on the investment strategy they should follow to achieve these objectives. Mention the types of investment which would be appropriate. Give reasons for your suggestions.

Suggested answer

The fund should be divided equally between fixed-interest and equity investments. High-coupon, long and undated gilts can be purchased to give a guaranteed income. Undated gilts are suitable because the income is guaranteed in perpetuity, which will meet long-term needs. The trustees should also consider local authority and company loan stocks for part of the fixed interest portfolio if yields are higher than gilts, but it is not advisable to place the whole of the fixed-interest element into such stocks even if their yields are higher, because these stocks can be less marketable. This could result in a lower selling price than expected if the need arose to liquidate stocks.

For the equity content equal amounts should be invested in at least 15 shares in different sectors, provided the trustees feel happy about managing direct equity investments. As an alternative, the trustees could consider CIFs which will provide professional management and diversification. If indirect investment is preferred, it would be wise to consider using two or three CIFs to minimize management risk. They could also use some investment trusts for the same reasons. The equity (or equity-based) content of the portfolio will help to achieve the objective of growth of capital and income. While the initial dividend yield from the equity base will be fairly low, the high income from the fixed-interest element will compensate. The trustees could also consider some overseas equity content to provide capital growth rather than income, and this should be included via unit/investment trusts/OEICs investing overseas or by or CIFs with some overseas content.

The fund should be reviewed regularly and changes made to take account of market conditions. The managers should also look at any new investment opportunities when the fund is reviewed. A certain amount of cash should be kept liquid. The amount will depend on the projected expenditure by the trust. The cash should be kept easily accessible in an account giving the highest gross interest, which may be a bank or a building society account.

Suggested portfolio

We shall assume that £5,000 cash is sufficient for immediate needs.

Investment	Amount (£)	% Gross rate	Gross return (£)
Bank/building society	5,000	4.5	225
High-coupon long-dated gilts	37,500	6.7	2,513
Company loan stock	10,000	7.5	750
Two/three CIFs	40,000	2.6	1,040
Unit/investment trusts/OEICs investing overseas	7,500	1	75
	100,000		4,603

$$\text{Gross yield on portfolio} = \frac{4{,}603 \times 100}{100{,}000}$$

$$= \underline{4.6\%}$$

21.6　Family trust and will settlements

A trust must have a clearly defined beneficiary or beneficiaries. If they are not ascertainable, the trust is void. The two main types of family trust are bare trusts and discretionary trusts.

Bare trusts

A bare trust is one where the beneficiary has an absolute right to the assets and income of the trust, but the trustees are the legal owners and hold the property as nominees. This type of trust is often used by parents or grandparents to make gifts to children under the age of 18. The child will then receive the money from the bare trust when he attains the age of 18. One of the advantages of bare trusts is that grandparents can transfer income-producing assets to use a child's personal allowance (note: it is not possible for parents to create a bare trust in this manner because the income would still be treated as the parents'). Another advantage of a bare trusts is that it overcomes the problem that many companies will not allow minors to hold shares in their own name.

A transfer to a bare trust is a potentially exempt transfer (PET) for inheritance tax purposes.

Discretionary trusts

A discretionary trust allows the trustees to use their discretion as to how the income and/or capital under the trust is to be allocated. On a discretionary trust no-one has the right to the income. It is the trustees' decision on how much, if any, of the income is distributed. The income from discretionary trusts is subject to income tax at basic rate + 10%, which is 32% for the tax year 2001/02. From 6 April 1999 dividend income is charged at the Schedule F trust rate of 25% of which 10% is covered by the tax credit, thus the trustees pay an extra 15% income tax on dividends. Any income paid to beneficiaries is paid with 32% tax deducted. If the income is less than the tax payer's personal allowance a refund will be made on the overpayment. If the beneficiary is a 40% tax payer there will be a further 8% income tax to pay.

Transfers to a discretionary trust are subject to inheritance tax as a lifetime chargeable event. The nil threshold band is offset against the transfer, provided that it has not already been utilized and the annual exemptions can also be offset against the transfer. If the donor dies less than 7 years from the transfer, inheritance tax due is recalculated at the full rate.

The rule against perpetuities

Perpetuity means forever. Where a trust could continue for a long time, e.g. a will trust with successive life tenants, there must still be a time when the trust will cease. Thus there must always be someone who will receive the capital of the trust at a future date on the death of the last life tenant. The trust cannot carry on forever. In fact, the only type of trust that can carry on in perpetuity is a charitable trust.

Will trusts

Most family trusts are created by wills, when the person who has died leaves a life interest in some property (which can be actual bricks and mortar, or cash or stocks and shares or any combination of these) to one or more persons, with the property reverting to another person or persons on the death of the person with a life interest. The person with a life interest is called the life tenant and the person to whom the property passes on death of the life tenant is the remainderman.

Trusts for minors

The other type of family trust, again often created by a will, is for a minor. A will often specifies that a person will receive his money only on attaining a certain age, which does not necessarily have to be majority (18 years). With such trusts the fixed-income element should be purchased with a maturity date around the date set in the will. The remainder of the fund should be invested in equities to provide growth of capital unless there is only a fairly short period of, say, two or three years, and a small sum available. In such a case equity investment is not really suitable because the stock market fluctuations in the short term may wipe out any capital gain. Discretionary trusts (i.e. ones where the income and/or capital is paid out at the discretion of the trustees) pay tax at the Schedule F trust rate of 25%, of which the 10% tax credit covers part, leaving an extra 15% to pay.

Powers of retention and postponer

When a trust is set up under a will, the testator, while limiting the trust to the statutory powers of investment, sometimes gives the trustees the right to retain any investments held at the date of death and postpone the sale of them. Other testators can instruct the trustees to sell the investments but give the trustees the power to postpone their sale indefinitely.

An example of a will trust is best understood by studying the following question and answer.

Example

(a) The life tenant of a will trust is a widow aged 55. The remaindermen are her two children aged 27 and 25. The trustees have wide investment powers. The assets consist of £80,000 cash. State with reasons the investment policy you would recommend and suggest suitable types of investment.

(b) The testator's grandson, aged six, has been bequeathed a legacy of £5,000 which cannot be paid to him until he can give a valid receipt at age 18. Income is to be applied for his maintenance, education and benefit. Indicate the investment policy you would recommend, and suggest suitable types of investment.

Suggested answer

(a) The trustees must balance the interests of the life tenant and remaindermen and not favour one over the other. They need to provide a reasonable level of income for the life tenant and protection and growth of capital for the remaindermen.

About half the sum, £40,000, should be invested in index-linked gilts which will also provide a real rate of return on both income and capital. (Note, virtually all fixed-interest gilts are over par, thus carrying a capital loss which would not be acceptable to the remaindermen.) As the life tenant is only 55 there needs to be a spread of medium and long dates in the index-linked gilts.

The remaining £40,000 could be invested equally in 15 different shares in different sectors which should provide both growth of income and capital in the long term. The shares should not yield more than the average gross dividend yield on the FT Actuaries All Share Indices in order to balance the interests of life tenant and remaindermen. Within the equity content, some overseas element could be introduced to provide a greater chance of capital growth, albeit with a lower income. The overseas element should be provided by unit/investment trusts and OEICs.

The investments should be reviewed regularly to ensure that they keep pace with market and interest rate changes. A liquid element is not needed because the only cash paid out is that generated by the trust itself.

Suggested portfolio

Investment	Amount (£)	% Gross rate	Gross income (£)
Gilts	40,000	4	1,600
Equities	30,000	2	600
Unit/investment trusts/ OEICs investing overseas	10,000	1	100
	£80,000		£2,300

$$\text{Gross yield on portfolio} = \frac{2,300 \times 100}{80,000}$$

$$= 2.88\%$$

(b) Half of the £5,000 should be invested in a gilt to mature around his 18th birthday. As income may be paid out during the life of the trust, a gilt yielding around 6.7% will provide a reasonable income but may show a capital loss.

The remaining £2,500 should be invested in two general unit/investment trusts/OEICs which should provide a moderate income to begin with, and growth of both income and capital in the longer term. The trusts/OEICs should also counter the effects of inflation in the longer term although this cannot be guaranteed. These investments will be easy to manage and fulfil the overall policy of protecting capital in real terms, plus provision of a reasonable income.

21.7 Probate valuations

The property to be included as liable to inheritance tax is valued on the general basis of the price it would fetch if sold in the open market on the day of the deceased's death.

Stock exchange securities

These are valued on the basis of the lower of the following two methods. Both methods must be used both in answering examination questions and in practice to arrive at the correct valuation.

Quarter (3) up method

The Inland Revenue accepts for quoted stocks and shares the prices ruling on the Stock Exchange (as quoted in SEDOL) at the date of death. Two prices are quoted – the market maker's buying price and the market maker's selling price. The value is obtained in the following way:

(i) take the difference between the two prices;

(ii) find one-quarter of this difference;

(iii) add (ii) (i.e. one-quarter difference) to the lower price quoted.

Example

Stock quoted	=	80-82
Difference	=	2
One-quarter of this	=	½
Add ½ to 80: value	=	80½

Middle-market price

This is the middle-market price of ordinary bargains recorded. If the prices of bargains were listed '79, 81, 82, 83', the valuation would be $(79 + 83) \div 2 = 81$. Thus the share would be valued at 81, the lower of the two valuations.

Note: when the Stock Exchange is closed on the date of death, the Stock Exchange Daily Official List (SEDOL) for either the preceding or subsequent business day is used. The price determined is the lower one shown from these two days' lists. Quoted shares that have not been dealt with recently are priced at the date when business was last done, as shown in SEDOL.

Foreign securities

The value of the investment in foreign currency is arrived at by adding one-quarter of the difference to the lower quotation. The price is converted into sterling on the basis of the exchange rate that gives the lowest value in sterling. For example, if the exchange rate is US $ 1.50 - 1.52, then the price is converted on the basis of US $ 1.505 to the £1.

Unit trusts

Holdings in unit trusts are valued at their bid prices.

'Cum div' and 'ex div' quotations

All quotations are presumed cum div unless expressly marked 'xd'.

With cum div quotations, the value of the stock is arrived at in the ordinary way. In the case of ex div quotations, the whole of the impending dividend or interest, less income tax where this is deducted at source, must be added to the value of the holding, because the whole of the next dividend is paid to the seller.

Example

To calculate the market value of a fixed-interest stock quoted xd, the following procedure must be used after the initial valuation on the basis of the lower of the quarter up and middle market price basis:

Date used for valuation purposes: 26 August

Interest payable: 1 March/1 September

Stock: £3,000 MYZ plc 6% Debenture Stock 03-07 probate valuation 54½

Valuation: £1,635 + net interest

$$= 1,635 + \left\{ \frac{3,000}{2} \times \frac{6}{100} \times \frac{80}{100} \right\}$$

$$= 1,635 + £72$$

$$= £1,707$$

Unquoted stocks and shares

Shares not enjoying an official quotation must be fairly valued and a certificate from a stockbroker or a letter from the company secretary must support the valuation. Either of these letters must show the basis of valuation, details of previous sales in the open market, or details of the last three years' dividends and of any bonus distributed. In the case of shares held in a private limited company, which by its articles imposes restrictions on the transfer of its shares, these restrictions are to be ignored, and the value of the shares on the open market must be ascertained. Similar particulars must be furnished, i.e. basis of valuation, dividends paid during last three years, bonus, if any, distributed, and amount of profits carried forward. The balance sheet may be required, and should be attached to the certificate from the company secretary. Where the deceased holds a controlling interest in a private company, the shares are valued by reference to the total assets of the company, and not by reference to the current open-market value. The shares held by the deceased are calculated pro rata on the net value of the assets.

The valuation of shares in a private limited company presents some difficulty. Unless the shares are dealt in (for example on OFEX), there is no true open-market value. Usually, a valuation has to be negotiated between the shares valuation division of the Inland Revenue and the deceased's personal representatives. Normally, the Capital Taxes Office will refer the matter to the Shares Valuation Division. The factors to be considered in such cases are as follows, the:

- Dividend record of the company;
- Asset value of the shares both on the balance sheet values and the actual value at the date of death;
- Proportion which the deceased's shareholding bears to the capital issued.

Where there is a liability for unpaid calls at the date of death, this liability may be deducted from the value of the other assets.

Other assets

The remaining assets are always valued on the basis of their realizable value in the open market at date of death.

● As regards money on mortgage, this is the principal value together with accrued interest.

● As regards freehold and leasehold property, a surveyor's valuation is accepted, subject to agreement with the district valuer. If, however, a property is to be sold within a short time (usually two years) of the death, then the proceeds of sale will be taken as the value as at the date of death.

21.8   Pension funds

A pension fund aims to pay out the best possible pension to its beneficiaries. The actuary to the fund stipulates the desired level of annual income which the fund managers should achieve to meet their liabilities. There are four key questions that must be answered before developing the investment strategy and asset allocation for a pension fund. There are:

● How long will the members of the scheme live?

● How big will their pensions be?

● What will the assets in the pension fund realize?

● What income will the assets generate in the meantime?

In order to answer these questions certain financial assumptions must be made. These are:

● The level of future investment returns

● The rate of future salary growth

● The size of future pension increases

● The future trend in inflation

● The rate of dividend growth

● The level of the future expenses of running the fund.

Obviously these facts will affect the investment policy of the fund managers. For example, an income requirement of 5% per annum cannot be met by the managers pursuing an aggressive capital growth-oriented investment policy.

The 'age' of the fund will also determine how much income is needed by the pensioners each year. A relatively new scheme will have few pensioners, thus the manager can look towards capital growth. A well-established, ongoing scheme will need to look at both income and growth, while a fund that has been closed to new entrants will diminish in value because the capital (and income generated on that capital) will be paid out to an ever-ageing workforce. The asset allocation of the fund will be set by the actuaries, taking into account the pattern of future pension payments against future pension contributions and an analysis of the risk profile of the fund.

The investment duties of pension fund trustees

The Pensions Act 1995 lays down the key duties of the pension fund trustees. These are:

- To take advice on the investment strategy of the pension fund;

- Consult with the employer;

- Consider the kind of investments; the balance between different kinds; risk; expected return; realization; diversification of assets; and the suitability of assets ;

- Choose, appoint and monitor the investment manager.

Capital growth

A pension fund is totally free of all taxes except for the 10% tax deducted at source upon dividends received. This taxation of dividends received by the pension funds has had an adverse effect on the income they receive and may impact upon the level of pension that they will be able to pay in the future. The distinction between income-producing assets and growth-oriented assets is clearer than it use to be when pension funds did not pay any tax. A fund can obtain overall growth in value by opting for high income-producing assets and reinvesting the excess income into other assets. Now this 10% tax on dividends can be seen as a disincentive to this method of obtaining growth.

Some pension funds invest in purely capital growth assets, e.g. paintings, but these are the largest pension funds. Some favour property investment to provide both income and capital growth, others favour overseas investment (which is more growth than income oriented). To a certain extent the split of the money in the fund will depend on whether or not the fund has its own trust deed or comes under the Trustee Act 2000, although it is rare today to see a pension fund governed by the Trustee Act 2000.

To enable the income requirement to be met, the fund managers will generate a large proportion of the income from fixed-interest stocks. It is not uncommon to see up to 25% of even a multi-million pound fund invested in high-yielding fixed-interest stocks. One particular type of fixed-interest stock held by pension funds to provide fixed-income in perpetuity (i.e. forever) is an undated gilt.

Although a large portion of the fund is held in fixed-interest stocks, this does not mean that the stocks are never changed. Pension fund managers will use anomaly and policy switching to keep the returns high.

Provided the pension fund complies with the Inland Revenue's rule that assets must not exceed liabilities by more than 5%, the pension fund will be an exempt fund, i.e. it will be free of all UK taxes (except tax on dividends at source). If the assets do exceed the 5% figure, the fund could consider a 'contribution holiday', i.e. a period of time when no further contributions are paid into the fund.

The trustees will also invest in equities, both UK and overseas, and in property. If the fund is large enough this investment will be direct investment. Smaller funds may invest directly in

UK equities, and indirectly in overseas equities and property.

Overseas equities

These are aimed at capital growth, thus forming part of the pension fund's long-term growth requirement to enable it to maintain and increase the level of pension paid. If the fund is small, it will use indirect investment via unit or investment trusts. Larger funds will invest directly, and thus need to be able to manage, not only the shares, but also the foreign currency exposure.

Property

Mortgages and ground rents are fixed-interest investments with a fixed expiry date, and although higher yields may generally be obtained on them than on gilts of comparable date, their relative unmarketability and the complications of purchase and management are generally considered to make them unsuitable investments for the ordinary pension fund. However, the large funds can, and do, invest in property.

Overseas property

The basic principles applying to UK property investment also apply if investment in overseas property is contemplated. However, apart from foreign currency and tax implications, each country has its own property laws, its own tax laws affecting property, and its own set of relationships between landlord and tenant. The whole structure of the property market in an overseas country can be very different from that in the UK so it is essential to have available expert and local advice on all these aspects. Only the larger funds such as BT are likely to contemplate direct investment in overseas property, but property unit trusts specializing in overseas property investments for pension funds are available as an alternative.

There is an accountancy problem associated with investment in overseas property for a UK-based pension fund with its published accounts denominated in sterling (i.e. the fund's reporting currency is sterling). The overseas property will initially appear as an asset in the published accounts at the sterling equivalent of the original purchase price. However, at future balance sheet dates the sterling value shown in the published accounts will vary because that amount will be based on the currency value of the asset, converted to sterling at the spot rate of exchange ruling on the balance sheet date. This exposure is called translation exposure and it may have to be managed. Such management has a cost.

'Underweight' and 'overweight'

The terms 'underweight' and 'overweight' are used to describe a position where the fund's exposure to an individual sector is more or less than the percentage that sector represents in the market capitalization of the market.

For example, if the total capitalization of the market was £100 million, and the capitalization of the banking sector of that market was £10 million, then the banking sector would represent 10% of the market. If a pension fund held 5% of its funds in the banking sector it would be 'underweight'. If it held 15% of its funds it would be 'overweight'.

For the UK stock market, weightings are usually measured by the FT Actuaries All Share Indices and if the pension fund weighting is the same as the FT Actuaries Indices, then performance will be in line with the market. This approach is a low-risk approach, and is gained by using index funds.

By taking a more active approach, a pension fund will be under- or overweight in certain sectors in order to try to produce a better-than-average performance. This strategy is higher risk but active management should produce better returns.

The problem for a large pension fund in taking the more active approach is the cost involved in employing specialist managers to look after the portfolio. One person cannot be an expert in all market sectors, so the fund has to weigh the cost of employing specialists against the chance of them producing gains in excess of the average and their salaries.

The approach taken by large pension funds is to index, say, 75% of their funds, and this is monitored by computers. They then give their fund managers a free hand with the remainder of the fund to try to outperform the market.

For a large pension fund, weighting is important in order to adequately diversify their funds. However, changing weightings is expensive and is less likely to be done if the fund is taking a long-term view of the market. Weightings may be altered by using the new money that flows into the fund.

An example of the considerations to bear in mind when investing for a pension fund is shown now.

Example

What points would you consider in forming and implementing an investment plan for a new company pension fund which has a starting capital of £5 million and which is expected to receive in future an estimated £1 million per annum in contributions from the company and its employees? The trust deed contains the widest investment powers. Give reasons in your answer.

Suggested answer

Points to consider in forming the investment plan

- The actuary's report; specifically the desired level of income specified.
- The pensioners' (beneficiaries') needs.

    (i) Is commutation allowed? If so, how many pensioners are likely to commute part of their pension? What amount of money will be involved because cash will be needed to meet this obligation?

    (ii) How often is the pension to be paid, e.g. weekly or monthly, because again cash must be available to meet the payments.

(c) While a certain level of fixed income is required, the need for growth of both capital and income must be borne in mind, along with the need for inflation protection.

(d) Who are the fund managers, and what are their charges? (With a fund of this size it will not be cost effective to employ in-house fund managers.)

(e) Will the fund receive Inland Revenue approval as an exempt fund?

(f) How frequently should the investments be reviewed, and by whom?

(g) How will the portfolio be spread? What proportion will be invested in fixed-interest, equities, property and overseas?

(h) In view of the size of the fund, will it be more appropriate to use the special property unit trusts available to pension funds and registered charities rather than direct property investment?

Points to bear in mind in implementing the plan:

(a) Division of the fund

Approx %

20-25% Fixed-interest which will include some undated gilts to provide permanent guaranteed interest, and index-linked gilts to give protection against inflation.

10%   Property – with this size of fund property unit trusts will give a better diversification plus professional management.

25-30% Overseas equities – again it may be wise to consider the use of unit trusts in view of the size of the fund, unless the fund managers have the necessary experience in investing overseas directly themselves.

40%   UK equities.

(b) Account must be taken that it meets the minimum specified by the actuaries.

(c) As with all investments, the timing of the purchases is crucial.

(d) Bearing in mind the cash flow required to pay the pensions and any commuted sums, the amount of liquidity required must be estimated. As this is a new fund, the initial liquidity requirement will be very low since there will be few, it any, pensions to be paid in the early years. However, account must be taken of future liquidity requirements.

(e) Once the initial £5 million has been invested, the plan must be actively monitored, and consideration of UK and overseas market conditions taken into account when new money is invested.

Appendix –

Useful Web Sites

http://www.hm-treasury.gov.uk The Treasury

http://www.fsa.gov.uk Financial Services Authority

http://www.bankofengland.co.uk Bank of England

http://www.coi.gov.uk Central Office of Information

http://www.inlandrevenue.gov.uk Inland Revenue

http://www.londonstockex.co.uk (London Stock Exchange)

http://www.ftse.com (FTSE web site)

http://www.marketeye.com price data which can be downloaded into spreadsheets and charting section. Also has traded options prices information.

http://www.uk-invest.com Access to share prices in the UK and overseas.

http://www.moneyworld.co.uk (this site offers a power search facility to dig out the best or worst performers from a specified group over a given time period)

http://www.trackdata.co.uk/mytrack.htm

http://www.bmiquotes.com and http://www.bridge.com (both useful for prices and charts)

http://www.icbinc.com (for free annual reports)

http://www.iii.co.uk (information on share prices, unit trusts, OEICs and investment trusts)

http://www.esi.co.uk (information on unit trusts, OEICs and investment trusts)

http://www.trustnet.co.uk (information on unit trusts, OEICs and investment trusts)

http://www.angelfire.com/co/simplewealth/buffettips.html a collection of Warren Buffet sayings

http.//www.economist.com/editorial/freeforall/focus/big_mac_index.html. A collection of articles about the Big Mac index.

http://www.fool.co.uk share prices, portfolio tools.

http://www.investment-trusts-magazine.co.uk/ Investment Trusts Magazine
http://www.thisismoney.co.uk – Daily Mail

http://www.the-times.co.uk The Times

http://www.ftyourmoney.com Financial Times – Your Money

http://www.guardian.co.uk The Guardian

http://www.telegraph.co.uk Electronic Telegraph

http://www.economist.com The Economist

http://www.google.com is a general search engine, but it has access to a wide number of sites that are relevant to this subject

http://www.finance.uk.yahoo.com (Yahoo is a search engine – this is a focused part of it).

INDEX

C